Soviet workers and the collapse of perestroika is a comprehensive analysis of the role of labour policy in the development and ultimate collapse of Mikhail Gorbachev's reforms. Drawing on a wide range of sources, Filtzer argues that initially perestroika was designed to modernize the Soviet economy while keeping the existing political and property relations of society intact, a task which required a thoroughgoing restructuring of the labour process within Soviet industry. To this end labour policy had four basic goals: the creation of a flexible labour market, including large-scale unemployment; an attempt to raise workforce morale through political liberalization and limited enter-prise 'democratization'; a recasting of the wages system in order to pressure workers to accept a higher intensity of labour; and the replacement of centralized planning directives by so-called 'market mechanisms'. As each of these policies failed, the regime in mid-1990 opted to move to a full-scale restoration of capitalism, a task which could not be fulfilled so long as the traditional work practices and work relations within industry remained unchanged. Filtzer argues that the collapse of the USSR has brought the solution to this problem no nearer, and that post-Soviet capitalism is rooted in corruption and speculation and cannot ensure long-term economic growth.

SOVIET WORKERS AND THE COLLAPSE OF PERESTROIKA

Cambridge Russian, Soviet and Post-Soviet Studies: 93

Editorial Board

Cambridge Russian, Soviet and Post-Soviet Studies, under the auspices of Cambridge University Press and the British Association for Slavonic and East European Studies (BASEES), promotes the publication of works presenting substantial and original research on the economics, politics, sociology and modern history of Russia, the Soviet Union and Eastern Europe.

Cambridge Russian, Soviet and Post-Soviet Studies

Series list continues on page 000

SOVIET WORKERS
AND THE COLLAPSE
OF PERESTROIKA

The Soviet labour process and
Gorbachev's reforms, 1985–1991

DONALD FILTZER

CAMBRIDGE
UNIVERSITY PRESS

CAMBRIDGE UNIVERSITY PRESS
Cambridge, New York, Melbourne, Madrid, Cape Town, Singapore, São Paulo

Cambridge University Press
The Edinburgh Building, Cambridge CB2 8RU, UK

Published in the United States of America by Cambridge University Press, New York

www.cambridge.org
Information on this title: www.cambridge.org/9780521452922

First published 1994
This digitally printed version 2008

A catalogue record for this publication is available from the British Library

Library of Congress Cataloguing in Publication data

Filtzer, Donald A.
Soviet workers and the collapse of perestroika: the Soviet labour process and
Gorbachov's reforms, 1985–1991 / Donald Filtzer.
    p.   cm. – (Cambridge Russian, Soviet and Post-Soviet Studies: 93)
Includes bibliographical references.
ISBN 0 521 45292 9 (hard)
1. Labor policy – Soviet Union – History. 2. Working class – Soviet Union –
History. 3. Soviet Union – Economic conditions – 1985–1991.
I. Title. II. Series.
HD8526.5.F539 1994
331'.0947 – dc20   93–5975   CIP

ISBN 978-0-521-45292-2 hardback
ISBN 978-0-521-05653-3 paperback

In memory of David, Elsie, and Lil
and for all those who miss them

Contents

Preface and acknowledgements

This book is the third volume of my three-part history of the Soviet working class and the evolution of the system of production relations that came to dominate Soviet industry from the 1930s onwards. When the ideas behind this study were first taking shape Mikhail Gorbachev's reforms were themselves only in their early stages of formulation and implementation. Like most observers at the time, I presumed that, however unstable the Soviet system might be, the Gorbachev era would last for some time. It would therefore be a logical extension of my previous research to investigate how the changes Gorbachev was introducing into labour policy and enterprise financing would interact with the traditional labour process within Soviet industry, which, I had argued, constituted one of the main causes of crisis in the Soviet economy and in the past had proven quite resistant to reform. My assumption was that the patterns of mutual dependency between workers and line managers in Soviet factories would throw up countless points, if not outright resistance to the reforms, then of distortions to these policies which could well subvert their intentions. At the same time, however, it was clear that one of the prime aims of perestroika was precisely to break down this pattern of labour relations, first and foremost the considerable control which individual workers or groups of workers were able to assert over how their work was organized and conducted.

As it turned out, this study was rapidly overtaken by events. The original policies of perestroika rapidly ran into difficulties at both macro- and micro-economic level. Nowhere was this failure more manifest than in labour policy. Perestroika had proposed radical changes to the Soviet workplace: modernization and rationalization would lead to massive layoffs and the creation of a flexible labour market; a reform of the wages system would widen differentials and force workers to exert themselves much harder to maintain their standard of living; and promises of enterprise 'democratization' would give workers a political incentive to accept tighter discipline and material sacrifices, as well as a new purpose to which to apply their labour. As we outline in Part I, by 1990 all of these policies lay in ruins: instead of unemployment there was a severe labour shortage; the wage reform was so routinely ignored that it had to be officially abandoned; and workers, unmoved by the false promises of 'democratization', had developed their own ways of influencing enterprise and government policy, namely strikes. Thus for Gorbachev and his wing of the reform movement the conclusion was now inescapable that reform *within* the existing system was no longer possible and it would be necessary to reintroduce capitalism into the USSR.

The rest is, as they say, history. Even without the abortive *putsch* of August 1991 it was clear that the Soviet system was fast unravelling and could not long survive such protracted and chronic instability. In this way what had begun as an open-ended inquiry into how the reforms and the inherited system of shop floor relations would conflict with and distort one another soon became an historical analysis of how these shop floor relations contributed to perestroika's collapse. This, then, is the theme of this book.

As with most books of this type, many people and institutions contributed to its completion. The research for it was financed by a major project grant from the Leverhulme Trust. The British Academy enabled me to spend six weeks in Moscow and Leningrad during the summer of 1991, where I carried out interviews and read factory newspapers. The research was begun at the centre for Russian and East European Studies, University of Birmingham, and completed at the School of Slavonic and East European Studies, University of London. I am grateful to the administrative and library staff of both institutions for the organizational backup which they provided.

As for the research itself, David Mandel has over the years provided invaluable assistance, introducing me to contacts in the USSR, reading and making detailed criticisms of drafts of articles and of the current book, and generally helping me to make the transition from social and economic historian to an analyst of modern Soviet society. He also made available to me a number of the interviews which he conducted in the course of his own research into the Soviet working class, and has kindly granted me permission to use this material. Simon Clarke has been equally generous in devoting time and effort to reading the manuscript and suggesting essential improvements. Judith Shapiro, a friend and colleague of many years, has been an ongoing source of ideas and criticism, not just for this book, but for my study of the Khrushchev period as well. Nick Lampert, with whom I collaborated on my Khrushchev-era project, gave much helpful advice on drawing up the formal proposal for my perestroika research.

This book could never have appeared but for the help of a number of Soviet friends and acquaintances. Anna Temkina and Nikolai Preobrazhenskii organized for me a number of meetings and interviews during my stay in Leningrad in the summer of 1991. They also taught me a great deal about what was then contemporary Soviet politics and the state of Soviet society under perestroika. Aleksandr Buzgalin helped me to set up similar interviews in Moscow. Further contacts were made possible through my association with Leonid Gordon. Sergei Agapov gave me indispensable insights into the operation of Soviet industry, drawing on his own experience as a worker. Naturally, I owe an equal debt to those whom I interviewed, as well as to Galina Pokrass, who transcribed the interviews. It will be immediately obvious to the reader just how big a contribution all of these individuals made to my research.

Jonathan Aves, George Blazyca, Michael Burawoy, and Elizabeth Teague read and commented on drafts of earlier discussion papers and articles based on this research, some of the material from which has also been used here.

Alastair McAuley, another colleague whose suggestions were indispensable to the preparation of my earlier book on the Khrushchev years, was kind enough to act as reader of the present manuscript for Cambridge University Press.

Much of the material in chapter 4 appeared originally as 'The Contradictions of the Marketless Market: Self-financing in the Soviet Industrial Enterprise, 1986–90', *Soviet Studies*, vol. 43, no. 6, 1991, pp. 989–1009, and has been used with the kind permission of the editors of that journal.

It goes without saying that none of those mentioned here bears any responsibility for remaining errors or shortcomings in the text or for my perhaps controversial analysis and conclusions.

Terms and abbreviations

FNPR Federation of Independent Trade Unions of Russia (Federatsiya nezavisimykh profsoyuzov Rossii)

glasnost literally, publicity, or the act of making something known; generally translated as 'openness'

goszakaz literally, state order – that portion of an enterprise's output which it had to sell to the state at official prices

KGB Committee for State Security (Komitet Gosudarstvennoi Bezopasnosti) – the secret police

khozraschet profit-and-loss accounting

kolkhoz collective farm (kollektivnoe khozyaistvo)

Komsomol *see* VLKSM

KPSS Communist Party of the Soviet Union (Kommunisticheskaya Partiya Sovetskogo Soyuza)

krai territory

KTU Labour Input Coefficient (koeffitsient trudovogo uchastiya – literally, coefficient of labour participation)

limitchik migrant worker on temporary residence permit

nomenklatura list of key appointments reserved for members of the Communist Party, used more generally to refer to those in privileged positions

oblast region (roughly equivalent to a province)

orgnabor organized recruitment

perestroika reconstruction, or restructuring

PTU vocational training school or technical college (professional'no-tekhnicheskoe uchilishche)

raion district (administrative sub-division within a city, oblast, or other larger territorial unit)

razryad wage and skill grade

RSFSR	Russian Soviet Federative Socialist Republic (Rossiiskaya Sovetskaya Federativnaya Sotsialisticheskaya Respublika)
SSSR	Union of Soviet Socialist Republics (Soyuz Sovetskikh Sotsialisticheskikh Respublik)
STK	Council of the Labour Collective (soyuz trudovogo kollektiva)
TsK	Central Committee (Tsentral'nyi Komitet)
VKP	General Confederation of Trade Unions (Vseobshchaya Konfederatsiya Profsoyuzov – successor to VTsSPS)
VLKSM	All-Union Leninist Communist League of Youth (Vsesoyuznyi Leninskii Kommunisticheskii Soyuz Molodezhi)
VPK	Military–Industrial Complex (voenno-promyshlennyi kompleks)
VTsSPS	All-Union Central Council of Trade Unions (Vsesoyuznyi Tsentral'nyi Sovet Professional'nykh Soyuzov)

Introduction: The roots and limitations of perestroika

In my two previous studies of Soviet workers in the Stalin and the Khrushchev periods,[1] I argued that the Soviet Union was neither an autonomous mode of production nor a variant of capitalism, but an unstable social formation with limited, and declining, historical viability. It derived its unique character from the fact that the bureaucratic elite, which took root following the collapse of the wave of revolutionary struggles after World War I and the resulting isolation and disintegration of the October Revolution, was unable to consolidate its position as a ruling stratum through either the capitalist market or genuine socialism, both of which would have negated the functions of the bureaucracy and displaced it in favour of another class: the bourgeoisie in the case of a capitalist restoration, or the proletariat in the case of socialism. The system that took shape during the process of Stalinist industrialization was thus deprived of any regulator of economic life. There was neither the spontaneous, albeit crisis-ridden and contradictory regulation of the capitalist market, nor democratic planning, through which society's members could collectively determine its aims and priorities and the methods by which it might achieve them. Unlike the bourgeoisie, which, through its ownership of capital, could reproduce its growing hegemony within the maturing capitalist system before it had actually conquered political power, the Stalinist elite did not own the means of production, and therefore had no economic mechanisms through which to secure and reproduce its expropriation of the surplus product. It could expropriate the surplus only by virtue of its political control over the means of production, which derived in turn from its political control over the state apparatus. This was by no means a peaceful process. The elite faced momentous challenges from both sides: from the private sector, in the form of peasant resistance to collectivization, and from industrial workers, who reacted against the privations and hardships of

1

forced industrialization. To overcome this opposition required the maintenance of a ruthless and ubiquitous repressive apparatus and the near-total atomization of society, in order that any collective challenge to the elite's rule should be impossible.

The society which emerged from this process had definable class relations – a ruling elite expropriating a surplus product and an exploited proletariat and peasantry which created it – but no stable means of reproducing them. In their own quite different ways both the market and socialism rely on independent decision-making by decentralized economic units. The elite, however, could only maintain control through hyper-centralization. Everything had to emanate from the centre, right down to instructions for every nut and bolt. Here there was a contradiction. Such a high degree of centralization presupposed both perfect obedience on the part of the managers and workers who had to execute these 'plans', and perfect information about resources and the results of production. As is now well known, neither managers nor workers had any incentive to provide such obedience. Managers lied about capacities and distorted production programmes to make nominal plan fulfilment much easier. Workers took advantage of the perpetual disorganization within the factories, coupled with the severe labour shortage and the absence of any threat of unemployment, to take back a certain amount of control over the labour process: they worked slowly, showed slack discipline, and turned out defective or low-quality products which deformed the quality of other products in whose production they were used.

The end result was an economy crippled by its huge wastefulness. Quality was bad; managers and workers resisted technical innovation; productivity was poor. There was growth, but it relied on the sheer quantitative expansion of the number of factories put up and, during the system's formative years, on the massive application of slave labour. More crucially, this growth was partially self-consuming. Because quality was so bad the economy needed more and more inputs of things like coal, steel, and building materials, just to keep production stable, much less to increase it. The end result was a vast industrial apparatus which could not feed, clothe, or house its population and which, by the end of the Brezhnev period, had fallen into a state of long-term decline.

There is little doubt that when Gorbachev came to power in 1985, he and his immediate entourage had a relatively clear perception of the crisis condition into which Soviet society had descended, as well as of its political origins. In this they were not unique. Some thirty years before Khrushchev had come to the same realization, and understood that without solving the problem of the population's low morale economic progress would be impossible. This necessarily meant lifting the terror and introducing political liberalization, in the hope that the population would begin to identify its own interests with the maintenance of the system as a whole. The dilemma facing Khrushchev, however, was that any such liberalization had to be controlled and hence limited: it must not go so far as to threaten the very existence of the bureaucratic elite and their hold on power. This tentativeness was to undermine every one of Khrushchev's political and economic reforms. Because they did not lead to any genuine democratization of society, they could only be implemented by bureaucratic officials whose privileges the reforms actually threatened. Thus even the better-intentioned of Khrushchev's reforms relied on the very people who stood to lose out from them, and therefore would not carry them through. More fundamentally, Khrushchev's very perception of what changes were needed was constrained by his own position as a member of a ruling elite that had come to power through the Stalinist system, and whose continued political domination over society depended on that system's perpetuation, even if in a more humane form.

If Gorbachev appreciated both the severity of the country's crisis and, as is probable, the political pitfalls into which Khrushchev had fallen, it is doubtful that he fully understood the essential question which Khrushchev's failure posed: could the Stalinist system be reformed while still preserving its underlying power and class relations? Here the fears of the conservatives – survivors of the Brezhnevite old guard and the younger conservatives (such as Egor Ligachev) who held an ambiguous attitude towards Gorbachev's reforms – were well founded. They had an instinctive awareness, which Gorbachev and his faction of the elite did not, that the system's coherence was so fragile that any relaxation would threaten to fly out of control. But the conservatives had no solution to the country's problems. Soviet society had fallen into a crisis so extensive and so deep that the very process of surplus extraction had become compromised. The official characterization of the Brezhnev period as the 'period of stagnation' was by no means an empty slogan. The economy had ceased to grow, which was both cause and effect of the population's demoralization and disgruntlement. Thus both the economic and political basis of the elite's privileges and its continued rule were threatened. The elite's very existence as a ruling group was in jeopardy if the system did not change. This was the basic truth which the conservatives simply could not grasp.

This book analyses these problems from a very specific vantage point. Its central argument is that the economic policies known as perestroika, together with the political liberalization which came eventually to be known as glasnost (literally, publicity), were above all else designed to restore to the elite greater control over the process of surplus extraction. This necessarily meant conflicts within the elite, since the reforms would inevitably threaten the power and privileges of certain groups, in particular the so-called old guard. However, as already indicated, reforms were unavoidable if the elite *as a social group* was to retain power over society.

In the Soviet context the issue of surplus extraction meant three things. First, it was necessary to increase the size of the surplus. Put simply, society had to produce more, and reverse the years of declining or zero growth. Secondly, there had to be a structural shift from the production of absolute surplus to relative surplus. The Soviet enterprise has traditionally been so resistant to innovation or the restructuring of work practices, that the expansion of production has relied on the application of a greater quantity of means of production and labour power (usually through the construction of new plant), rather than through the use of more efficient machinery and work methods within existing enterprises, which would allow a given unit of labour power to be more productive. Finally, the reforms would have to reduce the 'leakages' from the surplus caused by the wastefulness of the system: physical losses, overconsumption of fuel and materials, defective and poor quality output, and unnecessary expenditures of labour power.[2] None of these issues could be addressed, however, without a fundamental restructuring of the labour process within Soviet industry, which would give the elite greater control over the behaviour of managers and workers at the point of production. Fundamental to this task was reducing the control which the individual worker exercised over the organization, pace, and quality of work.

The issue of workers' control over the labour process itself has different dimensions to it. Numerous Western studies of the labour process under capitalism have emphasized the historical struggles that have taken place over job conception and job execution.[3] By closely guarding skills and their knowledge of processes, materials, tools, and equipment, workers in the nineteenth and early twentieth centuries were able to defend the practice of output restriction, through which they could limit the amount of effort they were required to exert, forestall cuts in wage rates, and determine the organization of their work. Management's response to this was the theory of so-called scientific management, which expressly sought to remove this specialist knowledge from the worker and make it the exclusive prerogative of management. In this way conception would be divorced from execution, and the power of the worker to limit the extent of exploitation severely curtailed. Despite the general success of this managerial offensive (the extent and form of this success have been the subject of much debate among labour historians and labour process analysts), both output restriction and informal shop floor bargaining over effort and remuneration have remained an essential part of industrial life.

Informal bargaining lies at the very heart of the labour process within Soviet industry as well, but its contours differ considerably from what we observe under capitalism. Historically, Soviet workers were stripped of their ability to design and organize their own work process during Stalinist industrialization of the 1930s. Yet, as we have described in some detail in *Soviet Workers and De-Stalinization*, the disorder and lack of coordination that characterize Soviet industry have constantly forced the worker to reassert his or her independence within the work routine. For a significant number of production workers, shortages, improper job specifications, incorrect designs, or faulty equipment all demand a willingness and ability to improvise and redesign processes and procedures, thus indirectly reestablishing at least a partial unity between job design and organization, on the one hand, and execution on the other. However, this exists alongside the dominant form of 'control', which is far more negative in character. The atomization of society by Stalinism had its counterpart in the hyper-individualization of work in Soviet factories. This created a situation where the atomized, alienated worker, deprived of any and all means of exerting collective defence of her or his interests within production or society at large, could and did assert substantial individual control over the organization and execution of work. Slow work, defence of inefficient work organization, toleration, if not exacerbation of disruptions to the work routine, and a general disregard for quality acted sharply to curtail productivity and the elite's ability to appropriate and dispose over the surplus product. Moreover, the worker's behaviour itself became a cause of distortions and bottlenecks, thus helping to perpetuate and reproduce this general work environment.

This brief statement of the argument, which forms the heart of all three of our studies of Soviet workers, must be augmented by two qualifications. First, we are not putting forth a reductionist analysis, attributing all the dysfunctions in Soviet industry to the behaviour of the worker. On the contrary, the combination of the high degree of bureaucratic centralization and the inherent instability of the Stalinist system of production forced both managers and workers to adapt to what confronted them as an externally given work environment and to protect their respective interests as best they could. Thus the disruptions to the work routine resulted equally from the actions of managers, who concealed capacities, resisted the introduction of new technologies, showed scant regard for the conservation of materials and equipment, and circumvented quality standards. This could and did involve considerable conflict between the two sides, but it also resulted in a high degree of enforced collusion. Managers needed the cooperation of workers not to aggravate the myriad dislocations to production; they also needed – given the chronic labour shortage that has perpetually plagued Soviet industry – to dissuade workers from quitting; finally, as noted, they depended on workers' readiness to intervene in the production process and actively assist in the rectification of shortages, poor quality, design faults, or broken equipment. As a result, management was prone to help protect earnings and to turn a blind eye to slow work, defective output, alcoholism, lax time-keeping, and other discipline violations. Workers, for their part, were dependent on management for the granting of these very favours; moreover, they depended on the enterprise for much of the so-called social wage, in particular housing, but also certain levels of health care, access to scarce consumer goods and foodstuffs, and holidays. This leads us to the second qualification. The range of defensive practices developed by workers to lessen the extent of their exploitation, especially against the rapacious labour policies of the 1930s, was by no means a form of resistance. On the contrary, it signified the reaction of a de-politicized workforce no longer able to act as a class in the pursuit of its own radical needs. Through this set of shop floor relationships workers became locked into a politically corrupting relationship with management.

In trying to confront this long-established pattern of shop floor relations perestroika came up against one of the fundamental contradictions of the Stalinist system. The elite, in order to maintain its political control over society, required the atomization of the population and of the industrial workforce in particular. In this sense the paternalistic, de-politicized relations between workers and management were both an expression of this atomization and a precondition of its perpetuation. The cost, however, was the elite's loss of control over the appropriation of the surplus product. In this sense the condition of the elite's ability to maintain its political power was the long-term undermining of the economic basis of that rule and of the elite's privileges.

Perestroika attempted to address this problem partly through the application of quite traditional labour policies, and partly by introducing fundamental changes in the way managers were to run their enterprises, all within the context of what by Soviet standards were far-reaching moves towards political liberalization. The most conventional of these policies was the 1986 wage reform, which sought to undermine the basis of shop- and section-level informal bargaining between workers and line management, by limiting payments for the overfulfilment of norms (output quotas), placing large numbers of workers into lower wage and skill grades, and widening differentials between different categories of workers and between workers as a group and technical specialists. The innovations were in the shift of enterprises to so-called self-financing, through which enterprises were to become less reliant on parent industrial ministries for the guarantee of funds, the allocation of supplies, and the direction of finished output to customers, and were instead gradually to cover the major categories of expenditure out of the revenues they earned. In theory this would put pressure on enterprises to cut costs and improve quality by modernizing plant and equipment and shedding workers – in the early days of perestroika it was estimated that some 16 million people (not all of whom would be industrial workers) would lose their jobs by the year 2000. In so doing, the reforms would also provide managers with both necessity and incentive to launch a frontal assault on the workers' control over the labour process.

It was perfectly clear that if these policies were successful workers would suffer. To this end perestroika had quite definite political preconditions. For their sacrifices workers were to be granted greater participation in enterprise affairs (the slogan 'workers must become masters of their enterprise' became common currency), together with the promise that the reforms would bring a higher standard of living. Perhaps equally important, general political liberalization throughout the society would create an atmosphere in which the elite could establish an ideological legitimacy for itself. In this sense there was much talk of the need to create a Soviet 'civil society', based on the free citizen enjoying political rights. Commensurate with this task, the reformers hoped to create what Gramsci termed a hegemonic ideology, through which the subordinated mass of the population would accept as normal and natural the organization of society which produced and reproduced its subordination. But here, too, the reforms were caught in a contradiction. The creation of a Soviet civil society and hegemonic ideology could only evolve through a protracted process, covering many generations, and would require not just political liberalization, but a rapid rise in the standard of living. But as the reformers recognized, the standard of living would only rise if the population overcame its feelings of atomization and exclusion – something it would only do if the standard of living were already seen to be improving. The reforms were caught in a vicious circle. Moreover, the economy was in such grave difficulties that the elite could not really wait for the evolution of such a civil society, with its 'self-motivating' mechanisms, to come into being. Industrial and agricultural output would have to improve now, which could only come at the expense of tighter discipline and an intensification of work.

As we shall see in chapters 1–3, the major aspects of labour policy under perestroika failed, and with them went any hope of restructuring the labour process in such a way as to permit a substantial increase in the surplus product. As this became evident, by mid-1990 at the latest, the elite, or at least its reform wing around Gorbachev, realized that structural adjustments to the old system would no longer work and it would be necessary to move full-scale towards capitalism and the market. Yet the collapse of the original concept of perestroika was only partly due to resistance by entrenched elements in the bureaucracy or to rigidities within the old system. It is true that industrial managers opposed numerous aspects of the reforms and distorted others. Workers, too, showed less than rapt enthusiasm, especially as they experienced few palpable benefits from the changes. Fear of popular discontent also played a major role, forcing successive governments to hold back from more drastic steps towards marketization – in particular, the ending of state subsidies on food and basic consumer goods. For all the importance of these different factors, the main problems with the reforms lay deeper within the system. They deprived the system of what tenuous coherence bureaucratic 'planning' had given it, but could not find an alternative mode of economic regulation. On the contrary, the tendencies inherent in the old system which subjected enterprises to constant disruptions to supplies, labour shortages, and uncertainties over the reliability of equipment or components, were now reinforced by decentralization and the market. The introduction of so-called market mechanisms and enterprise self-financing compelled enterprises to adopt the logic of the market without a real market actually being put in place. The decentralization of planning and decision-making regarding pricing, finding customers, sources of supplies, and the distribution of revenues between new investment, money wages, and social benefits led to the collapse of interenterprise coordination. As essentially monopolistic producers operating in an environment of chronic scarcity, enterprise after enterprise responded by cutting production and raising prices. Shortages of materials reached crisis proportions, forcing a further contraction of production. It was an economy on the verge of implosion. In this environment, with enterprises struggling just to maintain production, restructuring of the labour process became simply an impossibility, and it is doubtful if many managers even recognized it as a goal.

First of all, it was impossible to introduce a flexible labour market without new investment, yet such investment was one of the first casualties of self-financing. This is over and above the structural obstacle to modernization inherent in the backward technology characteristic of most of Soviet industry. Secondly, changes in the wages and incentives system soon became ineffective, since the disruptions to production endemic to the old system were now reinforced by the loss of workers – both skilled and unskilled – to the new cooperatives, which offered better wages and often better conditions. Whatever financial discipline the 1986 wage reform had imposed was soon cast completely aside, as managers had to raise wages in order to induce workers to stay. Moreover, there was now a new element in the equation. With political liberalization workers began to engage in strikes, and soon found that they could extract considerable concessions from management through industrial action.

By 1990 Gorbachev's original reforms lay in tatters, and the regime made a clear decision to introduce capitalism, despite all the uncertainties this posed for the elite as a social group. No other alternative was available. For this was not a case where the entrenched conservatism of the old system had subverted the reforms, and the situation would return to the *status quo ante*. Quite to the contrary, perestroika had undermined the basis of the old system once and for all, so much so that further attempts at its reform or restructuring became impossible. But the path to capitalism was also blocked. New struggles broke out between different sections of the elite over who would emerge as the new class of owners of the property that was now going to be privatized. Yet whoever wins this battle – and its outcome is still by no means clear – will find an economy that is too enfeebled to generate sufficient capital accumulation to make post-Soviet capitalism viable. Instead, the new capitalism will be a parasitic, corrupt, speculative capitalism, with no dynamic towards growth and development.

And what of the working class? Perhaps the great historical contribution of perestroika was that it unblocked the social stasis of the Stalin and Brezhnev years and created at least the conditions for a reemergence of class struggle. But this has proved an uncertain and tentative process. Workers soon learned how to initiate and organize collective action, but politically they remained highly tentative, reflecting six decades of political demoralization. Even the most militant sections of the new workers' movement had little clear vision of what positive goals to pursue, beyond dismantling the old system. What is more, the economy's collapse created new soil for many of the old shop floor relations to implant themselves more firmly. Patterns of informal bargaining over sanctions and concessions underwent remarkably little change because managers still required workers' cooperation to maintain production. For their part, workers became once again dependent on management and the official trade unions for the wherewithal to ensure the survival of themselves and their families. Thus the old paternalism was given a new lease on life.

What resulted, then, was a qualitatively new and highly unstable economic environment which by 1991 had left society in a state of stalemate. Even when the political logjam at the top of the system was eased in the aftermath of the August 1991 *putsch* and the ascendancy of El'tsin, the essential problem still remained unresolved. The failures of perestroika reinforced and consolidated those traditional shop floor relations which had always been a brake on the development of the productive forces and the creation and appropriation of the social surplus. No future capitalist class, even one presiding over the type of Latin American capitalism that is the former USSR's likely future, can circumvent the need to address this issue. To survive capitalism must accumulate, and this task will be impossible on the basis of the social relations that existed within Soviet industry. Sooner or later, therefore, the new ruling class will have to mount a frontal assault on these relations. But this will bring in its wake massive social conflict, the outcome of which no-one can yet predict. Stand-off and continued disintegration and chaos cannot be ruled out. We may well reach a situation where the organization of production will change only when the working class of Russia and the other ex-Soviet republics decides that it must change, that is, when it achieves a new political consciousness and places society under the collective, democratic control of its disenfranchised toiling majority.

The plan of the book is as follows. Part I examines the three major areas of labour policy under perestroika. Chapter 1 discusses attempts to create a labour market and introduce unemployment, and analyses why mass unemployment did not occur and industry was instead beset by a worsening labour shortage. Chapter 2 examines the 1986 wage reform and the reasons for its failure. Chapter 3 deals with the regime's strategy of trying to win working-class support for what were in effect anti-working-class reforms by allowing limited enterprise 'democratization'; this policy also collapsed, partly because no real democratization was on offer, and partly because the political liberalization of society at large gave rise to two waves of mass worker protest which shook perestroika to its foundations and rendered any restructuring of industry impossible.

Part II looks at the labour process under perestroika. Chapter 4 analyses the contradictions of what we have termed 'the marketless market', and shows how the policy of enterprise self-financing led the economy to the verge of total collapse, thus depriving the reform programme of any foundation on which to proceed. Chapter 5 analyses the political economy of working conditions in Soviet industry, focusing on two issues: (1) the implications which the economy's shortage of fixed capital, together with the perpetuation of arduous and unsafe working conditions have for any possible restructuring of production; and (2) the contradictory role which women workers occupied in the strategy of perestroika. To raise the standard of living the reformers had to concentrate resources on precisely those industries which manufacture consumer goods, industries which rely almost exclusively on female labour; yet these were precisely the industries which perestroika neglected and which suffered the worst from the crisis of self-financing. Chapter 6 investigates the labour process *per se*, looking in some detail at patterns of informal bargaining on the shop floor and showing how perestroika actually reinforced these relations, rather than undermined them. Finally, in the Conclusion we examine the implications which the collapse of perestroika and of the Stalinist system have for both the post-Soviet and international working class.

Part I

Labour policy under perestroika

1 Attempts to create a labour market: employment, unemployment, and the labour shortage

Since the first five-year plans the Soviet economy has been characterized by the seeming paradox of a severe and reproducible labour shortage alongside overstaffing within each individual production unit.[1] The paradox becomes explicable if we examine its principal causes. (1) Enterprises need to hoard labour as a hedge against taut periods, usually at the end of the month or planning period, when extra hands are required to meet production targets (so-called 'storming'). (2) The system suffers from a structural inability to mechanise auxiliary operations within production, leading to a swollen auxiliary apparatus. (3) Workers exercise a considerable degree of control over work speeds and labour organization, which impedes the introduction of modern equipment and rationalizations which might reduce the demand for labour power and otherwise weaken this control. (4) The system exhibits a general tendency towards waste, which causes Soviet production to consume considerably more inputs of means of production and labour power per unit of finished output than modern capitalist economies. To these basic factors must be added workers' virtual security of employment, which functions here as both cause and effect. Although since Khrushchev it has been legally very difficult to dismiss a worker, this has more to do with the persistence of the labour shortage than any legal guarantees, which both managers and workers have proven adept at circumventing in other areas of factory life. The labour shortage has been a prime factor in reinforcing workers' control over the labour process by undermining the effectiveness of any potential sanctions, including dismissal. Managers have been reluctant to discharge workers for discipline violations unless they are perceived as distinct trouble-makers, while the effectiveness of internal penalties is weakened by the threat that the worker might quit. It is this, the issue of control, which gives rise to the labour shortage's reproducibility. The labour shortage permits workers the freedom of action which, by causing or exacerbating tendencies towards inefficiency and waste, constantly recreates the conditions that require management to hoard labour, thus reproducing the labour shortage in each successive production period.[2]

It should come as no surprise that the creation of labour mobility and an unfettered labour market was a central goal of the economic reforms of perestroika. At stake were two issues. The first was how to free up the labour resources locked inside industrial enterprises in order to provide labour power for new industries and services. The second was how to end the labour shortage, so as to weaken workers' individual and collective power on the shop floor, itself a necessary condition for restructuring the labour process. Both these tasks required the introduction of large-scale layoffs and mass unemployment. According to the State Planning Commission's (Gosplan) initial forecasts, some 16 million people would lose their jobs by the year 2000, although not all would stay out of work.[3]

There were, in fact, two distinct, if not conflicting strategies among reformers concerning unemployment. According to the dominant strategy, which formed the basis of official policy, workers were to be let go as a result of technical modernization and a general streamlining of production, enforced in turn by the need for enterprises to show a profit under the new conditions of financial management. Redundant workers would, however, be reemployed almost *in toto* in other areas of the economy. According to this scenario, then, workforce reductions would not lead to long-term unemployment, but would merely release workers currently unproductively employed for the expanded production of use values or the provision of services. This was certainly the official position of the State Committee on Labour and Social Questions, Goskomtrud.[4] The other strategy, championed by the more strident of the marketeers, saw redundancies leading to genuine unemployment, which was to act as a disciplining vehicle and a means of coercing workers into surrendering shop floor prerogatives, similar to the strategy pursued by the Conservative government in Britain after 1979.[5]

Despite the considerable gulf between these two approaches (the first would do nothing to weaken workers' power, either individually or collectively on the shop floor), both saw the erosion of legal and *de facto* protection of employment as essential to introducing labour mobility and undermining the practice of labour hoarding. The successful implementation of either of these strategies had specific political and institution prerequisites which, as we shall see, were never

created. The issue of unemployment has always been politically sensitive among workers. If redundancies were to be introduced on a mass
scale it was essential that potential discontent be forestalled or defused
by providing an adequate system of unemployment benefits, job
placement services, and retraining. In the event, partly due to inadequacies of policy, partly because of the rigidity of the bureaucratic
system, and most importantly, because of the backwardness of Soviet
production, the regime failed even remotely to carry out this task. But
what finally undermined the reformers' employment policy were the
market reforms themselves, which by opening up alternative employment in cooperatives and at the same time precipitating a calamitous
fall in production, with a commensurate deterioration in working
conditions, led to an exodus from industry of skilled and unskilled
workers and a severe labour shortage which accelerated the
economy's downward spiral.

The plan of this chapter is as follows. Section 1 examines the general
state of unemployment during perestroika, together with certain
specific features of the Soviet labour market in this period: the problems of long-term unemployment in the Central Asian republics; the
vulnerability of specific groups to layoffs, in particular women, young
workers, and the disabled; and the position of migrant workers, on
whom so much of Soviet industry and construction has come to
depend. Section 2 looks at what might be termed the political infrastructure required for the successful management of unemployment,
namely, the provision of benefits and the job placement and training
networks, and analyses their failures and weaknesses. Finally, section
3 traces the emergence and worsening of the labour shortage, which
was both proof and cause of the collapse of reformers' original
employment strategy.

Specific features of the Soviet labour market under perestroika

The Soviet workforce, like the working class in every society,
is highly differentiated. As we show in chapter 5, there are deep
divisions along lines of skill and gender, not to mention those of
nationality, language, and race. The relatively skilled male workers,
concentrated in the heavy industries of the European republics,
enjoy significant privileges relative to weaker sections of the population. Women are marginalized into low-paying jobs in services and
industry, where they work under strenuous and often hazardous

conditions, and have little access to the acquisition of higher skills and other avenues of advancement. Since the mid-1960s many of the low-skilled and unattractive jobs in industry have been taken not just by women, but by migrant workers of both sexes, the so-called *limitch-iki*,[6] who come to the large cities from small towns or rural areas in the hope of settling there and acquiring permanent access to a higher standard of living. The position of the non-European republics is somewhat different. Since Stalin's time, if not before, they have suffered from a distorted development of both industry and agriculture which has left their economies dependent on monoculture and a handful of heavy industries, leaving large sections of their populations with only limited opportunities for gainful employment and desperately poor, even by Soviet standards.

To some extent the impact of unemployment during perestroika followed these divisions. While overall the predicted wave of mass redundancies never occurred, not all groups of workers were safe. Workers on specific investment projects or specific industries targeted for cutbacks, or in the small number of enterprises which underwent substantial reconstruction, did indeed lose their jobs, even if they were the exception. Equally, certain sub-groups within the workforce, namely the long-term unemployed of Central Asia, women, migrant workers, the young, and the disabled, in different ways saw their position made more tenuous by the market pressures of perestroika. Either, as in the case of Central Asia, they continued to bear the brunt of regional underdevelopment or, as with women, the young, and the disabled, they saw their existing jobs or access to new ones made far more uncertain. Yet here, too, the impact of unemployment was uneven: although there was a discernible tendency for enterprises to discriminate against young workers and women, within industry as a whole their positions were at least partially protected by the labour shortage.

Unemployment during perestroika: general results

At no time during perestroika did the regime produce precise figures on how many people were actually unemployed in the USSR. In spring 1990 the State Committee for Labour and Social Questions (Goskomtrud), put the number at around 2 million, but even Goskomtrud's own officials conceded that this was no more than just a guess.[7] A later estimate by the State Committee for Statistics (Goskomstat) claimed 4 million people who were either seeking work but were unable to find it or were simply unwilling to work in the state sector.[8] If nothing else, both these figures ignored the huge black labour market estimated by one specialist to embrace 5 million formally unemployed people and another 15 million 'hidden unemployed'.[9] The issue is further clouded by the existence of long-term structural unemployment and underemployment in the Central Asian republics which we discuss in the next section. In terms of the present discussion, we should note that, no matter how serious its social and political impact in the areas concerned, such unemployment is a separate problem from the use of redundancies to introduce labour mobility – and with it an assault on the existing pattern of shop floor relations – in established industrial centres.

Even at the beginning of perestroika redundancies did not develop as originally intended. For the economy as a whole, between 1986 and 1988 some 3 million employed persons lost their jobs, of whom 1 million were directed to new posts within the same enterprise (filling out second or third shifts or staffing new production units) and 1.5 million went to other branches of the national economy, including services and cooperatives. In all, only 370,000 vacancies were eliminated for the economy at large. The cuts fell proportionally heaviest on specialists and white-collar employees rather than on ordinary workers, although in absolute numbers more workers were released from their jobs.[10] Where production workers were concerned, a study by the State Committee on Labour and Social Questions (Goskomtrud) covering the period 1986–87, found that some two-thirds of workers who lost their jobs were redeployed to cover labour shortages in the same enterprise. Often normal transfers were listed as 'redundancies', merely to show compliance with the official campaign. Conversely, many of those who had been made 'redundant' did not even know that they had been let go or moved to other jobs. On the other hand, management often took advantage of workers' desire to avoid leaving the enterprise in order to impose worse pay or working conditions. Thus during this early period layoffs, or the threat of layoffs, appeared to have some 'disciplining' effect on workers within production, but it did not produce greater mobility, a key aim of employment policy at this time.[11]

There were widespread predictions that unemployment would rise sharply during 1990 and 1991. According to one Goskomtrud official, 1990 would see as many as 2.7 million unemployed,[12] while the head of the newly created Moscow Labour Exchange predicted that during 1991 1.2 million people would 'temporarily' lose their jobs in Moscow

alone.[13] In the event, the expected massive job losses never materia-
lized. In Leningrad, where the city authorities had expected as many
as 13,000 layoffs a month during the winter of 1991, the actual number
was just over 3,200, mainly among technical specialists.[14] In Moscow
the picture was the same. In October 1991, that is, four months after the
official start of registration under the 1991 employment law, there were
a mere 5,600 unemployed registered with the Moscow Labour
Exchange, the overwhelming majority of whom were women specialists over the age of 45.[15] In Zaporozh'e as of 1 October 1991, a total of
six people had registered as unemployed, all of them technical personnel.[16] Instead of witnessing mass unemployment, the country fell into
a steadily worsening labour shortage, which undermined even the
limited disciplining effect achieved during the early years of the
reforms.

However, this picture was not uniform across the Soviet Union.
Leaving aside the chronic structural unemployment of Central Asia,
there were cities, industries, or individual enterprises where layoffs
occurred on a significant scale. In Kazan, in the Tatar Republic, the rate
of layoffs accelerated towards the end of 1990 while vacancies contracted, and at least 4,000 people were unable to find a new job within
their first three months out of work.[17] A rise in unemployment to 4 per
cent of the working age population was forecast for the Krivoi Rog
basin in Ukraine in early 1991, due to conversion from military to
civilian production and an expected restructuring of the region's
industry.[18] Enterprises or enterprise sub-units on leasing were, of
course, encouraged to shed workers in order to economize on wages,
and many did so.[19] The atmosphere of impending catastrophe was
fuelled by those sections of the Party bureaucracy and the press which
were still sceptical about the market reforms. In July 1990 the paper
Rabochaya tribuna launched a Social Fund for Defence Against
Unemployment, which drew the support of many of the large industrial ministries, local Party first secretaries, enterprise directors, and
even Prime Minister Ryzhkov – all of whom demagogically tried to
present themselves as the defenders of ordinary workers.[20] In early
1991 the Ukrainian government pointedly announced that it was
unable to pass an employment law, since the republic's treasury had
insufficient funds to pay out the anticipated unemployment benefits.[21]

The combination of these expectations and the reality of redundancies in particular factories or shops was sufficient to create a genuine
fear of unemployment among some sections of workers, making them
vulnerable to management intimidation. Women at the local confec-

tionary association in Nizhnii Novgorod began putting in substantial forced overtime after the factory went on *khozraschet*, simply out of fear of losing their jobs.[22] Miners in the Magadan gold mines began avoiding health checkups, frightened that if they were diagnosed with silicosis they would either be let go or put on low-paying surface work.[23]

Such examples were augmented by more systematic cases, often involving large numbers of workers. As early as 1989 the jobs of 50,000–150,000 workers on construction of the Tyumen' gas pipeline (commissioned in the wake of the Chernobyl disaster) were threatened when the government, on the pretext of reducing its budget deficit, ordered the wholesale abandonment of the project. These workers were in an especially precarious position, since there was little alternative employment in the region. Even if new jobs could be found, either in the Far North or elsewhere in the USSR, many had been in the housing queue for over ten years and would have to begin their wait all over again at their new place of work. Despite threats of strike action, the layoffs eventually went through, although the exact number affected was not published.[24] The timing of the pipeline cutbacks in late 1989, that is, when it was already evident that the reformers' policy of inducing mass unemployment was not working, but before the deteriorating labour shortage had begun to cause serious bottlenecks in industry, suggests that this decision was not simply motivated by the desire to reduce the budget deficit, but was at least partly political. On this scenario, the government was using the Tyumen' workers as a test case, to see if it could introduce large-scale unemployment without provoking widespread protest, while at the same time acclimatizing the population to the general idea that further layoffs were to come.[25]

Long-term unemployment

In many ways the problem of long-term unemployment in the non-European republics does not properly belong to a discussion of employment policy under perestroika. Its roots are much more structural, in their long-standing domination by the metropolitan centre in Moscow. Chronic poverty, rural overpopulation, a top-heavy industrial structure, coupled with the extensive corruption of the local Communist Party machines, make this region the Soviet Union's 'third world'.

The bulk of long-term unemployment has long been concentrated in

Central Asia and the other Muslim republics, although it was only under perestroika that the problem was openly acknowledged. The actual magnitude of unemployment is difficult to ascertain. According to *Rabochaya tribuna*, for example, in early 1991 there were 500,000 people in Uzbekistan 'temporarily not working', that is, unemployed.[26] Yet a year earlier, when the employment situation was clearly better, a member of the Uzbek Academy of Sciences claimed that of the republic's 2.3 million residents not in employment, a full 1 million were looking for work.[27] In Azerbaijan at the end of 1990 there were 500,000 unemployed, with another 200,000 expected to lose their jobs during 1991.[28] In reality the situation is even more severe than these figures would suggest, for there is a large surplus population, most of it rural, totally outside social production. If in 1985, 8.2 per cent of Russians and 5.3 per cent of Balts of working age were not in employment, in the Central Asian republics and Azerbaijan the figure was from two to four times as high: 27.7 per cent in Tadzhikistan, 21.4 per cent in Uzbekistan, 21.3 per cent in Azerbaijan, 15.7 per cent in Turkmeniya, 15 per cent in Kirgiziya, and 13.5 per cent in Kazakhstan.[29] In most of these republics, by 1989 these figures had risen still further.[30] Moreover, because of their higher birth rate, more young people are entering the labour market with fewer opportunities to find work.[31] According to *Trud*, in Tadzhikistan some 30,000–40,000 young men and women join the ranks of the unemployed every year.[32] The situation was similar in Uzbekistan, where in 1985 only 13 per cent of graduates of rural schools found jobs in industry or construction.[33]

Although these figures are to some extent explained by the Muslim culture of these republics, and the discouragement of rural women from working, much of the problem lies in the distorted development of the region. Agriculture is based mainly on monoculture, namely, cotton for the Soviet Union's textile mills. Investment policy, determined by the centralized ministries in Moscow, concentrated on constructing large enterprises in the cities where infrastructure and public amenities are poor. Conversely, there have been few opportunities for non-agricultural employment outside the large towns. Most cotton, for example, was sent to the European part of the USSR for working up.[34] The result was an irrational industrial location structure, where urban heavy industry had thousands of unfilled vacancies, while in the countryside hundreds of thousands of people were out of work. In part this imbalance arose from the poor infrastructure of the towns, especially the lack of housing, which has detered rural families from seeking work in urban areas.[35] At the same time, however, the unemployed do not possess the skills which industrial enterprises require.[36] In theory they could easily be trained for many of these jobs, but the training network is weak. In Kazakhstan the All-Union departments so abjured the training and hiring of local people that they even brought their own secretaries and typists from outside the republic, giving them priority for housing and childcare places, much to the resentment of locals who had been queuing for many years.[37]

By the end of perestroika the labour shortage in the cities of Central Asia had become chronic. In Kazakhstan at the end of 1990 there were 200,000 unfilled vacancies.[38] Central Asian iron and steel plants reported a severe shortage of workers. Production lines at engineering factories in Frunze were standing idle for lack of people to run them.[39] The aviation factory in Tashkent reported a shortage of milling machine operators, turners, fitters, and builders, despite the existence of 67,000 unemployed in Tashkent alone. All its efforts to recruit local people, including television advertisements and bonuses offered to recruiters, were in vain. The reason throws considerable light on the complexity of the employment situation in this and similar republics. There is in Central Asia, as well as in many Russian cities, a thriving black labour market, where workers go to the bazaar to be hired for casual jobs, often in state enterprises. In Tashkent, at least, many workers considered the pay and conditions (up to 25 rubles a day, plus free lunch) better than at the aviation plant, which helped explain the latter's inability to recruit.[40]

It must be said that by and large the problem of long-term unemployment and the general underdevelopment of the non-European USSR were only peripheral concerns of perestroika. There is little evidence that either the government or the central ministries had any coherent policy to reverse these trends. Nor could the persistence of unemployment be used as an effective political weapon to impose tighter discipline among workers in the region's industry, for despite the surplus population, industry itself suffered from a labour shortage as severe as elsewhere in the USSR. Although its causes were in large part regionally specific, its impact was the same.

Groups vulnerable to discriminatory hiring and dismissal

Under the pre-perestroika wages system, where wage bills were guaranteed by the centre, enterprises were under little pressure to economize on wage costs or to demand high levels of productivity. With the shift to *khozraschet* this situation began to change. Suddenly

certain groups of workers became unprofitable to hire or to keep on
the payroll: women with young children, who might have to take time
off work to sort out family affairs or look after sick children; young
workers looking for their first job and needing training; the disabled;
workers seeking to return to work after prolonged sick leave; workers
fired for discipline violations; and ex-prisoners.[41] What they all had in
common was that, in the eyes of management, they were unlikely to
be able to carry a full work load and would thus be a drag on
enterprise performance. They were, in the words of two labour
specialists, the 'socio-occupational "ballast"' of the enterprise.[42]

In the early phases of the reform numerous commentators warned
that women with young children would be the first candidates for
redundancies when factories came to shed staff. Zoya Pukhova, chair
of the Soviet Women's Committee, told the 19th Party Conference in
July 1988, that such women, should they attempt to avail themselves of
flexible work schedules or part-time work, 'unwillingly enter into
conflict with management and the labour collective of the shop or
brigade, and are becoming undesired labour power. When establishments are cut, women are the first to be dismissed'.[43] Such fears
were echoed by other commentators, including a woman production
worker, who wrote to *Okhrana truda*, the trade unions' labour safety
journal, 'I'm 40 years old, and I've worked 20 of them as a machinist on
the conveyor. When men were scarce we were needed, but now
they're kicking us out'.[44] As we discuss in more detail in chapter 5, the
potential victimization of women placed the regime in a somewhat
contradictory position. On the one hand, it was clearly the strategy of
at least some sections of the elite to push women out of the workforce
and back into the home, both as a means of strengthening the family
and of introducing unemployment in a way which male workers
would find more acceptable. On the other hand, the early evidence of
discriminatory hiring and firing pushed the government in spring 1990
to offer pregnant women and women with dependent children
greater legal protection of their right to work. In the event, large-scale,
permanent layoffs of women workers did not, in fact, take place,
although many women were put on short time or sent on unpaid leave
in connection with the deepening supply crisis. This does not mean
that at individual enterprises workers were not made to bear the brunt
of marketization, especially during the early stages of the reforms. By
late 1991 and early 1992, unemployed women specialists and clerical
employees were to come up against these same obstacles.[45] But within
production the labour shortage became so severe, even among low-

skilled workers, that layoffs of either men or women became for managers a practical impossibility.

A similar, but less clear-cut pattern emerged with regard to young people. Under pre-reform regulations, enterprises were obliged to maintain a quota of jobs reserved for young, first-time entrants into the labour force, and to take on those sent to them by the planning authorities. With the State Enterprise Law of 1987, and the gradual shift of enterprises to *khozraschet*, factories were allowed independently to determine the number of workers they would hire and their skill and occupational composition. Thus, although the quota system was still in place and the Labour Code continued to bar factories from refusing to hire young people except in specially enumerated cases, enterprises were now under financial pressure to avoid these obligations, and were given the legal means to do so.[46]

In reality, pressures on the job market for young workers had been building up for some time: the number of new work places created each year declined from an average of 1,859,000 during 1960–70, to just 434,000 in 1985–6, and actually contracted in 1988.[47] With *khozraschet* these pressures intensified, as older workers became reluctant to take young people into their brigades, for fear they would be less productive. Factories also cut back on training, since this was now deemed a high-cost item with little immediate payoff. In 1988, that is, before the cutbacks imposed by *khozraschet* had really begun to bite, the number of first-time workers receiving training in industry fell by 365,000. Enterprises simply found it more profitable to poach skilled workers from other enterprises, rather than to train their own.[48] At the same time, young workers became early candidates for redundancy.[49] The effect of both these trends was to deflect younger workers out of more technically sophisticated enterprises towards those dominated by low-skilled work under poor conditions, although by mid-1990 even these factories were beginning to refuse to hire them.[50] It is clear that the 'market mechanisms' of *khozraschet* were storing up the for Soviet Union a serious future skills shortage. A new generation of skilled workers was simply not being trained.[51] While most school leavers were still finding some form of work, 1990 also saw the appearance of the first signs of structural youth unemployment. This was most pronounced in the Asian republics. But in the RSFSR and Ukraine, too, 1.3–1.4 per cent of school leavers were unable to find any sort of job at all. This may seem small by Western standards, but it represented only the beginning of a trend that will surely accelerate as the process of marketization advances. Yet, as we shall see in the last section, even here the picture was contradictory, for while many factories were reluctant to hire young workers, others were having great difficulty deterring them from quitting and coping with the bottlenecks their exit created.

The position of the disabled is somewhat different, since they are a group which has suffered long-term discrimination and exclusion from the labour force. Of the Soviet Union's 7.5 million disabled persons well under half were employed, even though most wished to work.[52] Legally, enterprises had to reserve 2 per cent of their work places (raised to 5 per cent in December 1990) for disabled persons,[53] but in reality few did so. The quota was simply unenforceable, since there were no penalties for ignoring it, and managers had little incentive or desire to invest in the adaptations and equipment that would allow the disabled to carry out a job. Where factories did employ them, it was in such mind-numbing occupations as watchpersons, caretakers, and cloakroom attendants. According to the head of the All-Union Society of Blind Persons, those who chose which jobs the disabled would do gave little thought to whether or not they would find the work satisfying.[54] This has led to the totally irrational situation where in Perm there are some 6,500 disabled children unable to obtain any schooling, while the city has unemployed disabled teachers.[55]

The Soviet Union actually had a policy of constructing special shops and enterprises in which the disabled could work, but they met only about 7 per cent of need. Worse still, they often exploited their disabled workers ruthlessly. In Perm, for example, the city's society for the disabled ran a workshop manufacturing cardboard boxes. It employed 134 people, 86 of whom were disabled, but conditions were appalling: premises were said to be the size of a bus in rush hour, there was no hot water, and only one toilet. Yet the enterprise was extremely profitable, with a turnover in 1990 of 6 million rubles a year.[56] Worse still was the Spetstrud (literally, special labour) Production Association in Moscow, which consisted of twenty-six separate enterprises officially classified as for the disabled, by virtue of which they received substantial concessions over taxes and the receipt of raw materials and equipment. In 1989 the Association recorded a profit of tens of millions of rubles, yet was actually laying off its disabled workers. Some of its enterprises, in fact, had few disabled workers. One, the Krasnogorsk fancy goods factory, employed only 197 disabled out of a workforce of over 1,000. Moreover, they were put on the least lucrative jobs (some earned as little as 30 rubles a month) in dreadful physical conditions. In effect, the factory used its grants and concessions to subsidize the wages of its able-bodied workforce, who not only enjoyed substantial wage rises, but whose bonuses alone were nearly twice the size of some of the disabled workers' total earnings.[57]

Migrant workers

Since the mid-1960s industry in the Soviet Union's largest cities, in particular Moscow and Leningrad, came to depend increasingly on the influx of migrants from small towns and villages, who sought access to the better supplies enjoyed by the large conurbations. Like migrants in other countries, they came to take the low-paid, arduous, and often hazardous jobs which locals would no longer do. In the past in the Soviet Union these jobs had been filled by women from the cities concerned, but as the service sector expanded, thus offering local women greater opportunities for non-factory employment, and as the scale of industrial investment continued to grow, eventually even this source of recruitment proved inadequate. Factories were allowed to recruit specific numbers of migrant workers, most of whom came from Central Russia, who were given limited residence permits, or *propiski*.[58] The individual allocations became known as the *limit*, after its English cognate, with the migrants being called *limitchiki*.

Even those familiar with the Soviet Union may not fully appreciate just how vital these workers are to the urban economies. In Leningrad as late as 1991 they made up virtually all of the city's construction workers, and most of its dockers, loaders on transport operations, street cleaners, policemen, and workers in the leather and rubber goods industries.[59] In Moscow they are half the workforce at the city's ZiL truck and limousine plant (many of the remaining workers are former migrants who obtained permanent residence), and an integral, if not the main component of workers at the AZLK automobile factory, the Serp i molot iron and steel works, the building materials industry, and enterprises in light industry.[60] In Ivanovo, the large textile town in Central Russia, the mills increasingly have had to rely on young girls coming in from the surrounding countryside.[61]

From the point of view of the urban authorities the system of migrant labour was not without its drawbacks. Although factories were able to recruit the required number of workers, the influx of outsiders placed huge demands on the infrastructures of the urban areas, in particular housing. The extra population also taxed the supply and distribution networks, especially as food shortages became more serious. As a result cities began to restrict the inflow of non-locals. In 1987 Moscow placed a ban on all temporary residence permits.[62] In Leningrad the city authorities did not impose an outright prohibition, but tried to deter recruitment through financial penalties: as of 1 January 1990, for each non-resident entering a factory vocational training school the parent enterprise had to pay the city 13,000 rubles and had to guarantee her or him the same amount of housing space as would apply to Leningrad natives.[63] Since these measures did nothing to induce local residents to take the jobs for which the *limitchiki* were needed, enterprises began to suffer labour shortages, made worse by the fact that, at least in Leningrad, the city no longer enjoyed a palpable supply advantage over other big cities, making it a less popular pole of attraction for migrant workers.[64] Factories were forced to cope as best they could. Some had to make up the short-fall by hiring 'temporary' workers, primarily ex-drug addicts and alcoholics.[65] ZiL was also able to extract a special dispensation from the Moscow city government, allowing it to bring in 5,000 *limitchiki* per year, many of them apparently recruited through swap arrangements with driving schools throughout the USSR: ZiL provided the schools with whatever they needed, and the schools recruited and sent to ZiL 'cheap, reliable labour'.[66] AZLK, which used to draw most migrant workers from the oblasts around Moscow, had to send recruiting agents to Uzbekistan, where, taking advantage of the high unemployment in that republic, it hired workers on three-year contracts, after which they would have to return home. In many ways this worked very much to the factory's advantage: it would never have to provide these workers with permanent housing (unlike the former migrants, they could not stay in the job long enough to earn permanent residence), and they proved politically extremely timid, for fear of losing their jobs.[67]

Another solution was to bring in workers from abroad. In early 1981 the Soviet Union began recruiting workers from Viet Nam, who if anything were even more brutally exploited than the workers from Central Asia. As of 1990 there were 90,000 Vietnamese workers in Soviet industry, evenly divided between women and men.[68] Both light industry and heavy industry were in large part dependent on them to keep production going. There were 13,000 Vietnamese in the tractor industry alone,[69] while large numbers worked at ZiL and other motor vehicle plants in Ul'yanovsk, Yaroslavl', and Tol'yatti.[70] In all cases they were hired on limited contracts: women could stay no more than four years, men no more than six. Most had to leave their husbands, wives, and children back in Viet Nam; they had the right to make one visit home during the length of their contract, but only with management permission. Changing jobs was practically impossible, since they were virtually indentured to the factories, which paid for their training and often gave them seed loans to ease them through the first months of their stay.[71] If they found their jobs completely intolerable, the only way out was to commit deliberate absenteeism, in an attempt to force their employer to fire them and send them home.[72] In addition to suffering from the more 'subtle' forms of racism – constant stares, fear of walking the streets at night[73] – they became involved in repeated conflicts with Soviet workers. Fights were not infrequent, sometimes ending in stabbings. Some reports accused the men of engaging in various forms of black market crime,[74] but other, more sympathetic commentators put much of this down to the low wages they earned in the Soviet Union, where they had come in the hope of earning extra money to send home to their families.[75] Whatever the reason, the clashes were often quite serious, with Soviet workers demanding that the Vietnamese be sent home.[76]

Even for Soviet citizens, the working and living conditions of migrant workers range from bad to dreadful. At ZiL, for the 'privilege' of a Moscow residence permit, such workers might drag around 9 tons of metal billets a shift, wash parts in toxic chemicals, or work in foundries where contamination and gas levels are seventy times the permitted maximum.[77] In Moscow's large commercial laundries, the women work in temperatures up to 60–70C in permanently damp conditions.[78] But it is housing which is their worst problem, and which is used by management to keep these workers under control. Almost uniformly these men and women live in dormitories, in cramped conditions, where they might stay for fifteen, twenty, or even thirty years.[79] Some of the dormitories are located in industrial areas where pollution makes them unsafe to live.[80] At ZiL workers receive just 4 square metres of living space, with a bed and a bedside table.[81] At Leningrad's Krasnyi treugol'nik rubber technical goods factory, families share a single small room, children and all, divided only by a screen and a wardrobe. There is a housing queue, but only those white-collar staff able to bribe the management are able to jump it, for which they might receive a room in four or five years. For *limitchiki* such possibilities are beyond reach.[82] However, these families are by no means the most unfortunate. Some workers live in men- or women-only dormitories, and are split up from their spouses.[83]

The predicament of the migrants was best described by *Komso-*

mol'skaya pravda, in an article about the Ozvobozhdennyi trud fine-cloth factory in Moscow. Playing on the factory's name, which means liberated, or freed labour, the paper wrote:

> At Ozvobozhdennyi trud there exist several levels of freedom. The first is that this Moscow factory is absolutely free of actual Muscovites. Here there is a 100 per cent *limit* – the most dependent part of the USSR's working class, deprived of any rights. The *limitchitsy* of Ozvobozhdennyi trud, like thousands of their colleagues at other enterprises, are free from everything: from a Moscow residence permit, from housing, from garden plots, and from labour which brings pleasure and satisfaction. They are free from a rewarding life. The temporary difficulties of these non-Moscow girls are temporary only because as the years go by they grow over into permanent ones.[84]

The article also made it abundantly clear just how this system is used to control the workers. Initially they receive a five-year permit. If during that time they avoid all conflict with the management, they might, if they are lucky, receive permanent residence. After another five years – or ten years in all – they have the right to join the housing queue. Then, after another fifteen or twenty years they may possibly receive a flat far outside of Moscow. *Komsomol'skaya pravda* remarked ironically that by the time they reach retirement the women might be able to start a family.

That this is no isolated incident is shown by a similar account from a worker at the Lytkarino optical glass factory (LZOS) in Moscow oblast:

> The town is based largely on *limitchiki*. People come from different regions, they live in dorms. Then they get married and receive apartments. Different people, various nationalities. And they say to themselves: 'Thank god, I have escaped from the backwoods, the provinces; I am living here now and that suits me'. They are mostly from the village, youth who have gone through the factory technical schools. Many have no rights at all. When they first get here, they are kept quiet by their lack of a permanent residence permit. They have to work five years in order to be able to live permanently in the city. Once they get the permit, the question of an apartment arises. If you fight with the administration, you won't get one. So they try to keep peace with the bosses, even if they are dissatisfied.[85]

With the exception of the disabled, who were quite extensively marginalized, each of the groups examined here posed serious problems for the successful implementation of the economic reforms. In the case of Central Asia, unemployment was peripheral to the aims and needs of perestroika, because it did not in the main affect industrial workers. By the same token, the regime never had any coherent policy for developing these regions and solving their deeper problems of economic backwardness and poverty. Where the other groups are concerned, although they might have provided a politically convenient method of introducing job losses, here, too (again excepting the disabled), the labour shortage preempted any large-scale layoffs. More importantly, to have driven these groups from production would have generated even greater problems than it might have resolved. It would have been quite impossible to have found local workers to fill the places of migrant workers, who were brought into industry precisely because the residents of Moscow, Leningrad, and the other large cities, would no longer do the low-paid and physically demanding jobs which predominate in so many areas of production. The same applies to women, whose expulsion from industry would have simply left many low-skilled, but essential jobs unfilled, as actually happened when they began leaving production voluntarily in the course of the labour shortage. For young people, the short-term gains to individual enterprises of not hiring, and therefore not training, young workers have been storing up a potential disaster for the economy as a whole by undermining its skill base, an issue we take up in more detail at the end of the next section.

The management of unemployment: political necessities and institutional realities

Perhaps the most enduring legacy of the system of informal bargaining in Soviet industry is workers' expectation of secure employment. It is probable that the Soviet elite has long understood the need to introduce unemployment if it were successfully to break workers' partial control over the labour process, but politically it has had no way to do this without running the risk of massive opposition. Despite the extensiveness of the repressive apparatus and the atomization of the workforce, to remove such a major element of security in workers' lives would have been fraught with dangers. This became even more true under Gorbachev, as the political relaxation made collective action by workers possible, at first on a limited basis, and then, after the 1989 miners' strike, with few enforceable obstacles or impediments. Under these circumstances the reformers had to find a way to make unemployment politically acceptable to the working class. The promise of a better standard of living and greater democratization was part of this, but more tangible measures were also essential, namely the creation of an appropriate infrastructure to make the loss of a job less traumatic and more part of 'normal' life. This meant, in short, putting in place a proper system of unemployment benefit, job placement facilities, and a training network for those who would have to acquire a new trade or profession or upgrade their skills. As we shall see, in each of these areas regime policy was marked by hesitancy and lack of planning, so that even after the collapse of perestroika, when the supply crisis and the drive towards the market threatened at long last to make unemployment a reality, none of the ex-Soviet Union's independent republics had erected the institutions which might have made it politically manageable.

Early unemployment regulations and the 1991 employment law

The regulations governing redundancy at the beginning of perestroika were relatively liberal. In addition to the long-standing (but often ignored) requirement of trade union approval of any dismissals, workers had to be notified in writing at least two months in advance of impending redundancy. If discharged they were in the first instance to be offered alternative work at the same enterprise or, if this were not available, at another enterprise in the same trade and at the same level of skill. If suitable work was not available, the worker was to be offered retraining in a new trade, with the guarantee of a job afterwards. Women with children up the age of eight were to be offered part-time work. If the worker did not agree to accept a new job at her or his old enterprise, management had the formal responsibility to consult with local job placement agencies and inform the worker where she or he might find work. Finally, once discharged, the worker was entitled to a one-off payment of one month's average earnings, and to keep her or his average earnings for up to two months while looking for another job. If the worker registered with the local job placement agency, and the latter could not within two months find her or him a job in the worker's former trade or skill level, then the worker would receive an extra month's pay. Workers made redundant because their enterprises were closed down were entitled to this three-month cushion in all circumstances.[86]

There were, however, distinctly coercive elements in this system. When letting staff go and deciding which workers would be kept on, enterprises were to give first priority to those with the highest productivity and skill. Only in cases where management had to choose between workers showing comparable skills and performance were other, social criteria to be taken into account: whether workers had families and dependents; whether the family had another wage earner; length of service at the given enterprise; disabilities; or whether workers had upgraded their skills at outside educational institutions without a break in production.[87] We should also note that in rulings of February and December 1988 the USSR Supreme Court considerably weakened workers' rights of appeal against unfair dismissal, transfers against their will, or discriminatory refusals to hire.[88]

These early regulations were supplanted by the new employment law, passed by the USSR Supreme Soviet in January 1991.[89] From the spring of 1990 until the law's final passage, its original draft had been subjected to considerable criticism by the official trade unions, VTsSPS, centring on three main issues. First, the unions wanted the new law to enshrine the right to a job for all Soviet citizens through job creation and public works projects. Secondly, the law had envisioned that unemployment benefits and public works would be paid for out of an Employment Promotion Fund, created out of deductions from the tax on labour resources – effectively a tax on the number of employees – which enterprises paid to the All-Union, republican, and local governments. The unions objected to this, on the grounds that it would jeopardize enterprise finances and, therefore, prospects for investment and maintaining employment. These burdens would fall especially heavily on those enterprises in the weakest financial position. Following this same logic, namely, that the state should bear the costs of protecting the unemployed, the unions vigorously opposed proposals to allow individuals to take out private unemployment insurance. Finally, the unions claimed that the level of proposed unemployment benefits was too low. According to the draft law benefits were to be based on a worker's basic wage at her or his last place of employment. Although this would include additional payments for meeting or overfulfilling piece work targets, it would exclude payments for overtime, working in heavy or hazardous conditions, various bonuses, and the traditional thirteenth monthly pay packet. The unions argued that these supplementary sources of income, which make up a substantial portion of earnings for most workers, should be included when making benefit calculations.[90]

It is a testament to the political marginalization of the official unions within ruling circles that the final law, composed essentially by Goskomtrud, took little account of their views. The law created a State Employment Service at All-Union and republican levels, the main responsibilities of which were: (a) to provide analyses and prognoses on the state of the labour market; (b) to compile a register of the unemployed; (c) to solicit information from enterprises and other employers regarding proposed changes or reorganizations which might result in layoffs; (d) to refer those seeking work to potential employers; (e) to direct the unemployed, on a voluntary basis, to paid public works projects organized by local soviets on the recommendation of the Service; (f) to pay, out of the State Employment Promotion Fund, the costs of professional training and retraining for those out of work, as well as a stipend to support them during their period of instruction; (g) to pay unemployment benefits. In addition, the Service had the right to recommend to local Councils of Peoples Deputies (local soviets) a six-month suspension of enterprise decisions to impose mass layoffs (the term 'mass' was not defined) if this would subsequently make it difficult to place the affected workers. One has to assume that this last clause was inserted to allow local soviets to try to forestall large-scale redundancies that might provoke popular discontent.

As for benefits, these were differentiated, according to whether or not recipients agreed to undertake retraining. Persons made redundant due to liquidation of their enterprises or establishment reductions were to receive their average wage for up to three months while they sought a new job, provided that they registered within ten days with the State Employment Service. If, upon finding new employment, they underwent retraining, they would preserve their average wage during the training period, with the enterprise deducting the costs from their taxable income. This part of the law was essentially a carry-over of previous regulations. For those unable to find work within the three-month period, and who thus had to register as unemployed, if they entered a retraining scheme and had children or other dependants they would receive a stipend of no less than 50 per cent of their average earnings at their last place of employment; for those without dependants, benefits were set at 50 per cent of their last basic wage. Benefits for the rest of the unemployed were set at 50 per cent of their last basic wage if they had a record of previous employment, and 75 per cent of the USSR minimum wage if they were first-time entrants to the labour force. Recipients could be deprived of benefits if they refused two job offers, took temporary work while receiving benefits without the permission of the Employment Service, or lost their jobs because they had violated discipline regulations or quit their last place of work without just cause. In all cases the period of eligibility was strictly limited: to six months for those who had lost an existing job or who wished to re-enter the labour force after a prolonged absence (usually women who had stayed home to look after pre-school age children) and three months for all others.

Having decreed these levels of support and compensation, the state was not, however, actually prepared to pay them. The law's benefit provisions were not to go into effect until 1 July 1991, and the State Employment Service was not to begin receiving state subsidies until 1992.[91] In response to this move, the Moscow city soviet declared a temporary moratorium on mass layoffs until 1 July, so that no one should be left without some form of financial support.[92] As with much local and national legislation, this was an empty gesture, since, given Moscow's labour shortage, there was little likelihood of large-scale joblessness in any case.[93]

With supply shortages and rapid inflation gripping the economy in early 1991, the real value of these benefits promised to dwindle to insignificance, especially for young people receiving less than the already paltry minimum wage. Had enterprises begun to let workers go in large numbers the hardship thus provoked would have been severe, not to mention what would have happened once recipients' period of eligibility ran out. The fact was that the authorities at both national and local level were totally unequipped to cope with even moderate levels of unemployment, as our discussion of the labour exchanges and the training system makes clear.

Job placement and the labour exchanges

For decades the Soviet regime had officially denied the existence of unemployment, so that when the issue pushed its way on to the political and economic agenda, the bureaucratic system was ill-prepared to put in place coherent and effective structures for assisting those out of work. Prior to the 1991 employment law, responsibility for placing those seeking work resided with agencies bearing the cumbersome name, Centres for Job Placement, Retraining, and Vocational Guidance of the Population. From the very start of their existence, the Centres (originally known as bureaux) were beset by numerous problems.

A small-scale Goskomtrud survey carried out during 1986–87, the first years the Centres were in operation, found that nearly half of those registering with them failed to find work; a further 22 per cent spent more than two months before they could land a job. These were curious findings, given that for every applicant to the Centres there were three or four vacancies.[94] Yet the trends here were confirmed by more complete statistics from 1990. The overwhelming majority of those using the services were those who had left their jobs voluntarily and were relatively easy to place. Less than 4 per cent were people actually made redundant, but of these the Centres found jobs for only slightly more than one-third, despite over 1.25 million unfilled vacancies in enterprises and institutions.[95]

Much of the problem lay in the fact that the Centres had no statutory power either to compel enterprises to notify them of vacancies or to accept the workers they referred. In general, enterprises reported only the low-prestige jobs; the better jobs they concealed, knowing that they could easily fill them at the gates.[96] In Kaluga and Ufa the city authorities tried to block this practice, banning all hiring except through the local Centres, but this, too, was doomed to failure, not the least because they could still not force enterprises to hire people whom the Centres sent.[97] In the words of one Moscow labour official, 'We give little help to the people who come to us. And those coming to us are those with no protection, with no chance to set themselves up through some patron. We lead them in circles: go here, go there, maybe they'll take you on. But we cannot really set someone up in a job.'[98] The head of a Centre in Moldova told the same tale:

> I write without hope that anything will change. We have been waiting for three years now, ever since we started up work. The worst thing is that the people who turn to us lose faith, and the workers in the Centre lose interest in their work. We have been placed in a situation where, instead of job placement, we collect information on those who've taken a job and then send the enterprises a bill. Who needs this kind of deception?[99]

The problems of the Centres were not simply statutory, however. They were hopelessly under-resourced. In early 1990 the Centres had just 11,000 staff, compared to 5,000 working in similar agencies in Australia, a country with one-twentieth the population of the USSR. Although by the end of 1990 their numbers had risen sharply, to 14,700, this was nowhere nearly enough to meet the need.[100] The workers they did have did not always have the skills required. The Centres needed labour economists, lawyers, psychologists, and sociologists, but, as one Centre director lamented, 'who is going to do this for 120 rubles?'[101] From the very beginning the Centres had no control over their budgets. In 1988 the government put the Centres on *khozraschet*, so that they were to obtain funding from two sources: first, from the payments which local enterprises made for their services, and secondly, from local soviet funding, raised from the labour-resource payments which enterprises made into local budgets. But this system made the Centres totally dependent on the enterprises, which either had no incentive to use their services or, in a minority of cases, did not have the funds to pay for them. As for the payments into the local budget, these funds went not to the local soviets, but into the treasuries of higher territorial units – oblast, krai, republican, or even All-Union budgets – which disbursed money to the Centres on a completely arbitrary basis.[102] Nor were the local soviets themselves overly anxious to spend their money on the Centres. In reality, the application of *khozraschet* to the employment services changed nothing, as the director of the Moscow oblast job placement Centre made clear:

> In practice, not a single district Soviet of People's Deputies in the oblast has fully resolved the problem of improving the material base of the employment services. The letter of the USSR Ministry of Finance and Goskomtrud, 'On financing the job placement services', which guardedly talks about the 'right' of Soviets to provide funds, does not in practice oblige them to do it. Payment for labour resources is distributed as they please, only not for work on the rational employment of labour resources. At the very start of the work of the state employment system, the service has found itself in an even more difficult situation than before. It is completely probable that behind the change of sign outside the door no fundamental changes have taken place. For the fact is that under conditions of cost accounting, no one wants to pay for the work of securing employment or providing vocational guidance ...
>
> At present the situation is this: The state has given the labour agencies the task of solving problems of efficient employment, while the financial agencies refuse to pay for it.[103]

The result was that the Centres were permanently short of funds for such essentials as computers, running advertisements, and providing proper information services.[104] The unemployed were well aware the placement system had little to offer: as of 1990 only between 5 and 6 per cent of those losing their jobs bothered to turn to the Centres for assistance.[105]

In a small number of cases local groups set up their own initiatives to try to circumvent the palpable inadequacies of the official system. In the middle of 1990 the local soviet in the city of Glazov, in the Udmurt Autonomous Republic, in north-central Russia, created its own local labour exchange. The heart of the city's economy were two defence plants, which were facing severe cutbacks as a result of conversion. In an attempt to cope with the expected unemployment, especially among young people looking for their first jobs, the soviet implemented its own system of public works and temporary unemployment benefits. The newspaper article reporting this, however, was quick to note that the city had received no formal assistance from either Goskomtrud or the latter's Scientific Research Institute of Labour, some of whose academics donated their time to the Glazov endeavour free of charge.[106]

With the implementation of the 1991 employment law the work of the job placement Centres, many of which now called themselves labour exchanges, continued to show the same problems as their predecessors. Responsibility for financing the Centres now fell on the republics, which received 90 per cent of the funds for their operation. This immediately led to disputes over the unequal provision of services. In particular, the six republics with the worst unemployment, namely Central Asia and Azerbaijan, had not allocated any funds to deal with the problem.[107] In the large cities the Centres continued to suffer from lack of resources. In Leningrad the entire city had but fifty to sixty staff to run its district employment centres. Computerization, without which an effective placement system is almost unthinkable, remained weak: as of April 1991 there were ten computers in Leningrad city and five more in Leningrad oblast. Its twenty-two district centres for retraining job seekers were still not operational a mere ten days before official registration was to begin on 1 July. Equally important, the system had little real power to affect the overall employment situation in the city. Most of those out of work were technical specialists, not workers, whom officials were reluctant to put to work on public works projects, such as road and building repairs. At the other end of the spectrum, the service was not yet able to offer adequate retraining to the low-skilled.[108] Similar difficulties were encountered in Moscow, where the district centres were hamstrung by shortages of cash, computers, and trained staff.[109] In Sverdlovsk (Ekaterinburg) officials told the same story. In addition to inadequate staffing and lack of funds, the service was squeezed into premises so cramped that it had no place to set up its Information and Inquiry Centre, without which it clearly could not function. It had no data on which enterprises were planning redundancies, or how many people might by affected. Public works were, in the words of the head of the Employment Service, a farce.[110]

The breakdown of the training system

One of the persistent weaknesses of Soviet industry has been its inability to construct a viable system of training those needing new or better skills and young workers preparing for entry into the labour force. On the one hand, the different institutions and programmes responsible for vocational training have consistently failed to prepare workers in the skills which industry needs, so that enterprises have often had to retrain these workers once they arrived at the factory. On the other hand, the backwardness of Soviet industry itself has meant that there are insufficient opportunities to carry out skilled work relative to the general educational level of modern school graduates, who become frustrated at the need to do low- or semi-skilled work with limited prospects for advancement.[111]

Officially each year some 40 million workers and clerical employees were raising their qualifications through various factory-run or outside training courses, and a further 7 million acquired a new trade. In theory this meant that the average member of the workforce raised his or her qualifications every two to three years. According to labour specialists, however, these were vastly over-exaggerated, since only a small proportion of those learning a new trade or skills did so in connection with the introduction of new technology or a more rational organization of production. Most enterprises retrained their workers simply because of the labour shortage in vital or mass occupations, shifting workers into areas where they could fill pressing vacancies. In line with this, for most workers the training was too brief and superficial to have any real impact on workers' skills: some 80 per cent of trainees were on short courses of less than three months and did their training while still holding down a full-time job. Use of computers or other modern training techniques was rare, and in factory-run courses almost non-existent.[112] Enterprises themelves had little clear conception of what skills they actually demanded, or which ones would be needed in the future.[113]

We have already noted that as enterprises moved to *khozraschet* the financial pressures to cut back on training of both new and older workers became even stronger. Money earmarked for retraining workers was diverted into wage funds, to allow factories to offer higher wages as a means of stemming their labour shortage. The quality of training also declined, as enterprises were reluctant to devote funds to improving or maintaining what in many cases were already inadequate equipment, premises, and teaching materials.[114]

Workers, too, had little incentive to engage in such schemes: few of those learning a new trade had their wages protected during the first months of working at their new job, while they were still trying to master it and earnings were likely to suffer; for nearly a quarter of workers their earnings failed to improve after retraining, and for another 10 per cent their wages actually fell.[115]

A further burden on the system was the total lack of any centralized coordination. On-the-job training was the responsibility of the industrial ministries and their departments; training in vocational training schools, the PTU, was under the State Committee for National Education (Gosobrazovanie); and there was no agency at all to administer retraining in the specialized secondary schools or technical colleges (*tekhnikumy*). All this led to duplication of effort, poor cooperation between different sections of the educational bureaucracy, and huge differences in educational programmes and methods. Any idea that the Job Placement Centres could somehow provide this missing coordination was, of course, utopian, given the crippling problems they had just trying to erect a basic placement service.[116] Perhaps indicative of their inability to provide effective help in this regard is the example of Omsk oblast, where, of the 25,000 people who registered with its Employment Service during the first ten months of 1991, only 14 agreed to retrain for a new trade.[117]

As grave as these various shortcomings were, even more serious was the state of vocational education. The simple fact is that it was impossible to modernize the Soviet economy given its traditional methods of preparing its young people for work. By the end of the Brezhnev period virtually all Soviet school children were receiving a complete secondary education, either in a general secondary school or by leaving school after grade eight (the USSR had a ten–grade system) and moving to a PTU (which provides training in workers' trades) or a *tekhnikum* (which prepares people for lower level technical occupations).[118] Where industrial workers are concerned, the PTU are, at least in theory, the centrepiece of the training network. However, like their predecessors, the Labour Reserve Schools of Stalinist times, they have never proved adequate to their task.[119] According to one recent report, over 40 per cent of young people were entering the ranks of the working class without any vocational training whatsoever. So unpopular had the PTU become that they were generally perceived as taking the 'rejects' whom the general secondary schools had neglected.[120] The reasons behind this have as much to do with the general backwardness of Soviet production as with the PTU themselves. Given the huge amount of low-skilled, monotonous, and often back-breaking and hazardous labour in Soviet factories, workers' trades have, in Soviet parlance, 'lost their prestige', that is, become highly unpopular with young people. Even many of those who enter PTU want to avoid going into a factory at all costs.[121]

However, the inadequacies of the training system, both in general secondary schools and the PTU, have contributed greatly to the ill-preparedness of the students they turn out. If throughout the Soviet economy workers were trained in over 1,000 trades, 62 per cent of school graduates going into industry studied either metalworking or sewing.[122] This, combined with the appallingly low level of instruction these students received, led to the fact that the vast majority had to be totally retrained from scratch by the factories themselves.[123] It is small wonder, then that factories were still recruiting and training directly more than three times as many new workers as they were taking from the PTU.[124]

Since their inception under Khrushchev, the PTU remained in a state of almost total neglect. Premises have always been inadequate. In 1989, some 2,000 PTU buildings were listed as 'decrepit', and another 900 required reconstruction. Nationally, the average PTU had only half the number of workshops it required. Their equipment was outmoded, consisting primarily of hand-me-down machinery which the base enterprises to which they were attached wished to scrap. PTU in both Moscow and Leningrad complained that their students had to work on equipment dating from the 1950s and 1960s, thus making it impossible for them to acquire the skills that would make them employable in the future.[125] Instructors as a rule were badly trained (many PTU heads and foremen have no previous experience in vocational training), and teaching materials were generally poor.[126] For many students, especially in construction, their 'practical work' consisted of carrying out only menial jobs; in some cases work was so badly organized they had no work to do at all.[127]

The difficulties with the PTU are closely bound up with the plight of migrant workers. As the PTU became more and more unpopular, they found that the only way to fill their rolls was to recruit young people from small towns and rural areas, who in turn used the offer of a place in a PTU to get around the restrictions on *limitchiki* in cities like Moscow and Leningrad. Even before these restrictions were imposed, outsiders made up over half of PTU entrants in these two cities, including well over 85 per cent of those training for construction and over 90 per cent of those in textiles. And although they were a smaller proportion of those in the engineering PTU, in various machine tool operator trades, for which recruitment is difficult, they were over 70 per cent. Very few of these young men and women enrolled in a PTU to acquire a particular trade (most could have received the same training at home), but simply to gain entry to one of the large cities.[128]

Given the combination of low motivation, inadequate career guidance and instruction, and the often gruesome conditions in which they had to work and live, it is little wonder that turnover among PTU students and graduates was high. Many failed to complete their course. Of those who did go into industry, about 30 per cent were fired for various causes during their first year of work; some 80 per cent never entered the trades for which they were trained.[129] The generally poor relations between PTU and industry also help explain the readiness with which enterprises began selling off or running down their PTU once they went on *khozraschet*.[130]

The training system in the Soviet Union was clearly in crisis long before perestroika. What can be said is that the economic reforms, which as one precondition of their success, had to find a means of training both experienced workers and young school leavers in modern trades with up-to-date skills, simply proved incapable of this task. While part of the cause lay in *khozraschet*, and the pressures it put on enterprises to trim back expenditures in this area, the real root of the problem was the technical backwardness of Soviet production, with its excessive share of unskilled manual labour and outmoded equipment. This low level of technique is not an historical accident. As we discuss in chapter 5, it is a direct result of the obstacles to modernization and innovation inherent in the Stalinist planning system, including the cheapness of labour power, which acted as a powerful disincentive to investment in labour-saving equipment, especially in industries and processes reliant on women workers. Even in the more narrow context of job training, the legacy of this system has been costly, for the Soviet Union, to paraphrase one commentator, has been training the next generation of its unemployed:[131] low-skilled workers prepared for trades which are of questionable utility even within the existing structure of industry, and which would be almost totally redundant were the country successfully to make the transition to a modern market economy. There is, of course, no guarantee, or even likelihood, that this is the type of economy towards which the former Soviet Union is evolving. Like the countries of Latin America, it may find its place in the international division of labour as a source of cheap manufacturing labour, where prior skills are of little importance, but flexibility and a willingness to work at any job become the chief determinants of employability. This would involve deskilling on a massive scale, while condemning a large part of the population to a marginal existence, all in the service of a new form of economic 'rationality', that of international capital.

The debacle of conversion

In 1989 the Soviet government acknowledged the existence of a huge budget deficit, together with plans to bring it under control. Such a move, while of limited significance within the old bureaucratic planning system, was essential if the Soviet Union were to obtain extensive foreign credits or attract foreign investment, neither of which would be forthcoming without a stable currency. Some of the effects of this policy we have already seen: the drastic cutbacks on the construction of the gas pipeline in Tyumen' oblast, with the threat to tens of thousands of jobs; and the inability (or claimed inability) of republican governments to finance unemployment benefits. Another we take up in chapter 3: the refusal of the USSR and Ukrainian governments to meet the Ukrainian miners' pay demands, which precipitated the 1991 miners' strike. The downward spiral into which enterprises could plunge was exemplified by the iron and steel works at Alapaevsk, whose reconstruction was halted due to the withdrawal of central financing, leaving the enterprise with heavy debts which it could not pay off, since it now had no factory in which to produce anything worth selling.[132]

Crucial to the campaign to reduce the deficit was a substantial reduction in the country's huge military expenditure and the conversion of large tracts of its so-called military-industrial complex (*voenno-promyshlennyi kompleks*, or VPK) to civilian production. This was vital for two reasons. First, military spending accounted for a large, if not the overwhelming proportion of the budget deficit. Secondly, as under capitalism, military production is a drain on future growth, since it soaks up vast quantities of means of production and labour power for the production of what are essentially extraordinarily costly consumer goods. Moreover, these are consumer goods of a very special type, since they are either kept permanently in storage, or 'consumed' in the process of destruction – both of themselves and the human beings, houses, factories, and infrastructure of the societies or peoples against which they are aimed. They cannot function as either means of production in a future production cycle or as means of consumption for the labour power that might set these means of production in motion. Their production is totally wasteful – it is a drain on resources which in no way helps restore the productive forces which it depletes.[133] To this extent the fate of perestroika in large part depended on the regime's ability to shift resources away from defence spending towards the production of means of consumption for the general population. At the same time, if conversion failed it threatened to engulf the labour market with tens, if not hundreds of thousands of unemployed workers (many of them highly skilled by Soviet standards), at a time when the regime had neither a strategy nor the structures for redeploying them, retraining them, or otherwise preserving their skills.

In the Soviet Union the problem of conversion involved special difficulties, related to the technological and geographical structure of military production. Whole cities – not just large conurbations like Leningrad and Sverdlovsk, but medium or small towns in the country's heartlands – were dominated by, and dependent upon the defence industry. In general the workers in these plants enjoyed special privileges in the form of higher wages or better access to consumer goods and housing; the factories, or at least those shops engaged in defence work, were better equipped and enjoyed preferential receipt of material supplies. This was not always the case, however. A detailed study of the machine factory in Ioshkar-Ola, which was slated for conversion in 1991, found that it differed little from ordinary engineering enterprises in terms of the advanced age of its equipment, its high proportion of semi-skilled workers (many of whom were women), and wages. The one noticeable difference was that management there was, if anything, even more authoritarian, and the workforce even more excluded from participation in decision-making, than at its civilian counterparts.[134]

No matter which category defence plants fell into – the comparatively prosperous and privileged or the 'rank and file' – sharp cutbacks in defence spending threatened them and their workers with severe hardships: reduced orders and cuts in wages; loss of pensions for those shifted to less hazardous work after conversion; deskilling; and in some cases actual unemployment.[135] Moreover, this was not a managed process. Conversion, such as it existed, was haphazard and planless, so that the dislocations suffered by those affected proved far greater than need have been the case.

To a large extent the problems of conversion were compounding a long-term decline in engineering production, made worse by the conjunctural pressures of self-financing. As enterprises and farms were forced to spend a larger share of profits on maintaining wage levels, they cut their demand for such basic engineering items as machine tools, tractors, and lifting and transport equipment. According to a 1991 study commissioned by the Leningrad City Soviet, demand for such equipment was expected to fall throughout the USSR by 30–60 per cent during 1992–3. In Leningrad itself this would have put nearly a third of those employed in Leningrad engineering – and one in ten of the city's total employed – at risk of losing their jobs.[136] Although layoffs on this scale did not occur, the crisis which conversion posed for the city were severe, and were typical of those confronting other centres heavily tied to the VPK.

In 1991, factories that were part of, or had close connections to the military-industrial complex possessed over half the stock of high-technology equipment in Leningrad industry and accounted for nearly 40 per cent of the output of its engineering enterprises. These enterprises fell into four main categories: radio electronics and instrument-making; shipbuilding; aeronautics and space; and purely military production. In all but space and aeronautics, where Leningrad-made aircraft engines were allegedly already competitive on the world market, the economic outlook under conversion was far from sanguine. In radio electronics export potential was limited by inferior quality relative to the West and still-extant Soviet export restrictions. The sector's main 'comparative advantage' was its rela-tively highly skilled, but low-paid workforce, but their profitable employment would require large-scale Western investment. The picture was roughly similar in ship-building: the chief factors offering it possible *entrée* to the world market were cheap labour power and cheap metal. More difficult still was the situation with military hard-ware. Although at the time this report was written the city still saw prospects in arms exports to Eastern Europe and the third world, there was no avoiding the need for what in Russian is termed 'reprofili-zation', that is, the restructuring of defence plants towards civilian production. Here lay the main difficulties of conversion, since such a shift would require a substantial replacement of equipment and tech-nology and a near-total retraining of the workforce.[137]

Leningrad's gigantic Kirov works was illustrative of this process. The Association produced two main articles: tanks and tractors. Neither had good long-term perspectives. Tank orders were being cut and attempts to take up the slack by producing road-building equip-ment were foundering on difficulties acquiring supplies. Tractor pro-duction was equally in crisis. Kirov tractors were too heavy and too expensive for Soviet agriculture, which, like industry, was suffering a financial squeeze. The City Soviet was trying to negotiate a possible deal with a Western car maker to assemble automobiles at Kirov using Western parts (the cars would have been exclusively for export), but this would have meant substantial deskilling of much of the workforce. Eventually, the Association started to manufacture a small tractor which it felt it could sell on the domestic market, but it could not put it into mass production, since it was unable to attract the required investment.[138]

Plans to convert enterprises to civilian production were badly thought out and executed. Enterprises had their existing defence production halted, often all at once, before the shift to new lines of production had been properly prepared. Factories were given plans to produce consumer goods without provision being made for the necessary raw materials, equipment, or centrally funded capital investment.[139] Some enterprises tried to shift to lines of production which would preserve the skills of their workforce and allow them to utilize their relatively advanced technology, but then found that there was no demand for what they made. The only solution was to switch once again, to the manufacture of marketable goods, but this could involve a complete squandering of skills and misuse of technology. Workers who used to make airplanes or high-technology components for space craft found themselves making vacuum cleaners or tennis rackets.[140] Steel workers wound up making jewellery or processing sheepskins.[141] Other engineering factories were told to make equipment for which their own machinery was totally inappropriate; they could meet these plans, but only by running up huge losses, which either had to be absorbed by the state budget or compensated by excessively high selling prices.[142] The pressure this put on wages was substantial, since production under such conditions necessarily resulted in poorer productivity. This trend was exacerbated by the fact that in the central plans each hour of civilian production was remunerated at one-third to one-quarter the level of defence production, so that the same volume of civilian production in terms of physical inputs and labour-hours would bring in far less revenue. The strain on wage funds was enormous. Factory after factory reported a loss of skilled specialists and workers as a direct result of conversion.[143]

Yet this was far from the worst scenario. For many enterprises conversion existed in name only. Defence orders fell, but were not compensated by a switch to new products. Some shops were able to survive in this climate, but only by relying on their ability to line up one-off orders.[144] Others were simply left with not enough work,[145] driving down earnings or increasing labour turnover even further.

The destabilizing effect of the failure of conversion was potentially enormous. For unlike the politically powerless sections of the workforce, namely, women and *limitchiki*, massive layoffs in the defence industry would of necessity have put out on the streets large numbers of male workers in heavy industry, a constituency whose response would quite literally have been unpredictable. That these layoffs did not occur was in no way a reflection of the coherence of regime policy. Rather, the breakdown of the system of enterprise self-financing allowed managers to maintain revenues by putting up prices and in this way to keep production going. This saved jobs, but in so doing perpetuated the severe structural imbalances inherent in Soviet industry.

The labour shortage

By 1990 it was abundantly clear that the employment policies at the heart of perestroika had virtually collapsed. As the economy slid further into disorganization and production contracted, modernization and reequipping came almost to a halt. On the other hand, if workers were not being displaced by machines, at least the fall-off in production, combined with the pressures of *khozraschet* and self-financing, should have produced the layoffs which the economic reforms could not. Yet reality proved quite different. Industry became gripped by a deepening labour shortage, as conjunctural factors drove large numbers of workers, both skilled and unskilled, out of production at a time when the structural and political pressures at the root of the long-term, secular labour shortage did not permit any appreciable reduction in the demand for labour power. The result was that the growing supply crisis and the shortage of workers reinforced each other to create or exacerbate often near-crippling bottlenecks within production. With inflation rising rapidly and living standards falling, managers could only hold on to workers by raising wages even at the cost of undermining the enterprise's medium- and long-term economic well-being. This trend was reinforced by the fact that the labour shortage greatly strengthened workers' bargaining power on the shop floor: in addition to the traditional weapon of threatening to quit, workers could now go on strike and bring production to a standstill.[146]

In January 1990, there were, according to official statistics, nearly 1 million vacant work places in industry, 654,000 in construction, 119,000 in automotive transport, and 245,000 in trade and catering. Labour turnover in the more labour-intensive branches of production was estimated at between 14–17 per cent.[147] In Moscow during 1990–91 shortages were reported in a vast number of trades: fitters, printers, cooks, cleaners, bricklayers, plasterers, carpenters, house painters, bulldozer operators, turners and milling machine operators, and loaders.[148] This was not, however, a local phenomenon. Shortages in the construction and iron and steel industries were universal.[149] In Latvia, where 95 per cent of the potential workforce was already in employment, the job placement bureaux – which, as we know, received notice of only a small share of vacancies – alone listed 24,000–25,000 openings, or 2 per cent of total employment in the republic.[150] In Omsk oblast, as late as November 1991, there were 9,851 vacancies, with the worst shortages in workers' jobs, especially those demanding low skills or involving difficult working conditions. Elsewhere in Siberia, and even in Central Asia, the situation was exactly the same.[151] It was not unusual for large numbers of vacancies to exist alongside unemployment, especially since most openings were for industrial or construction workers, while unemployment, such as it existed, was concentrated mainly among specialists and clerical employees.[152] Only during the first quarter of 1992 did the number of vacancies begin to fall alongside rising numbers of redundancies.[153]

The existence of unfilled vacancies has been an almost permanent feature of the Soviet economy, deriving, at least in part, from the need to maintain relative over-staffing as a hedge against storming. It was routine for factories to inflate investment requirements and accumulate equipment, much of which was never installed or properly utilized, largely as a means of justifying an expansion of establishments. Enterprises also used this practice surreptitiously to enlarge the administrative apparatus: they created workplaces through new construction, which was centrally financed and did not come out of enterprise funds, and filled them not with workers, but with so-called *podsnezhniki*, the Russian name for the snowdrop plant – the ironical usage presumably coming from the fact that the flowers bloom early and are buried under the snow. These were people who, on paper, were counted as factory employees, for instance, as instructors, service personnel, chauffeurs, storekeepers, or warehouse supervisors, but who were really doing something else, most often in or around the factory apparatus, primarily in the trade union, Komsomol, or Party committees, and whose wages were counted as part of 'production costs'. One author has estimated that a full third of the empty workplaces created between 1953 and 1987 consisted of such 'dead souls'.[154] What is significant about the complaints of unfilled vacancies towards the end of perestroika, however, is that they clearly had nothing to do with any of these subterfuges, but represented a real shortage of workers. This does not mean that if production were reorganized many of these empty positions could not have been streamlined and eliminated; what it does mean is that, under existing Soviet conditions, the vast majority of these workers were vital to production at some point in the monthly or quarterly production cycle, and their absence greatly aggravated problems of coordination and quality. This is extremely well documented, especially in the factory press.

Both of Moscow's motor vehicle factories, ZiL and AZLK, which had long depended on *limitchiki* and, more recently, on Vietnamese workers, were badly affected. During the last two years of Gorbachev's rule ZiL lost 4,000 people, leaving its main plant alone short of 14,000 workers. The press shop was so short of workers that, in addition to constant overtime and weekend work, technical specialists had to be drafted in to run the machines.[155] At AZLK, shortages of skilled machine-tool operators in repair and machine shops contributed to ongoing shortages of spare parts and stoppages on the conveyor. Assembly lines in the body-welding and press shops had to rely increasingly on temporary workers, mainly students, people recruited on short-term contracts (mostly from Central Asia on *orgnabor*), or so-called contract workers, who signed up for short stints at the factory in exchange for the right to buy a Moskvich car at the end of their stay. The factory was so short of unskilled transport workers that it was hiring ex-alcoholics and drug users on rehabilitative work therapy, who caused innumerable problems because they consistently delivered parts to the wrong shops.[156] However, the labour shortage was by no means confined to Moscow or the automotive industry. The Dneprospetsstal' iron and steel works in Zaporozh'e had more than 2,000 vacancies out of a workforce of 13,500, a shortfall of some 15 per cent. Brigades that should have had five people in them were working with just one. Here, too, the factory was importing ex-alcoholics.[157] A similar situation prevailed in the engineering industry in Khar'kov.[158]

In general it was the factories, shops, or sections with the lowest pay and/or the worst conditions which had the greatest difficulties recruiting. According to an electric welder at Leningrad's Baltiiskii shipbuilding factory, entire brigades were quitting because of poor working conditions, including one brigade of welders whose members had worked there for ten to fifteen years.[159] Even more dramatic was the case at the rubber-technical goods and instrument factories in Sverdlovsk, where key shops, including the rubber factory's power plant, were short of press operators, fitters, loaders, cleaners, transport workers, and maintenance mechanics, in almost all cases because wages were too low to allow them to replace workers who had quit.[160] In light industry, where the high intensity of labour and low pay had combined to make many branches of light industry, and the textile industry in particular, increasingly dependent on migrant workers, the labour shortage played a major role in the precipitous fall in consumer goods production, even before the supply crisis of 1990–1 led to a general contraction of output.[161] At one weaving factory in Kalinin there were times during 1990 when they had no one to start up the equipment.[162] By early 1991 the labour shortage in textiles was being 'resolved', but only due to the supply crisis, which saw over 600,000 women in the RSFSR alone temporarily laid off, put on unpaid leave, or working short time.[163] Yet even here it did not lead to long-term unemployment. Cutbacks in production put an end to overtime work and led to short-term layoffs, but not to permanent redundancies.[164]

The question is, why, when official policy had for some years been geared to prompting enterprises to introduce planned workforce reductions in line with modernization, did the reverse occur, leading to a labour shortage of such crisis proportions? The most commonly offered answer is that skilled workers left the factories *en masse* to take up jobs in cooperatives, where the pay was higher and the working conditions often better. There is no question that a major outflow of skilled workers did occur, as reported at a number of factories, and that factories found it almost impossible to replace them, even with young workers who could be trained in these trades.[165] As one line manager at the Steel Foundry in Kuibyshev stated, 'People are coming and going. We're hiring students, but that's hardly a solution – you get more high jinks out of them than output. And you can hardly put a student on a skilled job'.[166] Nor is there any doubt that many of them did, indeed, go to cooperatives, where earnings might be two, three, or four times those offered in state enterprises.[167] This did not always mean that workers changed enterprises. At Moscow's Rezina rubber-technical goods factory those shops where price constraints and/or the supply situation meant that profitability was too low to allow them to develop internal cooperatives lost workers to shops where cooperatives had proved viable.[168] Other workers stayed in the state sector, but went into construction, where they could acquire a flat if they worked there for four or five years.[169] The damage caused by this form of turnover was not simply to the shops or enterprises these workers left. In many, if not most cases, once in the cooperatives they no longer worked at the trades for which they were trained. Insofar as this was a mass phenomenon, it posed the prospect of widespread deskilling of a significant layer of skilled workers.[170]

Despite this evidence, it would be wrong to see this as the sole source of the problem. Firstly, the exodus was not simply of skilled workers. Many young workers were also quitting their jobs.[171] In at least one engineering factory workers entitled to early retirement, by virtue of the difficulties of their jobs, were in fact taking their pensions, rather than staying on, as is commonly the practice in the Soviet Union.[172] Perhaps more important, the exodus affected unskilled workers, as well as the skilled, for whom the extra pay offered by the cooperatives was an even greater lure.[173] It is certainly no accident, that many of the unfilled vacancies cited above were primarily for the low-skilled.

It is probable that at least two processes were at work simultaneously. First, workers, both skilled and unskilled, were indeed leaving state enterprises for jobs in cooperatives. The exact scale on which this occurred is impossible to tell, nor can all the claims be verified.[174] Given the size of the labour shortage at some of the factories we have cited, it is doubtful that the cooperative sector in 1990–91 was large enough to absorb all the workers who allegedly quit to find jobs there. But the size of this movement was surely significant. Secondly, there was a discernible movement of women workers, largely those in low-skilled, arduous, and hazardous jobs, out of industrial production altogether. It is impossible to say with any certainty why this should be so. A long-term trend in this direction had been discernible throughout the 1980s, suggesting that as older women reached retirement and left industry, there were fewer young women to replace them. Some went in to trade and public catering (where they could gain access to scarce foodstuffs), and even more went into the 'non-productive' spheres of education, science, social security, medicine, and culture.[175] Thus, insofar as rigidities within the factory workforce meant that only women had been recruited to do certain jobs – in particular those that were low-skilled and/or particularly arduous, when these women left there was no-one to replace them. However, women's exodus from industry appears to have accelerated during perestroika. As noted, many of those going to cooperatives were in low-skilled occupations, and many of these would have been women. But it also seems

probable that, at least for a certain proportion of women, the rapid
inflation and deepening shortages of 1990–91, which required them to
put far more hours into queuing for food, meant that the low pay they
received was simply no longer adequate compensation for the back-
breaking and often dangerous conditions in which they had to work.
Their wages were becoming relatively insignificant compared to the
cost of food and consumer goods, while time was at a premium. This
would have been especially true if their husbands were in a position to
win substantial wage rises through industrial action, as was becoming
more frequently the case.[176] Thus factories were being squeezed at
both ends. Skilled workers were fleeing to jobs with better pay, while
unskilled workers were either doing the same or, as in the case of
many women, simply forsaking production completely. For those who
remained this meant more pressure, as bottlenecks worsened and
factories found their financial position deteriorating. The labour shortage and the supply crisis began to reinforce one another. Although the
origins of the latter lay in the system of self-financing and the application of 'market rationality' to production and distribution decisions,
shortages of labour led to stoppages and cutbacks in production,
which in turn made the supply situation worse. And as supply shortages became ever more unmanageable, so, too, did working conditions, thereby increasing workers' incentives to leave.

In the face of what for many managers was becoming an increasingly desperate situation, enterprises tried to counter the loss of
workers through various devices, some of which were quite patently
counter productive. In one extreme case, the administration of the
Khar'kov tractor-motor factory temporarily transferred bookkeepers,
planners, economists, and other office workers to machine tool operators' jobs, with predictably disappointing results.[177] The main vehicle,
of course, was simply to raise wages, often combined with promises of
housing, on-the-job training, and other benefits. Thus the giant Rostov
agricultural equipment factory, Rostsel'mash, placed a large notice in
Komsomol'skaya pravda advertising for machine tool operators, fitters,
tool-makers, electric gas welders, electricians, and a number of other
trades, promising an average wage of 300–500 rubles plus a number of
other sweeteners.[178] In Dnepropetrovsk in late 1991, the Dneprospetsstal' iron and steel works placed advertisements in the local papers for
steel makers, steel makers' helpers, fitters, turners, forge hands, and
crane operators, offering wages of 600–1,600 rubles per month plus,
more importantly at a time of worsening shortages, access to food,
clothing, shoes, and other consumer goods. In effect the factory was

poaching workers from other plants in the region whose weaker financial position did not allow them to compete in terms of either wages or supplies.[179] Leningrad's printing and publishing equipment factory, Lenpoligrafmash, actually had a special fund for topping up the wages of key workers whom it could not provide with a full work load, but whom it wanted to deter from quitting.[180] In most cases, however, the process was more spontaneous, as evidenced by the sharp rise in wages in Moscow over the course of the summer of 1991, where even seamstresses could earn as much as 800 rubles a month, turners up to 1,000, and carpenters and truck drivers 1,500. Although for most trades average wages were about half these figures, and were barely keeping pace with the rapid rise in the cost of living, it does show that, in order to keep their workforces, factories were abandoning the financial caution which *khozraschet* was supposed to have imposed. Moreover, workers were demanding, and obtaining, promises of other concessions, so that their wages could be made 'real': free food and transport, medical care and access to sanatoria, and guarantees that they would be able to purchase scarce goods at their new place of work.[181]

Conclusion

Whether we look at the original stages of perestroika, which envisaged an economic reform using 'market mechanisms' within an essentially centralized bureaucratic planning system, or the later phases, when the elite declared its commitment to the market and the restoration of capitalism, the creation of a flexible labour market was central to the reforms' success. As the reforms and *khozraschet* failed to create the incentives towards reequipping, modernization, and the subsequent combing out of surplus staff, the elite's employment policies lay in tatters. As already noted, only in limited areas did factories embark on large-scale redundancies and, at least on the evidence at our disposal, primarily during the reforms' early years. We have already discussed those which came from attempts to convert military to civilian production, and the modest scale of layoffs in these industries. As for the restructuring of production, which was supposed to be the true driving force behind the release of surplus labour power, this, too, was confined to individual enterprises, some of which modernized plant and equipment, letting workers go in the process. In some cases this was the result of long-term enterprise development policy,[182] but in others it arose out of the hiving off of enterprise sub-units into leasing collectives or cooperatives, where there was an incentive to shed staff – often administrative personnel and not workers – simply to economize on wage bills.[183]

If conversion and enterprise reorganization – as limited as their scale was – could be deemed consistent with the essential aims of the economic reforms (although in each case the regime had no clear policy and allowed the situation to descend into chaos), this is by no means true of the unemployment caused by the country's deepening environmental and supply crises. As public awareness of environmental issues led to growing protests in the worst affected areas, some factories were faced with closure.[184] The impact of the supply crisis was deeper and more widespread. Although we discuss it in detail in chapter 4, its basic outlines are relevant here. During 1990 the breakdown of the command system of supply-allocation led to generalized shortages of materials and components throughout industry. The worst affected was light industry, where factories were sending workers home on unpaid leave or simply imposing layoffs. As already mentioned, in September 1990 some 600,000 workers in this branch were without work due to shortages of synthetic fibres, thread, wool, linen, leather, dyes, and other materials. In many cases the crisis was compounded by the lack of hard currency, needed to buy foreign raw materials.[185] The essential point about these layoffs – aside from their largely temporary nature – is that they had nothing to do with perestroika's original goals of impelling factories to shed workers by modernizing and restructuring production. Nor did they arise from the workings of a well-established market, at least as this market existed in the dreams of the liberal reformers. Instead they emerged out of unplanned events which were neither anticipated nor desired. In the case of environmental closures, this was the legacy of the decades-long neglect, if not the actual planned abuse of the environment rooted deep in the Stalinist planning system. As for the supply crisis, this, as we shall see in chapter 4, was the inevitable outcome of trying to erect a market economy on the basis of the ossified, bureaucratic structures of the old command system. This remained true even after Gorbachev's fall from power and El'tsin's headlong dash towards the market. The factory closures of early 1992 resulted not from the 'rational' operation of market forces (if market forces can ever be said to be 'rational'), with bankruptcy for the non-competitive and the inefficient, but because of the accelerating collapse of all economic ties between enterprises. There was simply no coordination of economic activity, whether on the basis of the bureaucratic command system or the market. The economy was in grid-lock. This was a process set in motion by the policy of self-financing, and only made worse by El'tsin's 'reforms' and the breakup of the old Soviet Union, with its subsequent plunge into regionalism.

2 Economic incentives: the disintegration of the 1986 wage reform

Since the early five-year plans the Soviet regime has consistently failed to develop a coherent and workable system of incentives. Under Stalin wages were seen as a bludgeon with which to coerce the workforce into accepting stricter discipline and a higher rate of exploitation. The overwhelming majority of workers were put on piece rates, with basic wages set so low that only massive overfulfilment of output quotas, known as norms in Russian, could ensure the worker a living wage. To ensure that workers did not eventually adapt to their higher targets and learn how to meet them without excessive strain, norms were raised and the rates for the job cut during annual norm 'revision' campaigns conducted every spring. In this way, with each piece now worth less money, workers would have to raise output by some 10, 20, or 30 per cent just to maintain earnings at their old levels. But such a policy produced its own reaction. The labour shortage, together with uncertainties over the non-arrival of supplies, the quality of materials, unanticipated plan changes, and equipment breakdowns – difficulties which routinely plagued every area of production – compelled managers to keep norms attainable, so that workers could overfulfil their targets by enough to earn an acceptable wage. Where manipulation of norm setting proved insufficient or too difficult, as in the case of time workers, for example, managers had other devices with which to augment earnings: fictitious bonuses, permitting claims for work not carried out (*pripiski*), or regrading workers into higher skill and wage grades (*razryady*). Despite the Stalinist regime's repeated attempts to break this system, concessions over wages became a key element within the general nexus of informal bargaining that evolved between workers and line management.[1]

With Stalin's death and moves to relax the social tensions caused by the terror, Khrushchev attempted to resolve the problem in a different way, by raising basic wages and offering incentives to both managers and workers to accept tighter norms and the increased effort that went with them. But this was hardly more successful. Because the regime could do nothing to eliminate the constant disruptions to production and the threat of lost earnings they brought with them, managers and workers continued to operate according to their old arrangements. Bonuses for plan fulfilment or meeting various quality indicators were paid so routinely that they amounted to no more than an automatic supplement to the basic wage. *Pripiski*, especially, but not exclusively, in construction, remained a vital lever for wringing concessions from workers, for example, their agreement to work overtime. Norms were kept relatively low. More essentially, managers remained unwilling to impose tighter, so-called 'technically-based' norms[2] in the face of the perpetual uncertainties of the production process, which could make fulfilment impossible and thus lead to conflicts with the workforce. Where the Khrushchev reform was fairly stringently applied, in particular in the engineering industry, workers responded with high turnover, creating shortages in key trades that severely exacerbated bottlenecks.[3]

Under Brezhnev the elite's policy was effectively to buy the cooperation of the workforce by taking a benign attitude towards wage increases, coupled with various ill-starred 'experiments' designed to prompt workers to accept the need for greater efficiency. One, based on the experience of the Aksai plastics factory in Rostov, attempted to coax workers into voluntarily agreeing to, and determining, their own norm rises, in exchange for relatively small-scale increases in bonus payments. Another, applied in construction (called Zlobin brigades, after their alleged founder), tried to create incentives for economizing on the consumption of raw materials. Yet a third, and perhaps the most famous, was the experiment carried out at the Shchekino chemical combine in Tula oblast, near Moscow, where workers were offered inducements to cut staff in return for sharing in the savings this brought to the combine's wage fund. Yet all of these efforts proved fruitless (at Shchekino the workers eventually wound up earning less than at other plants in the chemical industry which had not applied the reform), for the same set of reasons: management simply could not guarantee the conditions – regular supplies, availability of tools, reliable equipment – for smooth, disruption-free production, without which workers could not meet the targets needed to ensure decent earnings.[4] In short, the elite could not break the social relations on the shop floor, which were at one and the same time a response by managers and workers to the difficult situation within which they each worked and had mutually to coexist, and a cause of that situation's perpetuation.[5]

With perestroika the elite confronted an entrenched, if not totally dysfunctional wages system, where there was no longer any coherent correspondence between earnings and a worker's performance. Instead, the wages system was dominated by countless anomalies: because of variations in locally determined norm-setting and bonus procedures and the informal bargaining behind them, workers in identical trades, with identical skills, and working under allegedly identical conditions would often have very different earnings, while specific groups of skilled and unskilled workers in different enterprises or even in different sections of the same factory might earn very much the same. Although under Khrushchev the differentials between the highest and lowest paid widened, this was a short-lived phenomenon. Under Brezhnev they once again narrowed, as did those between technical personnel and manual workers. The issue here is not so much that the desired, planned differentials had been eroded, while unwanted ones grew up, as that they took on an almost random character and thus could not provide workers with an incentive to improve effort, output, or the diligence with which they worked.[6]

From the point of view of industrial managers, this absence of effective incentives was often of only secondary importance. Given the labour shortage, far more critical was the use of wage funds to attract or hold on to labour power. Here money wages could be less significant than the social wage provided by individual ministries or their subordinate enterprises (housing, health and recreational facilities, and access to scarce foodstuffs and consumer goods), for it was the availability of these which frequently determined workers' decisions whether to stay in a job or move elsewhere.[7] From the elite's point of view the effect of this system has been contradictory. On the one hand, successive policies designed to force management to adhere to uniform, centrally determined payment criteria have been consistently undermined, thus thwarting the elite's attempts to utilize wages to enhance its control over workers' behaviour within production, and hence over the process of surplus extraction. On the other hand, the informal, often highly personalized arrangements behind concessions over money wages, coupled with enterprises' near monopoly over the allocation of housing and social benefits, have made workers dependent on the enterprise. This has had a politically corrupting effect on workers and management alike, has reinforced workers' atomization, and thereby has strengthened the elite's political control over the system.[8]

The 1986 wage reform was a reflection of this very contradiction. As a product of the early phase of perestroika it sought to establish a viable incentives system through the use of traditional policies, essentially those employed by Khrushchev in the wage reform of 1956–62. Yet insofar as the strategists behind perestroika recognized the obstacles that workers' atomization and low morale posed to economic reform, it was coupled with attempts to 'democratize' the industrial enterprise by offering workers limited participation in the management of enterprise affairs. Neither aspect of policy proved successful. Democratization, as we discuss in the next chapter, was never more than a hollow promise, and never won the workers' trust. The wage reform collapsed because, having been implemented within the context of the 'market mechanisms' of profit-and-loss accounting (*khozraschet*), it could not survive the economic dislocations and disintegration which this policy created. In 1990 the regime conceded that the reform had been a failure and once and for all abandoned attempts to impose centralized regulation of wages.

The aims and provisions of the reform

The Gorbachev wage reform sought to address the problem of incentives by widening differentials between technical personnel and workers, and between different categories of workers, in the belief that the prospect of higher rewards would encourage workers to exert greater effort and would ease the problems of recruiting specialists in key areas. The main provisions of the wage reform were strikingly similar to those of the Khrushchev reform of 1956–62:[9]

1 To raise output quotas, together with basic wage rates, in the attempt to reduce the importance of overfulfilment payments, and thereby reduce the pressure on local managers to keep norms low.

2 To make more extensive use of quality and performance bonuses, so as to prompt workers to pay greater attention to economizing on materials and adhering to operating procedures. In many enterprises bonuses for fulfilling plans and norms were only to be paid if all output were defect-free.

3 To carry out a substantial regrading of workers, with many workers being put into lower wage and skill grades (*razryady*) as an inducement to upgrade skills in line with the demands of technological modernization. At the same time differentials between the more highly skilled and less skilled were to be widened sharply.

4 There was to be greater use of collective, or so-called contract

payments, whereby workers' earnings would be tied to the production results of their work team (brigade), shop, or enterprise, and each worker's individual share would be calculated according to a Labour Input Coefficient (KTU – literally, 'coefficient of labour participation'). In theory this would lead to better coordination between different links in the production cycle, since workers would no longer be concerned solely with maximizing individual results, irrespective of whether or not this improved overall enterprise performance.

5 In line with the contract system, workers were encouraged not to *overfulfil* plan targets (which merely exacerbated problems of coordination), but to achieve given targets with smaller labour costs, primarily by reducing the size of work teams or shop establishments. Under this system – as with similar schemes promoted in the 1970s – the remaining workers were to share part of the saved wages as a bonus.

6 In an effort to control wage overspending, in August 1989 the regime imposed a 3 per cent ceiling on wage fund growth and a tax on wage spending above this limit, unless accompanied by a commensurate rise in output. Light industry (Group B enterprises) was exempt from the tax.[10]

A major difference with past wage reforms, however, was the fact that these changes took place in the context of the transfer of enterprises to self-financing, where incentive funds were to be formed out of enterprise profits. During most of perestroika the bulk of enterprises operated on a system where basic wage rates were guaranteed, but bonuses were to come out of a material incentives fund, paid for out of profits. Eventually all enterprises were to move to a more radical set-up, where an enterprise had to earn its entire wage fund out of income, that is, where even basic wages were to be tied to brigade, shop, or enterprise performance.[11] As we shall see, the transition to this second variant of *khozraschet* encountered a number of difficulties, arising mainly from the fact that performance – and hence wages – remained heavily dependent on factors outside an enterprise's control, and certainly outside the control of its workers.

Results of the reform

By the end of 1987 some 29 million people in the non-agricultural productive sector had been made subject to the reform.[12] Two years later (1 January 1990) this figure had risen to 60 million, or 86 per cent (including 95 per cent in industry) of the total number due to shift to the new system.[13] Throughout this period the press was able to single out certain model factories where the reform had led to improved efficiency and higher earnings,[14] but on the whole it proved a failure, eventually being abandoned at the end of 1990. The main reasons for this failure are analysed below.

Differentials between workers and technical specialists

One aim of the reform was to restore the position of technical specialists relative to the wages of industrial workers. For many years technical specialists (known in Russian as Engineering and Technical Employees, or ITR) had seen their earnings fall behind those of skilled manual workers – a major source of resentment among the technical intelligentsia, who felt that what they regarded as their superior status in society should be rewarded in a more open and even-handed way than the old system of privileges, which depended on arbitrary networks of personal contacts.[15] The objectives of this part of the reform were not simply political: labour specialists have long been concerned at the wastage of skills due to large numbers of engineers choosing to work as ordinary workers, rather than in their area of expertise.[16] To some extent the grievances of the technical intelligentsia have been exaggerated, since disparities in money wages in no way reflect the higher standard of living they enjoy due to their superior access to goods through the closed distribution system, better housing, and educational opportunities for their children – although this has in no way diminished their perceptions of discrimination.[17]

Nevertheless, the disparity in money earnings between workers and ITR has been quite real. Before the reform the average specialist earned 96 per cent of the average worker's wage; in engineering the gap was even greater, with specialists' wages just 86 per cent of those of workers.[18] There are three main factors behind this trend. First, because of the labour shortage, managers have had to raise workers' wages, a necessity tacitly recognized by the permissive attitude towards wages taken during the Brezhnev period. This has been especially true of workers in heavy or hazardous jobs, even where such jobs are low-skilled: if these jobs did not pay relatively well, many would simply remain unfilled. Even where these jobs are done by women or migrant workers – who make up the bulk of the low-paid – the pay is still higher than these same workers would earn at other work.[19] Secondly, workers have been a potential political threat in a way that the intelligentsia was not. Prior to perestroika outbreaks of worker unrest may have been relatively rare, but the authorities, through their swift repression of such disturbances, made it abundantly clear that they took them extremely seriously.[20] Thirdly, specialists' wages have been held down by the fact that many of these professions have, since the 1960s, become increasingly feminized, which, given the prevailing wage discrimination against women in the Soviet Union, has served to reinforce their low status.[21]

On the surface, the reform appeared to reverse the wage gap in specialists' favour. By 1989 average workers' wages had risen 12.6 per cent, as against 21.2 per cent for ITR, although in such key industries as engineering, non-ferrous metallurgy, and machine-tool manufacture, specialists' pay was still lower than that of workers.[22] These figures are deceptive, however, because they include in the category 'specialist' not just ITR, but management, including enterprise directors and shop superintendents, and it was precisely they who enjoyed truly large pay rises, at the expense of their ITR subordinates, whose wages went up barely in line with those of workers.[23] The significance of this should not be underestimated, for it meant that a group which the Gorbachev wing of the elite had relied on to form a major part of its social base had its economic aspirations severely disappointed. This helps explain why the technical intelligentsia, like their more vocal counterparts in the liberal intelligentsia, grew impatient with what they saw as Gorbachev's hesitant march towards the market, and politically abandoned perestroika.

Problems of incentives

Whatever the political repercussions of the wage reform on the elite's relationship with the intelligentsia, its main failure lay in its impact on industrial workers and the labour process. One difficulty was the relatively weak response of Soviet workers to monetary incentives. This has been conditioned by a number of historical factors: the scarcity of goods on which to spend their wages; the long-standing network of concessions from shop floor management (often based on personal connections) designed to protect earnings from falling below tacitly agreed local minima; the manifest failure of past experiments aimed at modifying the wages system, and the resulting conviction that greater effort would not necessarily lead to higher earnings; and the general political demoralization that has characterized Soviet workers since the 1930s and led to the loss of any traditions of collective political action.[24] Moreover, there is a strong tradition of egalitarianism among the Soviet population, and most workers feel that they do not receive a 'fair' wage for the amount of work they do or in relation to their material needs. By the same token, workers tend to view top management as a parasitic stratum incapable of doing what it is allegedly employed to do, that is, manage production efficiently. To most workers managers are overpaid, and the differential between their own earnings and those of ITR is perfectly justified. According to one survey of engineering workers, most felt that the main criterion determining pay should be the severity of working conditions, rather than training: ITR should earn more only if their working conditions were worse than those of workers.[25]

For those workers who might have responded to monetary incentives, the opening up of market relations, particularly the legalization of cooperatives, partially undermined the potential rewards the wage reform might have offered: many workers were simply unwilling to invest the increased effort needed to achieve higher earnings when they could earn far more either in cooperatives or by working on the black economy.[26] Finally, those increases in nominal earnings which the reform did bring proved too insignificant to stimulate workers to improve their performance,[27] a factor whose impact almost certainly intensified with the rapid growth in inflation. For many groups of workers this trend was reinforced by their ability to win rises in their money wages through actual or threatened industrial action.

The reform of bonus systems met with similar obstacles. The aim was that bonuses for quality indicators and fulfilment of overall production targets should displace payments for individual norm overfulfilment as the major component of earnings. In this way it was hoped to improve coordination between different stages of the production process and neutralize the tendency to push for quantitative results at the expense of product quality. There was also to be a shift towards collective bonuses, as opposed to those based on individual performance. At the same time, the new system was designed to close various loopholes in the old bonus regulations, whereby enterprises could fail to meet their basic production and quality indicators, yet still earn substantial bonuses by fulfilling such specialized criteria as the collection and delivery of metal scraps, production for export, or meeting particular targets deemed by the planning authorities as especially important.[28] Like the bonus regulations of the Khrushchev period, the new criteria made little impact. Enterprises were said to be 'extremely unwilling' to switch from individual to collective payments.[29] In the

Donbass coal fields, pits refused to pay bonuses for economizing on materials and energy consumption, out of fear that if such economies were too substantial, their allocations of these inputs might be cut in subsequent years.[30] For many workers the payment of bonuses continued to appear quite arbitrary. One survey of young workers found large minorities – from one-quarter to one-third – who said that payment depended on relations with shop management and that the criteria used for awarding them were obscure.[31] There were also conflicts over the fact that bonuses could be made dependent on the work results of an entire collective, thus penalizing workers for the poor performance of sections or brigades with which they had no actual interconnection in the course of production, and over whose work they could exercise no influence.[32] Perhaps the greatest difficulty, however, was the fact that the bonuses were simply too small to have the desired impact on workers' motivation. In 1988 one of the open hearth shops at Magnitogorsk achieved 3 million rubles in economies in its consumption of ferro-alloys, for which each worker received the princely sum of 3 rubles a month.[33]

The weakness of incentives was reflected in the fact that at no time did the reform enjoy popular confidence or support, without which it was manifestly unworkable. According to the massive All-Union Monitoring survey of industrial workers, managers, and technical specialists, by 1988 no more than 15 per cent of respondents felt the reform had yielded positive results; by 1990 this figure had declined to 12 per cent.[34]

Distortions due to financial pressures on enterprises

On the whole, enterprises faced the problem of how to finance the higher basic rates and improved bonuses called for by the wage reform under circumstances where the shift to *khozraschet* was putting pressure on wage funds. Under Khrushchev the stipulated wage increases had been centrally financed (although not always adequately), but with perestroika this was true only for those enterprises on the first model of *khozraschet*, and then only basic wage rates were to be covered; all bonuses would have to come out of enterprise revenues. Eventually, as enterprises moved to the second variant of *khozraschet*, even these subsidies would stop, and enterprises would have to earn their total wage bill.

In theory the bulk of the extra money was to be found through improvements in productivity and imposing layoffs. However, part was also to come through tighter regrading of workers, to eliminate situations where the skills of the worker were higher than those demanded by the job being carried out. Soviet industry operated under a complex system of wage and skill grades (*razryady*). Each industry had a list of enumerated trades, and each trade had a grid, relating the basic wage rate (that is, before bonuses or payments for norm overfulfilment) in each skill grade to that in the bottom grade, with specific ratios between them. Most trades worked with a six-grade scale, although the reform reintroduced an eight-grade scale in engineering. The basic wage rate within each *razryad* could vary, depending on whether the work was paid at piece or time rates and was performed under normal or hazardous conditions. Basic rates also varied by trade and industry, so that a fitter in the textile industry might earn less than a fitter in engineering, even if they were in the same *razryad*. Similarly, workers in the upper grades of less favoured industries (textiles, food processing, light industry) might earn less than workers in lower grades in industries that were financially better off (heavy industry). Under Stalin the wages system had been dominated by a plethora of different rates and wage scales, with separate specifications for virtually every operation carried out within industry. These were considerably simplified under Khrushchev, but still were left open to manipulation by managers, in some cases to boost the pay of workers whose earnings might fall below the generally accepted minimum or, conversely, to cut workers' pay where economies had to be made. In general this was done by moving workers into higher or lower *razryady*, but earnings could also be regulated by putting workers on jobs where the skill rating deviated from that assigned to the worker. In such cases for both piece and time workers the basic rate was to be paid according to the skill level of the work being performed, while all other payments (bonuses and extra payments for night work or years of service) were paid at the skill grade of the worker. This left considerable room for manoeuvre. For skilled workers doing simpler work, although they were paid at the lower skill grade the simplicity of the work they were doing often allowed them to achieve substantial norm overfulfilment. Workers doing jobs more complex than those for which they were trained obviously enjoyed the higher rates that went with them.[35]

The 1986 reform sought to tighten up in precisely this area, demanding that workers be regraded to bring their *razryady* into line with their actual work, while in many cases simultaneously lowering the skill grade assigned to specific operations, as set out in a new Wage-Skill

Handbook, which stipulated the skill levels and wage rates of every job in the economy. It was inevitable that such a campaign, if actually enforced, would lead to conflicts, since it attacked the very fabric of informal understandings between management and workers. Where workers did jobs rated lower than their actual *razryad* this was not necessarily the result of managerial caprice, but of production necessities, and reflected a need to retain flexibility in a situation where workers frequently have to be shifted from one job to another, depending on the availability of parts and supplies, plan changes, urgency of orders, and the like. In such situations shop floor managers had to be in a position to protect workers from possible cuts in earnings which such uncertainties might cause.

Given this reality, it is perhaps surprising how many managers used the regrading to drive down wages, primarily to offset the higher basic rates imposed as a compensation for tighter norm-setting. Surveys suggested that nationally between 10–12 per cent of workers had their *razryady* cut, while 4.5 per cent moved up.[36] Although it is impossible to determine in how many cases the regrading conformed to the letter of the new regulations, we do know that conflicts over alleged abuses were common. To some extent this could be attributed to the 'campaign mentality' with which managers typically applied policy changes in the USSR: implement the campaign first, blindly and bureaucratically, so as to demonstrate one's diligence, and then make the necessary adjustments later on. It is clear, however, that much, if not most of the impetus was financial: because the main intended source of extra money – improved productivity and redundancies – did not materialize, managers saw massive downward regrading as the most convenient alternative. In some construction trusts from two-thirds to nine-tenths of workers had their *razryady* reduced. Often management did not even go through the formalities of regrading procedures, but just announced that, thenceforth, all workers in a particular shop or section were being moved into lower grades.[37] Hypothetically those workers placed in lower skill grades were to have earnings protected by the higher basic rates stipulated by the reform, but for many workers the new rates failed to balance their loss of pay,[38] while others receive no compensation at all.[39] It is significant that at least some managers were prepared to resort to this same tactic later on, after the April 1991 price rises (that is, when the wage reform had already been abandoned), in order to finance the wage 'increases' they now had to pay to compensate workers for higher meal prices in factory canteens.[40]

The financial pressures on enterprise wage funds went far beyond the problem of regrading. In many cases enterprises were able to maintain their social development funds (out of which they finance housing construction, for example) only by cutting back on essential expenditures within production, in particular improvements in working conditions.[41] This problem was most pronounced in light industry, whose enterprises continued to turn over the lion's share of their revenues to the state treasury, despite, under *khozraschet*, now having to finance wage increases and the provision of essential amenities out of their own coffers.[42] Other enterprises ran into difficulty because management was too quick to shift brigades (work teams), shops, or whole enterprises to *khozraschet* without first ensuring that their production operations were financially viable. Workers suffered wage cuts, which in turn became a major cause of the strike wave that hit the USSR during 1989.[43]

Even allowing that some of these enterprises may have been extreme examples, evidence suggests that during 1986 and 1987 the wage reform was having at least part of the intended effect, as wages rose perceptibly slower than productivity.[44] By 1988 and 1989, however, this trend had been dramatically reversed: in 1989 wages rose twice as fast as productivity for the economy as a whole,[45] and three times as fast in industry (and nearly six times faster than total industrial output).[46] In fact, the discrepancy was greater than these figures suggest, since much of the 'increase' in industrial production was due simply to inflation and the rise in factory prices, rather than to increases in output in physical terms.[47] This wages–output 'scissors' widened further during 1990 and 1991, as average money wages continued to grow while total industrial production actually fell. Thus it is clear that by the end of the reform's third year the pressures on managers to raise wages in most industries had become irresistible. As the labour shortage worsened and workers began increasingly to resort to strike action to push their demands, managers had little choice but to make concessions. Perhaps more important, despite the imposition of *khozraschet* factories were finding the money to finance these increases: by skimping on other areas of factory expenditure (investment or housing), by driving up prices, by receiving subsidies from parent ministries,[48] or by fraudulently claiming wage funds for factory sub-divisions which they had in fact hived of as self-financing cooperatives.[49]

Norm setting

At the heart of all attempts to reform the wages system lies norm setting, for it is here that the questions of incentives and control over the labour process most closely coalesce. Norm setting has been a constant three-way battleground in Soviet industry, between the state, factory management, and workforce. The central authorities have always recognized tighter norms as the main vehicle for raising the rate of exploitation. By the same token, management, no matter how much it might have wished to benefit from the greater control over the workforce which such norms would have allowed, has proven in the main unable to impose them because of its own imperfect control over the labour process and the subsequent need to make concessions over earnings and work speeds. Traditionally, the main vehicle for protecting workers' earnings has been the toleration of slack norms. Even in textiles, which has perhaps the highest intensity of labour and the lowest average norm fulfilment of all Soviet industries, it was common for management to keep norms relatively loose to allow women to achieve a tolerable level of earnings and to ensure an influx of workers.[50] Yet it is precisely on this issue that the failure of the reform was most transparent. Managers did not in all cases prove willing to raise norms as stipulated by the reform. Although some factories (for example the ZiL truck plant in Moscow) imposed tighter, so-called technically based norms, with resultant low levels of fulfilment,[51] in general managers resisted pressures in this direction. Some raised norms by less than the rise in basic wages, thus granting their workers a *de facto* wage rise.[52] Others increased them merely in line with the rise in the basic wage, keeping earnings more or less guaranteed without putting any pressure on workers for extra output.[53] Still other factories continued to use outdated norms, which new technology had made easier to fulfil, or to apply so-called correction coefficients, which allowed them to adjust norms downwards to compensate workers for what were alleged to be special circumstances impeding proper norm fulfilment.[54]

The main problem, however, was enterprises' continued unwillingness to impose genuinely 'technically based' norms.[55] The reality is that such norms have always been unenforceable given the uncertainties of Soviet conditions of production. Production is inherently arhythmical, with long periods of inactivity followed by overtime and storming. Until the collapse of the Communist Party and its factory organizations, it was also common for workers to be taken off production and sent to help out in the fields of nearby collective farms. In all these situations, if technical norms – which make no allowance for typical losses of work time – were stringently applied, there would be several days each month where workers would earn virtually nothing at all.[56] At the other extreme, because of the strict legal limits on overtime, factories conceal it by crediting output achieved during storming to workers' normal working hours, thus artificially inflating their performance and earnings and rendering reported levels of norm fulfilment almost meaningless.[57] Nor could fulfilment always be accurately measured, even where production was running smoothly. As technology has become more complex, reliable estimation of the labour content of various jobs has come increasingly to require computerization, an area in which the Soviet Union is notoriously weak.[58] Also, the nature of certain types of production does not lend itself to systematic norm setting. This was certainly the case in small-batch production, which accounts for a large part of output in the engineering industry: because equipment and components are not mass produced, it becomes extremely difficult to calculate their labour content, making norm setting at best an arbitrary exercise.[59]

Since at least 1989, if not earlier, there was a clear tendency for managers to ignore norm revisions altogether, a trend that intensified with the subsequent decentralization of norm setting, which freed managers from the obligation to impose centrally established norms and norm-setting criteria.[60] So long as the features of the production cycle remained fundamentally unchanged – with the availability of materials made more and more uncertain by the developing supply crisis, and the advanced age of Soviet equipment leading to ever-more frequent breakdowns – such resistance was inevitable, especially as managers were increasingly threatened by the loss of skilled workers to cooperatives offering higher wages, and saw low norms as one of the best means by which to inflate earnings and cut turnover.[61] Again, *khozraschet* itself undermined attempts to tighten up norm setting, since enterprises could now boost their incomes – and with it their wage funds – simply by raising prices, thus allowing them to 'finance' slack norms.[62] This, more than anything else, signalled the ultimate unworkability of the wage reform, for without the imposition of more rigid norm setting the elite had no prospect of exercising greater control over production.

Collective payment systems

A major part of the wage reform entailed the shift from remuneration for a worker's individual performance to collective payments according to the so-called contract system.[63] Like similar experiments in coal mining and construction in the 1960s, and in various branches of manufacturing industry in the 1970s, the system involved a work team taking responsibility for an entire complex of jobs, receiving payment for the total result, which was then to be distributed among the collective's members according to each person's skill grade, hours worked, and individual contribution to this total. In the past such arrangements had failed because the ability of workers to fulfil their contracts depended on too many external factors which disrupted production schedules and thereby jeopardized workers' earnings.[64] The rationale behind this system was to give workers a material incentive to cut establishments. If brigades could meet their contracts with fewer people, they would still receive the total contracted payment for the job, and would share out the extra savings in increased earnings. Like its predecessors, however, the contract system under perestroika came up against near-insurmountable obstacles, which we discuss in detail in chapter 4.

The use of collective payments was also intended to obviate some of the more intractable failings in the norm-setting system. In theory, since payment was by final results and depended on collective effort, workers would have no incentive to pressure line management to keep norms low. In practice, however, the new system led to considerable discontent and helped reinforce the contract brigades' limited popularity. The calculation of wages was a complex, and often arbitrary operation based on three factors: hours worked, skill grade, and the KTU. All workers in a brigade received the basic wage according to hours worked and their skill grade, while bonuses were distributed according to the KTU, which in turn assessed each worker's particular contribution to brigade results, for example, if workers had combined jobs or performed work of particularly high quality. In the Brezhnev period the KTU was calculated by the brigade council, but during the 1980s individual enterprises and shops had their own variations, depending on the balance of power between rank and file, brigade leaders, and shop management. Thus in some brigades the KTU was decided by a general meeting of the entire work team, in others by the brigade council, in still others by the brigade leader, or even by the foreman or shop superintendent.[65]

That such a highly subjective category became the focus of constant conflicts should come as no surprise. Both the basic wage and the KTU were based on workers' skill grades, yet the very nature of brigade work, where workers combined and rotated jobs, meant that workers in different *razryady* tended to do the same, or comparable jobs of identical degrees of complexity. Thus workers wound up with different earnings for the same work.[66] In some enterprises, foremen or section and shop superintendents usurped the right to determine the KTU and the distribution of wages, allegedly ignoring decisions of general brigade meetings or brigade councils.[67] Workers understandably distrusted such arrangements. A survey of building workers in Vladivostok found that where each worker's KTU was agreed at a general brigade meeting, nearly 90 per cent of workers were satisfied with the result, but only 75 per cent approved when the brigade council decided, 62 per cent when the decision was made by the brigade leader, and only 44 per cent when the KTU was set by the foreman.[68] Other factories reported similar attitudes.[69] In still other workplaces workers evolved their own local systems of job rotation, which rendered calculation of the KTU virtually impossible.[70] In the end, the use of KTU was virtually abandoned: in some cases formally, where it was replaced by other indicators, equally difficult to assess; or, as in most factories carrying out small and medium-batch production, simply by artificially adjusting it to allow earnings to gravitate towards the customary average wage, thus negating its very rationale, namely the undermining of alleged 'egalitarianism'.[71]

The fall in the standard of living and the collapse of the reform

By late summer 1990 the regime was forced to admit that the reform had been almost a total failure. As of January 1991 both wages and norm-setting were decentralized and devolved completely to enterprises; centrally set wage rates were to serve only as guaranteed minima.[72] Although from the regime's point of view this step contained the real danger that enterprises would distort wages policy even further – a danger, we should add, that was largely realized – it was a necessary move if the economy were to shift completely to a market, including a market for labour power.

It was not simply the need to marketize wages that explained the reform's abandonment. As we have seen, in almost all its particulars it had become simply unworkable. Incentives were weak and norm setting was in near chaos. Wages were shooting up far in excess of industrial output. Perhaps most important of all, there was no evidence that the reform had even the slightest impact on the mechanisms of informal bargaining on the shop floor, a topic we take up in chapter 6. Intended as a means of effecting a restructuring of the labour process, in the end the wage reform fell victim to the very shop floor relations it was supposed to have reshaped.

Unlike the wage reforms and experiments of the Khrushchev and Brezhnev periods, which were strangled by the intractability of the Stalinist system, the collapse of the Gorbachev reform revealed a more volatile dynamic. For it was imposed as part of a general economic reform whose effect was to throw many of the traditional institutions and *modi operandi* of the Stalinist system into flux. If it proved still-born this was as much to do with the new circumstances of economic disintegration which the reforms created, as with the structural rigidities of the old system. We have already mentioned the effect of the worsening labour shortage and workers' increasing use of industrial action to press their demands. Another, yet closely related, factor was the precipitous fall in the standard of living, which undermined many of the traditional mechanisms through which management exercised political control over the workforce.

The Soviet Union has always been characterized by the low standard of living of the mass of the population alongside the visible affluence of members of the ruling elite. Among average citizens, male workers in heavy industry were relatively privileged, although life was still a struggle. If in 1987 the average industrial worker earned 219 rubles a month, underground workers in coal mining or oil drillers made between 400–500, while women in the baking and confectionary industries could earn as little as 130.[73] For those like pensioners or young people just starting their working lives, poverty has been an ever-present reality.[74]

The stagnation of real incomes, as reflected in growing shortages and concealed inflation, was a long-term phenomenon, dating back at least to the late 1960s.[75] Whereas previously this trend had manifested itself in declining rates of growth of personal income, under perestroika living standards fell absolutely, as inflation accelerated and the output of food and consumer goods contracted. Officially prices rose by between 8.4–10 per cent in 1988, and 10–14 per cent in 1989, depending on the source of the estimate. However, for many items the figures were meaningless, since they were simply unavailable except on the *kolkhoz* or black markets, whose prices were out of reach for most families.[76] During 1990 and 1991 the situation deteriorated still further, so that by the end of 1991 the average monthly food bill for a family in Perm oblast was nearly 70 per cent of the wages of a skilled steel worker; a pair of children's winter boots would cost this same worker a week's wages.[77]

In fact, up until the runaway inflation of 1991, most price rises on foods and consumer goods were concealed, as factories resorted more and more to the tried and tested practice of cutting (or altogether ceasing) production of cheaper lines, and expanding their output of more expensive items under the so-called 'N' or 'D' labels (applied to new products or to goods deemed particularly 'stylish').[78] Often this involved the mere reclassification of old goods as new, although the quality could be abysmal.[79] In the clothing industry, for example, between 1987 and 1989 the number of different types of clothing manufactured fell by 23 per cent, while the spread between the cheapest and most expensive narrowed. It was the same with food products: prices on sausage went up 22 per cent between 1987–9, while production fell, on some types by a full third.[80] The increase in the proportion of output devoted to 'N' and 'D' lines was indeed consider-able: in the light industry of Leningrad and Leningrad oblast they accounted for 38 per cent of all goods produced.[81] Since clothing factories at least were still required to produce a certain amount of clothing for children and the elderly for the *goszakaz* (the state order, that is, the output obligatorily delivered to the central authorities at state-determined prices), most of the cutbacks came in low-price gar-ments designed for the general population.[82]

This behaviour was a logical outcome of *khozraschet*, especially when applied within the old, authoritarian framework of ministerial tute-lage. Under the centralized planning system enterprises in light indus-try were planned to earn high 'profits', the bulk of which were then transferred to the central treasury. Thus with the shift to *khozraschet*, these enterprises were left with totally insufficient resources to finance new investment, wage increases, housing, or other aspects of the social infrastructure.[83] One way around this problem was to take advantage of the consumer goods shortage and put up prices: this would allow enterprises to cut production (often bringing it more realistically into line with actual capacities) and at the same time acquire much needed extra revenue – most of which was still syphoned off by the Ministry of Light Industry.[84] In doing this enterprises were reacting perfectly rationally to the new economic circumstances. But the root of the problem did not lie with them alone. The strategy of cutting output and pushing up prices was the official policy of the Ministry of Light Industry, which in 1987 began incorporating substantial price rises and cuts in output into enterprise plans.[85] In theory this would provide funds with which enterprises could undertake reconstruction and reequipment while continuing lavishly to subsidize the Ministry's bureaucratic apparatus. In practice, however, enterprises in light industry behaved just like their counterparts in other branches of the economy: they used the extra money to finance wage rises, in an effort to stem turnover and counteract what was becoming an increasingly serious labour shortage.[86] By 1991 this trend of falling output and rising prices had gathered a momentum of its own: reproduced throughout the economy, it led to growing supply shortages, compelling factories, especially in light industry, to cut production even more, thus further depressing the standard of living.

As the basic fabric of economic coordination unravelled, the implementation of a coherent wages policy became simply impossible. The wage reform had been designed to introduce clear-cut and easily comprehensible differentials between different categories of workers, to spur them to improve their performance and accept tighter discipline on the shop floor. What happened instead was that the old anomalies, dictated by local traditions and the specific relations between workers and management within each factory sub-unit, were either reinforced or replaced by new ones, as managers and workers both scrambled to protect their respective positions. For workers the situation presented a cruel paradox: wages were rising, yet because of shortages and inflation their standard of living was falling, and they could not live on what they earned. As we saw in the previous chapter, many responded by leaving state enterprises and going to cooperatives, thus increasing the pressures of work for those left behind. Others resorted to industrial action and strikes. In Vladimir oblast, for example, as early as 1989 half of all strikes were over wages.[87]

The regime's response, as we have noted, was to attempt to place a ceiling on all wage rises not supported by increased output. Yet managers found that if they attempted to enforce these regulations, or to impose similar economies – for example, paying wages late or using profits normally set aside for workers' thirteenth pay packets to pay off bank loans and strengthen the factory's credit position – workers either left or threatened industrial action.[88] And so in most cases, as the global figures on wages and output show, the most effective action was simply to concede wage rises, even if this had to come at the expense of investment. But this became a highly uneven and almost unpredictable process. Differentials within and between enterprises now had far more to do with the enterprise's ability to withstand the financial pressures of *khozraschet* or with workers' collective strength at the point of production. To some extent this had always been the case, as large enterprises in heavy industry and the defence sector were distinctly favoured over smaller or less strategic units, especially in light industry. As we shall see when we examine the problems of conversion and self-financing, in key areas this pattern broke down, as previously strong enterprises were now plunged into economic uncertainty, as orders and wages both fell.[89] This randomness became even more pronounced following the price rises of April 1991. Although the only mass protests occurred in Minsk, workers throughout the country struck (or threatened to strike) at factory level in an effort to extract compensation from local management, and their relative success or failure varied enormously from workplace to workplace.[90]

The breakdown of coherence of traditional wages hierarchies was also true of the social wage, that is, the provision by enterprises of such essential services as housing, the distribution of scarce foodstuffs and consumer goods, child care places, medical clinics, and (via the trade unions) disability benefits and access to recreational facilities, including workers' holidays or summer camps for their children.[91] This system, which dates back to Stalin's time, has served a vital political function. It was central to the strategy of Stalinist industrialization that the standard of living – not just food, but housing and consumer goods – be sacrificed to the interests of accelerated accumulation in heavy industry. Consumption, both individual and collective, was to be determined by what the Soviets call 'the remainder principle', that is, by what resources were left available after meeting the needs of investment. At the same time, given the low level of provision, its concentration in the hands of individual ministries and enterprises was used as a weapon to try to control the workforce. This was most blatant in the 1930s, when labour regulations stipulated that workers guilty of absenteeism were to be dismissed from their jobs and evicted from enterprise-owned housing and deprived of ration cards,[92] but even with de-Stalinization it continued to form one of the bedrocks of worker–manager relations within Soviet factories.

Essentially, enterprises have used their ability to deliver social benefits to quell potential discontent and to compete for workers under conditions of permanent labour shortage. Unequal social provision, rather than simply wages, has always been a major cause of labour turnover, as workers abandoned enterprises with poorer housing or closed distribution systems to look for jobs where the social infrastructure was better. Conversely, enterprises used this infrastructure to deter workers from quitting. This is most obvious in the case of *limitchiki*, who are dependent on their employer for residence permits and a place to live, but in reality it applies to all workers, and has even been termed a modern version of serfdom.[93] Perhaps ironically, the enterprise has been in a stronger position precisely because of the country's backwardness in the social sphere. So long as a worker is still in the housing queue she or he remains dependent on keeping her or his job, whereas once the worker acquires a flat she or he is free to go.

In general, enterprises paying the highest wages also had the most generously endowed social and material incentives funds: defence factories and other strategically vital plants in heavy industry at the one extreme, versus light industry at the other.[94] These were planned disparities, designed to guarantee a flow of labour power to what the elite deemed were key sectors, although even here there were important exceptions, in particular coal mining, where the appalling state of housing was one of the main grievances behind the 1989 strikes.[95] To some extent these basic inequalities were actually reinforced by the financial crisis induced by *khozraschet*. Light industry, already stripped of most of its profits, had little left over for such social necessities as building flats. By contrast, the Komsomol organization at the huge Uralmash engineering works in Sverdlovsk was able to finance the construction of a new block of flats, half of which were reserved for young workers, in an attempt to curb their high turnover.[96] These variations in the social wage were also a major factor behind workers' reluctance to abandon the official trade unions in favour of the more radical independent unions and workers' organizations which sprang up during perestroika: however bankrupt they perceived the official unions to be, they feared the loss of benefits whose disbursal was under trade union control.[97]

Nevertheless, there were important areas where this system was badly disrupted. When, in December 1989, the government decided substantially to raise charges for freight transport, and fuel, and to increase enterprises' social insurance contributions, iron and steel works were left not only unable to meet their wage bills (threatening steel workers with pay cuts of between 25 and 100 rubles a month), but without the funds needed to put up housing or provide child care facilities.[98] Thus for many enterprises, *khozraschet* seriously weakened their control over workers' behaviour in this area, as well.[99] The haemorrhage of workers, both skilled and unskilled, continued, while discipline at shop floor level worsened.

It was this growing dysfunction of the wage reform, as much as the requirements of the move to the market, which led to its ultimate abandonment. In effect, the reform was an economic and political anachronism. It was conceived at a time when the elite's strategy was to try economically to reshape the Soviet system while preserving its traditional political and property relations. This is why it resembled the Khrushchev reforms so closely. The idea, however, was that by situating the reform within the context of *khozraschet*, while at the same time providing workers with greater political motivation to identify with the need to restructure production, the pitfalls of the Khrushchev reforms could be avoided. Reality was to prove otherwise. *Khozraschet* led not to a more functional system of incentives, but to the ultimate disintegration of economic coordination which rendered all incentives inoperative. By the same token, attempts to give workers the political grounds to identify with the aims of perestroika, in particular experiments with enterprise democratization, failed dismally. Democratization never took place, and workers perceived this quite clearly, with a subsequent loss of morale. Instead, taking advantage of the political relaxation signalled by glasnost, they came more and more to rely on collective action, at least at shop floor level. This did not supplant, but rather grew up in addition to the long-standing problems of poor individual discipline and the jealous protection by workers of traditional work practices. Thus both strands of the elite's strategy of cooption – embodied in its policies of economic and political incentives – fell effectively into chaos.

3   Political incentives: enterprise 'democratization' and the emergence of worker protests

Almost from the beginning of perestroika sociologists and economists spoke openly, and often with considerable insight, about the legacy which atomization and the estrangement of workers from decision-making power had bequeathed to the Soviet economy. As one senior journalist succinctly put it: 'The workers paid back this alienation from the means of production, this formal access to the management of their own enterprise, with a corresponding quality and quantity of labour'.[1] Yet the connection between low morale and workers' attitudes towards production was no discovery of perestroika. Upon Stalin's death, not just Khrushchev, but virtually all those vying for power recognized that the terror and the demoralization and fear which it engendered were a major obstacle to improving the country's poor economic performance. A sullen and browbeaten population would never show great enthusiasm for its work and would never willingly abandon the various manoeuvres and devices through which individuals protected themselves from the regime's overbearing presence at work and in society at large. A major aim of Khrushchev's policy of de-Stalinization was, therefore, to try to relegitimate the regime in the eyes of its people, and to encourage a revival (albeit tightly controlled) of social activism. The terror was removed, censorship was eased, and efforts were made to rejuvenate the Communist Party as the sole forum through which people could attempt to influence if not the formation of policy, at least the method of its implementation. For industrial workers this general liberalization was coupled with specific measures designed to break down the intense alienation felt by most of the workforce towards the ruling elite. Criminal penalties on job changing and absenteeism were repealed, regulations protecting workers against unfair dismissal were strengthened, and the trade unions underwent a 'reform', designed to make them nominally more responsive to their members. The impact of these changes was distinctly limited. Steps towards liberalization and 'democratization' offered no real avenues of popular participation in decision-making, either at the workplace or in general political life, which remained the province of the Communist Party and the bureaucratic elite. Workers had little opportunity to influence their trade unions, which continued to function as an arm of the state, with the primary task of expediting the fulfilment of centrally dictated production plans. Nor could workers go outside these structures and form independent unions or political organizations, much less engage in spontaneous protest. When they did so, as in the strikes and demonstrations in Novocherkassk in 1962, they were ruthlessly repressed. And so the problem of morale remained unresolved.

In its basic approach the strategy of perestroika was similar to that pursued by Khrushchev. Elements of economic coercion were to be combined with political liberalization to both prod and entice workers to accept the need for tighter discipline. During the first two years after Gorbachev's arrival in power – that is, until the State Enterprise Law of 1987 – this policy appeared as little more than a revival of the measures adopted by Andropov during his brief term as Soviet leader, when the government had demanded stricter discipline at work, in exchange for a campaign to clean up the much-hated corruption among top officials and enterprise managers. Even had Andropov lived, it is doubtful that such a policy would have born fruit: for the workers such a *quid pro quo* had little to offer. Yet Gorbachev at first seemed to be following precisely this path with his ill-fated campaign against alcoholism, which had no palpable effect on the economy other than to create a shortage of sugar.

At the same time, however, Gorbachev and his reform advisors were putting in place a more sophisticated policy, which demonstrated that they had indeed drawn important lessons from Khrushchev's failures. On the economic side the attempt to tie wages more closely to work effort through a Khrushchev-style wage reform was to be counterbalanced by a projected rise in the standard of living – hence the emphasis on economic modernization. On the political side, it was clear that these economic levers, even if successfully put in place, would not in and of themselves be enough to persuade workers to accept a restructuring of the labour process and the attack on their shop-floor traditions which such a restructuring would entail. Economic incentives would have to be supported by gestures towards liberalization, which in turn would have to be far more sweeping than anything mooted in the post-Stalin years. As argued in the

Introduction, this entailed the attempt to construct a Soviet equivalent
to bourgeois civil society, with a hegemonic ideology through which
the workers would come to view the prevailing class relations of the
society as a 'natural' and acceptable state of affairs. This strategy did
not evolve smoothly. Even limited democratization contained the
danger of how to introduce changes substantial enough to win
workers' support, but not so far-reaching as to fly out of control and
threaten the foundations of the elite's overall hold on state power.

It is the appreciation of this danger that explains both the extreme
caution with which Gorbachev introduced political liberalization, and
the fact that democratization proceeded much more rapidly within the
workplace than in society at large. Workers, through so-called Councils of Labour Collectives (STK), were offered the opportunity to
participate in key decisions on plans and the use of enterprise
resources, and to elect their managers – long before they received the
chance to vote in even semi-free elections for a Soviet parliament. The
slogan, workers must feel themselves the 'masters of the enterprise',
resounded throughout the press and labour journals. And while the
use of such terminology necessarily involved no small amount of
cynicism on the part of policy-makers, it nevertheless reflected a
general perception of perestroika's central problem.

By 1988 this strategy was already proving unworkable. Its
institutional limitations, coupled with entrenched managerial resistance to curbs on their authority, meant that enterprise democracy
never acquired more than a formal existence. Yet the general liberalization of glasnost emboldened workers to press their real grievances
more directly through strikes and other forms of industrial action.
Although this new-found militancy only rarely broke through to give
rise to a mass movement expressing advanced organizational forms
and political awareness, it meant the death of any strategy of 'incorporating' the working class and winning its cooperation in perestroika as
a long-term economic and political project. Workers' alienation from
the regime persisted, even as they began to overcome the atomization
imposed on them by six decades of Stalinism. Although the miners'
strikes of 1989 and 1991 showed the capacity of Soviet workers to
transcend this history and develop the potential nucleus of a new
working class movement – a potential that remained largely
unfulfilled – in most enterprises militancy over immediate shop-floor
issues coexisted with, and even reinforced, the long-standing political
demoralization and the recourse to largely depoliticized forms of
individual action characteristic of the workforce under Stalinism.

Where this was not the case, as in the miners' movement, workers displayed a contradictory consciousness: the strikes threw up extremely radical forms of working-class organization in the pursuit of demands, many (though by no means all) of which were pro-market and even pro-capitalist.

As with the wage reform and the disintegration of Gorbachev's incentives policy, to a large extent it was the market reforms themselves which doomed his political strategy to failure. As the reforms created deepening economic dislocation and crisis, workers came under ever-greater pressure to protect their precarious standard of living through strikes or the threat of industrial disruption. At the same time, the economic decline gave new foundations to growing demoralization and political despair, which undermined once and for all moves to coopt the working class into the elite's strategy for economic modernization. Once it became clear to the elite that it would have to abandon its original conception of perestroika and introduce the market, the initial experiments with enterprise democratization also had to be discarded, since worker self-management, even in the emasculated and ultimately powerless variant of perestroika, was incompatible with the private ownership of the means of production on which the market would have to be based. This gave rise to a new type of worker struggle – over who would own and control industrial enterprises – which will almost certainly become more frequent and more intense as the post-Gorbachev move to capitalism accelerates.

We begin this chapter by examining the failure of Gorbachev's policy of enterprise democratization and the struggles over ownership which arose once the policy of introducing the market was firmly put in place in mid-1990. We then move on to analyse the mass strikes of the miners in 1989 and 1991 and the protests against the April 1991 price rises. We conclude with an analysis of local workplace struggles and the political and ideological limitations inherent in worker protests during perestroika. We should stress that our account here, especially that of the two miners' strikes, is in no way comprehensive. Nor do we provide a detailed examination of the new workers' movement which emerged from the first miners' strike of 1989. These would be a massive undertaking far beyond the scope of this book, involving not just a detailed review of the press and journal material, but large-scale interviews with participants. Rather we have concentrated on those aspects of worker protests which have directly affected worker-management relations within the enterprise and help cast light on the dynamics of the labour process under perestroika.[2]

The false promise of enterprise democratization

The Councils of Labour Collectives

Discussions over worker participation in management, including a few highly circumscribed experiments with the election of managers, had been appearing in the Soviet literature since the late 1970s. Under Andropov there was a Law on the Labour Collective, which gave brigade members, either directly or through elected brigade councils, the right to decide how they organized their work and distributed payment.[3] As Yanowitch points out, however, these various reforms and proposals were never intended to give workers real power over the work environment. They were managerialist strategies, designed to make the Soviet enterprise run more efficiently.[4] The same could be said of the reforms introduced under perestroika, which set up the formal institutions through which workers could participate in decision-making at brigade, shop, and enterprise level, while leaving the reins of real power firmly in the hands of management.

The centrepiece of this policy was the State Enterprise Law, passed in June 1987, and which became fully operative in January 1988. According to this law the labour collective, which included all of an enterprise's personnel, from director down to ordinary workers, was the sovereign power in the enterprise. Between general meetings authority was to reside in Councils of Labour Collectives (STK). Each sub-unit, that is, brigades, shops, and the enterprise as a whole, were to have their own STK. In small enterprises the STK was to be elected by a general meeting of the collective. In larger enterprises, where such meetings were deemed impractical, the trade union committee and the factory administration were to convene a delegate conference, themselves deciding how many delegates would be selected from each shop. Once the new STK was elected, the convening of future conferences were its responsibility. No more than one quarter of STK members were to be representatives of management, although there was a loophole here, since managers elected to the STK as representatives of any of the factory's social organizations (the Communist Party or the trade union), did not count against the administration's quota. There were, however, some legal protections to defend STK members from managerial harassment: they could not be dismissed, transferred to another job, or subjected to disciplinary penalties without the STK's agreement.[5]

The actual powers of the STK were extremely ill-defined: collectives, either directly or through their STK, were invested with the right to make key decisions over approval of production plans, disposal of profits, and use of social development funds. In theory the STK, as the 'sovereign power' in the enterprise, was to act as its 'legislative' arm, setting general policy, while management functioned as its executive. But management's right to execute was not to be challenged or interfered with. Collectives could still influence managerial actions through their right to elect middle management and enterprise directors, but these elections had to be confirmed by higher authorities.[6] As might be expected, such elections were relatively rare events. As of late 1988 only 20 per cent of enterprise directors had been elected, and 5–8 per cent of shop superintendents and foremen.[7] Thus of the few contests that occurred, most were for top management only, with workers having almost no say in the appointment of those with whom they had the most direct dealings on the shop floor. With hindsight it can be said that the principle of election posed no real threat to the power and privileges of managers at any level, although this was not how it appeared to management at the time. As we note below, managers on the whole resisted any restrictions on their power and prerogatives posed by the STK.[8] In late 1989, as perestroika entered its more 'radical', pro-market phase, the Soviet government did away with these elections altogether, six months before the STK themselves were stripped of their few remaining functions.[9]

As of 1989 there were over 140,000 STK elected at enterprises in industry and the service sector, in construction organizations, and in institutions. Some 90 per cent of these had been set up in the course of 1988, which gives some indication of the rapidity with which they were created. In all, these STK represented just 4.7 million people, including 3 million workers, not all of whom would have been in industry. Thus even at the movement's high point the STK would have embraced an extremely small percentage of the country's 31 million industrial workers.[10] The first STK were overwhelmingly headed up by management, and there were charges in the press that elections of the Councils and Council chairpersons were undemocratic, if not rigged: voting was done by lists, sometimes even by acclamation (what one newspaper called 'voting without voting'), and councils were packed with management representatives.[11] A foreman at the AZLK automobile plant in Moscow described just how this worked in practice. At AZLK the STK was elected by a conference of the labour collective, delegates to which were supposed to be elected at shop meetings. In his particular shop there had not been a single shop meeting in over two years, save for the yearly routine trade union elections, which few workers attended. Rather, delegates to the conference were chosen by shop management, Party workers, and trade union officials, who handed out 'invitations' to foremen, a few of the latter's hand-picked drinking buddies, and older, so-called 'cadre' workers who have a special relationship with shop managers. Where shop meetings were held, workers tended to stay away from them, in his view because they had a sense of their own lack of organization and feared that if they spoke out against managerial wrong-doings and failed to receive support from other workers they would leave themselves open to victimization. Thus the meetings were dominated by 'cadre' workers close to management, foremen, and office staff, who then elected pro-management delegates to the conference. At the factory's initial conference the STK was elected in the following fashion:

> The administration prepares in advance those people who will nomi-nate candidates to the Council of Labour Collectives. These people stand up and call out the names of the candidates off of a piece of paper already drawn up by the administration. Voting is usually by list. So in our case there were 150 candidates for the STK. To discuss each one of them the conference would have to drag out for three days, but it has to be got through in two and a half hours. It's a big hall, everyone's tired, so when they say, 'how shall we vote', every-one says: 'read out the list and let's vote'. And naturally the over-whelming majority in the hall votes 'yes', in order to be out of the conference quicker and get home as fast as possible. So they elected 150 people to the Council of Labour Collectives and said that the Council would meet and elect from its own members a presidium of the labour collective of 25 people. And when they elected this pres-idium of 25, the presidium elected a chair of the STK, who turned out to be our factory director.[12]

This type of overt managerial control over the early STK was clearly becoming a political problem, for in February 1988 Goskomtrud and VTsSPS issued a 'recommendation' that enterprise directors should not serve as STK chairpersons.[13] After this, more workers and ITR were chosen as STK leaders, but this did not make the councils more representative of rank-and-file interests. The domination of councils by enterprise directors merely gave way to domination by middle-level management and specialists, who acted as proxies for their superiors. As of 1989 still only 30 per cent of STK were headed by 'rank-and-file' workers, as opposed to 33.5 per cent chaired by subdivision managers, 20 per cent by 'representatives' of management, and 16.3 per cent by directors themselves.[14] Even these figures substantially overestimate workers' real influence, since it was common for the STK chairperson to be a worker and all of his or her deputies and heads of STK committees to be representatives of the factory administration.[15] Moreover, such workers were themselves often administration stooges. This was the case at AZLK, where the director was forced to give up his post as head of the STK, but engineered the election of a worker with close links to management to replace him. In the words of the above-cited foreman, 'he was not a bad chap...he never spoke out, but just sat tight and kept his mouth shut'.[16]

Given their political make-up it is not surprising that the STK never achieved even the limited degree of worker autonomy within the enterprise originally proclaimed as their objective. They had, for example, no legal means to enforce adherence to their decisions, by either management or ministries.[17] Their powers were equally circumscribed in the realm of finance. According to the State Enterprise Law labour collectives had the prerogative to decide a range of issues relating to the use of enterprise investment, incentive, and social development funds, but found these rights either restricted by qualifying legislation or rendered nearly inoperative by the fact that superior ministries could limit the amount of money available through their power to decide what proportion of profits and amortization funds would be syphoned off into the central treasury.[18] As for their other functions, STK played little role in working out production plans or influencing other major areas of enterprise life: they rarely dealt with questions of wages and incentives, other than in a consultative capacity, and almost never took up questions of investment or technical modernization.[19] Indeed, both management and the trade unions pushed on to the STK matters which were not the councils' responsibility, but which could lead to conflicts with the workforce: housing allocations, distribution of deficit goods, dismissals for violations of labour discipline, the issuing of bonuses, compliance with safety regulations, and the organization of rest breaks.[20] In effect, if managers had to take decisions that might be controversial or of questionable legality, they could avoid responsibility by having the STK take the decision instead. In some cases this meant using the STK to legitimate what were in fact normal managerial responses to *khozraschet*, namely

distorting production plans and refusing to fill mandatory state orders
(*goszakaz*); boosting enterprise revenues by pushing up prices, rather
than increasing output; or diverting profits from investment to paying
higher wages. Others bordered on open corruption: speculating in
deficit goods through their own cooperatives or transferring fixed
assets into cash.[21] Summarizing these tendencies, *Trud*, in an article
ironically entitled 'Democracy of Second Freshness', concluded that
managers merely used the STK to compel workers to solve production
problems which management had created or could not deal with:

> If we take a careful look at what these STK were occupied with –
> besides the fact that they duplicated trade union work – then it is easy
> to see that, once again, just like the brigades in their day, upon this
> semi-social formation were thrown production and organizational
> defects. That is, the workers themselves have to create the conditions
> of normal work, rather than those whose job it is to be responsible for
> this. Fine democracy indeed![22]

Such manoeuvres were facilitated by the fact that many STK members,
including their chairpersons, had only vague and unclear notions of
their rights and obligations.[23]

That managers should have resisted any transfer of their powers to
labour collectives was to be expected, and managerial hostility and
distrust of worker participation in decision-making is well documented.[24] The result was demoralizing for workers, too, and there is little
evidence that the distrust and apathy which they first evinced towards
the STK diminished over time. One study of Moscow workers showed
that some 80 per cent felt that the STK did not express their views and
had no clear knowledge of precisely which issues the councils dealt
with.[25] A survey of workers in Perm oblast found that only 2 per cent
of workers felt that perestroika was making progress in their enterprise. A worker and STK member at the Soda Factory in Berezniki –
allegedly one of the most active councils in the oblast – stated that not
a single STK initiative had come from rank-and-file workers, who in
turn did not see the STK as a vehicle for resolving their problems.
Many felt that the creation of the STK was just another routine
campaign, similar to those they had seen all their working lives.[26]
Workers, and even STK officials, at other factories described this same
sense of powerlessness. The head of the STK at the electric locomotive
factory in Tbilisi, a brigade leader in the assembly shop, put it bluntly.

> What kind of chairman am I, you laugh? I just clock myself in, I don't
> do a thing. From the very beginning it was clear that the STK was a

forgery. The worker was never master over production, although they spent decades trying to convince him otherwise.[27]

These views were reflected in a more general trend towards demoralization, as reflected in different national surveys. According to one, only half of respondents voted in elections for the STK of their sub-divisions, and only one-third took part in elections for the STK of their enterprise at large.[28] The annual All-Union Monitoring surveys showed this trend even more sharply: each year from 1988 to 1990 the proportion of respondents disillusioned with perestroika, and with the work of their STK rose appreciably. By 1990 some 85 per cent felt that the economic reforms either had achieved nothing or made the situation worse; 79 per cent said the same regarding social policy. A staggering 98 per cent said that perestroika at their enterprise had either produced no material results 'as yet', or had still not been implemented. As for the STK, 50 per cent said that they had 'still not fully manifested themselves', and a further 29 per cent said their elected councils were inactive.[29]

There were instances, however, where this disenchantment led rank-and-file workers to protest against their STK's inactivity. At AZLK, for example, the managerial domination of the factory STK contrasted sharply with the STK in individual shops, which attracted independent people able and willing to argue with management, although even here they had to proceed with caution to avoid possible victimization.[30] One such person was a brigade leader and head of the shop STK in the factory's automobile assembly shop, who tried to lead a protest against management's plans (supported by the factory STK) to privatize AZLK and turn it into a joint-stock company.[31] Demands to reelect the STK were central to a number of factory disputes. At the Voronezh machine-tool factory workers went on strike over management's corrupt use of privileges, and, having no faith in either the local trade union or the STK, formed a workers' committee.[32] Similar committees were formed at the Siberian heavy electrical engineering works, Leningrad's Kirov factory, and the electrical engineering factory in Kovrov in Central Russia. In all three cases the grievances were the same: the STK did little and were divorced from the needs of the workers (at the factory in Kovrov the STK had only two workers on it).[33]

Despite the manifest weakness, if not impotence of the STK, the regime nevertheless saw them as incompatible with its decision to change the direction of perestroika towards the outright introduction of capitalism. In June 1990 the 1987 State Enterprise Law was super-seded by a new Law on Enterprises,[34] according to which enterprises – including those belonging to the state – were to have owners who alone had the right to select managers. STK were no longer mandatory institutions, although general meetings of work collectives had the right to form them if they wished. STK powers were left undefined, but the new law left little scope for them to exercise independent initiative. Rather, the STK were replaced by an Enterprise Council, consisting of an equal number of representatives designated by the owner and elected by the labour collective. The Councils took over many of the functions previously assigned to the STK (specifically, the determi-nation of the 'general direction' of the enterprise's economic and social development and the distribution of the enterprise's profits), plus a number of new responsibilities specifically tied to the transfer to the market: the issue of shares, the creation or hiving off of new sub-divisions. Most importantly, the Enterprise Council was to resolve labour disputes arising between management and the workforce. In all cases it was expressly barred from interfering in the 'operational-management' functions of the enterprise administration.[35]

It is worth noting that, although these sections of the law were to come into effect immediately (the rest of the statute came into force only on 1 January 1991), the STK at a number of enterprises appear successfully to have ignored it. According to two miners' leaders with whom we spoke during June 1991, the STK in many Ukrainian mines were still continuing to function.[36] In at least two factories the STK organized conferences of the labour collective to pass votes of no confidence in their directors and to have them removed. In one of them, the Razdol production association in Ukraine, the vote was actually confirmed by the factory's parent ministry (Agrokhim All-Union Association, formerly the Ministry of Fertilizer).[37] In the other, the Sverdlovsk Turbo-Motor production association, the ministry instructed the STK to organize a conference of the labour collective to vote on the issue, because it had declared a previous decision to fire the director, taken at a meeting of line managers, to be illegal.[38] Yet both of these dismissals were clearly prohibited by the new Enterprise Law.

Struggles over property

The attempt to denature the STK provoked a more serious protest, however, which gave birth, at least momentarily, to a mass national organization formed in late 1990, in an effort to have the new

Enterprise Law modified, if not repealed. Although the restoration of the STK's lost functions and prerogatives was one of its major demands, the main focus of its attack was the emerging wave of enterprise privatization carried out by managers and/or their superior ministries, by converting their enterprises into joint-stock companies with themselves as majority share holders. Thus the issue of worker self-management became inseparably linked to emerging struggles over property.

As we discuss further in chapter 4, once the transition to the market became inevitable, industrial managers and ministries rapidly worked out a mechanism by which they could secure their privileged position even after their main functions under the old command system had been eliminated or severely curtailed. Although the cases of such *nomenklatura* privatization were relatively few while Gorbachev was still in power, it became very widespread from 1992 onwards. It was to have profound implications for the content and structure of the capitalism which would emerge in the USSR and its successor states, for it meant the preservation of the country's old monopolistic institutions with many, if not most of the same bureaucrats and managers in charge. Only now they would exercise their control not through administrative right, but through titles to property. Thus from the start the new Soviet capitalism was doomed to become a quasi-parasitic capitalism with little dynamic for development. Based on monopolistic producers operating in an economy of perpetual shortages, there were simply too many opportunities to acquire wealth through corruption and speculation for it to provide any drive towards innovation, investment, and modernization.

Indeed, many of the early joint-stock companies were simply fictitious. Existing production associations or parent ministries and administrations (*glavki*) sold shares to subordinate or outside enterprises with the aim of attracting additional financial resources, while keeping the controlling packet of shares in the hands of their administrative apparatus. Enterprises buying shares paid for them with state funds taken out of their budgets. In virtually all respects the structure, status, and administrative personnel of the production associations and their constituent enterprises remained unchanged.[39] It is unclear if at this early stage management exploited the potential for interlocking control and ownership which the practice of enterprises buying shares in each other presented. Such possibilities were certainly contained in the conversion of the Kama River Motor Vehicle Factory (KamAZ), which was turned into a joint stock company by a decree of the USSR Council of Ministers in June 1990. Shares were sold in two stages: during the first phase only members of the factory's 140,000 member collective could buy them, while in phase two they were offered for sale to KamAZ suppliers and to enterprises whose shares KamAZ had itself acquired. In this way the administration was effectively buying shares in itself.[40] An even more extreme case was that of the pharmaceutical industry, whose ministry, Minmedbioprom, prior to being wound up formed itself into a private company (not even bothering with the joint-stock fiction) and bought up, or in some cases simply expropriated, most of the enterprises under its jurisdiction, with most of its former administrative directors holding prominent positions in the new firm.[41]

A later and more widespread variant of joint-stock company creation was for enterprises or ministries to issue shares, giving the workforce the right to buy a minority of the shares, but reserving the controlling package for themselves. A classic example of this was the Leningrad Printing and Publishing Equipment Production Association, Lenpoligrafmash, where 80 per cent of shares were to be owned by the factory's parent ministry (the USSR Ministry of Heavy Engineering), and only 18 per cent offered to the labour collective.[42] This was by no means an isolated example. We have already noted the strike at AZLK, one of the chief demands of which was to halt management plans to turn it into a joint-stock company. The workforce at the Novolipetsk iron and steel works similarly refused to accept a management plan to transform it into a joint stock company with its ministry holding 51 per cent of the shares. As the deputy head of the factory's trade union explained, workers were being offered the right to purchase up to 1,000 rubles worth of shares each. Even if all of them could afford this, which in fact they could not, this would have accounted for just 40 million rubles in share capital out of a total worth of 6 billion.[43] Even where the workforce was allotted a mathematical majority of shares[44] this still left the balance of power with management. For as share holders the workers could only operate as atomized individuals; the use of shares as a collective tool for determining policy and controlling management would have been almost impossible.

It was precisely this issue which sparked the largest of the protests over bureaucratic privatization, that at the Volga Automobile Factory, VAZ. Located in the city of Tol'yatti in Central Russia, VAZ was originally built by the Italian firm Fiat and produces the Lada and Zhiguli cars. Unlike other Soviet car plants, its technology, though now old, was said in its day to have been of relatively advanced design and its production processes well integrated. At the time of the dispute it had a total workforce of around 130,000, and in 1990 accounted for about 1.5 per cent of the total national income of the USSR.[45] In 1990 VAZ management drew up a plan to turn the Association into a joint-stock company, with a substantial block of shares – perhaps the majority – to be sold abroad for hard currency. The STK opposed the move and declared the factory the property of the entire collective. More specifically, it wanted the state to privatize the factory and give it to the collective without repayment. As the new owner, the collective would hire and fire management. The STK also wanted the factory 'depoliticized', that is, the Communist Party removed from the enterprise and its shop cell structure dismantled. Moreover, the STK had specific grievances against management, relating to corruption and mismanagement. It alleged, for instance, that the administration appropriated a certain portion of the factory's cars, which it used to buy favours from important political allies. It further claimed that if management plans went through VAZ's workers would become merely cheap labour for Western entrepreneurs. Management and the Ministry of Motor Vehicles and Agricultural Equipment (Minavtosel'k-hozmash), for their part, claimed that the STK had no authority to make such a declaration, and that the sale of stock abroad was essential to ensure the Association's future.[46]

In February 1991 a delegate conference voted to approve the management scheme, including the right of management to sell a minimum of 40 per cent of shares to foreign interests. Only 29 per cent would be sold to the workforce. The struggle was now for all intents and purposes over. An attempt by the STK to set up an independent trade union met with little success, as did its efforts to provoke a walk-out from the delegate conference. How democratic the delegate selection was we do not know, although *Komsomol'skaya pravda* claimed that the discussion indicated considerable confusion on the part of delegates over just what the main issues were.[47] In June the Soviet press reported that Gorbachev had concluded a tentative deal to sell 40 per cent of VAZ to Fiat for a mere 2 billion dollars, the low sum allegedly having been agreed as a means of persuading the Italian government to extend 5 billion dollars in credit to the Soviet government.[48] After the *putsch* of August 1991, the agreement was apparently later modified, with Fiat and VAZ forming a new joint-stock company. Fiat was still scheduled to receive 40 per cent ownership, but the price to be paid was not disclosed.[49]

Although the struggle at VAZ was eventually lost, the incident helped catalyse the formation of a national movement to oppose the 1990 Enterprise Law and the process of *nomenklatura* privatization. The First All-Union Conference of Representatives of Councils of Labour Collectives and Workers' Committees took place in Tol'yatti on 31 August–4 September 1990, with delegates from sixty-five enterprises, located in forty-six different cities, which between them employed 1.2 million people. On the issue of STK, the Conference condemned the 1990 Enterprise Law as undemocratic: no draft was published before its adoption and there was no public discussion of its contents. It deprived labour collectives in state enterprises of even the meagre rights they had enjoyed under the 1987 law, at precisely the time when 'labour collectives...must become active and equal participants in social transformations and the stabilization of the economic situation'. As to the issue of property, the Conference demanded that labour collectives themselves be allowed to determine the form of property of their enterprise, and recommended two alternatives: either enterprises should be transferred to collectives without compensation, so that the labour collectives would function as owners; or the state should continue to own enterprises, but delegate its functions to the labour collectives and their STK, which would run them on the principles of worker self-management. To press its demands the Conference called on STK to oppose implementation of the new Enterprise Law, and appealed to the USSR Supreme Soviet to suspend the law's operation until a new version could be drawn up, taking account of the Conference's objections.[50]

Over the ensuing three months the movement appeared to expand. In December it held the Founding Congress of what now became known as the Union of Councils of Labour Collectives (Soyuz STK), attended by 588 delegates from enterprises scattered over the entire USSR. It reiterated the positions adopted by its autumn Conference, but now located the attacks against the STK and the principles of self-management in what it termed the 'usurpation of power' by the old *nomenklatura*. 'By this means', read the main Congress Resolution, 'the germs of self-management by labour collectives are being liquidated and they are left only with the role of waged labour power'.[51]

Politically the new organization represented a peculiar amalgam of ideas and individuals. It established a democratic structure and was highly critical of the unrepresentativeness of the official trade unions. Yet at the same time it was opposed to strikes, welcomed Luk'yanov (Chair of the USSR Supreme Soviet and a conservative who was later implicated in the abortive *putsch* against Gorbachev) to address the Congress, and adopted a decidedly ambiguous attitude towards republican autonomy. Formally it declared itself in favour of transforming the USSR into a voluntary union of sovereign republics, and called on the separate republican Supreme Soviets (as opposed to just the Supreme Soviet of the USSR) to block implementation of the 1990 Enterprise Law.[52] However, as one of the union's new leaders explained, this meant the delegates were in favour of a strong central authority and preserving the USSR, but insisted that this could not be done from above, with truncheons and decrees, but only from the ground up through economic ties built up by autonomous labour collectives.[53] Most problematical of all, however, was the organization's insistence that workers' self-management should be situated within a general system of market relations.[54] As with all schemes for so-called 'workers' control', if extended to its logical conclusion this would merely have reproduced the same anarchy of the capitalist market, only among enterprises that were nominally owned by the collective, rather than private individuals. Thus, while the Union seemed to possess a clear idea of the implications that existing methods of privatization had for ordinary workers and the further development of democratization, it was not prepared to extend its concept of self-management beyond the issue of democratic control within each individual enterprise. Perhaps because of its own internal contradictions as an alliance of activists from different political viewpoints, it effectively remained trapped within a 'Stalinism or capitalism' dichotomy. At no point did it present an alternative vision of democratic control by society over the means of production as a whole.

For all practical purposes the STK movement subsided quite quickly after the defeat at VAZ. Although in Leningrad, and perhaps also other towns about which we have no information, it managed to maintain an episodic presence, its influence was always marginal.[55] The Union held a Second Congress in October 1991, at which it reiterated its attack on *nomenklatura* privatization, but did not oppose the principle of privatization *per se*. Perhaps more significant, its social composition had altered, so that this later gathering was dominated by representatives of middle-level management opposed to the continued rule of the old bureaucracy.[56] This group was thus beginning to articulate its own interests distinct from both top management and rank-and-file workers, and to stake its claim in the race to reap the benefits of the new capitalism.[57]

The mass strikes of 1989 and 1991

One of the most important consequences of the political liberalization introduced by Gorbachev was the speed with which workers learned to use strikes and workplace protests as a weapon in struggles against management and the government. Perhaps the earliest manifestation of this was the *de facto* general strike in Armenia in the summer of 1988, in protest at events in Nagorno Karabakh. Although these strikes were over nationalist, rather than class demands, they almost certainly provided an important lesson to other Soviet workers of the possibilities now open to them. In 1989 the Soviet economy as a whole officially (the real figure may be much higher) lost 7.3 million person-days in strike action, including 5.4 million in industry and 914,000 in construction. Almost all of this, however, was due either to the miners' strike of that year or to nationalist unrest in the Caucasus (Georgia, Armenia, and Azerbaijan).[58] During 1990 these figures increased sharply: between January and September some 1,700 enterprises were hit by strikes, involving losses of 13.7 million person-days, or 2.5 times the daily average for 1989.[59] These data are all the more remarkable in that 1990 saw no mass strike wave equivalent to the miners' strikes of the year before. Although many of these losses were the result of continuing ethnic conflicts, there can be little doubt that workers were increasingly resorting to strikes to press their demands.

Under the Stalinist system strikes had been brutally suppressed. If they did break out, the policy of the regime, even in the 1930s, was to contain them as quickly as possible: especially in the large urban centres, this often meant acceding to the strikers' immediate demands in order to defuse the situation and prevent news of the disturbances from spreading. Then the secret police would move in and arrest the leaders. In peripheral localities, where containment was intrinsically much easier, the repression was correspondingly swifter.[60] This policy was facilitated by the power relations of the centrally administered economy. Because local management could concede very little, all strikes quickly became *political* conflicts with the central authorities, which alone could satisfy workers' grievances. It was workers' knowledge of this, and the fact that the government would meet such confrontations with severe repression, which acted as the main deterrent to strike action.

The first miners' strike of 1989 very much followed this pattern. The miners were quick to realize that their economic grievances (declining real wages, inadequate housing, and poor social infrastructure) could not be resolved within the traditional structures of local management and the official trade unions. Only by going outside these structures and dealing directly with the government could the miners hope for any success. At the same time, however, the changed political mood of perestroika and glasnost soon weakened the fear of reprisal, allowing the strike to develop into the first genuine mass strike movement since the early 1920s.

As the economic reforms and *khozraschet* proceeded, however, this political boldness was matched by a drastically changed economic situation. Under self-financing local management now had something to concede, while the deteriorating economic situation (including the labour shortage) made workers far more prone to resort to militant action, especially since they were now secure in the knowledge that they were unlikely to face repression or even legal retaliation. Although these same grievances were shared by many workers, there were, outside the mining regions, no structures for generalizing them. Thus more and more workers were able to press their economic demands without this necessarily leading to political action. On the contrary, with the exception of coal mining and the April 1991 strikes in Belarus', strikes remained essentially localized affairs, often involving just a brigade or a section downing tools temporarily until their demands were met. Attempts by the regime to retain some degree of control over events through the imposition of a strike law in October 1989, proved fruitless. The law gave the official trade unions a pretext to avoid leading strikes, but it had little deterrent effect on the rank and file.

The first miners' strike: The awakening of a mass movement

The July 1989 strike in four of the USSR's five main coal mining regions – the Donetsk basin (Donbass) in the Ukraine, the Kuznetsk basin (Kuzbass) in Siberia, Vorkuta in the Komi ASSR in northern Russia, and Karaganda in Kazakhstan – was, outside of the Caucasus, the first large-scale, organized eruption of industrial unrest during perestroika.[61] Embracing some 400,000 coal workers, it lasted for two weeks and permanently altered the course of Gorbachev's reform strategy. The strike totally discredited both the Ministry of the Coal Industry and the official miners' trade union. In order to pursue their struggle the miners were forced to bypass these traditional structures and build their own grass roots organizations, the strike committees, which in some areas took over nearly full responsibility for running their localities. It also led to the country's first genuinely independent trade union, the Independent Union of Mineworkers, whose aims and politics reflected the contradictions of a working class just entering the process of its historical reconstitution after years of atomization.

The strike grew out of decades of pent-up grievances, and was by no means a sudden explosion.[62] Between the end of 1988 and 1989 there had been some fifteen local strikes in the Kuzbass, lasting from a few hours to two days, over demands for better food and living conditions. Local strikes had also broken out in the Ukrainian coal fields of the Donbass.[63] In March, miners at the Severnaya mine in Vorkuta went on strike, which was only ended when the Minister of the Coal Industry, M. I. Shchadov, came to the area. This strike was an important precursor to subsequent events, for local Party, trade union, and soviet officials had shown themselves totally helpless at dealing with the situation. As in the Kuzbass, the complaints of the Vorkuta miners were indicative of a long-standing crisis that was just waiting to erupt: bad housing, no cultural or social facilities, frustration at seeing the fruits of their labour go to support the swollen bureaucracies of the ministry and local management, and anger at the authorities' perpetual refusal to act on their demands, which the workers had presented on several occasions over the previous five years.[64] At the root of all these grievances lay an even deeper resentment, namely that the state had always treated the miners and their settlements as nothing more than vehicles for extracting the maximum amount of coal, irrespective of the human and social costs. As an electrician at a mine in the Kuzbass town of Berezovskii put it:

> Not long ago our Berezovskii greeted guests with the brave slogan, 'The city born at the dawn of communism will be a communist city'. Neither the guests, nor even more so the inhabitants believed this slogan. Because the city, born at the dawn of communism, instead of flourishing has withered at the roots. Indeed, they built it not for the good of its inhabitants, but with one aim only: to pump out coal as quickly as possible. Such was the fate of Prokop'evsk and Kiselevsk, Belov, and Mezhdurechensk. And this predatory administrative economic system destroys not only the town, but human souls.[65]

The strike began on 10 July, when about 300 workers at the Shevyakov mine in the Kuzbass city of Mezhdurechensk stopped work. The previous week they had presented a list of twenty demands to the administration, demanding wage increases for evening and night shifts, a common day off for all miners, improving supplies of soap and work clothes, and food while underground. When management and the local trade union ignored their demands they struck. The next day four other mines in the town joined their walk out, and led a demonstration of 12,000 miners in front of the local Communist Party headquarters. On 12 July Shchadov arrived from Moscow to negotiate with the strikers, and after protracted and difficult bargaining, including the miners' initial rejection of their strike committee's recommendation to return to work, they eventually went back on 14 July. However, by then the entire Kuzbass – 158 mines and 177,000 workers – was out on strike, partially in answer to an appeal for a Siberia-wide stoppage issued by the strike committee in Mezhdurechensk. Shchadov then went to Novokuznetsk to negotiate with the newly formed regional strike committee. The miners would only negotiate if Gorbachev and Ryzhkov, then his prime minister, would join the talks. They refused, but sent a member of the Politburo, Slyun'kov, in their stead. As in Mezhdurechensk, the strike committee recommended a return to work, stating that most of the miners' main demands had been met, but a third of the miners still stayed out, going back only on 21 July.[66]

Meanwhile the strike was spreading to the other major coal fields. The strike in the Donbass was provoked by fears that the deal worked out between the government and the Kuzbass miners would not apply to them. It began on 15 July, in the mining town of Makeevka. Initiative groups of strikers organized meetings and formed strike committees, and sent representatives to neighbouring pits and other towns in the oblast, so that the strike soon spread to mines in Donetsk, Gorlovka, Dzerzhinsk, Enakievo, Krasnoarmeisk, Selidov, Kharsysk, Shakhtersk, Torez, Snezhnyi, and Dobropol'. On 18 July it spread further to Voroshilovgrad and Dnepropetrovsk oblasts, and two days later to the mines in Western Ukraine around L'vov. Thus, by the time the government's negotiating team reached Donetsk on 20 July, 300,000 Donbass miners were on strike. An accord was signed on 22 July, but again it took several days before all miners agreed to return to work. By now the strike had spread to the Karaganda fields in Kazakhstan and to Vorkuta, both of which also returned to work by 24 July.[67]

Almost everywhere the demands of the miners were the same as those voiced by the Vorkuta miners in early 1989: better housing conditions, food supplies, wages, and working conditions. In the Donbass new housing construction was 20 per cent lower than it had been in 1964, so that housing queues had lengthened by 50 per cent just since 1980. In the Kuzbass the situation was much the same.[68] Typical was the Yuzhkuzbassugol' production association in the southern Kuzbass, where 11,800 families out of a workforce of 60,000 were in the housing queue. Thousands lived in ramshackle buildings and barracks. More than 6,000 children were waiting for pre-school places. Medical care was in a 'neglected state', and working conditions were unhealthy and unsafe.[69] Workers equally resented what they saw as inadequate pay relative to the difficulties of their job and the glaring inequalities between themselves and management, who in the workers' eyes were earning huge salaries and lived in luxurious conditions while carrying out their jobs incompetently.[70] At the same time the miners clearly linked these problems to the highly centralized and authoritarian way in which their industry was run. Mines were totally subordinated to their parent production associations: a director of a mine employing perhaps thousands of miners did not have the right to approve expenditure of more than 100 rubles without permission from a higher authority. All coal was given over the Ministry of Coal on the *goszakaz*. The industry was planned to run at a loss, and the price paid by the state was simply insufficient to allow pits to show a profit. Under the old command system this might not have had such serious consequences, but with the shift of the economy to *khozraschet* this was shackling the mines with severe financial difficulties. This was especially the case in the Donbass, which had long been the victim of planned underinvestment, making its coal increasingly expensive to extract. Henceforth the mines would simply not have the resources for new equipment or incentive funds.[71]

It was this connection between the desperateness of their material situation and the bureaucratic way in which the industry was managed that led the miners to link their economic demands with political ones: a genuine transfer of power to local soviets; an end to the election of People's Deputies from the so-called social organizations;[72] direct and secret elections of chairpersons of both the USSR Supreme Soviet and local soviets; the abolition of Article Six of the Soviet Constitution, which affirmed the Communist Party's 'leading role' in governing the country; the abolition of privileges for all people in posts of responsibility; and the rapid drafting of a new USSR constitution. In addition, the miners in Karaganda demanded a rapid end to nuclear testing in the Semipalatinsk region of Kazakhstan.[73] Finally, one other demand emerged which was eventually to assume considerable political importance: economic independence for individual mines.[74] The miners wanted an end to centralized ministerial control, and believed, to a large extent naively, that if they were free to market their own coal at whatever prices they could obtain, either domestically or abroad, they would have the funds to finance capital investment and their social infrastructure. Ironically, although the demand seems initially to have received greater emphasis among Donbass miners, it was the Kuzbass miners who eventually made it a main plank of their movement, for their pits were more modern and could mine coal more cheaply than those in the Donbass, and stood a better chance of surviving in a market economy.[75]

In almost all cases the miners' hopes were to be cruelly disappointed. The agreement between the government and the miners was codified in an accord, containing nearly 400 points.[76] Although many of its minor provisions were met (although haphazardly and bureaucratically),[77] most of the government's promises remained unfulfilled. As of October 1989 only the demand to have travel time between pit head and coal face paid had been implemented. Supplies of foodstuffs and consumer goods remained poor and no progress had been made on the issue of economic independence.[78] In October the Regional Council of Donbass Strike Committees narrowly voted down a proposal to resume the strike.[79] A November meeting between representatives from workers' committees throughout the country and Ryzhkov proved fruitless.[80] At the end of October the Vorkuta miners declared a 24-hour warning strike over the non-implementation of the August agreement, followed by a total strike in November.[81] However, the strike did not spread outside the region, and the miners' primary grievances remained largely unresolved.[82]

Far more important than the fate of these demands was the political transformation which the strike brought to the entire pattern of relations between workers and managers and workers and the state. This was most immediately evident in the strike committees. Perhaps for the first time since the 1920s, workers had established their own independent combat organizations, which in many locales filled a power vacuum left by the impotence of the local Party and trade union bodies. They ran not just the strike, but many aspects of public life, including maintaining law and order and tending to the day-to-day problems of ordinary citizens who turned to them for help with the local bureaucracy.[83] The committees survived the strike and in many cases were transformed into semi-permanent Workers' Committees, which were to play the central role in organizing the second miners' strike in 1991. In the Kuzbass the Workers' Committees formed the core of the Union of Kuzbass Toilers, founded in the autumn of 1989, which attempted – albeit with little success – to create a new, alternative movement, linking workers in different industries.[84]

The second great political transformation brought about by the strike was in the make-up and public posture of the trade unions. One of the principal complaints of the strikers was over the political corruption of their official union, the Trade Union of Coal Industry Workers, which like all other unions in the USSR was merely an arm of the state. This had become even more transparent during the strike: not only had the union refused to support it, but it actually participated on the side of the government during negotiations with the strike committees. In some cases the miners were able to take their vengeance: following the strikes there was a wave of reelections of mine trade union committees, and many former union officials were turned out in favour of militants who had backed the struggle.[85] The lesson was not lost on the official unions either in coal mining or other industries. With militant and spontaneous strike action now a real possibility, the unions began to adapt their profile, if not their actual politics, so as to appear as defenders of their members' collective interests – a task eventually made easier by the apparent threat to jobs contained in the move to the market.

The government faced a similar dilemma. It was now forced to recognize the legitimacy of strike action, while at the same time trying to contain it. The result was the strike law of 9 October 1989.[86] Strikes were now legal, but only if strikers had first exhausted a complex set of conciliation procedures, had won a two-thirds majority in a secret ballot, and had given management five days warning in writing. The law also banned strikes in a wide range of industries and services: railways and public transport, civil aviation, communications, energy, and defence industries. In theory this encompassed probably the majority of Soviet industrial workers. In addition the law banned picketing, and prohibited strike committees from 'usurping' those rights which were the competence of management or organs of state power. In short, it attempted to outlaw the situation of dual power which had arisen in the mining regions during the strike. In many ways the law proved symbolic of the entire experience of perestroika: despite all its strictures, at least in major disputes it proved almost unenforceable.

This was the true legacy of the miners' strike. It showed that workers could engage in mass struggles and in the process were capable of developing sophisticated bodies of self-organization, even if the wave of militancy and heightened consciousness displayed during the strike did not continue. Such forms of mass struggle were still a relatively new discovery for Soviet workers. But the climate of workplace conflicts was now changed forever, even if most strikes under perestroika remained overwhelmingly non-political.

The second miners' strike: Workers' ambiguities towards the market

The 1989 miners' strike reflected the very real contradictions of a labour movement emerging spontaneously after virtually six decades of political atomization. The strike had thrown up quite radical forms of working-class organization, coupled with a relatively clear understanding of the economic and political dead end into which the bureaucratic system had led both their industry and the country at large.[87] But beyond this the movement could not go. It was essentially a reaction against the old Stalinist system, but it had not yet worked out its own autonomous conception of what type of society should replace it. More specifically, the miners' movement and the new independent labour movement which it spawned, became heavily influenced by sections of the liberal-democratic intelligentsia who identified socialism with Stalinism, and hence viewed 'civilized' capitalism as the USSR's only path of development, but, unlike the majority of intellectuals, insisted that the democratic character of this new system could only be guaranteed by a strong labour movement.[88] No significant current in the new workers' movement saw independent working-class power as either a possibility or a desirable goal.

This revealed itself quite clearly in the developments leading up to the miners' strike of March–April 1991. The miners' increasing frustration with the government led to their demands becoming more and more political. But because large sections of the movement were at the same time committed to the establishment of the market, they tended increasingly to ally themselves with El'tsin and the so-called 'democrats' in the Russian parliament, rather than seek to pose an alternative to both the old *nomenklatura* and the new Russian bureaucracy which was seeking to supplant it.

In April 1990 the official union, now renamed the Trade Union of Coal Industry Employees (rather than workers), held its extraordinary Fifteenth Congress in Moscow. It was an extremely acrimonious affair, so much so that delegates refused to listen to the union central committee's report or even to allow its chairman to chair the proceedings.[89] A number of delegates walked out, demanding the formation of a new miners' union open to workers only, claiming the present union was dominated by management and gave no voice to rank-and-file workers.[90] Despite the election of a new Central Council (which replaced the old Central Committee), the dissidents began preparing a new miners' conference for June.

This conference, officially called the First Congress of Miners, took place in Donetsk on 11–15 June. It expressly declared its independence from the official union,[91] and called for the creation of a new miners' organization, the League of Miners. It empowered an organizing committee to prepare a second congress for October.[92] Its official resolution called for the resignation of the government and the creation of a new government taking into account the views of 'all strata of the population'. Its economic programme demanded the abolition of most ministries, including the Ministry of the Coal Industry, and a transition to the market to be financed by substantial cuts in military spending and in foreign aid to 'totalitarian' regimes. Its specific demands for the coal industry were not especially market-oriented, however, but rather called for proper prognostication of the industry's future development, greater investment in housing and social amenities, and efforts to deal with the ecological catastrophe in the country's mining regions.[93] Despite the document's restrained attitude towards the market, nearly 90 per cent of delegates were reported to favour some form of market economy, despite the fact that virtually all of them recognized this would bring with it unemployment and perhaps also rationing.[94]

The League of Miners proved a still-born organization, but the discontent in the coal fields which its putative leaders reflected was real enough. On 11 July 1990 – the first anniversary of the outbreak of the 1989 strike – the workers' committees called a one-day political strike which, in addition to long-standing economic grievances, in many of the coal fields now included demands for the resignation of the USSR government; the depoliticization of the army, the KGB, the Ministry of the Interior (which controlled the police), and the education system; and the removal of Party committees from the pits. Support for the strike was variable, but it was by no means a failure. Nearly all the mines in Vorkuta came out and approximately half those in the Donbass and Kuzbass. These were joined by mines in the smaller coal fields, for example, the Russian Donbass around Rostov-on-Don, and by the large bauxite mine in Sverdlovsk. In addition, many 'non-striking' pits stayed open to carry out necessary repair work, but extracted no coal.[95]

The Second Congress of Miners took place in Donetsk at the end of October, and was attended by over 1,000 delegates. It was dominated by one overriding issue, whether to split from the official union and use this congress as the founding congress of a new union. Support for a split came from the Vorkuta and Kuzbass delegations, and was based on the old complaint that employers and workers could not be in the same union. Despite considerable opposition to this proposal, on the final day of the Congress the Vorkuta–Kuzbass delegates won a majority and announced the creation of a new union, the Independent Trade Union of Mineworkers (*gornyaki*).[96]

The Second Miners' Congress did not, however, herald an unambiguous revival of industrial militancy. On the contrary, the mood of the miners, as within the working class as whole, had become much more sombre since the 1989 strike. The economic situation was worsening almost daily. Politically, Gorbachev seemed to be allying himself increasingly with conservatives: at the end of 1990 he installed the 'hard liner' Pavlov as Prime Minister and the even more sinister Pugo as Minister of the Interior, and sanctioned the use of force against the break-away movements in the Baltic. Although the conclusion drawn by many observers, namely that this 'turn to the right' signalled an abandonment of the market was fundamentally mistaken, there was no denying the authoritarian direction in which Gorbachev and his government were now moving.

It was against this background that the strikes of March–April erupted.[97] In the meantime one other important event had occurred, namely, in January 1991 the Ukrainian pits were transferred from the jurisdiction of the USSR Coal Ministry to that of the government of Ukraine. This was to have a significant influence on the course the strike took, both inside and outside Ukraine.

The spring strike really began as two separate struggles. It broke out first in the Donbass, where the demands were exclusively economic: a 200 to 250 per cent wage rise and extension of the right to retire after twenty-five years service to all workers in the industry, and not just face workers. The strike then spread to the Kuzbass, Karaganda, and Vorkuta, where the demands were primarily political: the resignation of the USSR government, and, where the Vorkuta and Kuzbass mines were concerned, their transfer to Russian jurisdiction.

Ironically, the Donbass demands had grown out of an attempt by Donbass mine managers to coopt simmering discontent in the coal fields. In January 1991, the general directors of Donbass coal associations issued an appeal to labour collectives protesting against the fact that, as in other industries, coal prices for 1991 were being kept at their 1990 level, while costs for fuel, electricity, equipment, and transport were going up. The directors threatened to halt coal deliveries for twenty-four hours if the situation was not reviewed by 10 January. The appeal claimed to have won wide support among coal workers, while the Donetsk gorkom of the Communist Party expressed its solidarity with the 'miners' (though not a single miner signed the appeal).[98] Even if the directors had vastly inflated the extent of their rank-and-file support, the confidence with which they acted on an issue over which Donbass miners were deeply worried was a barometer of how far rank-and-file militancy had declined. It is worth speculating whether the eventual strike would have been so bitter and so protracted had the directors stuck to their original strategy and supported the strike when it broke out, instead of opposing it. In the specific case, the directors' demands were taken up by the Ukrainian branch of the official miners' union, which extracted from the Ukrainian coal ministry the promise that coal prices would be raised sufficiently to allow a 20 per cent increase in wages, in line with the estimated rate of inflation.[99]

It was apparently out of these discussions and their totally inadequate outcome, that, in mid-February, the Ukrainian miners first put their own demands, the principal one being a rise in wages not of 20 per cent, but of 200–250 per cent. The Regional Council of Donbass Strike Committees had called a one-day warning strike for 20 February. If this did not have the desired effect, there would be an all-out strike on 1 March. The Ukrainian government responded to these demands by reiterating its offer to double the price of coal, but insisted that, with a budget deficit of 15 billion rubles, 12 billion of which were due to subsidies to the mines, it could not afford the wage increases the miners were demanding.[100] The 1 March strike call was not especially well-heeded, although figures appearing in the press underestimated the actual number of pits supporting the action, since some continued to work but refused to ship coal, while at others the strike was partially supported by miners on different shifts.[101] What is clear, however, is that gradually more and more mines joined the strike, in frustration at the intransigence of both the Ukrainian and USSR governments to negotiate over the miners' demands. The strike also spread from the central Donbass to Western Ukraine (where the nationalist movement, Rukh, opposed it) and the Russian Donbass around Rostov-on-Don.[102] By the beginning of April, when the two governments finally agreed to enter into talks, nearly a quarter of Ukrainian pits were out.[103]

In the Karaganda region of Kazakhstan the strike unfolded in similar fashion, although more rapidly. The mines there had also been placed under republican jurisdiction. On 1 March the territorial council of the official trade union, the Trade Union of Coal Industry Employees, together with the oblast workers' committee called a warning strike over a combination of economic and political demands: the immediate conclusion of a Union treaty, granting autonomy to the USSR's republics; a Kazakhstan law indexing wages to the cost of living; wage rises of 200 to 250 per cent; and an increase in the per capita meat allowance to 75 kilograms per year per resident. As in Ukraine, the republican government claimed the demands were unaffordable. The strike was supported by twenty of the region's twenty-six pits.[104]

Like in Ukraine, the strike in the Kuzbass, where leaders of the independent miners' union had attempted an unsuccessful political strike on 18 January in protest at government repression in the Baltic,[105] at first spread haphazardly. Beginning as a temporary strike in solidarity with the Ukrainian miners' demands, it eventually grew into a political strike calling for the government's resignation, and the transfer of power to the USSR Council of the Federation.[106] By mid-March it embraced about a third of Kuzbass pits, and over half by the beginning of April.[107] Support in Vorkuta followed the same pattern. The coal fields there, which had been among the most militant in 1989, did not strike until 7 March, and then only in Inta; the two largest Vorkuta mines, Vorgashorskaya and Severnaya, which had led the Vorkuta strikes nearly two years before, now carried on working, and even earned the epithet of strike breakers from the majority of Vorkuta mines, which went on strike from mid-March onwards.[108] As in the Donbass, the catalyst for the strikes' continuation and growth in Russia appears to have been the government's dogged refusal to negotiate. Prime Minister Pavlov and the coal ministry further inflamed the situation by threatening to prosecute those on strike and to file suit to have the strikes declared illegal – a move which played a major role in prompting the Vorkuta pits to join the conflict.[109]

At the end of March, however, the Soviet government finally entered into negotiations with miners' 'representatives', who included the official miners' union, which supported the miners' demands but not the strike itself, and delegates from non-striking pits. Under these circumstances the agreement they hammered out was unlikely to bring the strikers back to work. It called for a staged increase in wages over twelve months, expanded the list of occupations eligible for early retirement after twenty-five years on the job (but did not extend this right to all miners, as the strikers demanded), and offered higher compensation for the April price rises than that being paid in other industries. In addition mines were allowed to sell 7 per cent of output (5 per cent if coking coal) on the domestic or foreign market at free (so-called contract) prices.[110] The agreement was almost universally rejected, partly because of the unrepresentativeness of the miners' side in the negotiations, partly because the wage rises were made dependent on plan fulfilment, a condition which only *non-striking* pits were in a position to meet, and partly because of anger at the April price rises, which had provoked an explosion of industrial unrest in the Belorussian capital, Minsk.[111] An agreement between the Ukrainian government offering broadly similar economic concessions plus an amorphous pledge to enshrine the principle of Ukrainian sovereignty in any new union treaty, met with an identical lack of support.[112]

What finally brought the strike to a halt was a combination of two factors. First, as we discuss below, the strike wave in Belarus' against the April price rises ran out of steam and the factories gradually returned to work. This ended any hopes that the miners' strike would break out of its isolation and lead to a generalized strike wave. The second was the agreement worked out between El'tsin and Gorbachev, the so-called 'nine-plus-one' accord, which called for the drafting of a new union treaty and new government elections. El'tsin, on the basis of this arrangement, travelled to the Kuzbass, and on 1 May 1991, signed an order transferring all Russian mines to Russian jurisdiction and promising them economic independence.[113] Many pits in Ukraine and Russia had already decided to end their strikes during the last week in April. By 5 May only two Ukrainian pits were not working.[114] The Russian mines had all returned to work by 10 May.[115]

From the point of view of the strikers' original demands the strikes would appear to have been a defeat. Only in Karaganda could the strikers claim some success: they had suspended their strike on 3 March, pending negotiations with the Kazakhstan government, and won certain concessions over wages, pensions, and the promise to be allowed to export a certain percentage of their coal. They did not resume the strike.[116] The strikers in Ukraine and Russia did not fare so well, however. The Ukrainian miners won virtually nothing. They did not extract the pay rises they had sought and the Russian miners' demand for a transfer of jurisdiction was irrelevant to them, since they had already been put under Ukrainian authority at the start of 1991. The Russian miners also won very little. They failed to force a change of government and extracted few economic concessions that would improve the miners' situation even in the medium term. Effectively they had had their struggle coopted and defused by their political reliance on El'tsin. Yet it is important to keep in mind that the miners did not return to work because they had been defeated. In the face of immense hostility from government, most of the press, and the official trade unions in a number of industries,[117] not to mention tremendous financial hardship (unlike the 1989 conflict, the government this time was not afraid to suspend strikers' pay during the strike), they had persevered and organized themselves with skill and sophistication. The strike did not enjoy the universal backing of two years earlier, but it won enough support to force the government to a standstill. The press campaign notwithstanding, the strikes also won active solidarity from workers in other industries, especially in the Urals.[118] Thus the strikes showed once again the strength of rank-and-file organization among the miners.

On the other hand, the miners failed to transform their struggle into a mass strike wave, even in the wake of the April price rises. By the end of April they were politically isolated. This, coupled with the naive faith in El'tsin held by many of their leaders, had been enough to push them back to work. They simply did not understand the nature of El'tsin's manoeuvring and how he was using their struggle to enhance his own position in his contest with Gorbachev. This is not to say that the strike did not have an important impact on Soviet politics. The judgement of the Conference of Kuzbass Workers' Committees, held in Kemerovo on 7 July, was probably correct when it said that the strike had helped thwart the advance of 'reaction', that is, the conservative offensive of Pavlov and Pugo, and had made possible the conclusion of the 'nine plus one' agreement between the USSR's different republics. The Conference was equally aware of just how fragile the miners' 'victory' had been. For another outcome of the 'nine plus one' accord had been Gorbachev's edict on tightening up discipline in essential industries, coupled with proposals to place further limits on the right to strike. Warning of the dangers of such 'antidemocratic' moves, the Conference reiterated its view that the miners' strike had not ended, but was only suspended, and could be resumed if the agreement reached between government and strikers were violated.[119] In sum, the miners' political struggle had been played out exclusively within the context of existing Soviet politics, where different factions within the national and republican bureaucracies vied with one another for influence and power, and where a new putative capitalist class was struggling to affirm its position against the old order. What was needed was to transcend this level of politics and to pose a different solution to the Soviet Union's growing crisis, based on the formation of mass, democratic workers' organizations capable of assuming control over both the state and the economy. But most of the miners' leaders saw no long-term answer other than a shift to the market and the creation of what they thought of as capitalism – that is, 'free' prices for their coal and the right to sell it to whomever they wished, but without the unemployment and bankruptcies that the market actually brings. As a result of their conceptual confusion, a scenario where workers would pose an independent political alternative never appeared to them as either possible or desirable. And without that there could be no question of evolving any long-term strategy for countering the suffering that inevitably had to follow. The practical result is with us still. Unable to take power in their own name, workers have had to shoulder the disastrous burden of the post-Soviet power struggles over how the old USSR would move towards capitalism and who would become the new owners of what used to be state property.

The prices protest of April 1991

It was symptomatic of Gorbachev's underestimation of the strength of the miners' strike that on 19 March 1991, that is, with the strike already three weeks old, the Soviet government should have proceeded with plans to double, triple, or even quadruple prices on most foods and essential consumer items from 2 April.[120] In principle the price rises, which amounted to a full or partial removal of state subsidies, were to be compensated by wage supplements. However, coming in the wake of Gorbachev's hated 5 per cent sales tax, protests against the increases were almost inevitable.

The impact on the population was severe. In both Kiev and Moscow, for example, literally tons of salami and sausages, which at the time were one of the main sources of meat in the Soviet diet, were being returned unsold to packing houses because the public could no longer afford to buy them.[121] For workers the most immediate repercussion was the sudden three- to four-fold increase in the price of meals at factory canteens. The official trade union federation, VKP, issued a number of demands on the central government, including setting a realistic minimum wage, generalized wage rises of from 170 to 200 per cent, repeal of the sales tax, and the exemption from tax of those parts of enterprise consumption funds devoted to social and cultural benefits for their workers.[122] At no time, however, did the VKP threaten to back up its proposals with industrial action.[123] This was left for the workers themselves, and they did so at a number of factories, either spontaneously or through the local trade union committee. In some places the conflicts were resolved without striking. At AZLK, for instance, management announced general wage rises for all personnel, and set a minimum wage for industrial workers of 250 rubles per month.[124] At least two factories in Kemerovo worked out agreements whereby management offered workers financial compensation, to be paid for out of enterprise profits or by hiding it in the general wage fund.[125] In other enterprises, however, the workers resorted to strikes, although the nature of these also varied from factory to factory. At some, such as the Lieutenant Shmidt oil equipment factory in Baku, the Sverdlovsk Turbo-Motor factory, or the radio parts factory in Arzamas, the workers merely sought to claw back their financial losses.[126] Workers at other factories, however, showed themselves to have been clearly influenced by the miners' strike. At the Sverdlovsk instrument factory workers demanded, in addition to a doubling of wages and compensation for the price rises, that the factory be transferred to Russian jurisdiction and made the collective property of the entire workforce.[127] Workers at Leningrad's Kirov works went even further: they wanted the dissolution of the Congress of People's Deputies, the reelection of the USSR President (Gorbachev's post), the resignation of the USSR government, and the transfer of the factory to Russian control.[128]

With the exception of Belarus' a clear pattern seemed to be emerging, as exemplified by the Bryansk engineering works. On 2 April, the day the price increases went into effect, the workers spontaneously downed tools, demanding both compensation for higher meal prices and a two- to three-fold rise in wages. They set up a Strike Committee which also declared its support for the political demands of the miners, a two-thirds reduction in the number of administrative staff, and the exclusion of the Party committee from enterprise territory – a move supported by Party members themselves. Rather than allowing the confrontation to get out of hand, management defused the situation by making major concessions, including shifting the factory to Russian jurisdiction and turning it into a joint-stock company. It also agreed, along with other factories in the city, to abolish compulsory work on Saturdays (so-called Black Saturdays), to limit the work week to forty hours, and to give workers an extra six days holiday a year. Management equally persuaded the Strike Committee to accept its contention that its budget could not afford the wage rises they were asking. Although the Strike Committee did not drop this demand, it agreed to

a return to work while negotiations continued.[129] It was the duplication of this pattern across the country that undoubtedly explains
why the expected mass protests against the price rises did not materialize. It was not that workers did not air their grievances or take militant
action, but that management quickly moved to prevent potential
trouble by granting concessions. Such action was consistent with the
general policy of meeting strikes over wage rises by acceding to
workers' demands and recouping the money by putting up prices or
diverting funds from capital investment.

The one exception to this trend was in Minsk, which demonstrated
to the government the dangers that could occur when this policy of
local concessions was not followed. It was often asked why the strike
wave should have broken out in Minsk, a normally quiet industrial
town not known either for nationalism or industrial militancy. Part of
the answer no doubt lies with the intransigence of management at the
Kozlov electrical engineering factory, where the strike began, but it
also reflected long-simmering local grievances rooted in Belarus's
position in the USSR's peculiar geographical division of labour, which
made it especially vulnerable to the supply crisis caused by *khozraschet*.
The republic's industry is dominated by engineering: automobile and
tractor production, machine-tool manufacture, assembly line construction, and various consumer durables (refrigerators, for example) produced within heavy industry. To manufacture these items Belorussian
factories were totally dependent on steel, coal, oil, and gas from other
parts of the USSR: it produced not a gram of metal within its own
borders. When the economic reforms led to a breakdown of the old
supply networks overseen by the large industrial ministries, Belorussian enterprises found it harder and harder to acquire the materials
they needed. Suppliers would only provide metal or other vital inputs
on a barter basis, usually for consumer goods like refrigerators or
televisions, which the Belorussian factories could not get hold of: they
were already in short supply inside the republic, since almost all
consumer goods made in Belarus' were 'exported' to the rest of the
USSR via deliveries on *goszakaz*. Thus for some time, the earnings of
engineering workers had been falling due to shortage-induced stoppages. In this context the April price rises came as the last straw.[130]

The strike began on 3 April, at the Kozlov engineering works, over
the three-fold rise in canteen prices. The workers began to hold
meetings in their shops, which spilled over into the passageways. As
management would not allow them to continue meeting on factory
premises, the workers gathered in the streets, where they were joined

by workers from the automatic line factory, the gear factory, and three shops of the tractor factory. That same evening they formed an organizing committee whose task was to create a city Strike Committee. Strike committees were also set up at individual enterprises. Their basic demands, formulated at meetings with representatives of the Belorussian government and the city soviet were: (a) the price increases must not lead to a fall in the standard of living; (b) within Belarus' those suffering from effects of the Chernobyl disaster should be exempt from the 5 per cent sales tax; (c) at least a 15 per cent reduction in the share of enterprise profits paid into republican and All-Union budgets; (d) a one-third cutback in the administrative apparatus in both enterprises and parent ministries; and (e) the resignations of the USSR President (Gorbachev), the USSR Cabinet of Ministers, and the Belorussian government, and the dissolution of the USSR Congress of People's Deputies and the Supreme Soviets of both the USSR and Belarus'. According to one report, the original strikers had expressed a willingness to return to work while the republican government considered their grievances, but on the evening of 3 April, the workers of the Minsk automobile factory decided to join the strike, at which point the movement snowballed, with workers from virtually all the city's major enterprises converging on the Belorussian Supreme Soviet in Lenin square on the morning of 4 April. There they were joined by students from higher education and vocational training schools. The government's official position was that the republic had a huge budget deficit and therefore no money with which to raise wages, pensions, or student stipends. Not surprisingly, when V. Kebich, the chair of the Belorussian Council of Ministers, attempted to address the crowd, the workers refused to let him speak. Two other factors were significant in this early stage of the movement. One was the relative passivity of the official trade unions, which let the initiative pass completely into the hands of the organizing committee. The second is that at those factories where management quickly gave in and offered financial compensation, the workers did not join the strike.[131]

On 5 April, the strike was officially suspended while negotiations proceeded, but was resumed again on 10 April, when they broke down.[132] However, already on 9 April the Belorussian Potassium Association (Belarus'kalii) in Soligorsk – the USSR's largest manufacturer of potassium fertilizers – went on strike in support of the workers in Minsk and the miners' strike, followed one week later by workers in the Association's mines. This was of some significance, since the Association's management had acted early on to forestall discontent, first, by offering its factory workers 36 rubles per month to offset their higher meal costs, and then later by doubling the wages of its miners. The workers, however, were joining the strike in support of its political demands.[133] Meanwhile, also on 9 April, workers at a number of Minsk factories staged a warning strike to press the Belorussian government to honour a promise to grant the Strike Committee fifteen minutes' air time each day on republican television. On the following day, 10 April, the mass meetings in Lenin Square resumed.[134] When, on 11 April, the Strike Committee was finally given its promised television slot, it had expanded its demands, to include a total repeal of the 5 per cent sales tax; an urgent economic reform with the transfer of property 'to the people'; the removal of the Communist Party from all state structures on Belorussian territory; the nationalization of Party property; an end to Party and KGB control over the media, and free access to all political forces in the republic to television and radio; and finally, protection of strikers from direct or indirect persecution. At the same time the committee expressed its total no confidence in the official Belorussian Federation of Trade Unions.[135] These positions were formally reiterated, together with a declaration of support for the political demands of the striking miners, at a conference of the Belorussian Strike Committee (SKB) on 13 April, at which it also announced its intention to set up free trade unions at enterprise level.[136]

Still, the Strike Committee and the Belorussian government remained deadlocked. The heads of the strike movement called a political strike for 24–26 April, the fifth anniversary of Chernobyl, in conjunction with which striking workers at Orsha blocked the main rail line from Leningrad to Brest, the blockade only being lifted by the Orsha Strike Committee after twelve hours.[137] But then, surprisingly, the Strike Committee in Minsk suspended the call for a general strike, claiming that it feared the use of violence against the Orsha workers. Instead it postponed the strike until 21 May, the date of an extraordinary session of the Belorussian Supreme Soviet, although this was later put off further until 25 May.[138] However, the strike was never resumed.

It is difficult to understand just why the Minsk Strike Committee suspended its action – a move that was certainly opposed by a number of the city's larger factories.[139] What is clear, however, is that the fate of the Minsk protests and the miners' strike were closely interconnected. The cancellation of the political strike in Belarus' came just ten days after an appeal by Ukrainian miners for a one-day general strike in Kiev on 16 April had met with only partial success, and a similar call by miners in Vorkuta and the Kuzbass for a nation-wide political strike found little support, save for brief sympathy stoppages in the Urals.[140] It seems probable that, with little prospect of initiating a general strike wave across the USSR, the decision to end the strikes in Belarus' – the one hotbed of workers' activity outside the mines – strongly influenced the miners' decisions to go back to work, even though they had won few tangible gains. Conversely, with the miners' strike having ended in early May, the Belorussian Strike Committee must have seen itself as increasingly isolated, thus making the success of its strike call for late May highly questionable.

Whether the situation might have been different if the Minsk Strike Committee had stuck to its original plan for a political strike on 26 April is difficult to say. The miners' strike was already waning, and some mines were returning to work, even before the agreement with El'tsin had been formalized.

The limits of worker protests

In a formal sense the mass strikes of 1989 and 1991 achieved few of their stated objectives. The most important parts of the 1989 accord reached between the miners and the government were either never implemented or were soon eroded by inflation and the collapse of the economy. This helped provoke another strike two years later. When that occurred, and the miners made political demands the centre of the struggle, they eventually returned to work with Gorbachev still in power, and with a handful of promises from El'tsin which he, too, was never to keep. Yet it would be wrong to consider these strikes as a defeat. The miners set an example for other workers and, at least briefly, made it possible for them to win major concessions. While the 1991 strike was going on, for example, a series of local strikes broke out in the iron and steel and non-ferrous metals industries over low wages and poor working conditions. Although the metallurgical workers' official trade union quickly moved in to coopt this struggle and prevent the unrest from spreading, it was able to do this by winning from the government a 50 per cent rise in enterprise consumption funds.[141] At a more fundamental level, the 1989 miners' strike accelerated and made permanent a radical transformation of relations between workers and management on the shop floor. Strikes had already become what the sociological journal called 'a new social reality'[142] long before the first miners' strike, but it was this strike which, precisely because of its mass character and its political implications, forced the government to concede the *de facto* right to strike, irrespective of what laws it might put on the statute book. In this sense, the mass strikes bequeathed a weapon to all workers, which they used to influence the balance of power on the shop floor in their favour – even if for the majority of workers militant action did not involve them in mass struggle or political challenges to the regime.

Strikes broke out over a vast range of local issues, ranging from overtime, wages, and working conditions, to protests over managerial authoritarianism or corruption. They were in almost all cases small-scale, and rarely, if ever, posed the threat of growing into the type of mass strikes waged by the miners or the workers in Minsk.

Probably the most explosive issue behind these disputes was wages. The wage reform, of course, provoked considerable conflict wherever its strict imposition led to a fall in earnings.[143] But struggles over wages were not simply a product of government or enterprise wage policies. Because earnings in Soviet enterprises are so dependent on working conditions, the state of equipment, the availability of supplies, and the organization of production, these issues, too, necessarily became inextricably linked with discontent over pay.

The issue of overtime and storming has always been a main source of resentment among Soviet workers, in particular the imposition of so-called Black Saturdays, where workers are forced to give up their day off in order to make up backlogs in a factory's plan fulfilment. In one factory in Voroshilovgrad workers simply refused to accept a management plan to work twenty-one Saturdays over the course of the year.[144] The issue provoked ongoing conflicts at the Yaroslavl' motor factory, which we discuss in more detail below. The conflict there was typical: management insisted that without the overtime the factory could not meet its plan, while the workers maintained that the overtime would be unnecessary if management were doing its job and organizing production properly.[145] The other side of this problem was wages lost because of enforced stoppages, which provoked a number of strikes in the building materials industry in late 1989.[146] The strike at Moscow's AZLK car plant in early 1991, which, as we have already noted, was partly provoked by management's plans to turn the enterprise into a joint-stock company, also demanded an end to piece work: losses of work time at the plant were so great (nearly a quarter of workers complained of losing two to three hours each day just waiting for job assignments or the rectification of disruptions) that, in a period of mounting inflation, workers could no longer tolerate the loss of earnings.[147] In general, workers were becoming increasingly dependent on the smooth operation of production at precisely the time when the supply crisis was making this virtually impossible. They wanted either compensation for the time they were idle or for management to guarantee them a full work load. If management could not ensure these conditions, the response of many workers was to strike.[148] 'If in the past', said one worker at Leningrad's Arsenal Production Association, 'stoppages were paid at the average wage and this provided you with the necessary standard of living, now wages are virtually frozen but prices are rising. The situation is completely different'.[149]

As consumer shortages became acute over the course of 1990 and 1991, this, too, became a cause of confrontation. During 1990 there were a number of strikes in Ukraine over shortages of supplies, with workers at some factories demanding that their town or oblast be put in the priority category for supply allocations.[150] In the summer of 1990 oil workers in Tyumen' oblast threatened to cut deliveries through the pipeline by 10 per cent if food supplies to the region were not improved.[151] During the same period workers in the Kuzbass struck over shortages of tobacco, wine, vodka and – remarkably enough – bread.[152]

The question is, why, despite the frequency of these local strikes and protests, with but two brief exceptions, they failed to expand beyond their immediate confines and to lay the basis of a durable mass movement. The question becomes particularly acute when we consider that the strike activity was occurring at a time of worsening material hardship and alienation from Gorbachev and the rest of the political leadership. Part of the answer we have already touched on, when we noted how, following the April 1991 price rises, management at many enterprises conceded to workers' demands in order to head off more militant action. Most strikes were short-lived and over issues which workers perceived to be specific to their factory or their shop, even if, in reality, the same grievances were being expressed by workers elsewhere. If workers could not improve their situation through industrial action, they could always quit, and many did so. But this alone cannot explain what emerged as a long-term trend.

The fact is that the Soviet working class was in many ways historically unique. It was not a 'new' working class in the sense of the working classes that were formed during capitalism's industrial revolutions. Rather it had been through a turbulent history of creation under Tsarist capitalism, destruction and atomization under Stalinism, and re-formation under Gorbachev. Obviously a workforce existed, but it was not a class in the marxist sense of the term, since it lacked internal cohesion and even a primitive consciousness of itself as a coherent social group with its own distinct interests. This was reinforced by the strong 'corporatist' character of Soviet labour relations. The other side of workers' political atomization was their dependence on management for a whole range of essential goods and services, most notably housing, but also ranging from scarce consumer goods to holidays. This paternalism tied workers to the enterprise and helped defuse potential discontent: in its crudest form workers would have to think long and hard before challenging management or the local trade union if this would jeopardize the well-being of themselves and their families. There were clear signs that this was beginning to alter even at the end of the Brezhnev period,[153] but it nevertheless left a particular ideological and institutional legacy which made itself felt in both local struggles and the mass strike waves of perestroika.

In many, if not most local disputes, protesters faced not just the opposition of management and the hostility (or at best, prevarication) of the official trade unions, but also the demoralization and apathy of their comrades. This points up the contradictory impact of perestroika and glasnost on a workforce previously kept in check by its thoroughgoing political atomization. Political liberalization gave workers the opportunity to transcend this atomization and develop collective forms of struggle. At the same time, however, the political legacy of the old system made such a development haphazard and left many workers cautious and unclear about their aims and how to achieve them. As a result workers frequently found it difficult to win the solidarity of their workmates, a factor which helped reinforce the tendency for workplace struggles to remain localized within a single shop, section, or even brigade.

The difficulties this posed for mounting sustained struggle and forming permanent shop floor organization was shown by the experience of worker militants at the Yaroslavl' motor factory. As already mentioned, at the end of 1987 workers in some sections had gone on strike over the management's imposition of Black Saturdays. Out of this struggle a group of workers formed a Workers' Club and sought support from the factory's trade union, which refused to give the club more than verbal backing. As the issue of Black Saturdays continued to fester, in different shops over the period 1988–91 groups of workers mounted protests over the issue of stoppages and storming, but the militants at the head of these struggles found it difficult to maintain workers' morale; some of these leaders eventually themselves became so demoralized that they quit the factory. What undermined their position, and that of the Workers' Club in general, was the combination of opposition from the official trade union, which workers knew full well had total control over the disbursement of benefits, such as child care places, help in acquiring a flat, or the purchase of scarce consumer goods, and the general frustration at the factory's irregular work regime. The militants found it almost impossible to maintain solidarity: some workers might take action over a pressing grievance and refuse to carry out a specific job, and then someone working alongside them would agree to do it. Despite this situation a new strike broke out in late 1990 or early 1991, out of which workers set up a Workers' Committee which posed a number of demands, including an end to management's authoritarian style of behaviour and strict management and trade union accountability over the distribution of consumer goods, cars, and flats, and over management's plans to shift the enterprise to the market.[154]

The predicament of the activists was summed up by a quality controller at the factory who, though not a production worker, supported the Workers' Club:

> At the Yaroslavl' motor factory we still face the prospect of a long, despairing struggle, perhaps not so much with the administration as with our own comrades at work. We have much to overcome, much convincing to do, and a powerful personal example to set. We must try to show [them], we must succeed in putting in place our own defensive structure before the shift to the market, and precisely at the lower levels, where people work. Otherwise the cheapest commodity on our market will turn out to be our working hands.[155]

Accounts of other struggles suggest that this was a common problem. After the January 1991 strike at AZLK in Moscow, workers who had supported the strike enthusiastically were extremely reluctant to join the workers' side in negotiations with management because they feared reprisals.[156]

The trade unions played a major role in reinforcing this demoralization and parochialism, as well as stifling potential strike action. Although a detailed account of the reorganizations that took place inside the industrial unions and the national and republican trade union federations is beyond the scope of this chapter, the miners' strike had taught the official unions a bitter lesson. The leaderships of the major All-Union industrial unions, while recognizing the need to alter their image, if not the actual content of their work, continued to be dominated by old-line conservatives. Even *Trud*, the trade union paper, could not avoid berating them for their failure to abandon the habits and practices of the so-called administrative-command system.

If in the past the unions had operated by making appeals to their respective ministries, they now addressed their pleas to the Supreme Soviet, coupled with the occasional (and largely empty) threat to go on strike. But there was little real change in their internal functioning.[157] At factory level the situation was far more complex, depending on local circumstances. At most enterprises the old union structures continued to play a conservative role, provoking considerable worker frustration and hostility,[158] while at some the union supported workers' demands.[159]

More important, however, was the way the unions adapted to the collapse of their traditional relationship with top management and the state apparatus. With *khozraschet* neither management nor the central authorities required their services as expediters of plan fulfilment, at least not to the same degree as in the past. At the same time the unions were being subjected to intensified pressure from below to protect their members from the impending ravages of marketization, in particular unemployment and a plummeting standard of living. As a result the official unions came to adopt a militant rhetoric as the defenders of their members' interests while remaining, in effect, lobbyists for management, especially at local level. One of their main tasks, therefore, became to intervene in labour disputes and to prevent them from spilling over into more open conflict.

In virtually all cases the tactic was the same: sensing serious grievances among workers in an industry and the danger that workers might begin electing rank-and-file strike committees, the unions rushed to coopt the workers' demands, to present themselves as the sole champions of the workers' cause, and to take over the role of negotiating their grievances with the government. This was certainly the case in the gold mines of Magadan, where there had been a series of strikes during 1989. When a new strike loomed in April 1990, over the government's unwillingness to meet the miners' demands, the oblast trade union council consciously intervened and assumed leadership of the dispute. According to the VTsSPS journal, *Sovetskie profsoyuzy*, had it not done so, labour collectives would have by-passed the trade unions and assumed 'self-management' through their strike committees.[160] The same occurred on the railways in September 1990, where the railway workers' union threatened a strike, demanding the exemption of its members from the ban on strikes in vital services and industries; after government concessions on a number of points, but not the right to strike, the union called off the action and affirmed that – as a rare exception in Soviet industry – it would thenceforth pursue its struggle using 'legal, constitutional methods'.[161]

By far the two most important interventions of this kind occurred in the iron and steel industry and textiles, where the economic repercussions of *khozraschet* provoked so much discontent that spontaneous all-out strikes became real possibilities in both industries. The crisis in the steel industry arose during the end of 1989, when the government announced that, as of 1 January 1990, enterprises would have to pay sharply higher prices for transport, fuel, and electricity, as well as increase their contributions into social insurance funds. Although this was to apply to all of industry, the worst hit sector appears to have been Ukrainian iron and steel. Production costs were set to rise steeply, while the revenues earned for their own products were fixed by the prices set by the *goszakaz*. Throughout the sector factories were faced with having to make sharp cutbacks in housing construction, the provision of child care, and other social benefits; more alarming, workers at some steel works were facing wage cuts of from 25 to 100 rubles per month. Workers at a number of plants either declared warning strikes or began electing strike committees. At this point both the Ukrainian branch of the Metallurgical Workers' Union and VTsSPS took up the 'struggle', by issuing a protest to Ryzhkov and the USSR Council of Ministers, out of which emerged a conciliation commission to look into the issue. The result was that the government agreed partially to compensate the iron and steel and building materials industries for their extra costs, and to allow 'certain' enterprises to defer their payments to the state budget for two months. After further meek protests from Shalaev, the then head of VTsSPS, the agreement was accepted and the strikes were averted,[162] although the price rises went through and had serious repercussions for enterprises throughout the Soviet Union.

The cause of the unrest in light industry was the deepening supply crisis, which by the end of 1990 had left many textile and garment factories working short time, sending workers home, or temporarily closing down.[163] According to the Russian branch of the Union of Workers in Textiles and Light Industry, the 'majority' of enterprises were electing strike committees.[164] Whether these were genuine grass roots bodies or their formation was being orchestrated by the trade union, we do not know, but the claim no doubt received credence from the fact that spontaneous strikes had broken out in the light industry factories of a number of cities during 1989.[165] The union now declared its readiness to defend the workers and issued a call for a warning strike on 17 December. The union was backed by the Federation of Independent Trade Unions of Russia,[166] which interceded on its behalf with the RSFSR government. Like the earlier crisis in the steel industry, the parties set up a conciliation commission, and the Russian government promised to guarantee 70 per cent of factories' required raw materials at subsidised (state) prices. On the basis of this pledge the strike call was rescinded, although the worsening supply situation rendered it unfulfillable.[167]

It is important to note that in both of these disputes not just the unions, but also industrial management could and did claim to represent the interests of their 'labour collectives'. Thus the pressures of *khozraschet* acted to reinforce traditional paternalism. As we have already argued, the same might have been the case in the coal mines had management supported the 1991 strike, rather than opposing it. This trend was to become even more pronounced after the collapse of the Soviet Union, as industrial managers used the deepening crisis in industry to recement their corporatist ties to their workforce, arguing that both sides had a common interest in keeping production going.[168] Even during the final years of perestroika this trend had considerable significance. What limited scope had existed for workers to transcend the parochialism of their local conditions, to articulate their own demands, and to develop their own organizations through which to fight for them was further restricted by the political conservatism and institutional power of the official unions. This was reinforced by the fact that, as the economic situation deteriorated, the unions became even more important than in the past as a source of distributing scarce consumer goods at prices below those on the free market. in this way, too, they helped to restore old paternalistic relations and bind workers to management.

The political and ideological legacy of Stalinism had an equally great impact on the mass strike movements. The miners' strikes showed the potential within sections of the Soviet working class rapidly to transcend its atomization and wage an organized, rank-and-file-based struggle through its own organizations. But, as we have noted, this was a potential that remained largely unrealized. The strikes did not lead to the creation of a permanent mass workers' movement or of independent working-class political organizations and parties. Insofar as the strike movement had an ideology, it was highly plastic and amorphous. In its very beginning the strikers showed a discernable, but by no means unambiguous understanding of themselves as workers with distinct grievances and conflicts of interests with the elite

and its institutions of power. To some extent this reflected an unarticu-
lated and contradictory synthesis of aspects of the formal ideology of
Stalinism, with its crude, and indeed cynical affirmations of socialism
and its egalitarian rudiments of a 'welfare state', and the 'them and us'
consciousness spawned by workers' alienation from, and hostility
towards, the ruling elite. In this sense the workforce showed signs of
emerging as a class-in-itself, characteristic of the early stages in the
history of every working class – that is, a class aware of its existence as
a group separate from other groups in the society, but not yet able fully
to articulate its own independent needs and goals and self-consciously
to act to achieve them (a class for-itself). Between the first and second
miners' strikes this ideology showed signs of change, but never transcended these boundaries. The movement, or at least its leadership,
became increasingly pro-market and pro-capitalist and expressly anti-
socialist, although its underlying conception of capitalism was naive
and idealized, and bore no resemblance to the concrete capitalism of
the modern world or to the actual process of capitalism's introduction
into the USSR and its successor states. On the contrary, as the reality of
the new Soviet (or post-Soviet) capitalism began to emerge, workers at
many enterprises (and not just those who had engaged in the strike
waves of 1989 and 1991) protested at what they saw as the *nomenklatura*'s robbery of state property and demanded that the factories become
collective property – all, however, within a capitalist market economy.
That this demand was internally contradictory merely reflected the
confusion in people's minds – created by six decades of Stalinism –
over just what capitalism and socialism actually mean.

Unable to develop and articulate a consciousness of itself as a class
with its own *independent* needs and objectives in opposition to the class
rule of the old elite or the new capitalists, the new labour movement,
such as it existed, placed itself under the ideological tutelage of other
groups in Soviet society – primarily the pro-democratic minority of the
liberal intelligentsia, but also embracing elements of the pro-market
beliefs of the intelligentsia's authoritarian majority. What it did not see
was the necessity or possibility of a new form of social organization –
socialism as it was classically understood before the advent of Stalinism: that is, the collective, democratic determination by society of its
needs and priorities and of the means and methods to be used to fulfil
them. This would have to await the next phase in the historical
reemergence of the Soviet working class. But if workers were still
unable to pose their own vision of the future or to create the social and
political institutions needed to realize it, their actions effectively

negated the entire political fabric of perestroika. Through their behaviour on the shop floor they helped to render their enterprises unmanageable; through the threat of mass action they severely retarded the government's implementation of marketization. The workers thus brought society to a state of stalemate. They could render the elite's various reform programmes unworkable, but they could not provide an alternative to the disintegration into which Soviet society was rapidly sinking.

The immediate result was the abortive *putsch* of August 1991, from which El'tsin and his wing of the Russian bureaucracy gained the upper hand over the All-Union bureaucracy. The way was then clear for a more concerted assault by the survivors of the old *nomenklatura* to implant capitalism on the carcass of Stalinism. This could serve only as the precondition for the evolution of a genuinely independent working-class movement, but it is not a guarantee. Despite the massive social and economic hardships which befell the economies of the ex-Soviet republics during 1992 and 1993, new independent workers' organizations had yet to appear.

Part 2

Perestroika and the industrial enterprise

4   'Market mechanisms' and the breakdown of economic regulation

In his seminal work, the Soviet marxist economist, Evgenii Preobrazhensky, argued that there were only two possible regulators of economic activity: the law of value of the capitalist market, and what he called the planning principle.[1] By planning Preobrazhensky had in mind not the bureaucratic nightmare of the Stalinist system, but the democratic determination by society over its priorities and the methods by which they would be achieved within both the overall economy and the individual production unit. In the transitional phase between capitalism and socialism these two regulators would coexist within the same social formation, giving rise to certain hybrid forms, but these would by their nature prove unstable and the one principle would ultimately have to oust the other. As a general orientation, the subsequent history of the Soviet Union has proved this argument correct. Although far more durable than Preobrazhensky, or anyone else at the time could have predicted, the particular hybrid of Stalinist 'planning' (which its early critics referred to not as planning, but as 'planlessness'[2]) failed to generate a regulator of economic life specific to it as a system of production. Unable to avail itself of either market or plan, the ruling elite could only attempt to organize the economy through its control over the means of production, a control which, in the absence of formal titles to property, it could only exercise through its control over the state. This, as we have argued elsewhere,[3] proved to be a system incapable of achieving rational coordination of the economy's different parts and sectors. At the most basic level, a system based on driving individual workers, factory sub-units, and entire enterprises to achieve maximum output, cannot possibly achieve proper proportionality between all the products whose production and distribution are essential to a complex economy. The overproduction of certain machine components, for example, was rendered useless by the relative underproduction of others that were equally essential to the assembly of a finished product. But the system also foundered on the social relations of production which formed its basis. The arbitrary, bureaucratic nature of the system placed both managers and workers in a position where the only way they could fulfil basic indicators, and at the same time protect their individual interests, was to distort central instructions through informal, often *ad hoc* arrangements. Plans were drawn up on the basis of false information: false, because enterprise managers lied about their capacities and final plan fulfilment, and false because the centre had no way to enforce its decisions and compel either managers or workers to abide by central directives. Factories produced the wrong types of materials and equipment, in the wrong quantities, and of a quality that seriously distorted – if not totally negated – their functionality at subsequent stages of production. Thus the results of the activity of each individual unit within the production process had only haphazard connection with the plans issued by the central authorities and with the other units to which they were economically linked.

Implicit in perestroika was the recognition that the command system was incapable of providing the required economic coherence and coordination. As originally conceived the Soviet elite's plans for economic modernization sought to rely on the use of so-called 'market mechanisms', but without the actual introduction of a market, predicated, as the latter must be, upon exchange between independent commodity producers. The hope was that the rigorous application of profit-and-loss accounting would make enterprises more sensitive to cutting costs, in particular labour costs, which were to be reduced through equipment modernization and widespread redundancies. At the same time, the overhaul of incentives systems, combined with limited democratization, were designed to coax and persuade workers to surrender the partial control over the labour process that they had built up over generations, and which was perceived as a direct impediment to economic reform. From the point of view of the early reformers what was essential was that the implementation of these changes leave the basic property and power relations within Soviet society intact: the ruling elite, despite potentially drastic changes in its personnel, were, by virtue of its domination over the state bureaucracy and industrial enterprises, to remain the expropriators of a surplus product created by an exploited workforce. The reluctance to shift wholesale to the market and the eventual restoration of capitalism was a reflection of the uncertainties this would pose, not just for the personal positions of those individuals in the elite who would not be able to guarantee their entry into the new class of capitalists, but for the elite as a social group, whose hold on power would no longer be guaranteed under a system of private ownership of the means of production.

This solution, based on the creation of a 'marketless market', was beset by massive internal contradictions, which doomed it from its outset. For all its incoherence, the command system had not been an arbitrary creation, but the only means by which the bureaucratic elite could attempt to control the process of surplus extraction. It was, therefore, a system appropriate to the property and class relations of Stalinist society, but by the end of the 1970s it had reached the limits of its viability and had proved itself an historical cul-de-sac. As the process of dismantling it began, more and more of the functions previously fulfilled by the large industrial ministries – primarily the allocation of supplies and investment resources – were to be devolved to the growing network of market relations. Reality, however, proved more complex. The old links between suppliers and customers gradually came unstuck, but the 'market mechanisms' failed to fill the void that was then created. On the contrary, enterprises and production units began to function according to the *logic* of the market, but without a market having been created. This led to significant distortions in production and distribution, which in many ways made the economy less viable than it had been under the old system. Many of these difficulties we have already described. Enterprises sacrificed long-term investment in fixed capital, social infrastructure, and workforce training, in order to raise wages and stem the labour shortage. They cut production and raised prices in order to maximize revenue without undertaking large-scale new investments. Most important of all, they ceased to honour the delivery contracts inherited from the ministerial system, knowing that with production falling in an economy already plagued by chronic shortages, they could dispose of their output wherever they could obtain the most advantageous terms, often on the basis of barter.

Once the old economic connections began to unravel, the process acquired a dynamic of its own. By the end of 1990 virtually every enterprise was complaining of crippling shortages, which fed through the system like a chain reaction: factories could not meet orders because of supply bottlenecks, caused because their own suppliers had been unable to obtain materials and components from the enterprises on which they themselves depended. Even before the Soviet Union's formal dissolution in the wake of the August 1991 *putsch*, republics and regions, in an effort to save the industries under their jurisdiction, had begun to impose bans on the 'export' of goods and materials to other parts of the USSR. Given that much of Soviet industry was based on monopolist suppliers located in a single town or region (so that, for example, the country's entire production of particular lines of equipment was often assigned to a solitary factory), this led to a virtual famine of certain types of materials and machinery, and the contraction of industrial production accelerated. By the end of 1991 the economy was approaching a position of gridlock.

This process was reinforced by important social changes, already described in chapter 3. As it became increasingly obvious that the initial strategy of perestroika was unworkable and that only a full-scale transfer to a capitalist market could save the elite's position, heads of ministries and large enterprises began rapidly to manoeuvre themselves into a position of preeminence within the emerging class of entrepreneurs. They divested themselves of their ministerial functions, but continued to draw off funds from the enterprises still legally under their control. More crucially, they initiated a process of '*nomenklatura* privatization', acquiring control and ownership of an evergrowing number of concerns, firms, and joint stock companies. The Communist Party, too, began using its vast financial resources to buy up firms and create various holding companies, in anticipation of the impending privatization of state assets. This was to be a development of extraordinary significance. For the new market that was emerging became dominated by the institutions and personnel of the old command system, who, with the economy still governed by large monopolies operating under shortage conditions, had little incentive to provide the impetus towards renewal or investment that the ideologists of the market had imagined the reforms would bring. Instead, the emerging class of capitalists, like the Russian bourgeoisie before 1917, has been incapable of creating a dynamic capitalism which could develop and modernize the productive forces. The capitalism of the post-Soviet Union has promised to be a static, dependency economy, characterized by underinvestment, cheap labour, and the domination of foreign capital.

Self-financing within the industrial enterprise

At the end of 1990 Gorbachev made a discernable turn towards more authoritarian government. Soviet troops violently attacked pro-independence demonstrators in the Baltic states, while in Moscow,

Gorbachev shook up his cabinet, appointing the hardliners Pavlov as Prime Minister and Pugo as Minister of the Interior. He also railroaded through the election as Vice President of G. I. Yanaev, the totally incompetent ex-chair of VTsSPS, who was later to serve as the figure-head for the *putsch* of August 1991. These events led most Western observers, together with the Soviet liberal intelligentsia, Gorbachev's erstwhile allies, to conclude that Gorbachev had abandoned market reforms. This interpretation was profoundly mistaken. The govern-ment had certainly moved in a more authoritarian direction, but the institutional preparations for the implantation of the market pro-ceeded with little delay, even if the fears of popular protest continued to force Gorbachev to move more cautiously than his more radical pro-market advisers wished.[4]

In June 1990 the new Law on Enterprises supplanted the 1987 State Enterprise Law, and established the rights of owners to appoint their managers without challenge or interference from the workforce, whose own representative institutions, the STK, had their powers severely curtailed. A few months later, in October, the government repealed the 1986 wage reform, so that, for the first time since industrialization in the 1930s, the setting of wage rates and norms was totally decentralized.[5] In December there was a new law on invest-ment, which established elaborate guarantees protecting investments and provided for compensation if either national or local legislation caused losses to investors or if investments were subsequently nation-alized.[6] This was followed in January 1991 by the law on employment, which set up procedures and regulations governing the management of unemployment, and in February by the publication of draft legisla-tion on the denationalization and privatization of state enterprises.[7] In short, the market was going ahead, not along the path of so-called liberal democracy, but imposed from above by arbitrary methods. The heroes of economic policy were no longer the Social Democratic welfare states of Scandinavia, but such paragons of democracy as South Korea, Franco's Spain, and Pinochet's Chile.[8]

These legal changes had for some time been preceded by shifts in policy towards enterprise financing and the position of individual production units within the larger system of economic planning and coordination. Originally the new arrangements, which in varying degrees made enterprises responsible for earning their own budgets through production and sales, were part of the overall strategy, already mentioned, of attempting to use 'market mechanisms' without introducing a full-scale market. This strategy proved unworkable.

Self-financing and *khozraschet* so destabilized the economy that the elite was left with little alternative but to change direction and attempt to transform the Soviet Union into a capitalist economy.

As already noted in chapter 2, the 1986 wage reform and the 1987 State Enterprise Law had defined two methods by which enterprises could apply profit-and-loss accounting, or *khozraschet*. On the first model, enterprises would be guaranteed basic funds for investment and wages, but bonuses and additional funds for social development (housing or child care, for example) had to be financed out of profits. Eventually all enterprises were to evolve to a second, more rigorous model of *khozraschet*, according to which enterprises were to finance all expenditures out of revenues, including wages, replacements of fixed capital, and investment. In line with this transition the *goszakaz*, or state order, was de-emphasized. From the point of view of production, many enterprises or their sub-units were now free to dispose of output over and above their planned deliveries to the state wherever they could find customers, and could use the extra revenues to increase their material incentives funds (that is, pay out extra bonuses), invest in plant and equipment, or augment funds for social development. The other side of the declining importance of the *goszakaz*, however, was that ministries were guaranteeing enterprises with ever-smaller proportions of their planned supplies of raw materials, components, and other essential means of production; enterprises had to acquire the rest by signing independent contracts with potential suppliers. Indeed, in light industry the USSR Ministry of Light Industry was actually disbanded, and its tasks devolved to the Ministries of Light Industry of the USSR's constituent republics – a move which eventually brought enterprises in that branch of production to a near standstill for lack of essential supplies.[9]

Within this scheme, in 1986–87, enterprises began putting sub-units, ranging from shops down to individual brigades, on to self-financing arrangements. Initially this was done primarily through the contract system [*podryad*], where work collectives contracted to fulfil specific production targets and would receive enhanced bonuses if all quantitative and quality criteria were met. Savings achieved through rationalization and shedding labour were shared by those remaining. Management for its part was, at least in theory, obligated to provide contract collectives with all supplies and equipment needed to allow them to meet their contracts.[10] Unlike later leasing arrangements, collectives on contract work did not manage their own wage funds or budgets.

The contract system was not an invention of perestroika. The contract brigades differed little from earlier experiments in the Khrushchev and Brezhnev years (when they were used primarily in construction) and many of the problems they encountered then were repeated under Gorbachev. While the collectives had specific obligations before management, the latter did not have binding responsibilities to the brigades.[11] The most serious impediment was the irregularity of supplies, which made it difficult, if not impossible, for management to guarantee collectives the materials they required to meet their contracts. A brigade in one of the assembly sections of AZLK in Moscow, for example, had to abandon the contract system because of the large number of defective components it received from the foundry.[12] Moreover, supply problems meant that managers had to maintain the ability to manoeuvre resources to meet changing production circumstances, which introduced further instabilities into the work of collectives.[13] Brigades became discouraged by the absence of accurate accounting procedures and the frequent unwillingness by managers to allow them to distribute earnings as they saw fit. In some cases management so manipulated the terms of the contracts that workers stood to gain little by meeting them.[14] But the logic of contract work also dictated a specific life cycle, where brigades could achieve substantial economies by cutting numbers, but, once these reserves were exhausted, could obtain no further improvements in performance – and hence in earnings – without technical innovations, the investments in which were outside their control. Many, therefore, broke up after a short life span, often within two or three months of their formation.[15] The contract system also aroused considerable hostility among both management and workers: the former, because they did not always want to take on the extra work involved, especially where they might not be able to meet the terms of the contracts;[16] the latter, because contract work usually involved a greater intensity of labour which many workers were unwilling to accept.[17] As a result, in early 1988 less than 5 per cent of all brigades in industry were on contract arrangements.[18] As a further reflection of the system's declining importance, press and journal discussions of contract work became increasingly infrequent over the course of 1990. Although contract brigades continued to survive at some factories,[19] they were usually only cited as a transitional stage to leasing.[20]

As a result of the limitations inherent in contract work, the regime began to place increasing emphasis on leasing arrangements (*arenda*). The publicity they received in the press, especially in the paper

Ekonomika i zhizn', far outweighed their actual numerical significance, so it is clear that leasing became seen as the wave of the future, at least in the absence of total privatization of state enterprises. Under leasing schemes, enterprise sub-divisions, or even entire enterprises, contracted out of their parent organization (the enterprise or production association). They undertook to provide the parent body with a specified volume of goods or services, and were free to sell all output over and above this amount wherever they could find customers. They also controlled their own wage funds. In some cases, especially where enterprises had been operating at a loss, they were given their means of production,[21] in others they leased them. They also paid for materials and centrally provided services, such as maintenance and technical advice, according to 'internal' prices. In all cases lessees were required to pay the parent body a leasing fee, often of punitive proportions. Some enterprises took the system even further and hived off certain shops or sections as cooperatives, run on strictly private lines, which sold their services to the enterprise.[22]

Finally, as the advance to the market progressed, some enterprises were turned into joint stock companies, the details of which – and the struggles which this provoked – we have already described in chapter 3.

At the end of 1989 approximately 8.5 per cent of Soviet enterprises and production associations were on so-called full *khozraschet* – that is, the second variant, where all costs were to be met out of revenues – and a further 4 per cent were on leasing. Together they accounted for approximately 11 per cent of total industrial personnel and just over 10 per cent of industrial output.[23] In the engineering industry take-up was particularly low, although exact figures were not published.[24] The number of enterprises and enterprise sub-divisions on leasing increased substantially during 1990 and 1991, but still accounted for only about 12 per cent of industrial production.[25] It is noteworthy that units on leasing in 1989 did marginally better at cutting costs per ruble of output and at raising wages than the average for industry as a whole, but the results were hardly spectacular.[26]

Nevertheless, it is clear that some enterprises used the new system to good advantage, achieving considerable improvements in quality, productivity, and wages, often with substantial redundancies (generally viewed favourably in the literature as a sign of progress).[27] Many reported better labour discipline and lower turnover rates as productivity and wages went up.[28]

A more detailed insight into how the more well-developed leasing contracts worked is provided by those enterprises and associations which shifted all of their sub-divisions – rather than isolated units – to the system. At the Gidromash engineering works in Novokuznetsk, which went on leasing in March 1989, all sections signed contracts with one another under which they paid each section for whatever services it provided. Payments were settled according to a system of intra-factory prices. Some sections, for example, all those involved in main-tenance and construction, were hived off as cooperatives. Out of its gross revenue from sales of output and services a section would deduct its outlays on raw materials, equipment maintenance, and services from other shops, plus its leasing payments to the enterprise. The balance would go to cover the section's wage fund, a fund for 'economic risk', and a centralized fund for 'stimulating' technical progress.[29] At times the creation of market relations *within* enterprises could be taken to quite extraordinary lengths. Many factories allowed shops or shop sub-divisions to file damage claims against one another for defective supplies, late deliveries of parts, or similar violations of contractual arrangements. Claims were paid out of the offending unit's *khozraschet* income, thus presumably hitting wages and bonuses.[30]

Despite these examples, the experience of leasing was not an unqua-lified success. In many cases the leasing collectives found themselves confronted with the same problems as the old contract brigades. Obligations tended to be one way. If collectives failed to meet their contracts they could suffer heavy penalties, but management faced no sanctions if they did not provide equipment, supplies, or raw mater-ials.[31] Conversely, managers in Kuzbass coal mines were accused of refusing to allow collectives to go on leasing precisely because of fears that they would not be able to meet terms of the contracts.[32] The contracts themselves were often poorly drawn up, or bureaucratically imposed by top management. This was the case with several enter-prises in Penza, where shop managers and foremen were so badly informed about the contracts that they had no idea how production costs were composed or by what criteria wage funds were to be formed. Formally they were on leasing, but in fact neither the organi-zation of production nor the wages system had changed from the previous system.[33] A similar situation befell the erection and rigging section of shop no. 423 at Leningrad's Arsenal Production Association. Its workers, who carried out repair and erection work throughout the Association, first discovered that they were on leasing when told by factory journalists. Management had simply imposed the transfer by fiat, without any prior preparation. The shift brought no change in the way they worked: they had no control over the distribution of earnings or work organization, and earnings did not go up. In fact, the imposition of *khozraschet* weakened their position considerably, since the Association's constituent factories and sections now had fewer funds for buying new equipment or for purchasing the section's services: they preferred to carry out repairs and rigging themselves.[34]

Leasing units equally faced a number of financial difficulties. Leasing payments by enterprises to their ministries, or by enterprise sub-divisions to their parent enterprise or production association were as a rule exorbitantly high. In some cases the payments merely replaced the old planned exactions from profits, and ministries used these to subsidize loss-making enterprises.[35] One construction trust in Karaganda was paying 8 million rubles a year to the State Construction Agency (Gosstroi) in leasing fees, but received back only 70 to 80 per cent of the materials it required and only 5,000 rubles worth of equipment out of 1.5 *million* stipulated in the lease contract.[36] The fixed capital passed to leasing collectives was usually in an advanced state of depreciation, forcing them to shoulder the added burdens of high repair and maintenance costs.[37] These problems were further compounded by the partial deregulation of prices (discussed in more detail below), whereby leasing units were faced with steeply mounting costs for materials and equipment, which they could only cover by putting up prices on their own goods, thus exacerbating the general prices spiral which was gripping the Soviet economy.[38] Where this proved impossible because the prices charged by collectives were still controlled by the state, their higher production costs were not matched by increased revenues, thus threatening their financial position.[39] Inflation in general tended to undermine the basic rationale of leasing, namely the higher wages that collectives could guarantee their members: the extra 20 to 50 rubles a month that workers might earn was no longer an adequate incentive to improved performance.[40] Finally, collectives had difficulty managing their internal finances because of poor accounting procedures. At Leningrad's Lenin factory, shops and sections were converted to small or medium-sized enterprises, or shifted to self-financing, contract work, or leasing, without setting up proper bookkeeping services, taking prior inventory of resources, or training specialists in how to work under market conditions.[41] At a more mundane, but no less important level, Soviet factories have few metres for recording usage of electricity, steam, water, or fuel (most factories, for example, have but two or three electricity metres for the entire plant), thus making it almost impossible accurately to measure the materials consumption of individual sections or shops.[42]

The obstacles to leasing were not purely economic. Ministries and production associations in many cases attempted to obstruct enterprises from transferring to leasing and thus leaving their jurisdiction.[43] In some examples cited in the press, these were profitable collectives whose financial support ministries and associations were reluctant to lose.[44] In others, ministries did not want to see their power-base weakened, even where the enterprises concerned were operating at a loss.[45] At times the opposition by higher bodies was so fierce that they tried to block the move to leasing by locking out the local management or even seizing the 'offending' factory using hired thugs.[46]

To sum up, while the press touted individual successes, the evidence suggests that units on leasing suffered from a number of structural, financial, and political weaknesses which jeopardized the system's general viability, and even caused collectives to refuse to accept it.[47] More important, however, was the impact of self-financing on the economy's underlying mechanisms of coordination and regulation, the breakdown of which acquired crisis proportions.

The breakdown of *Khozraschet* and the supply crisis

The difficulties of self-financing, although disruptive for the enterprises affected, were in many ways merely symptomatic of the deeper disruptions caused by marketization and the pressures it placed on management to base decisions on short-term financial considerations, rather than the enterprise's long-term development. Because of the extensive interdependency between sectors and enterprises such decisions impacted not just on the enterprise concerned, but on all those which it supplied. In a growing number of cases factories proved either unable or unwilling to fulfil contracts which in previous years had been dictated to them by the *goszakaz*. As the process hit more and more enterprises it began to take on a dynamic of its own, so that by 1990 the entire fabric of inter-enterprise supply connections was in crisis.

The Enterprise Law of June 1990 made enterprises responsible for acquiring their own supplies through direct contracts, wholesale trade, and intermediary organizations, including state agencies responsible for so-called material-technical supply. Except in certain strategic areas of production, the *goszakaz* was to be phased out. Henceforth, enterprises were to deal with each other through the market. The loss of the *goszakaz* was significant at both ends of the spectrum. It meant the loss not only of guaranteed supplies, but also of guaranteed customers. Thus the problem was not always that traditional suppliers refused to provide materials or equipment; in some cases factories could no longer *pay* for what they needed because they could not sell their own output.

The outlines of the crisis became increasingly visible over the course of 1990, as a growing proportion of enterprises in different sectors failed to meet their contracts for deliveries. By the autumn of 1990 this included 39 per cent of enterprises in the fuel industry, 42 per cent in engineering, 51 per cent in metallurgy, and 54 per cent in chemicals.[48] These figures actually improved slightly during early 1991, but only because a large number of contracts – some 12 per cent for industry as a whole – had still not been concluded.[49] Yet these general figures fail to convey the true magnitude of the crisis at enterprise level. An enterprise like the Chelyabinsk tractor factory relied on 1,200 different suppliers for some 13,000 components, and it required the non-delivery of only one of these to bring the entire conveyor to a halt.[50] Such reports became routine. In automobiles, chemicals, general engineering, building materials, and construction, factories and building sites were idle because such vital items as steel, aluminium, copper, chemicals, and timber were simply unobtainable.[51]

There developed a chain reaction, where a holdup in the supplies coming to one factory would, like falling dominoes, cause a whole string of other enterprises to be idle in its wake. Thus the Dinamo engineering works in Moscow received cable from the Moskabel' cable factory and ball bearings from the First State Ball Bearing Factory, both also in Moscow. The ball bearing factory simply refused to deliver the bearings; Moskabel', on the other hand, was unable to obtain copper from its usual suppliers because government departments were selling the copper abroad for hard currency. The result, of course, was that Dinamo was unable to fill its own contracts, including a large order of 300 excavator motors to Leningrad's Izhora works.[52] We can only speculate as to the fate of the construction projects which were waiting for Izhora's excavators.[53]

Especially vulnerable were those enterprises which lost their access to supplies through centralized channels, yet whose own output had to be sold on *goszakaz* at controlled prices. Instrument making was excluded *in toto* from the *goszakaz* in 1991, which meant that its enterprises were no longer guaranteed deliveries of materials, components, or equipment. The conclusion of independent contracts was hindered by the stringent conditions imposed by potential suppliers, for example, advance payment before orders would be filled. By late 1990 instrument factories were already cutting back production and defaulting on deliveries to major industries, including meat packing and iron and steel.[54] A similar problem befell the electric locomotive factory in Tbilisi, which produced exclusively for the USSR Ministry of Railways. During the course of 1990 the prices it had to pay for essential machinery were raised substantially, on some items by 300–1,000 per cent, while its own revenues were fixed.[55]

Similar difficulties were caused by the loss of Eastern Europe, which brought in its train the collapse of long-established trading patterns, whereby the Soviet Union had paid for East European imports either in rubles or in kind. As the new East European regimes set about introducing their own forms of marketization, they demanded all payment in hard currency. They had no need for rubles and the quality of most Soviet manufactures was simply too low to make them worth accepting. Since for most Soviet enterprises hard currency was desperately scarce, those which were dependent on East European equipment or components, for example the combine-harvester factory in Ternopol', the tractor-frame shop at Leningrad's Kirov works, the Rezina rubber-technical goods factory in Moscow, and the metro-car factory in Mytishchi (Metrovagonmash), were suddenly left without suppliers. Although in some cases they succeeded in finding alternative Soviet sources, it could still take several years before they actually received the equipment.[56]

The breakdown of ruble exchange eventually extended to Soviet factories, which increasingly refused to deliver output to customers unless the latter could pay in dollars[57] or offer something they needed by way of barter. The Sverdlovsk transformer factory, for example, would not deliver transformers to the Uralmash engineering works unless the latter could provide it with a long list of items, including piping, scrap metal, kitchen fittings, rest home passes, and even a telephone for the flat of the doctor looking after the director's wife.[58] Iron and steel works would despatch metal only in exchange for food, consumer goods, or even carloads of vodka.[59] Leningrad's Arsenal factory traded compressor stations for refrigerator cars full of vegetables or sausage.[60] Bricks, too, became a virtual second currency: engineering enterprises even began manufacturing brick-making equipment specifically for barter with brick factories.[61] In general, those enterprises producing 'deficit' items were in an especially strong position. According to *Rabochaya tribuna*, factories holding stocks of paper could exchange it for anything from French cosmetics to automobiles and video equipment. By the same token, such material-intensive industries as machine-tool production, electric locomotives, and mining equipment found their situation becoming more and more desperate.[62] Barter arrangements became increasingly complex: enterprises would swap their output for intermediate items which they could not use directly, but which they could trade with a supplier. The Kuibyshev footwear association, for example, swapped a large consignment of shoes for automobiles, and then traded the cars for leather. The Perm garment association was told that it could receive the cloth it needed if it could come up with airplane engines – a condition it was unable to meet, thus forcing it to go without the supplies.[63]

By the end of 1990 the supply situation had become so grave that Gorbachev tried to stem the tide with a presidential edict which guaranteed supply contracts at their 1990 levels through the first quarter of 1991. The order declared equally invalid all decisions at All-Union, Republican, or local level which impeded the delivery of supplies (for example, bans on the export of raw materials outside a particular Republic), coupled with the promise to import sufficient raw materials to maintain coordination between different branches and industries, and to impose sanctions on the sale of raw materials abroad without the required export licenses.[64] The edict had not the slightest effect whatsoever. As the foundations of economic coordination crumbled still further, pressures towards regional and republican protectionism mounted. A shadow trade war developed between republics as each, in an effort to ensure that its own factories received top priority, banned the 'export' from its territory of what it deemed to be essential supplies. This inevitably provoked retaliation from the other republics. Given that for many of the factories which fell victim to such manoeuvres there existed virtually no alternative suppliers, the economic chaos this caused was considerable – all the more so, since the embargoed raw materials or semi-finished goods often would have gone to manufacture finished products which were themselves necessary to the republic which had imposed the ban. Thus, in early 1991, Ukraine failed to sanction the shipment of stainless steel to Russia. The latter countered by blocking the shipment to Ukraine of rolled metal, even though Russian factories were themselves dependent on the Ukrainian products fashioned from the Russian metal.[65] Similarly, the Krasnyi aksai agricultural equipment factory in Rostov-on-Don manufactured 70 per cent of the USSR's cultivators, for all crops and climatic zones. Half its metal came from Ukraine, and in late 1990 this supply halted, leading to a chronic shortage of spare parts for cultivators, including in Ukraine itself.[66] This outbreak of parochialism was by no means confined to Russia and Ukraine. Practically all inter-republican supply relations were affected.[67] In April 1991, Gorbachev intervened with yet another edict, but it was symptomatic of his declining authority that this time he merely 'proposed' to republican and regional authorities that they repeal their decisions banning the export of goods outside their boundaries.[68] His appeal was no more successful than his directive of four months before.

The two industries most severely hit by the supply crisis – or at least, the two where the crisis was most thoroughly documented in the press – were light industry and iron and steel. The crisis in light industry, which threatened to spill over into mass unrest among the industry's workers,[69] had a long history, dating back to 1989, when the All-Union Ministry of Light Industry was disbanded and replaced by the State Committee for Light Industry (Goskomlegprom). Many of the former ministry's functions were then devolved to the individual republics, some of which subsequently abolished their own ministries of light industry. As the general supply situation deteriorated and republics began imposing restrictions on the sale of raw materials beyond their borders, light industry factories began to suffer severe shortages.[70] By the third quarter of 1989 the textile industry, for instance, was already short of literally tens of millions of metres of cloth, satin, flannel, linen, and coat linings.[71] When in spring 1990 the Russian Ministry of Light Industry attempted to sign bilateral agreements with other republics, whereby they would supply Russian textile mills with raw materials in exchange for finished cloth guaranteed by the Russian government, this led to a jurisdictional dispute with Goskomlegprom, which declared these agreements null and void.[72] But the supply contracts then mediated by Goskomlegprom proved unenforceable: suppliers would not send raw materials to the textile plants or other branches of light industry. *Trud* estimated that throughout light industry enterprises had been able to negotiate contracts for 1991 covering only 20–60 per cent of their needs.[73] For some items, such as raw cotton, the situation was extreme: as of 15 January 1991, completed contracts for raw cotton came to only 8 per cent of total purchases during 1990, a year during which supplies had already fallen.[74]

As with other industries, factories came up against three basic problems. Most commonly, as just noted, suppliers either would not conclude contracts or would not deliver contracted materials. In other cases suppliers were willing to honour contracts, but either only on a barter basis or at vastly higher prices, which the garment, footwear, and other processing factories could not afford, especially since their own wholesale prices were being frozen, while raw materials prices had been freed. Thus by early 1991 the price of thread was actually lower than that of the cotton used to make it.[75] Finally, sources of foreign raw materials had dried up because of the shortage of hard currency. In reality these three difficulties were closely interrelated, affecting factories at different stages in the production process. Typical was the crisis which hit the woollen industry when, in early 1991, the Krivoi Rog yarn factory had to lay off its entire workforce of 4,000 people because it could no longer get hold of raw wool, much of which was imported. The factory also made heavy use of foreign equipment, which the press elliptically noted had 'gone out of service', pre-sumably because the factory could no longer obtain spare parts. The root of the factory's difficulties lay in the country's heavy reliance on imported wool, cotton, and synthetic fibres, which made up some 38 per cent of total consumption. As sources of hard currency dried up, so, too, did purchases of these raw materials. Yet there were no alternative domestic suppliers. Krivoi Rog was able to meet only 16 per cent of its needs using Soviet wool, and the quality was poor. To make up the shortfall the Soviet Union would have to increase its sheep herds by 40–50 million head. As one commentator remarked, 'Who, other than God, knows how to do this?' Knock on effects were quick to follow. The factory was simply unable to honour its contracts with the ninety or so textile and knitwear factories throughout the USSR that it supplied, and which were themselves now badly affected. In Ukraine, some tried to switch to synthetic fibres, but these, too, had to be imported, and the Ukrainian government would not – or could not – provide the hard currency.[76]

As the crisis deepened layoffs began to mount, as more and more enterprises in light industry and textiles were forced to put workers on short time or send them home on unpaid leave.[77] In February 1991 the government of Georgia went so far as to declare that all the republic's light industry enterprises would have to close for two months because of a lack of electricity, although we do not know if the threat was actually carried out.[78] For those still at work, wages, of course, fell because of lengthy stoppages.[79] By January 1991 between 750,000 and 1 million light industry and textile workers in Russia alone were out of work, although as we noted in chapter 1, these layoffs did not prove permanent. By the autumn those still out of work due to supply shortages was less than half the January figure, although the supply situation was progressively worsening and output continued to fall. In August 1991 the volume of production in textiles and light industry was 10–12 per cent down on the already dismal results of 1990.[80]

The difficulties besetting the iron and steel industry had an equally long history, and were rooted in two main factors: the tenuous financial position of most of its enterprises, and its dependence on coal, which left it especially vulnerable to the aftershocks of the two miners' strikes and the coal industry's own supply problems. The industry suffered from severe structural weaknesses even before the introduction of *khozraschet*. Its plants are old and their equipment worn out, making production excessively labour-intensive. The former USSR Ministry of Ferrous Metallurgy (Minchermet) took billions in amortization payments from the factories, but doled little of it back for capital investment and reconstruction. Moreover, plants were still making high amortization payments even after the Ministry began relinquishing its traditional responsibilities of guaranteeing enterprises with necessary supplies. Energy and materials costs were high. Thus at the start of 1991, the Kuznetsk iron and steel combine, constructed at the start of the First Five-Year Plan, required root and branch reconstruction, costing nearly 1.2 billion rubles. Yet its profits for that year were planned at only 106 million, of which it would retain just 64 million. Many of the older Ukrainian steel works were in a similar position.[81]

The underfinancing of the industry grew to crisis proportions thanks to the various 'market mechanisms' of *khozraschet*. In late 1989 the government announced massive price rises on fuel and transport costs which threatened severely to cut into funds available for investment, housing, social benefits, and even wages. Although trade union protests managed to win temporary subsidies, the price rises were eventually imposed.[82] Then, in 1990, the government created a so-called 'economic stabilization fund', to which enterprises had to contribute a sum equal to 20 per cent of their amortization funds. To this was added Gorbachev's 5 per cent sales tax. These payments hit all of industry, but for the older iron and steel works and coke by-products factories, much of whose equipment, though still in service, was fully depreciated and demanded replacement, they raised the prospect of financial disaster. For the Krivoi Rog coke by-products factory, the stabilization fund payments alone would mean each year not replacing three or four of its coking batteries. As for the sales tax, with raw materials and fuel making up some 85 per cent of production costs, paying an extra 5 per cent on top of the already higher charges for these items would wipe out half the planned profits for the entire Ukrainian iron and steel industry.[83]

It is against this backdrop – that is, an industry already deeply mired in financial and structural difficulties – that the specific character of the supply crisis in iron and steel must be analysed. Steel production in the Soviet Union has always been heavily dependent on the recycling of scrap metal, a reflection of the huge wastage of metal within the economy. In part this stems from the poor quality of metal and the careless working of it in subsequent stages of production, especially casting, with the result that metal components are themselves of poor quality, and a large proportion of them have to be resmelted. In part it comes from the waste of metal within production. Castings are frequently over-sized, so that in engineering, for example, much of the metal winds up on the floor as shavings. Prior to *khozraschet* factories actually had plans for the delivery of scrap metal back to the iron and steel industry – this was both an official recognition of the dimensions of waste and an incentive to its reproduction (factories were penalized if they did not generate enough scrap).[84] With perestroika this system virtually collapsed. Under the old arrangements deliveries had been overseen and expedited by directive of the local Communist Party. As the Party lost its power and influence, especially within the enterprise, this lever of command was removed, but no new financial incentives were created to encourage enterprises to carry on with scrap deliveries. On the contrary, many found it more profitable to export their scrap for hard currency. Although the government tried to counter this trend by belatedly raising the ruble price by 50–100 per cent, it is doubtful that this proved more attractive than the prospect of foreign earnings.[85]

It was coal, however, which lay at the heart of the steel industry's supply problems. Neither the coal industry nor the iron and steel enterprises which depended on it, in particular coking plants, had recovered from the 1989 miners' strikes when the 1991 strike broke out. During 1990, coal production was 95 per cent of its 1989 level, a disastrous result considering the amount of production lost during the 1989 strikes. In Ukraine alone this left coke and coke by-product factories with a shortfall of 3.5 million tons of coking coal. Worse still, for 1991 orders already placed accounted for less than half the industry's needs. The rest the mines were prepared to sell only at free, or 'contract' prices, which the coke factories could not afford to pay.[86] In the Kuzbass the story was the same: during January–February 1991, that is, before the outbreak of the second miners' strike, coal extraction in the Kuzbass was down 2.2 million tons over the same period in 1990. Iron and steel output was hit severely. Production of basic steel was down 4 per cent over 1989, rolled steel down 3 per cent, and steel pipe down 5 per cent. The decline accelerated during January and February 1991. Quality also deteriorated: because of the shortage of coking coal, coke by-product factories were providing blast furnaces with charges of inferior quality, leading to an overconsumption of scarce coke. Moreover, the decline in steel production fell disproportionately on metal produced by more modern, less metal-consuming methods (cold-rolled sheet steel and low alloy rolled steel).[87]

Not all of the shortfall in coal production was due to the 1989 strikes. The coal industry was itself victim of supply problems, in particular metal and timber for pit props, and spare parts for its equipment. In mid-1990 Donbass miners claimed that many pits were on the verge of shutting down because they had no wood for roofing. Such claims may have been exaggerated, but the depth of the problem was not: delivery plans for 1991 were a full 30 per cent below the amount required to meet the plan for coal.[88]

Under these circumstances the 1991 miners' strike was bound to have a devastating effect on the steel industry and those industries, in particular automobiles and engineering, which were the heaviest metal consumers. Coal production, already depressed before the strike began, fell by 11 per cent during January–March and by 20 per cent in April. Production of coking coal during April was down by 39 per cent.[89] In both Ukraine and the Kuzbass, coking plants, which had been working well under capacity, were now faced with the prospect of having to shut down batteries, an extremely costly move since to start them up again would require practically full reconstruction, which could take up to two years. Despite this, by the end of March, eleven batteries in Ukraine had been taken out of action, in order to conserve enough coal to run the others. Even these had to be run at lower temperatures and extended coking times, sharply cutting productivity and quality. The economic impact on the coking plants was equally severe: revenues were slashed and jobs placed under threat.[90] The chaos soon spread to the iron and steel mills. In April Azovstal' sent 5,000 workers and technical staff on unpaid leave.[91] Magnitogorsk and Nizhnii Tagil began shutting down blast furnaces, open hearth furnaces, and rolling mills, at the risk of causing extensive damage. Engineering and automotive factories soon began following suit, since they had insufficient supplies of metal to manufacture machinery, parts for agricultural equipment, refrigerators, or vacuum equipment. Industries and processes which used coke also had to cut back production, including the manufacture of light bulbs and certain pharmaceuticals.[92]

Although the immediate threat of plant closures subsided with the end of the strike, the general disintegration of the economy continued. As the breakup of the Soviet Union became a fact, regionalism and galloping inflation made the maintenance of stable supply relations almost impossible. The economy of the former USSR had been too highly integrated to permit factories to find local suppliers for all their needs. In September El'tsin issued a Presidential Edict barring 'exports' from the RSFSR to other republics until the internal needs of Russian industry had been secured. This left Ukrainian factories, from textiles to automobiles, almost idle because of their dependence on Russian materials and components.[93] Russian factories were hit just as badly. The Podol'sk accumulator factory, which made accumulators for tractors and combines manufactured in Minsk, Chelyabinsk, Khar'kov, and Volgograd had to suspend production because it could not obtain lead from Kazakhstan. The Elektrokabel' plant, also in Podol'sk, ground to a halt because it could not get hold of tin, aluminium, or insulation materials.[94] Coking plants were once again placed under threat, only this time not because of a lack of coal, but because of a shortage of refractory bricks for their furnaces.[95] Where suppliers were willing to fulfil contracts, the prices now charged were in many cases prohibitive. Components for agricultural equipment had become so expensive that manufacturers had to charge from 200,000 to 300,000 rubles for a tractor, against the usual price of 7,000.[96] Farms simply could not pay such prices, and instead of buying new equipment, tried to survive by patching up their old machinery. In this way the worst effects of the supply crisis, governmental parochialism, and the anarchy of the evolving market combined to send the economy into near total collapse.[97]

Conclusion

We have argued here that the supply crisis was the inevitable result of the attempt to impose a market upon the bureaucratic structures of the Stalinist system. There were a number of reasons why this was so. First, self-financing and the imposition of *khozraschet* drove both individual enterprises and many parts of the central planning network to operate according to a market logic in the absence of functioning market structures. Throughout the economy this led to a dismantling of the old bureaucratic planning network without the creation of any viable regulator of economic activity. The state strove to cut its budget deficit, and individual enterprises tried to maximize their revenues, but at the expense of coordination between the different 'cells' of the economic organism. Put another way, free rein was given to the greed generated by the market, without any of the market's disciplining mechanisms, such as bankruptcy, shareholder retaliation for loss of profits, or even prosecutions for corruption.

Secondly, as we have discussed in the introduction to this chapter and the chapter on worker protests, and take up further in the Conclusion, the group best placed to rise to prominence in the new market economy was the old *nomenklatura*, in particular high-ranking personnel within the industrial ministries, and enterprise directors. To the extent that privatization was already beginning to take place during the final phase of perestroika, these people assumed control over the newly privatized means of production precisely through the monopolistic – both in a political and economic sense – structures of the old command system. In a shortage economy this could have only one result: the drive to maximize revenues and personal wealth without any impetus towards dynamic innovation, modernization, or development of the productive forces. The supply crisis was merely an expression of this tendency, which manifested itself more fully after the collapse of the Soviet Union and the scramble for ownership under El'tsin's market reforms.

Thirdly, as with virtually every other aspect of perestroika, the reforms were undermined by the fact that the Soviet people, in particular the working class, did not react to them as passive cyphers, but as active agents, trying to protect their individual and collective interests. This is perhaps less obvious in the case of the supply crisis and the centrifugal disintegration of self-financing than with worker protests, but it proved a key factor. Neither perestroika nor the market which was to supplant it, could succeed without a restructuring of the labour process and the traditional relationships between line managers and workers. We have already shown how the key elements of Gorbachev's labour policy – over employment, wages, and enterprise 'democratization' – failed to impose such a solution. Marketization equally contributed to this outcome. By perpetuating and even exacerbating the internal dislocations plaguing Soviet production, *khozraschet*, too, made it extremely difficult, if not impossible to achieve the restructuring of the labour process upon which economic reform and the successful introduction of the market would depend. For management was both unable and unwilling to launch a frontal assault on traditional labour practices when faced with such critical uncertainties, since an enterprise's survival continued to rely on workers' cooperation in dealing with them. Thus moves towards the market threw up barriers to their own development: they gave renewed force to precisely those aspects of the production cycle which reinforced workers' partial control over the labour process.[98]

This last point has another aspect to it. It was impossible to introduce a market without the free mobility of commodities (a virtual impossibility given the decrepit infrastructure of the Soviet economy) and the existence of a universal equivalent through which commodities could acquire a value expression. But such an equivalent arises historically with the evolution of commodity production and exchange and the emergence of abstract labour – that is, labour whose social significance is no longer its capacity to produce concrete objects of use (use values), but its ability to be reduced to the one common property shared by all labour in the capitalist mode of production, its ability to create exchange value. Under capitalism the concrete utility of what labour produces becomes irrelevant; its social importance lies only in its capacity to create commodities, each of which is interchangeable with every other because each embodies the social abstraction of value, the social property through which equivalence can be established for purposes of sale and exchange. By contrast, the Soviet economy, as an economy without commodity production and exchange, could not generate a universal equivalent. Indeed, it is doubtful if it was ever the aim of perestroika, at least in its original conception, to transform the economy into one based on the private ownership of the means of production and commodity production. Enterprises were to sell to survive and find their own customers and suppliers, but they were still to have plans, and prices were to continue to be determined centrally. They were, in effect, to operate as partial commodity producers, a goal as internally contradictory and utopian as the 'civilized capitalism' of the more democratically minded market reformers.

Under the Stalinist system labour power was not abstract, but concrete. Goods, including labour power, circulated according to bureaucratic dictate, not according to value or the quest for value maximization. Enterprises sought them for their concrete properties, as steel, glass, wood, paper, electric cable, machinery, and so on. Enterprises often engaged in black or grey market exchange, swapping surplus items for scarce goods held by another factory, but such exchanges were not based on the abstract value of goods as commodities. On the contrary, the 'price' or production costs of what was exchanged were immaterial, for in an economy dominated by scarcity the important thing was to acquire whatever would allow management to keep production functioning. This helps explain what otherwise appears as the cavalier attitude adopted by both workers and management towards resources, the waste of which became an intrinsic drive of the system.

One of the striking features of *khozraschet* was its singular failure to alter either the nature of the product or the behaviour of management within the process of circulation. What we observed was the seemingly contradictory phenomenon, whereby the introduction of marketization and market criteria led to a breakdown of economic regulation and coordination which enterprises could only try to overcome by making increasing use of barter. As under the old Stalinist system, such barter was based not on an exchange of value equivalents, but strictly on the exchange of things for their useful properties: metal or raw materials to allow production to keep going; food and consumer goods to maintain the workforce and stanch labour turnover during a time of worsening labour shortage. In this sense, too, attempts to introduce the market turned into their opposite. Rather than breaking down concrete labour and replacing it with abstract labour, the dislocations which it produced made abstract labour – the *sine qua non* of a market economy – more and more of a chimera.

As we discuss at the end of chapter 6, this gave rise to a peculiar hybrid form of the social product: a product which aspired to become a commodity but which remained trapped in its use-form as a defective, or deformed product. To understand this more fully we need to examine the Soviet labour process which creates this product and, in particular, the failure of perestroika to achieve a fundamental restructuring of that labour process. As with enterprise behaviour in general, perestroika did not leave the labour process untouched. Like management, workers adapted to the new conditions, but in such a way as to preserve and consolidate the essence of the old social relationships within production, so that in the end they became the primary block to the full transition to the market.

5 The labour process under perestroika: 1 The political economy of working conditions

Attempts by management to restructure the labour process, whether under capitalism or in the Soviet Union, do not just hinge on the political struggle at shop floor level over work practices and control, but are bounded by the technical parameters of production, most importantly, what is being produced and by what process, the type of technology employed, and its deployment and organization. Clearly these two areas overlap. One of the aims of so-called scientific management has been to secure for management greater freedom to impose new types of technology which, irrespective of its direct impact on profitability, would help to break down workers' control over the labour process.

In the Soviet Union, the question of working conditions acquired acute importance. At stake was not just the question of health and safety, but the elite's capacity to restructure production. The uneven mechanization of different stages in production and the backward technology employed in most Soviet factories perpetuated a particular division of labour between production and auxiliary workers which had long been a drain on productivity and on the regime's ability to impose rationalization of production. The age and decrepitude of equipment and the extremely hazardous and unhealthy conditions under which a large proportion of workers had to labour affected both the long-term state of the society's supply of labour power and the effectiveness of its application within the production process itself. Complicating the issue still further is the particular role which female labour has played in regulating the process of surplus extraction, a role which is reinforced and reproduced in large part by the dismal conditions prevailing in many, if not most female industrial jobs.

Yet for all its importance, the topic has received relatively little attention from Western writers on the Soviet economy; it has only recently achieved modest prominence among Soviet specialists. In this chapter I examine the issue of working conditions in some detail, not in order to catalogue the poor state of health and safety in Soviet factories, but in order to show the relationship between these conditions and certain central aspects of the labour process. In the first section I look at the crisis of underaccumulation which beset Soviet industry, as the age of its fixed capital stock reached the point where the society no longer had (or has) the productive capacity to renew it. In the second section I present a general picture of working conditions and analyse some of the major factors behind their reproduction and persistence. Finally, the third section extends this general argument to the specific role of female labour in the process of economic regulation and how this became one of the primary contradictions undermining perestroika.

The crisis of underaccumulation

Ever since the period of Stalinist industrialization in the 1930s the Soviet economy was characterized by the hypertrophied production of means of production and the neglect of its consumer goods sector.[1] During the 1930s this was the result of deliberate policy, as consumption was squeezed in order to extract resources for accumulation. As the system matured these political priorities were reinforced and perpetuated by structural rigidities which inhibited attempts to redress this imbalance: the empire-building of the large industrial ministries; resistance to technological innovation; and the enormous wastefulness of production, which required a *de facto* overproduction of means of production to compensate for the overconsumption, poor quality, and unreliability of metal, raw materials, and machinery.[2] Up until the very end of perestroika it was still official policy to syphon off the bulk of revenues from light industry to subsidize investment in Department I. With the shift of enterprises to *khozraschet*, or profit-and-loss accounting, enterprises in light industry found themselves left with few resources with which to undertake new investment.[3] These financial constraints were reinforced by the planning system, which made inadequate provision for the equipment needs of light and food industries, which, in order to expand, had to resort increasingly to the import of foreign equipment, squandering scarce hard currency.[4]

From the very beginning, this disproportion created a fundamental contradiction within the political strategy of perestroika, whose success was predicated upon raising the standard of living by increasing the output of food and consumer goods. The regime could not hope to expand the output of consumer goods without improving the motivation of workers in both heavy industry, which would provide means of production for Department II, and light industry, where the consumer goods themselves were actually to be produced. Yet any improvement in morale and productivity would depend upon the *prior* expansion of the supply of consumer goods. The obstacles in the way of breaking this vicious circle lay not simply in those factors which had traditionally led to the retardation of Department II. Perhaps more damaging was the deepening crisis of underaccumulation of fixed capital which had been gestating throughout the 1970s and 1980s, and which manifested itself with full force in the economic crisis of perestroika.

In its broad outlines the nature of the problem resembled the crisis of underaccumulation of the NEP period. The expansion of the production of consumer goods required the prior investment in consumer goods industries, which in turn demanded the prior expansion of that part of Department I which manufactures means of production for Department II. This, however, came up against the obstacle that Department I did not actually have the spare capacity to shift resources to this type of production. As we shall discuss, its own fixed capital stock was, and remains badly depreciated and in need of massive renewal. Thus expanded investment in the consumer goods industries of the former Soviet Union requires a prior massive expansion of Department I *for which Department I does not have the productive capacity.*[5]

Unlike NEP, where the boundaries of the crisis were defined by the weakness of the country's industrial base within an overwhelmingly backward peasant economy, the current crisis has emerged in a country which, since the 1930s, has been characterized by hypertrophied investment in Department I and an apparent overaccumulation of means of production. The fact is that most of the plant and equipment in Soviet and post-Soviet factories is physically and morally depreciated and has been kept in service long after it should otherwise have been replaced. According to one economist, during perestroika 45 per cent of the equipment in heavy industry and 38 per cent in light industry was *totally* worn out.[6] The list of major enterprises working with equipment dating back to the 1960s, 1940s, or even before the October Revolution was almost endless. Typical in this regard was the Siberian Heavy Engineering Association (Sibtyazhmash), which in 1987 had 32.5 per cent of its equipment over twenty years old and a further 24.4 per cent older than ten years, in an industry where the normal period of moral obsolescence is calculated at seven years.[7] This situation arose from a long-standing trend for new equipment manufacture to lag behind needs for replacement, a tendency which dates back to the early 1960s.[8] Under perestroika this trend clearly accelerated, so that long-term declines in the rate of investment actually turned into positive disinvestment.[9]

As Lavrovskii has pointed out, this need not have been a negative development, had it led to the scrapping of worn-out plant and equipment and its replacement with more modern, productive technology. This is not, however, what happened. Firstly, the tendency in the Soviet economy had long been to purchase new machines while leaving older ones in use. When managers did replace machinery they usually retired only individual pieces of equipment, rather than modernize entire production systems.[10] This tendency was reinforced by managerial and worker resistance to innovation, which might have threatened in the short term to jeopardize plan fulfilment and may subsequently have entailed long-term reorganizations of the production process which would undermine workers' partial control in this area. For this reason, when enterprises introduced new technology or new lines of production they had to erect entirely new shops or factories, rather than attempt to modernize existing production units.[11] This helps explain the country's enormous volume of unfinished capital construction, as enterprises initiate an almost endless succession of new projects without the resources actually to complete them. Moreover, during perestroika the lag in completing projects worsened, so that by 1989 only about half of the units planned to come on line were able to do so. As one economist put it: 'As in the past, we are spending our basic energies and resources on erecting boxes, rather than on renewing equipment'.[12]

The result was to increase fixed capital stock without improving its effectiveness or productivity. New equipment was not intended to *replace living labour power*, but required *more* labour power to run it. Thus the labour shortage, which under perestroika reached crisis proportions in Soviet industry, arose not just because workers were quitting production, but because of this cumulative expansion of work places. Another side of this was the continued rise in the amount of uninstalled or underutilized machinery,[13] leaving an estimated one in every four work places 'surplus'.[14] This seemingly irrational behaviour had always been a logical response to the realities of Soviet production. The irregularity of supplies deliveries, which gave rise to the famous Soviet phenomenon of 'storming', meant that factories had to keep on hand both excess equipment and excess workers in order to meet plan targets at the end of the production period. The availability of labour power was here more important than reserves of machinery, but the former could not be incorporated into wage plans without the latter. Equally important, the unreliability of Soviet equipment, the non-standardization of parts, and the general non-availability of spare parts from equipment manufacturers, meant that factories had to erect and maintain their own machine shops to produce parts and carry out repairs. These machine shops, of course, had to be equipped, usually with universal machine tools of advanced age, and which were badly underutilized.[15]

Secondly, the characteristics of new machinery provided factories with little incentive to institute sweeping rationalization. The huge lags in bringing planned innovations into production meant that 'reequipping' often involved the purchase of obsolete, albeit 'new' machinery.[16] Another problem, as we discuss in more detail in the next section, is that labour power in the Soviet Union was cheap, so that the mechanization of unmechanized jobs made little economic sense from the point of view of the individual enterprise. This was especially true of auxiliary operations, primarily loading and warehousing jobs, where such equipment as electric cranes and electric loaders were becoming increasingly costly, while the wages of the workers (mainly women) who carried out this work remained extremely low.[17] Moreover, the performance potential of much of Soviet machinery was poor: equipment costing two or three times the machinery it might replace would routinely lead to only a modest 10 or 15 per cent rise in actual output.[18]

These problems were particularly severe in the cases of machine tools with numerical controls, and robots. The former, despite their excessive cost, often could not be properly utilized because of a shortage of skilled specialists to programme, set, and run them, or because factories could not guarantee the correct physical environment essential to their trouble-free performance. Their actual degree of utilization was low, and when they were used it was often not to carry out the complex, specialized operations for which they were intended, but to turn parts which could be machined on universal machine tools.[19] Moreover, workers showed a marked reluctance to work with these machines because of the potential loss of control their use might bring.[20] Similar difficulties were encountered with robotization. The robots were so expensive, yet so limited in their productivity and the range of operations which they could perform, that one study estimated they would only cover their costs in 500 years.[21] In many cases the robots went out of action, often for lack of spare parts, so that the workers they initially replaced were forced back on to their old jobs.[22] Attempts to circumvent some of these problems by importing robot systems from the West were subverted by the low level of technique of the operations into which the robots were supposed to be integrated, thus negating their potential benefits. At AZLK gaskets on gear boxes were fitted by robots; however, because the factory could not fashion the lids in the correct shape, the robots could not do the job, and the factory had to employ a special worker to knock the lids on with a hammer.[23]

Thirdly, although the tendencies described here date back to the origins of the Stalinist system, perestroika simply had no mechanism by which to induce either managers or workers to alter their attitudes and behaviour towards rationalization. On the contrary, Gorbachev's economic reforms led to precisely the opposite result. The old All-Union industrial ministries were either dismantled or divested of their previous functions of coordination and tutelage over the enterprises under their jurisdiction. These functions were supposed to be fulfilled indirectly through so-called market mechanisms, primarily through the system of enterprise self-financing, whereby enterprises now had to cover equipment replacement, supplies purchases, new investment, and wages out of earned revenue. In fact, this system reinforced disincentives to renew capital stock, as enterprises consistently opted to divert revenues to short-term aims, primarily by raising wages or purchasing consumer goods as a means of stanching the haemorrhage of labour power. Many enterprises were left without the funds even to buy adequate supplies of raw materials, much less new machinery.[24]

The practical effect of all these trends was to discourage investment in more modern technology, the rate of growth of whose output steadily declined from the mid-1980s onwards, leading to a further accumulation of old, physically and morally obsolete fixed capital stock.[25] Moreover, according to Lavrovskii, by the perestroika period the 'reserves' of equipment allegedly indicated by the huge volume of uninstalled and underutilized equipment no longer represented real spare capacity. On paper they existed because dilapidated machinery had never been written off, but they could not be mobilized to boost output.[26]

In the past successive Soviet regimes attempted to improve the efficiency of equipment use through various campaigns designed to induce or compel enterprises to discard surplus equipment (the so-called certification of workplaces) and to use their fixed capital more intensively. In the main such campaigns had little impact.[27] The experience of perestroika showed little improvement in this regard. The amount of old equipment taken out of service through certification continued to fall.[28] A similar campaign to increase equipment utilization through the extension of work to second and third shifts met with an equal lack of success. The logic behind this latter campaign was to expand output through the more intensive use of equipment, and at the same time to accelerate the depreciation of old machinery.[29] While some improvement was reported at individual factories in Leningrad, Kiev, Ulyanovsk, Irkutsk, and other cities,[30] overall results were disappointing. Coefficients of utilization[31] for industry as a whole in 1987 rose from 1.26 to 1.46, a not inconsiderable jump of 13 per cent.[32] But utilization was lower in key engineering centres like Leningrad; worse still, machine tools with programmed controls were often utilized least efficiently of all.[33] For most managers the economic incentives to expand multi-shift work were weak or non-existent. Bottlenecks caused by irregular deliveries of materials and spare parts and by shortages of skilled tool setters tended to be worse on evening and night shifts, so that increased output did not cover extra costs. There was also evidence of conflicts provoked by worker discontent at new shift schedules. Needless to say, these difficulties became exacerbated by the deepening supply crisis within Soviet industry from 1990 onwards.[34]

On balance, the failure of these campaigns under perestroika, for all their negative impact, must be seen to have had less economic significance than in the Khrushchev or Brezhnev periods. The problem afflicting Soviet industry was, and remains, far more fundamental: the pattern of normal replacement of worn out equipment has been so badly disrupted for so long that, especially when coupled with the antediluvian technology of much of 'new' Soviet machinery, the demands for replacement now exceed the country's production capacity.

We have already outlined how this helped to undermine the political strategy behind perestroika, namely the attempt to use rising standards of living as an inducement to persuade workers to accept an attack on traditional work practices. However, the crisis of accumulation also affected the labour process in a more immediate way, by perpetuating the traditional occupational structure within Soviet industry, in particular its heavy reliance on unmechanized manual labour and the perpetuation of strenuous and dangerous working conditions.

Working conditions in Soviet industry

It has long been known that working conditions in Soviet factories are among the worst in the industrialized world. Under Stalin, and far more so under Khrushchev, such issues as industrial accidents and the drudgery of manual labour became the focus of periodic press campaigns designed not so much to improve the appalling state of health and safety at work, as to demonstrate the regime's alleged concern over the issue, while shifting the blame on to negligent managers or local officials. In fact, no less than under capitalism, the dreadful conditions which confronted so many Soviet workers were the logical consequence of the economic system: in this case, bureaucratic 'planning' and the premium it placed on gross production, record-setting, and investment in plant and equipment at the expense of safety devices, ventilation systems, and proper work clothes. During *glasnost'* discussions of working conditions became both more open and more urgent, as labour economists and other commentators began to emphasize the enormous costs which bad working conditions were inflicting upon production efficiency, the workforce, and the general environment. Thus V. D. Roik, one of the few Soviet specialists to write extensively on this topic, has asserted that such problems as social passivity, alienation, and drug and alcohol abuse 'are in no small degree connected with poor working conditions, monotonous and uninteresting work, and unsatisfactory interpersonal relationships within labour collectives'.[35]

The scale of the problem almost defies description. Workers constantly work amidst filth, noise, and toxic fumes. In Leningrad's Sevkabel' cable works the air in some shops becomes so polluted the workers are ordered to stop work.[36] At the Cherepovets iron and steel combine, shops are said to be so dirty that crane operators are unable to see their hoists.[37] These factories are by no means exceptions. In the worst smoke-stack industry towns of the Urals or the Kuzbass factories annually emit from 600 to 1,500 kilograms of pollutants per resident. During Gorbachev's visit to Nizhnii Tagil, near Sverdlovsk, in April 1990, workers complained that the sky was never blue, but red or yellow. In Novokuznetsk the rate of cancers rose twenty-six-fold between 1975 and 1990; cases of bronchial asthma increased six-fold. A staggering 23 per cent of all children born in the city in 1990 were born with some form of illness.[38] Work-related deaths and disabilities occur on an equally massive scale. In the Soviet Union as a whole, every year some 14,000 to 15,000 people died in accidents on the job, 700,000 were maimed, and between 30,000–32,000 were permanently disabled due to accidents or occupational disease. As several commentators pointed out, more Soviets died in one year on the 'production front' than were killed during the entire Afghan war.[39] Not all of these accidents were in industry; as in the West, agriculture accounts for a large share, although the exact proportion is unclear.[40] By the same token these figures clearly understate the true situation, since many accidents and cases of occupational disease go unreported.[41] Nor do the statistics take account of those who die each year from illnesses contracted on the job.

Although comparative statistics are not available, the industry worst affected appears to be coal mining. During the late 1980s approximately 600–800 coal miners died each year, although this figure fell to 450 for the first 11 months of 1990. For the industry as whole this means an average of one life lost for every million tons of coal dug out of the ground. At older, smaller pits the death rate is much higher: the press recently cited one mine with one death per 80,000 tons of coal, and another with an incredible three deaths per ton! If one considers that some 7 to 10 million tons of coal are lost each year just falling off coal cars during transport, the pointlessness of these deaths gives even greater cause for outrage.[42] Coal mining, of course, is a hazardous occupation in any country, but its intrinsic dangers are made worse by pressures of the wages system and managerial negligence. Thus in December 1989 and April 1990 miners in two different Donbass mines were overcome, leading to three deaths, when toxic fumes from the Gorlovka chemical factory seeped into the mine works.[43] In June 1990 eleven miners were drowned in a Kuzbass mine when water burst through the coal face.[44] It was incidents like the latter which prompted the Independent Union of Mineworkers, formed in the wake of the 1989 miners' strike, to demand an end to piece rates in the mines. Irregular deliveries of supplies forced miners to bend safety regulations during end-of-month storming periods as the only way to meet their plans and maintain earnings.[45]

The situation in coal mining, though perhaps extreme in the scale of its casualties, in fact is typical of the rest of the Soviet economy. As late as 1991 the Soviet Union was one of the last industrialized countries in the world still to use asbestos as ballast on the railbeds of its railway network, exposing both repair workers and train passengers to high levels of asbestos dust.[46] In factories safety standards were (and almost certainly still are) notoriously lax: as of 1990 the Ministry of Health had issued exposure limits on a mere 1 per cent of all the chemical substances used in industry.[47]

Table 5.1. *Major manual auxiliary operations in Soviet industry, 1 August 1985*

Quality controllers	908,000
Ancillary workers	882,000
Loaders	675,000
Storeroom attendants	422,000
Carters and transport workers	363,000
Packers, stackers, baggers, and weighers for bagging operations	289,000
Sorters	166,000
Washers	72,000
Weighers	52,000

Source: *Trud v SSSR* (Moscow, 1988), pp. 63–65, based on enterprise surveys covering 25,980,000 industrial workers, or 83 per cent of all workers in industry.

However, for the mass of workers the persistence of the heavy and hazardous conditions in which nearly half of them work is directly tied to the advanced age, backward technology, and poor utilization of machinery, alongside a wide range of jobs for which no equipment exists at all. In 1985 virtually half of all workers in industry were employed on auxiliary operations, some 15 per cent in just nine trades (Table 5.1). Nearly 35 per cent were doing heavy manual labour. Another 14.1 per cent worked manually as tool-setters or maintenance mechanics, both skilled occupations (Table 5.2).[48] All three of these phenomena reflect the antiquated nature of Soviet production. The poor quality and generally decrepit state of machinery demand a huge army of repair and maintenance personnel – not just mechanics and electricians, but machinists and other support workers in the vast number of repair shops servicing every factory. Transport, warehousing, and loading work is almost totally unmechanized. Such jobs are a drain on surplus extraction not just because auxiliary operations create constant bottlenecks for more highly mechanized production shops, but because these workers enjoy considerably greater control over how they organize and carry out their work, even where the job is difficult and tedious.

The statistics convey nothing of the actual content of this labour. It is almost impossible to exaggerate the extent of technological primitiveness of many of these jobs. At Moscow's Moskabel' cable factory, the cable was manufactured on a French assembly line, but the copper

Table 5.2. *Percentage of industrial and construction workers doing manual labour, 1 August 1985*

	I	II	III
Construction	40.0	56.4	3.6
Industry (total)	51.0	34.9	14.1
Including:			
Electric power	50.0	16.3	33.7
Oil extraction	66.8	14.4	18.8
Oil refining	55.0	23.1	21.9
Coal mining (underground pits)	32.5	47.6	19.9
Coal mining (open cast mines)	46.6	37.7	15.7
Peat	59.9	28.9	11.2
Iron and steel	48.8	28.6	22.6
Extraction and enrichment			
of ores for iron and steel	49.9	25.0	25.1
Non-ferrous metallurgy	55.3	23.7	21.0
Chemicals and petrochemicals	48.4	30.3	21.3
Engineering and metalworking	53.1	4.5	12.4
Timber	43.1	48.5	8.4
Woodworking	54.0	36.3	9.7
Cellulose and paper	51.4	29.5	19.1
Building materials	52.9	31.7	15.4
Glass and porcelain	40.5	47.1	12.4
Light industry			
(excluding textiles)	60.8	33.4	5.8
Textiles	53.7	31.3	15.0
Food industry	42.7	46.1	11.2
Printing and publishing	51.3	41.6	7.1

Column I Workers working with machinery and mechanical devices or tending automatic equipment.
Column II Workers performing manual labour, including manual operations connected with machinery and mechanical devices.
Column III Workers on repair and setting of machinery and mechanical devices.
Source: Trud v SSSR (1988), p. 252, based on a survey of industrial enterprises comprising 25,980,000 workers, or 83 per cent of all industrial workers, and 5,747,000 construction workers, or 66 per cent of all construction workers.

cores were trimmed using the 'stone age technology' of an axe and a sledgehammer.[49] In the tractor shops of Leningrad's Kirov works (the rest of the factory manufactured tanks), scale on ladles in the foundry was knocked off with a sledgehammer, while motors and radiators were mounted using what the factory newspaper called 'prehistoric' crowbars. Conditions in the factory's railway shop, where workers unloaded incoming freight, were so dangerous that, according to managers, the workers had to risk life and limb just to keep production going. In the words of one shop superintendent, 'if we kept to the letter of the [safety] manual we would have to halt production'.[50]

Some safety regulations, such as, limits on how much weight women may lift in the course of a shift, are simply unenforceable because the equipment does not exist that would make adherence to them possible.[51] The same applies to the mechanization of manual jobs in general.[52] For those workers using machinery, including working on conveyors, the advanced age and dilapidation of equipment adds to the burdens of work and raises the incidence of accidents or occupational disease.[53] Some equipment is so hazardous in this regard that maintenance personnel try to avoid repairing it.[54] How this translates into the reality of working life is made clear by the following account:

> My wife works at a very old machine-building factory in the stamping shops. Young girls come who had hoped to enter some institute. A few weeks go by, and they lose a finger or a hand. That happens a lot there because the equipment is in terrible condition. It is old. You are supposed to insert the metal piece with special forks, but the women are in a rush and do it by hand. The older ones want to earn more, and the younger ones simply want to have a smoke. If the machines ran normally, nothing would happen. They'll be inserting the part as the press is rising, but it suddenly falls on their hand because it is out of order.[55]

The situation is made worse by the poor design and manufacture of machinery, so that even when new it is often lethal or harmful to users. According to Roik, citing statistics from the official trade unions (the former VTsSPS) and the All-Union State Standards (Gosstandart, which used to set quality and safety standards), one in three construction projects, one in four enterprises brought on line, and eight in ten units of installed equipment had serious safety faults. Of 2,000 models of machinery and mechanical devices serially produced by the USSR's twelve engineering ministries, only 8 per cent met safety requirements.[56] Many of these defects originate in the design stage: new equipment lacks protective guards and interlocks, and routinely exceeds limits on vibration, noise, and dust creation.[57] Foreign equipment purchased in the attempt to ease the burdens of manual labour sometimes cannot be utilized because it is incompatible with existing machinery or premises.[58]

The Stalinist 'planning' system was so constructed as to provide both managers and workers with strong disincentives to improve working conditions. First and foremost in this regard is the simple fact that labour power in the Soviet Union is cheap. For managers it has been far more economical to employ large numbers of low-skilled manual workers, many of whom are women at the very bottom of the pay scale, than to invest in safety equipment or the mechanization of manual jobs. This is especially true of loading and warehousing jobs, where the prices and running costs of such equipment as electric cranes and electric loaders had been constantly rising even before hyper-inflation set in towards the end of 1991.[59] These pressures are intensified by the long-term neglect of equipment: in order to introduce even simple improvements, equipment might be in such an advanced state of disrepair as to make it necessary to close down an entire section, something which neither management nor workers are keen to do.[60]

By the same token the sanctions on managers for violating safety regulations have been virtually non-existent. Fines for safety violations used to amount to no more than 10 to 50 rubles.[61] Only one in five fatal accidents ever resulted in a prosecution; if there was no fatality legal proceedings were virtually never instigated. In serious cases some lower-ranking manager might be temporarily transferred to another job.[62] Where an accident resulted in substantial injury it was actually cheaper for the factory if the worker died. It then made a one-off payment of 300 rubles, while the state paid the family a pension for the loss of its bread winner, whereas if the worker survived the enterprise had to shoulder the burden of medical treatment and compensation.[63]

The introduction of market conditions and enterprise self-financing only acted to reinforce these tendencies. As more and more enterprises now had to cover equipment purchases and investment, as well as wages, out of their gross incomes, they were less and less willing to put money into safety improvements. In 1989 industrial enterprises cut outlays on mechanization, automation, and other improvements to working conditions by a third.[64] This was graphically described in the coal mining industry, where, following the granting of financial independence to pits in the wake of the 1989 miners' strike, mines began curtailing investments in ventilation equipment, instruments for measuring dust and gas levels, and safety education for workers and supervisory personnel. Individual mines simply did not have the financial power to commission designs for new, safer equipment from scientific and research institutes, causing the latter to become bogged down in small-scale projects with little future pay-off for mining technology.[65] The pressures of self-financing even pushed shop, factory, and oblast trade union committees to demand cutbacks in the numbers of doctors and safety inspectors employed by them, as a means of trimming their hard-pressed budgets.[66] But cutting outlays on safety was not the only means by which enterprises sought to strengthen their financial position. According to the labour safety journal, *Okhrana truda*, many factories attempted to maximize revenues by lengthening the work day or compelling workers to work extra shifts, with a corresponding rise in accident rates and a deterioration in workers' fitness for work.[67]

Nearly half of all Soviet workers used to receive some form of benefits in compensation for working in heavy or unsafe conditions. In 1985 46.9 per cent of workers in industry were granted supplemental leave; 42.4 per cent received higher wage rates; 33.1 per cent had the right to free milk or comparable food products; 24.1 per cent had the right to early retirement or a higher pension.[68] Yet for the typical industrial enterprise it was far cheaper to pay workers danger money than to invest in improvements; what is more, as the labour shortage worsened during 1990 and 1991, managers came to rely on their ability to offer these 'privileges' as a means of attracting and holding on to workers.[69] As a result of these various pressures, the average enterprise during perestroika was spending four times as much on compensation as it did on safety. This led to an ever-widening gap between the cost of modernization and what enterprises were actually spending: according to Roik, in 1989 enterprises spent between 30–100 rubles per workplace on improving conditions, while the average cost of these improvements had risen to 7,000–10,000. At these levels of expenditure it would take sixty to seventy years to make all existing workplaces safe, and then only on the unrealistic assumption that the number of unfit places did not grow. Kul'bovskaya calculated that for the economy as a whole the bill would come to 130 billion rubles, yet even this was cost effective given the country's annual outlay of nearly 20 billion rubles on compensation payments and special work clothes – not to mention the costs of maintaining those with occupational disabilities, treating illnesses like silicosis or skin cancer, or the lost production incurred by their exit from the labour force.[70]

The problem is that this system had a corrupting effect on the workers themselves, who were reluctant to see improvements in conditions if these would cause them to lose such privileges as higher wages, better food supplies, or early retirement.[71] This was especially

true of women, who, as we discuss in the next section, often depended
on these supplements to augment their otherwise meagre pay.
Moreover, with self-financing many workers, especially women, faced
the added fear of losing their jobs. If they pressed for safety improvements they might lay themselves open to victimization;[72] if enterprises
made such improvements, this might jeopardize their financial position, forcing them to make economies elsewhere, namely through
layoffs.[73]

As with other aspects of marketization, the economic reforms, rather
than countering tendencies created by the Stalinist system, acted to
reinforce them. The economic logic of the bureaucratic plan and the
premium it placed on the pursuit by managers of their own self-interest,
was replaced by the self-interest of the market. It is safe to say that full-
scale marketization and the restoration of capitalism will only worsen
this situation, unless workers themselves make conditions a central
focus of collective protest. Before perestroika the emphasis on gross
output and investment in production shops at the expense of auxiliary
operations resulted in the cumulative neglect of health and safety at
work. At the same time, toleration of bad working conditions became
part of the informal bargaining between line management and workers.
Unable even to contemplate collective action to force improvements in
this area, workers opted for an individual solution: higher wages or
early retirement in exchange for agreement to work in unsafe conditions. It was, in effect, an exchange of the worker's long-term health
for a slightly higher standard of living. In the end this exchange proved
dysfunctional, both for the workers themselves and for the system. As
Kul'bovskaya noted, the country was caught in a vicious circle. Wages
were low because labour was inefficient and badly organized. But it was
inefficient because people were working in terrible conditions, and so
worked unproductively and with bad quality. 'It is a vicious circle. And
instead of breaking it with a system of state measures for improving the
work environment, we exploit cheap labour power that makes no
demands, enticing it with an extra tenner on its wages'.[74]

Yet however accurate this assessment may be, it ignores one
important aspect of the problem. A large proportion of the workers in
this situation were women, whose hyper-exploitation proved
economically rational not just from the point of view of the individual
enterprise manager, but from the point of view of the Soviet elite, for
whom female labour had long been an important means of regulating
the mechanism of surplus extraction and compensating, at least in
part, for its otherwise imperfect control over this process.

Working conditions and the regulatory role of female labour[75]

In my study of workers in the Khrushchev period I argued that women workers occupy a specific place in the political economy of the Soviet system.[76] On the one hand, they carry out most of the low-paid, low-skilled jobs, often under heavy and hazardous working conditions, which men refuse to do. On the other hand, 'feminized' industries – primarily textiles and other branches of light industry, but also including such female-dominated trades in heavy industry as press operators, or assembly line work in light engineering – are by the nature of the technology involved and the greater political docility of the women who work in them, characterized by a higher intensity of labour, so that the women in these industries have fewer opportunities to exercise the degree of control over their labour process which men do. The elite, therefore, has had greater control over the process of surplus extraction in these industries and trades, which historically allowed it partially to compensate for its otherwise imperfect control over that part of the surplus created in high-priority, male-dominated areas of production. Moreover, these two areas of female productive labour exist in symbiotic relationship to one another. It is only the existence of the large pool of low-skilled and arduous female jobs which, by narrowing the scope of alternative employment, has up to now ensured the steady flow of women into high-intensity branches of industry.

This is not to say that certain characteristics of this general portrait did not change in the years after Khrushchev. The slow, but steady expansion of the service sector opened up new jobs for women, both in clerical work and the trading network. Both are low-paid, but their conditions of work are in most cases preferable to work in the factories. Where this is not necessarily the case, for example, in retail trade, the better access to supplies, especially food, made these jobs nonetheless attractive. Moreover, as we shall discuss below, there is evidence to suggest that as the sphere of non-factory employment grew, industries like textiles found it increasingly difficult to recruit new workers from the traditional urban population, and began more and more to rely on migrants from small towns and rural areas. In the case of light industry these new entrants were also women; in heavy industry the migrants, the so-called *limitchiki* discussed in chapter 1, have been of both sexes. Despite these changes in the structure of female employment, the essence of women's role within production has remained unaltered, as illustrated by the following contemporary description of a brigade of women in the distributor casing shop of the Ul'yanovsk motor vehicle factory:

> In general women are very profitable labour power, as we can easily illustrate from the example of this brigade. They do not squander work time on smoke breaks, since they do not smoke. Their dinner break lasts only 15 minutes, since they eat right there in the shop, in a little enclosure, where they spread out on the table food they have brought from home. Granted, saving work time in this way, at the expense of their own stomachs, is not explained by any principled dislike of public eating, but simply by the fact that the shop canteen is closed for repair, to which there is no end in sight.
>
> And yet another plus. The women do not drink. Everything they earn they take home to the family. And in order to earn more they come to work early and stay behind afterwards, as well as cutting back on the legal dinner break.
>
> And how unpretentious and patient they are! Surrounded by noise, din, and dirt, worn out equipment, a mass of manual labour, drunkenness and lack of discipline on the part of tool-setters, rates which are cut from year to year...Who would even begin to put up with such working conditions, where there is not even any ventilation over the machinery, and, instead of ventilation, glass has been knocked out of the roof? No, not every male would endure this. But they do. How long, as they say? And who will replace these hard-working women, who uncomplainingly adapt to 'temporary difficulties', when they give up work and take a well-deserved (and really well-earned) rest? Even now the shop has a severe shortage of working hands. Things have got to the point where they have sent several engineers and technicians to lend a hand, and even Vietnamese – of whom there are about three thousand at the factory – are helping out.[77]

The original reforms of perestroika did not address these or any of the other main problems confronting women workers. On the contrary, it was part of the reforms' initial strategy to impose a rationalization of production largely at the expense of female unemployment, while at the same time neglecting working conditions within precisely those branches of industry – light industry and the food industry – whose improved performance was essential to the discipline-for-consumption bargain which Gorbachev sought to strike with the working class as a whole. Thus even at the outset, the failure to confront the problems of women in production was a source of internal contradiction within the reforms. As events unfolded this neglect, and women's reaction to what in many cases was their deteriorating position at the workplace, became a factor accelerating the reforms' collapse.

Women were especially vulnerable to the imposition of so-called market mechanisms on the Soviet economy through *khozraschet* (profit-and-loss accounting) and enterprise self-financing, and many of those concerned with women's issues were quick to predict that women would be the first to be made redundant if mass unemployment became a reality. There is some evidence that this did occur in the early days of the reforms, but on the whole when women faced layoffs they were temporary and due to the totally unanticipated – and unwanted – impact of the supplies crisis, rather than to workplace rationalization. Permanent, widespread female unemployment failed to materialize. When unemployment did begin to set in in late 1991, it was confined almost exclusively to women engineers and technical specialists, a group among which the market reformers had neither expected nor desired job losses.[78] The non-appearance of unemployment stemmed partly from the fact that women were already leaving production in response to a combination of bad working conditions, low pay, high inflation, and food shortages. Together these reduced the value of their wage packets relative to the effort involved in earning them, while putting a premium on the acquisition of more free time for queuing and shopping.

For those women who remained in production the reforms led to a downward spiral. The exodus of women put added strain on those left behind, who had to meet production targets in working conditions which were steadily deteriorating due to lack of funds for new investment and the worsening supply crisis. Thus the pressures to leave production became intensified. At the same time, the general collapse of the economy exacerbated women's domestic burden, so that the time spent on housework has actually risen since 1980, mostly because of difficulties finding food.

Finally, the specific conditions which made women vulnerable to unemployment, although they did not lead to this result under perestroika itself, almost certainly will do so during the final stages of the transition to the market.

The marginalization of women in employment

The basic morphology of female labour in both home and factory has not changed since the 1960s. According to one economist, in the late 1980s the population of the USSR was expending 275 billion person-hours each year on domestic labour, as opposed to 240–50 billion person-hours in social production. Already in the mid-1980s, annual losses of time from queuing exceeded the total number of hours put in by industrial workers.[79] While the average amount of domestic labour fell by about a third between 1963 and 1987, the fall was proportionately equal for both men and women, leaving women still doing nearly three times more housework than their male partners (approximately twenty-seven hours per week versus ten hours for men).[80] Moreover, virtually all of this reduction was achieved during the 1970s,[81] so that between 1979 and 1987 women enjoyed no diminution of their domestic burden. In fact, a study carried out in March 1990 indicated that the amount of women's domestic labour, in particular the acquisition and preparation of food, was once again rising,[82] even before the calamitous food shortages of winter 1991–2.

However, it is not the scarcity of food alone which accounts for the heavy work load in the home. The poor availability and even poorer quality of domestic appliances means that housework requires an even larger amount of time than would otherwise be the case. Thus as recently as 1989 only 72 per cent of households had a washing machine and only 46 per cent had a vacuum cleaner.[83] In Minsk the wait for a new, locally-built 'Minsk' refrigerator is ten years.[84] Even this fails to take into account the primitive design of appliances: over half of all *new* Soviet washing machines still require hand ringing, and only 4 per cent are fully automatic; most refrigerators are small, and have only one compartment. But the strain does not stop there. Their quality is such that even new machines involve a huge investment of time and effort coping with frequent repairs.[85] Nor is this lack of appliances compensated by adequate public services. Public laundries, because of their deficient number, run-down equipment, and appalling working conditions, can meet only a fraction of demand, and the quality of their service is poor. Self-service laundries remain a rarity: for Moscow's 9 million inhabitants there were in 1990 a grand total of 65 self-service laundries, a full third of which were dilapidated and falling apart.[86]

There is, of course, a more basic point, namely that given the large amount of domestic labour the sexual division of labour within the home is strikingly unequal, leaving women in a subordinate position which is reproduced in the workplace. Like capitalism, the Soviet economy shows a sharp division between 'female' and 'male' sectors. Thus in 1985 women were 46 per cent of industrial workers but 87 per cent of employees in credit and insurance, 82 per cent in trade, 81 per cent in health and physical education, and 75 per cent in education.

Table 5.3. *Women as a percentage of industrial workers by major industry, 1985*

All industry	46
Cement	36
Engineering and metalworking	42
Cellulose and paper	46
Food industry (including baking and confectionary)	56
Leather, hides, and footwear	69
Textiles	70
Baking	71
Confectionary	72
Garment industry	89

Source: Trud v SSSR (1988), p. 106.

While their share in industry is quite large compared to most capitalist countries, within industry there is a very clear division by gender (table 5.3). Women also make up over half of workers in the chemical industry and nearly three-fourths of those in printing and publishing.[87] In construction they are 78 per cent of house painters and 69 per cent of plasterers.[88]

As we discuss below, the industries with the highest concentration of women workers are precisely those with the lowest wages. Irrespective of the industry in which women work, however, in each case they make up a disproportionate share of workers doing low-skilled, manual operations. Women are three-quarters of unskilled workers in industry and some 58 per cent of those doing manual labour, both far in excess of their share of industrial workers as a whole.[89] Forty-four per cent of women did manual labour in 1985, as opposed to only 27 per cent of men.[90] At the other extreme there are few women in skilled manual trades, such as tool-setters, maintenance mechanics, and electricians. Although detailed statistical evidence of this trend is available only for the 1960s,[91] anecdotal evidence suggests that the situation has not changed. We know from interviews with workers and other factory personnel that such large-scale enterprises as the Arsenal engineering works and the Krasnyi treugol'nik rubber goods factory in Leningrad, and the Lytkarino optical glass and AZLK car factories in Moscow, have virtually no women tool-setters, even where, as in the case of Krasnyi treugol'nik and Lytkarino, women make up between 60–70 per cent of the workforce.[92] Thus when factory newspapers mention women in skilled manual trades these are almost certainly still exceptions.[93] Moreover, it has long been the case that when low-skilled, arduous manual jobs are mechanized women are frequently taken off these jobs and replaced by men.[94] Where women are kept on newly mechanized jobs it is no guarantee that working conditions actually improve: in one survey a third of women whose jobs had been mechanized claimed that, although the work became easier, they suffered increased monotony while the work became no healthier; on balance they considered that they were actually worse off than they had been before.[95]

Women equally suffer from wage discrimination. Women industrial workers on average earn about 70 per cent of what men do, a picture which has not changed since the 1960s, and which differs little from women's relative position in the West.[96] The low wages of women workers are a major cause of hardship. A trade union survey from the early perestroika period claimed that for 37 per cent of married women workers their wages were the main source of family income. In addition, there were throughout the USSR a further 10 million single-parent families where the woman was the sole wage earner.[97] A number of factors explain this situation. First, a large proportion of women are in low-wage 'feminized' industries, such as light industry or textiles, which have long suffered from the Stalinist policy of favouring heavy industry at the expense of the consumer goods sector. Secondly, women, as we have seen, make up a disproportionate share of low-skilled manual workers. Many of them are migrant workers from small towns or rural areas (limitchitsy) who are able to find work in the large cities by taking the heavy or hazardous jobs which local residents will not do.[98] Thirdly, even in industries and trades where women work alongside men they are marginalized into the lowest wage and skill grades (razryady), and have few prospects for advancement.

The most glaring discrepancy is that between industries, as shown by table 5.4, which presents average wages in major industries in 1987. Wages in light industry (which excludes textiles) were 21 per cent below the all-industry average and 25 per cent lower than those in heavy industry. Those branches of heavy industry, such as chemicals and electrical engineering, where women are a majority or a near-majority of the workforce, also paid below-average wages.

This discrimination against light industry (taken in its broad sense) dates back to the beginnings of Stalinist industrialization, when consumption was deliberately squeezed, at times down to starvation

Table 5.4. *Average wage in rubles of workers in selected industries, 1987*

All industry	219.2
Heavy industry	230.0
Fish	349.9
Coal mining	346.2
Gas	318.8
Oil extraction	313.5
Non-ferrous metallurgy	308.4
Timber	250.7
Iron and steel	244.5
Machine-tool manufacture	229.7
Tractors and agricultural equipment	228.9
Cellulose and paper	228.6
Engineering	226.7
Automobiles	226.0
Building materials	221.3
Instrument making	218.9
Woodworking	215.9
Petrochemicals	211.8
Chemicals	210.4
Electrical engineering	210.3
Oil refining	204.7
Leather, hides, and footwear	189.9
Meat and dairy	187.4
Textiles	182.5
Food and gustatory	179.6
Light industry	172.2
Garments	155.3

Source: Trud v SSSR (Moscow, 1988), pp. 189–95.

levels, in order to finance investment in heavy industry. This policy has continued in less brutal form up to the present: prices on consumer goods are high, while wages in light industry are extremely low. Thus a seamstress in 1990 received 2 rubles for making a man's suit which in 1989, that is, before the ensuing year's high inflation, sold for 135 rubles.[99] Planned profits in light industry were thus high, but the vast proportion (some 80–90 per cent) was syphoned off into the state treasury, leaving factories with little money to pay bonuses or provide amenities out of their so-called material incentives funds.[100] With the shift to *khozraschet* and self-financing, the financial crisis of most enterprises in this sector became even more critical, as they now had to finance their own investment and wages, but were deprived of the necessary resources – a situation with which they eventually coped by cutting back on the production of cheaper items and sharply raising prices.[101]

Even before the crisis of self-financing a skilled weaver near the top of her scale was earning less than a semi-skilled foundryhand in heavy industry.[102] This same pattern was observed within individual industries, as indicated by the considerable gap between the average wage and skill grades of men and women workers. Within Soviet industry's six-grade scale, women in the late 1980s lagged from 0.5 to 1.9 grades behind men.[103] Some of the worst disparities were in industries where women predominate, a reflection of the fact that such highly skilled jobs as mechanics and maintenance fitters are reserved for men. Thus in the cellulose and paper industry the average *razryad* was 2.75 for women and 4.10 for men. In building materials the equivalent figures were 3.17 and 4.05; in light industry, 3.0 and 4.17; in the food industry 3.0 and 3.89. In cellulose and paper over 40 per cent of women were in the first and second skill grades; in light industry and the food industry about a third; in building materials one quarter. Yet in each of these industries the share of men in these bottom grades ranged from 10 to 16 per cent.[104] The same pattern is observed in engineering, where 70 per cent of women workers (who make up over 40 per cent of the workforce) are in grades 1–3, and only 1.3 per cent in the top grade, grade 6.[105] Often such discrimination exists in shops where men and women work alongside each other and do the exact same work. A graphic illustration is the Stupino iron and steel combine, where in one of its forge shops men and women work on the same job sheet, but the men are all in skill grade six and work with the best equipment, while the women are all in grade three and work with outmoded drop hammers.[106] Of course, low wages are enforced not simply through regrading. In early 1991 piece rates in the fastenings shop of the Sverdlovsk turbo-motor factory were so low that the most skilled women machinists could earn no more than 220 rubles a month; there were other women in the shop who made barely half that much.[107]

This marginalization of women into low-skilled and/or low-waged work is bound up with a number of often mutually reinforcing factors: expectations of women and employers, education, access to vocational training, family circumstances, and opportunities to enhance skills once on the job. In the past low wages were attributed to lack of skills, in turn put down to the relatively low educational level of many women.[108] Certainly by the 1970s such a proposition could no longer be taken seriously, as the extension of general education made completion of secondary school the norm for young men and women alike. In fact, average education levels of women workers have for some time been slightly higher than those of men. Yet men occupy the most prestigious jobs. Even in professions where women predominate, such as medicine or teaching, top posts of responsibility belong to men.[109] This same dichotomy is reflected among industrial workers. Although to some extent the concentration of women into low-skilled work still reflects the fact that many are older women with less education and vocational training who have not yet retired, these same patterns are discernible among women in younger age groups who are entering the workforce with equivalent qualifications to young males. Thus a survey of young women workers in Taganrog in the late 1970s found that 42 per cent of women aged 24 or younger were in the lowest two wage and skill grades [razryady], versus just 14 per cent of young men.[110]

Far more important than basic education are the traditional patterns of expectations and women's limited access to vocational training. The Taganrog study, for example, found that once leaving school nearly two-thirds of young women obtained their training through brief on-the-job programmes, and only one-third through extended courses of vocational study. For young men the ratio was virtually fifty-fifty.[111] In fact, the imbalance is even greater than these figures suggest, since a large proportion of young women attend vocational training schools (PTU) attached to 'feminized' industries, primarily textiles. These inequalities become even greater after women begin work, and especially after they have children. Between 1986 and 1990 a mere 17 per cent of women workers in the Soviet Union took courses to raise their qualifications, or just over 3 per cent a year.[112] In part this is due to the unequal division of labour within the home, which allows women little time for outside activities. But it is also due to women's keen appreciation that such efforts are an almost total waste of time. A 1990 survey of working women found that, of those who had improved their qualifications, 65 per cent considered it had brought no change in their work situation. Even more staggering, 90 per cent reported that improving their skills led to neither promotion nor a rise in skill grade, and 81 per cent said it brought no rise in wages.[113]

It should come as no surprise, therefore, that for the vast majority of Soviet women the primary motive for going out to work is instrumental: to augment the family income. Although women tend to derive considerable satisfaction from the social contacts they find at work and have consistently proved reluctant to leave the labour force, they obtain little intrinsic fulfilment from the content of the work itself.[114]

Working conditions of women workers

As noted at the beginning of this discussion, an analysis of the working conditions of women workers must differentiate between two sets of factors. First, there are the conditions confronting the millions of women in industry who carry out heavy manual labour and/or work in unsafe conditions. Officially women make up 44 per cent of all workers in this group in industry and 17 per cent in construction.[115] Second, there is the issue of the intensity of labour, characteristic of the textile and garment industries, as well as assembly line work or press operators in engineering.

By official estimates, of the roughly 14.5 million women industrial workers in the Soviet Union in the late 1980s, 3.4 million were deemed to be working in hazardous conditions, including over a million exposed to high levels of dust and toxic fumes; 1 million working in high or very cold temperatures; and 800,000 working with excessive noise or vibration. Approximately 3 million were doing heavy physical labour. In all, between 20 and 50 per cent of work places employing women did not meet the Soviet Union's already relatively lax safety standards, depending on the branch of industry.[116] Moreover, there is evidence that the situation deteriorated over the course of perestroika: in Sverdlovsk oblast between 1986 and 1990, the number of women workers on heavy jobs in metallurgy and electrical engineering doubled, and in light industry it tripled. Similar, but much more modest increases were reported in certain industries in Belarus'.[117]

Regulations imposed in 1982 and 1986 reduced the maximum load which women could lift to 10 kg for individual items, and 7 tons over the course of a shift.[118] Not surprisingly, they are routinely ignored. Women in the building materials industry will lift and transport 20 to 40 tons of bricks a shift. Women roadbed repairers on the railways must handle sleepers weighing 100–200 kg.[119] It is the same with exposure to toxic substances. Women surface workers in coal mining, as well as women in engineering, footwear, textiles, and other industries work with acids and caustic substances without adequate protection, suffering not just skin damage, but loss of teeth.[120] In foundries, chemical plants, paint shops, and other areas of factory work women are exposed to high levels of toxic fumes, made worse by the poor functioning of Soviet ventilation equipment.[121] Workers are also victims of managerial corruption. Women at the Lytkarino optical glass factory (Moscow oblast) have to clean lenses with ether because managers steal the alcohol intended for this job. In order to cover up the true cause of the substitution, the ether is officially deemed not harmful, and the women receive no extra pay.[122] Hazards equally arise from faulty equipment design. The incidence of accidents on textile machinery rose eleven-fold in the fifteen years prior to 1989. Textile workers in Kazakhstan refer to some of their spinning equipment as 'killer machines'.[123] Moreover, much of the equipment used by women is designed for use by the 'average' man, so that weavers have to stand on tip toes to reach bobbins, while women crane operators cannot see over the dashboard.[124]

Women also bear the brunt of night work. In 1988 there were 3.8 million women – approximately one in four women industrial workers – doing night shifts, despite the fact that by Soviet law night work for women is banned other than in 'extreme necessity' or as a temporary measure.[125] While it is doubtful that Soviet women work more night shifts than their Western counterparts, they nonetheless do two to three times more night work than men.[126] Although various industries were allegedly attempting to eradicate night shifts for women, one commentator noted that this was proceeding at such a pace that it would take 74 years in the coal industry, 144 years in iron and steel, 90 years in chemicals, and 322 years in petrochemicals.[127] The disadvantages of night work are clear. They disrupt family life and lead to greater fatigue, longer illnesses, and more accidents. Thus at the KamAZ motor vehicle factory women on night shifts have twice the accident rate of men, a fact the local trade union attributed to the extreme tiredness these women suffer as a result of the need to combine night work and domestic labour.[128] In textile towns, where women work sliding schedules involving nights and weekends, they seldom have days off in common with their families. As the manager of one Ivanovo textile mill commented, 'On Sunday father and children are at the theatre or going for a walk, while mother is at work, at the loom'.[129] At the same time excessive night work among textile workers has been blamed for an alleged rise in juvenile delinquency and even male alcoholism, a highly tendentious argument advanced by those wishing to push women out of the workforce and back into the home. However questionable, or even reactionary, these particular conclusions may be, one underlying point is valid: women doing regular night shifts have even less time to spend with their children than those working days, while losing virtually any possibility to find free time for study and upgrading their skills.[130]

It is the textile and garment industries, in fact, in which the problems of unsafe working conditions and a high intensity of labour are most visibly concentrated and systematically documented. The work is often monotonous, high-stress, and requires women to work a majority of the time in uncomfortable positions, subject to deafening noise and vibration, in temperatures often reaching 37–40 °C.[131] Probably no other Soviet industry has such a high intensity of labour: equipment utilization in textiles is from 50 to 80 per cent greater than in engineering; over 90 per cent of shift time is spent in productive work, far higher than male-dominated industries.[132] Improvements in equipment, rather than leading to an easing of work loads, have simply been matched by higher norms: if in the past a weaver might tend 8–10 looms, she will now tend 20 or 30, walking some 10 kilometres over the course of a shift.[133] The work requires intense concentration and agility. A winder on some types of winding machines will replace empty packets over 1,200 times a shift. The process takes 7.6 seconds and requires the worker to bend over some 1,500 times, spending almost half her shift in this position.[134] Quality controllers must inspect cloth passing by at a rate of 22 metres a minute,[135] work which is both stressful and probably of questionable value, given the difficulty of detecting flaws at such a speed. Weavers and spinners can spend as much as 75 per cent of their time repairing thread breaks, a job which demands speed and dexterity and which the women carry out in a bent position. The difficulties of this operation are made worse by the poor quality of raw materials – cotton or wool – which increases the amount of breakage.[136]

The impact of these conditions on workers' health is marked. The high noise and vibration levels, microbial contamination of raw materials, and the heightened strain of the work have left textile workers with a wide range of job-induced diseases: hearing damage, respiratory ailments, hypertonia, nervous disorders, heart disease, arthritis, varicose veins, anaemia, skin ulcers, and infertility and a high rate of birth abnormalities. Yet none of these are actually recognized as occupational diseases, entitling the women to compensations such as higher wages or early retirement, beyond the general provision that women with long years of service in the textile industry may take their pension at age 50, instead of 55.[137] The result is that Ivanovo oblast has one of the highest rates of sickness in Russia, with the average worker losing 10.4 days off work per year.[138]

The combination of bad working conditions, low wages, and the financial squeeze on the provision of amenities, in particular housing, has over the years led to a long-term exit of women from light industry. Cities such as Ivanovo, which for generations had seen the children of its weavers and spinners following their mothers into the mills, have come increasingly to rely on migrant workers from outlying areas and, more recently, temporary workers from Viet Nam. As the manager of one weaving factory in Ivanovo commented: 'What mother who has experienced all the "delights" of a weaving or spinning shop is going to send her own daughter there?'[139] According to an official of the Light Industry and Textile Workers' Union, 160,000 workers had fled light industry during the five years 1986–90, this coming on top of a long-term decline beginning in the late 1970s.[140] It has long been the case that few women stay in production trades in textiles past the ages of 40 or 45.[141]

The toll which unsafe conditions take on women workers extends far beyond light industry, however. A 1990 survey indicated that fully a quarter of female urban residents over the age of 40 suffered from some form of work-related illness.[142] The life expectancy of Soviet women, as it is for Soviet men, is far below that of other industrialized countries. Soviet women live on average 67 years, as opposed to 77 years for women in the United States and 79 years in Japan. The maternal death rate is twenty-seven times higher than in Denmark and ten times higher than in the United States.[143] The birth rate is similarly affected. Women in the rubber, chemical, paint and dye, plastics, and synthetic fibre industries are 50 to 100 per cent more likely than the average Soviet woman to suffer complications with childbirth, still births, and other gynaecological disorders. Among women in the non-ferrous metals industry the incidence of premature births is four times the Soviet average.[144] Women themselves are painfully aware of what they sacrifice by taking the types of jobs which Soviet society has had to offer. In the words of a woman electroplater at the Cheboksary instrument factory, 'Who is going to give us back the teeth that have fallen out, our damaged stomachs? Not to mention the fact that many of us have lost the most precious thing for any women – the ability to become a mother'.[145] Yet, like men, they are equally aware that they have become victims of a system which virtually compels them to accept these conditions. Perhaps more than men, they are dependent on the extra pay and privileges to which night shifts and work in heavy or unsafe conditions entitle them. If they took other jobs they would be lucky to earn half of what they receive now. Thus the trimmers in the foundries of Moscow's ZiL truck and limousine plant are all women: as of early 1991, that is, before the April 1991 price rises, they could earn 300–350 rubles a month and retire at the age of 45. Men simply refuse to do this work, because they find it too difficult.[146] Women, therefore, have steadfastly resisted attempts to induce them to take other, cleaner jobs, or to accept improvements in working conditions or limitations on night work for fear of losing their higher wages or their place in the housing queue.[147] Thus women have become the prime victims of the vicious calculus we described above: even if paid their danger money their labour power is cheap. And so for factory managers and industrial ministries alike it has been economically rational to substitute what seemed like a plentiful supply of female labour for mechanization and improvements. The contradictions into which this policy helped lead the Stalinist system of production we shall deal with at the end of this chapter.

The unfulfilled promise of female unemployment

Already in the Brezhnev period Soviet commentators were split in their policies towards women's employment and the family. Confronted with evidence of a falling birth rate in the European parts of the USSR, yet keenly aware of the economy's dependence on women workers, there emerged, according to the analysis of Gail Lapidus, three distinct schools of thought. One camp was occupied by the pro-natalists, who wanted women to leave the workforce and have more children. Another camp stuck to the traditionalist view that if Soviet society could provide more social amenities (such as public laundries and public catering) and household appliances, the burdens of domestic labour could be reduced without forcing any fundamental restructuring of family relationships. Finally, a third, minority position, was occupied by those who identified the problem precisely in the relations between men and women within the home, and called for men to take a more equal share of domestic burdens and women to be offered the options of part-time work.[148] These controversies were resuscitated under perestroika, as the more relaxed political climate allowed more open and forthright discussion of the 'women question'. The early policy of perestroika was clearly directed towards encouraging women back into the home. This reflected a convergence of three different political currents. First, certain conservatives sought to explain what they saw as the disintegration of the social order, in particular rising crime and juvenile delinquency and the Soviet

Union's high divorce rate, by an alleged decline in the role of the family. As late as mid-1988 *Pravda* could still defend the old Stalinist principle, 'the stronger the family, the stronger the state', and insist that the woman must return to the home.[149] Secondly, these concerns were buttressed by the pro-natalists, who saw a back-to-the-home policy as a way of raising the birth rate, at least among the Slavic population. Finally, with perestroika initially envisioning the rapid onset of mass unemployment, coaxing women out of the labour force was a way to make unemployment politically acceptable to men.

Such policies contained their own internal contradictions. Given the large proportion of women in jobs that men refuse to do, who would replace them if they gave up work? As for the birth rate, it is not just women's double burden which discourages families from having more children, but the housing shortage and the generally low standard of living.[150] Even if the Soviet Union had been able to solve these problems, this would not in and of itself have guaranteed that family plans would alter: the experience of pro-natalist policies in Nazi Germany shows clearly that women who took advantage of the lavish benefits offered if they gave up work for homemaking did not necessarily repay the government with more children.[151] Finally, there are the attitudes of women themselves, who, despite the conditions in which many of them work, have shown no willingness to surrender what little satisfaction they derive from their jobs in favour of the social isolation of the household.[152]

In April 1990 the Soviet government adopted a number of measures designed to encourage women to leave work. Maternity benefits were raised to the level of the minimum wage, and were to be paid for each child up to the age of 18 months, while women looking after children younger than 14 were given the right to request part-time work.[153] At the same time, however, the government felt compelled to respond to protests that women with young children were being unfairly dismissed when enterprises made redundancies. The old regulations, which made it illegal to dismiss or refuse to hire a woman on the grounds that she was pregnant or had a child under 18 months, were now extended to cover married women with children up to the age of 3 and single mothers with children under 14 (16 if the child was disabled). The only grounds for discharge became the liquidation of the entire enterprise itself.[154]

Various attitude surveys of women workers have found that, while large numbers of women might welcome the opportunity to work part time, very few have been eager to give up work altogether. Thus a trade union study carried out among women workers and engineers in the textile industry during the early years of perestroika claimed that among workers a quarter would stay at their present job, a third would want to work part-time, and 30 per cent would try to find a more attractive job.[155] A study of women workers at the KamAZ motor vehicle factory, where women are over half the workforce and some 40 per cent are employed on jobs which fail to meet elementary safety standards, only 3 per cent said they would give up their jobs if the opportunity arose, versus 20 per cent who wanted to stay at their current job, and 57 per cent who would work part time.[156] The fact is, however, that whatever their desires – and there is a significant minority of women who still find social satisfaction in their work – women simply must carry on working on a full-time basis. In reality there are few opportunities for part-time work in the Soviet economy: in the mid-1980s only 1 per cent of women had such jobs.[157] Yet even if such work had been more widely available few women could have afforded the intolerable fall in family income it would have imposed.[158] For despite the low average earnings of most women compared to men, this still far exceeded the paltry level of child benefits.[159]

Nevertheless, as I have already noted, there has been a discernible movement of women out of production. In the past the need for all family members to work has been partly neutralized by the poor provision of childcare facilities, which has caused a certain percentage of women to remain out of the workforce when they otherwise might have chosen to work. Although the childcare network was more extensive in the Soviet Union than in the West, it still was never able to meet demand. In 1989 the total number of places in pre-school establishments met only 64 per cent of actual need. In fact, demand is artificially depressed by the poor state of most institutions, which are overcrowded and often located in dilapidated premises.[160] These difficulties are compounded by the late school entry age, where children start school only at the age of seven. However, the economic collapse of perestroika added a new element to these long-standing, traditional problems. For some women, even though low skilled, work in the cooperative sector offered wages (if not conditions) which state industry could not match. Moreover, as inflation accelerated and food became increasingly hard and more time-consuming to find, the relatively low wages of at least a section of women workers proved less and less able to compensate for the harsh conditions in which they worked. This will have been especially true for married women whose husbands may have been able to wrest considerable wage rises from management through industrial action.

More important, the move out of production under perestroika was not accompanied by any large-scale attempts by enterprises to impose redundancies and shed women workers. As discussed in chapter 1, the long-anticipated advent of mass unemployment did not materialize. Where layoffs occurred they came as a result of supplies shortages, and not from rationalization or bankruptcies. As such they were episodic and not especially welcomed, and certainly had nothing to do with any modernization of production. On the contrary, the financial incentives for enterprises to continue relying on cheap female labour power remained, but the women themselves were becoming increasingly unavailable. The result was a squeeze on industry, causing labour shortages and bottlenecks among unskilled, as well as skilled workers.

The special position of women workers was to bequeath both perestroika and its new capitalist successor two intractable contradictions. First, there can be no hope of modernizing the economy without a radical restructuring of industry's technological backwardness, which implies first and foremost doing away with heavy unskilled work. This will remain a problem irrespective of the gender of those who do these jobs. However, so long as these workers are women, and so long as women face such multi-dimensional discrimination and exploitation within Soviet and post-Soviet society, the pressures not to modernize these jobs will remain overwhelming.

Secondly, as we have stated on a number of occasions, the entire strategy of *perestroika* was predicated upon the possibility of improving the standard of living. Yet the working and financial conditions under which enterprises in light industry operated constantly undermined this objective. In the main, these enterprises were badly hit by the introduction of *khozraschet* and self-financing, since they were now responsible for their own investment, wages, and incentive funds, but continued to see the major part of their revenues syphoned off into the state budget. Enterprises continued to work with old, outmoded equipment, suffered high turnover due to their poor working conditions, but could not afford to invest in modernization, especially in the face of rising costs for equipment. Some were even unable to maintain their kindergartens, while investments in new housing (many women live in old, dilapidated dormitories) were out of the question.[161] The result is that light industry has remained a low-wage sector where morale is poor and technical modernization slow. The impact this had on the fate of the economic reforms was aptly described by one commentator:

> The reform, which is based on strengthening incentives to workers, has barely penetrated that branch of industry which has to turn out goods for the materialization of these incentives. The government then has to take measures to limit wage rises, trim back incentives, and in essence, trim back the reforms in every industry.
>
> The logic of things states that it is precisely those enterprises which turn out goods for popular consumption which should be the leaders in the fundamental reconstruction of economic activity, which should prepare the basis for the others. What we now see on the shelves is a consequence of violating the order in which the reform should proceed, of not knowing how precisely to define priorities.[162]

Thus the role of female labour, which was vital to the elite's attempts to regulate the economy, came to pose a major obstacle to its plans for economic reform and recovery. It presented itself, in fact, as one of the central contradictions of perestroika. Historically the elite required the marginalization of women workers into the twin armies of high-intensity labour and low-skilled manual workers. Even in its new capitalist guise, it will continue to do so until it can break down the partial control over the labour process exercised by workers in the rest of industry, construction, and transport. Yet a precondition of achieving this latter, more fundamental objective is the transformation of the conditions of female labour – but this would then deprive the elite of an important regulatory mechanism through which it partially compensates for its lack of control elsewhere. It is a vicious circle whose potential resolution lies not in the elite and its policies, nor even in the development of a new Soviet capitalism, but in the workers themselves in the course of their developing class struggle.

6 The labour process under perestroika: 2 The failure of restructuring

Previous chapters have examined the different policies at the heart of perestroika which, we argued, were essential to the elite's attempts to restructure the labour process, but ultimately failed in this objective. Having then, in the last chapter, described the work environment in some detail, we now move on to explore the labour process itself. We begin with an investigation of the position of the worker within the labour process: the use of work time; labour discipline; the division of labour; and the forms and mechanisms of informal bargaining between workers and line management. We then examine the social form of the product which emerges from this process, that is, the deformed product and the phenomenon of waste. We analyse how perestroika modified this social form, intensifying its already high degree of internal contradiction, thus depriving production of any driving force and sending the economy into a phase of declining reproduction.

The organization and use of work time

Since the creation of the Stalinist system, the labour process in Soviet industry has been characterized by the high proportion of work time lost to production.[1] Such losses take a number of forms: the large amount of enforced idleness due to equipment stoppages or non-arrival of supplies; time wasted rectifying defects in production or repairing machinery; time during which workers must leave off production in order to hunt down or queue for parts and tools, or make them from scratch if they prove unavailable; time appropriated directly by workers to lessen the intensity of labour, for example, extensive smoke breaks, little excursions to chat with friends, or leaving early for dinner break or at the end of the shift. The seeming distinction in this list between losses caused by 'objective', as opposed to 'subjective' causes is artificial. As we shall see, what confronts one group of workers as an 'objective' cause of lost work time, is often the result of the 'subjective' behaviour of workers, managers, or technical specialists at an earlier stage of production or circulation. In addition to negligence by operators themselves, equipment stoppages may occur because of faulty design, construction, or repair. Supplies may not arrive because of lack of diligence on the part of workers or managers at supplying factories or in the distribution network. Workers may have to waste hours redesigning production processes because of errors in drawings or the improper specification of parts, materials, or equipment operating procedures. In short, the problem of lost work time is an expression of the underlying social relations of production on the shop floor, which compel and allow workers and managers alike to circumvent formal instructions or regulations in order to protect their individual positions. It is this that explains why enterprises can undertake extensive reconstruction of production processes, including the construction of new buildings and the introduction of new technology, without any fundamental alteration in working arrangements, systems of management, or relations between line management and workers.

The exact dimension of lost work time has always been difficult to quantify because enterprises routinely under-report stoppages.[2] In 1989 industry as a whole allegedly lost 38 per cent of 'calendar' time, that is, the time potentially available to production.[3] This is only an approximate measure of how the working day is used, since it includes, besides stoppages and other interruptions to the work routine, normal breaks in production, for instance, time spent mounting metal components on to a lathe for machining. It does, nevertheless, give some general indication of how much slack existed. Actual time-and-motion surveys of enterprises from this same period found losses of work time in the more narrow sense – that is, abnormal interruptions and stoppages – came to between 10–20 per cent, as opposed to the 0.5–0.6 per cent that factories officially reported. Thus the average worker lost between 1.5–2.5 hours out of each seven–hour shift, a figure almost unchanged since the 1960s. This is equivalent to an additional twenty-three to forty-six days idle per year without ever leaving the work place.[4] These figures will almost certainly have deteriorated further during 1990 and 1991, as the labour shortage and the supply crisis made themselves felt.

Much of the disruption within Soviet factories had little or nothing to do with the actual organization of production. At one Leningrad factory management efforts to 'improve' time-keeping forced workers to knock off work 20–30 minutes early in order to collect their passes from the timekeeper.[5] At Leningrad's Arsenal Association workers routinely left early for dinner because the queue was 30 minutes long and if they arrived at the assigned time there would be nothing left to eat.[6] The general economic crisis under perestroika also caused workers to take time off production to do essential shopping. Factories, keen to deter workers from quitting by providing scarce food-stuffs and consumer goods, tolerated the distribution of such goods during work time. A shop superintendent at the Voskresensk fertilizer factory (Minudobrenie) described the situation there as follows:

> Perhaps I cannot give you an exact figure, but right now at our work, for example, at least 10–15 per cent of work time is spent each month [on shopping]. We have barter deals through which we receive produce and various commodities. And the distribution between people takes place here, directly at the enterprise, not in the shops, and diverts 15 per cent of work time. That is, people aren't working, but running to get a slab of meat, a jacket, a television, or canned goods.

According to other factory personnel, the stress created by this system led to constant fights over who would get what goods, with the losers sometimes storming out of work. By the same token, the workers were usually paid for the time lost off work during such shopping runs.[7]

The main obstacle to smooth operation, however, was the near impossibility of coordinating the work of interdependent sections and shops. Assembly line production was especially vulnerable. Some lines were idle for hours, days, or even weeks at a time because of shortages of components, mostly from other sections of the same factory.[8] The problem was perhaps most acute in the car and tractor industries because of the large number of components which have to be assembled and the poor integration of the various stages in parts production.[9]

Thanks to the extensive coverage which its newspaper gave to the factory's perpetual production difficulties, the AZLK car plant in Moscow provides a rare insight into the complex morphology of lost work time. The factory was subject to constant stoppages and disruptions. Most significant is the fact that the causes changed almost every day. Thus there was no one problem area on which management could concentrate attention in order to make production and assembly run smoothly. During the first quarter of 1991, for example, the main conveyor lost the equivalent of ten full working days out of sixty-six because of the non-availability or late delivery of polymer products (steering wheels and other fittings made out of plastic), gear boxes, joists, and assemblies.[10] A time-and-motion study of the forge shop in April 1991 found that equipment was out of action on average 44–47 per cent of the time on the first shift, and 59 per cent on the second, because of the irregular supply of components, the need to wait for mechanics and electricians to repair equipment, a shortage of workers, and the absence of specific job assignments.[11] Nor was this a new situation. A portrait of the main conveyor carried out a year earlier, in May 1990, detailed the following chain reaction: on one particular day final car assembly was held up because there were no gear boxes; the gear boxes, in turn, were delayed because of a shortage of flanges; the flanges could not be made because there were no cams coming from the machine and tool shop, which claimed it was too inundated with work to meet all its orders. However, on another day the problem was different: the cars could not be assembled because there were no petrol tanks. The factory did not have the plastic out of which they were normally manufactured; it tried to switch production and stamp them out of metal, but there was no metal either.[12] On still another day the conveyor stood for 2 hours 40 minutes because there was no grease for priming the cars.[13] On several occasions during 1989 and 1990 the bottlenecks became so serious that in some shops whole shifts had to be sent home because they had no parts with which to work.[14] It is small wonder, then, that when a strike broke out at AZLK in early 1991 one of the demands was for an end to piece rates, so that earnings would not suffer from excessive stoppages.[15]

Some of these problems no doubt arose from the worsening supply situation, and indeed, the factory did have constant difficulties getting hold of metal, causing line managers to improvise and alter the size and specification of parts which now had to be made by other methods.[16] But most of the factory's problems appear to have been due to internal disorganization and the relations between workers and shop management and among the workers themselves which had developed on its basis. Some of these we discuss later in this chapter, in the section on informal bargaining, but others warrant mention here. No small role was played by lax discipline and negligence. The failure of machinists to clean equipment and production lines increased the frequency of breakdowns.[17] Workers on evening shifts left work well before the end of scheduled work time.[18] Shortages of parts, for example, gear boxes, were exacerbated by the fact that workers stole them.[19] In addition to poor discipline, the factory encountered numerous difficulties due to its reliance on foreign equipment. A number of its production lines were foreign-made, and AZLK simply could not afford or otherwise obtain spare parts for them.[20] Yet far more fundamental than all of these was the web of informal relationships that existed between workers within and between shops, which made production workers dependent on the good will and cooperation of manual workers, auxiliary personnel, and line management.

The section of AZLK which caused the greatest bottlenecks was Machine and Assembly Shop No. 2 (MSP-2), which assembled gear boxes and other key components for the Moskvich car. The shop, as already indicated, was itself the victim of shortages and holdups generated elsewhere in the factory, and its losses of work time were considerable. The morning shift officially started at 8 am, but it was not unusual for production in this shop to begin one to two hours later.[21] Coordination with other shops, usually mediated through despatchers and hence dependent on personal relations between them, was dreadful. In general these shops were in no hurry to respond to MSP-2's requests for urgent orders and often cavalierly misplaced parts earmarked for MSP-2 which only showed up after several days' searching.[22] This same network of personal relations existed within MSP-2, especially when it came to expediting repairs to equipment. The procedure was both highly bureaucratic and highly instructive of how certain groups of workers could exercise control over their labour process when other workers could not. When machinery broke down it had first to be assessed by the shop's 'energetics and machine department' (energomekhanicheskii otdel). This department would then inform the Shop Maintenance Department of what parts were required. The latter would then place an order with the Maintenance-Machine Shop, which would manufacture spare parts. The problem was that for many parts the machine shop would take on this work only unwillingly. This was especially the case with parts for the newer imported production lines, for which the factory administration had not yet set norms and for which, therefore, there were not yet agreed rates of payment. As a result, if work in the machine shop was slack, it would take on MSP-2's order; if this presented any difficulties (the machine shop was itself short of machine-tool operators), it would refuse.[23] The situation here was clear. The workers in the machine shop, who were relatively skilled and in a strong bargaining position, could effectively determine which jobs they would carry out and which ones would receive bottom priority. In short, they could exercise considerable control over their labour process. Upon the behaviour of this small group of people the success or failure of an entire day's production might depend.

The significance of repair and maintenance, and the rectification of defective production to which analytically it is closely related, extends far beyond the issue of informal bargaining, however. The poor quality of Soviet production constitutes one of the most important drains on the surplus product. Although we analyse this topic in more detail in a later section, two aspects of it are relevant here: the labour power expended rectifying defective output, and the time lost to production because of equipment breakdown and the excessive need for repair.

The labour lost due to defective production takes two forms. First, the defective parts or products must be detected and, at least in theory, taken out of production. This can be inordinately time-consuming, as workers have to rummage through whole batches of parts, weeding out the usable from the unusable components.[24] The production line for gear boxes at AZLK actually employed a special fitter who did nothing but remove faulty components from the conveyor and make good the defects.[25] Sometimes, however, the faults are only detected after the finished product has already been assembled. At Leningrad's Kirov works, whole batches of tractors had already gone through final assembly before it was discovered that the hydraulic systems were defective and had to be stripped out.[26] Second, the defects must be rectified, although in many cases, as with defective metal, this is not possible and the objects in question must be sent back through the production process. A women brigade leader at the Sverdlovsk rubber-technical goods factory described the routine in her shop:

> The customer has specified that the calendering process pass through cooling drums, but the drums have been so designed that it is impossible to work with them. Here's what happens: The roller operators turn the rubber into junk. They're penalized for it and the rubber is sent to the warehouse. But afterwards they send us this same rubber and demand good quality. From just one batch we lose god-knows how much time picking out rubbish, metal fragments, and other bits by hand.[27]

Such incidents are duplicated in every Soviet factory, irrespective of the type of production, as workers are constantly having to modify faulty parts and components received from other factories or make good the defects created by themselves or their workmates.

Repair and maintenance occupy a specific role within Soviet production. As noted in chapter 5, some 14 per cent of industrial workers are engaged directly in the repair of equipment. To these must be added the vast army of support services whose main or exclusive task is to facilitate repair operations, predominantly machine tool operators and auxiliary workers in machine shops. Soviet industry exhibited a long-term trend for the repair sector to grow relative to the rest of the industrial labour force,[28] a phenomenon which Soviet commentators in the days before perestroika used to attribute to the 'natural tendency' for machinery to oust manual labour in the course of 'the development of the productive forces'. The reality was somewhat different. The swollen repair apparatus arose essentially from the high rate of breakdown of Soviet equipment, itself the result of the interaction of a number of factors: (a) the poor construction of Soviet machinery; (b) the reluctance of managers to take equipment out of service for preventive maintenance, routine servicing, and minor repairs, thus storing up long stoppages and major repairs later on; (c) the abuse or negligent handling of equipment by workers; (d) the lack of spare parts, which compels each shop or section to keep its own machine shop; and (e) the poor work of the repair workers themselves, causing machinery to go back out of service soon after it has been fixed.[29] More recently, additional problems have arisen from the fact that many Soviet fitters and electricians lack the training to work on newer models of equipment, in particular those imported from abroad. According to a worker from the Stupino thermoplastics factory, new equipment there suffers longer stoppages than old machinery, despite the latter's intrinsic unreliability, simply because they do not have the personnel trained to fix it.[30]

The costs to production of frequent breakdowns and prolonged repairs need little elaboration. It is, however, worth looking at the conditions of labour of the repair workers themselves. Despite being highly skilled – at least, by Soviet standards – they are not particularly well-paid, and at AZLK, at least, this was acknowledged as a major cause of their half-hearted approach to their work.[31] In compensation, however, they have enjoyed considerable control over the organization and execution of their labour. This has involved not just the ability to dicker over which jobs they would do, as the example from AZLK shows, but jurisdictional disputes with other workers and line managers over who would do which jobs.[32] Much of this independence derived from the chronic absence of spare parts, which greatly increased the strain under which they worked, but at the same time enhanced their bargaining power. The shortage of spare parts was a constant fact of industrial life in the Soviet Union, as the planning system gave factories no incentive to provide spare parts for the equipment they produced.[33] Where foreign machines are concerned, Soviet enterprises, as we have seen, did not always have the hard currency available to purchase parts from abroad. The advanced age of Soviet equipment poses an additional problem, since in many cases the machinery, and the spares for it, are no longer produced. As a result individual shops and sections have had to set up their own machine shops in order to manufacture the missing parts themselves – something they can do only at great cost and extremely poor quality.[34] For the time lost is not just in making the part. This assumes that the wherewithal for this – drawings, metal, machine tools, and cutting tools – are already to hand. This is far from always the case, as a repair fitter at AZLK explained:

> We run through the whole factory looking for some sort of alloy. What's more, there are no drawings for the parts, we make the sketches ourselves and from them we manufacture what we need as quickly as possible. People understand the situation and pitch in: they stay behind after hours without any conditions, spending the night here. But why do we have to put right other people's mistakes and miscalculations?[35]

Not all repair workers showed such dedication, as the other press accounts show, but the conditions described here are in no way exceptional. The intrinsic wastefulness and inefficiency of the Soviet system generated a hypertrophied demand for repair and maintenance, which in and of itself represented severe losses to surplus extraction through idle equipment and idle workers. But this same system subjected the repair apparatus itself to the same conditions of labour, thus dragging out repairs and lowering their quality even further.

This brief analysis of the contours of the work regime suggests the perhaps unremarkable, but nevertheless important, conclusion that the policies of perestroika failed to alter the decades-old patterns of shop floor organization. Production continued to be characterized by excessive disruptions of the same type, magnitude, and etiology as in the past: poor discipline, shortages of supplies, weak coordination between factory sub-divisions, excessive defects in production, frequent breakdowns of equipment, and lengthy and poorly executed repairs. This environment produced, and was itself reproduced by, specific relations between workers and management, which we examine in the following two sections.

The deterioration of labour discipline

In the introduction to chapter 3 we described how, under perestroika, sociologists and labour specialists openly linked the Soviet Union's traditional problems with shop floor discipline to the atomization and alienation of the population. Labour discipline is an amorphous concept, especially as used in Soviet discussions, since it covers a wide range of phenomena: alcoholism, theft, absenteeism, insubordination, leaving work early, slack work, disregard for operating procedures or equipment, and even changing jobs. None of these are peculiar to the Soviet Union, but the social and political context in which they manifest themselves – namely, the atomization of the workforce and the absence, until recently, of any opportunity for workers to act collectively – makes it especially difficult to identify the motivations and causes behind them. How do we distinguish simple 'bloody-mindedness' from attempts by people to exercise some sort of control over their living and working environment in a situation where the choices of action were decidedly limited? Even in the 1930s, this fact was tacitly conceded by policy-makers and academics specializing in labour affairs, who at one and the same time branded labour turnover a 'discipline' violation, while claiming it to be a perfectly rational response to poor pay, housing, or working conditions. The same is true of negligence at work, which has been seen as both cause and effect of the constant disruptions and irrationalities with which people must cope.

Rhetoric about the need to tighten up 'production discipline' played a major role in the propaganda of perestroika, although the analysis was more sophisticated. The stress was now on poor motivation, and sociologists described how work had become an increasingly peripheral part of people's lives.[36] Moreover, it was now acknowledged that problems with discipline affected all workers, and were not just concentrated among the young and inexperienced, as had been claimed for generations.[37] With this the proposed solutions also became more subtle. Coercive measures (the campaign against alcoholism, the attempt to create mass unemployment, and the wage reform) were recast in the context of using 'market mechanisms' and limited worker participation to provide the missing 'stimulus to labour'. People would earn according to how well they worked; growing differentiation would provide the incentive for people to work better. This approach crashed upon the rocks of the labour shortage and economic disintegration. As workers once again became 'scarce', as the factories were beset by mounting problems just keeping production going, and as workers discovered the efficacy of localized protests, shop floor discipline remained lax, and in some areas clearly deteriorated.

The press reported an approximately 20 per cent rise in unauthorized absenteeism in industry and construction between 1986 and 1990, and a more than 100 per cent jump in absences sanctioned by management, although the figures cited suggested the incidence was still relatively low: far less than half a day off per worker.[38] Given the extent to which foremen routinely cover up violations these are probably a vast underestimate, but the deterioration to which they point is quite striking. Far more important has been the behaviour of workers while on the job. Work time, as we have already seen, was if anything used more poorly under perestroika, both because of stoppages and disruptions, and because of workers' ability to take advantage of the general disorder to appropriate more free time for themselves. Indifference towards the work routine has cost factories vast fortunes in equipment damage, spoilage, and defective output. One technical specialist detailed to us how workers in steel production routinely cut out certain stages in the smelting process, leading to lower-quality steel which would still pass quality control.[39] At AZLK a batch of gear boxes could not be assembled because a tool-setter had been careless when setting the production line and the holes for the bolts were too small. On another occasion parts were allowed to rust because the machines which clean them went for months without anyone filling them with the proper cleaning solution. In still another case, newly assembled cars were damaged because no one had filled the appropriate tanks with grease for lubricating them as they came off the production line.[40] Equally great is the amount of wastage and harm caused by auxiliary workers during loading and transport operations. To a large extent this stems from management's own indifference towards constructing proper storage facilities, forcing workers to leave raw materials and equipment out in the open air or under leaky roofs, where they spill or rust.[41] But these problems are clearly compounded by the indifference of auxiliary workers themselves. Sacks are thrown around so that they split; materials are spilt or left outside in wet weather. The result is extensive spoilage, which either compromises the quality of finished output or makes production impossible from the very outset.[42]

The attitude of these auxiliary workers is understandable if we consider how little they earn and the conditions under which they work. As late as mid-1991, some drivers who fetch and haul parts from one part of an enterprise to another were earning as little as 100–150 rubles a month. Many could not have survived had they not been able to supplement their incomes by stealing from the factory.[43] In fact theft, which is uncategorically characterized in the press as one of the gravest violations of labour discipline, is an integral part of factory life and involves an intricate network of social relations. The scale of thieving is enormous. One shop at the Khar'kov tractor parts factory had 3,300 generators stolen during 1990.[44] A shop at the Lenin works in Leningrad had 300–400 units of finished output stolen every month.[45] The factory paper at Arsenal complained that if certain equipment was not properly stored it would be stripped down to the last screw.[46]

Workers steal partly because they see it as part of factory culture, as their way of redressing their lack of power with regard to management. As one worker explained:

> The majority of people steal. We call it the 'socialist disease', when if you leave the factory and don't take something with you, then you think the day's been wasted, it's gone by in vain. You've got to take at least some little nut out with you, then you can feel you haven't worked the whole day at the factory for nothing.

But stealing also has an instrumental side to it. It is a means of supplementing not just money wages, but of expediting exchanges for scarce goods or essential favours.

> It is simply a fact of life that the relatives and friends of people who work at the factory are constantly asking them for parts because they're not for sale in the shops. And life is such here that everybody has to help one another not just in the factory, but outside as well. I'll get you some part and you'll help me buy meat at the store, or someone will help you get your kid into a kindergarten. And so when friends and relatives ask us to nick a piece of iron or something, we steal it. We go up to one another and ask if such and such a piece of iron is available, and often we'll help each other out without any mercenary motives, although there are people who'll only do it for money.

Such practices are carried on openly and involve considerable solidarity among the workers. In the locker rooms, right in front of their workmates, workers hide things in their jackets or trousers and walk out of the factory with them. At the factory where this person worked, it was almost unheard of for a worker to turn in another worker for theft. More than that, those, such as drivers, who are in a position to help other workers smuggle things out, would usually do so without asking any reward. But the workers are protected by more than their solidarity. As our informant pointed out, management could catch the regular offenders and put them in jail, but then whom could they get to take their place?[47]

While stressing the importance of the sub-culture of theft, it would be wrong to romanticize it. This same worker stressed the general demoralization of the workers at this factory and their lack of interest in politics. We merely wish to point out the 'rational kernel' of the sub-culture around theft which, like many other 'violations' of labour discipline, is rooted in the particular organization of factory life. Moreover it highlights the conditional sense in which we must use the concept of atomization. Such forms of non-cooperation as theft, infringements of timekeeping regulations, and output restriction (discussed below), while essentially individualistic responses by people for whom collective action and collective organizations had been excluded, nevertheless involved no small amount of solidarity and collusion from fellow workers. But such solidarity had definite limits. It was in large part passive, and, at least prior to perestroika, operated within tight boundaries, what we might call the collective defence of the individual. The collective pursuit of collective goals remained an impossibility. With perestroika this situation changed. Collective action became possible, but the soil which had produced the tendency for workers to act primarily as individuals remained, and was even reinforced by workers' new-found political freedom, in particular their ability to increase their wages through strike action without having to offer management the *quid pro quo* of either higher productivity or better discipline.[48]

There seems no doubt, for example, that alcoholism and drinking on the job have indeed become worse. These, of course, have long been serious problems at the Soviet workplace, and most factories have 'drying-out' stations where they send workers who show up too drunk to work. According to one specialist at Leningrad's Krasnyi treugol'nik rubber goods factory:

> Perestroika has had absolutely no impact on labour discipline, on alcoholism. We can even point to the following phenomenon. Preparatory production is very heavy work. We make rubber out of chemical ingredients, gas and dust levels are high, and the worker constantly works without a respirator. Such jobs are not very attractive, and so we get people who, let us say, other enterprises won't take on,

people fired for alcoholism, for absenteeism, people just released from prison. And here they suddenly raised these people's wages. It was a preemptive measure, that is, they wanted to see if these people would start to work better. Because our administrators, unfortunately, had in their head a model of economic man: I'll offer better pay and he'll work better. But the effect was just the reverse. People just got drunk. For whole shifts they drank, and even the foreman went drinking with them. Work was disrupted. And our general director for the very first time came up against the human factor...It turned out that they just didn't need the money, as soon as they had some spare cash they immediately drank it all up.[49]

To some extent this situation is perpetuated by foremen, some of whom have close social ties with their workers and regularly go out drinking with them.[50] But there are more functional reasons as well, to do with the complex fabric of mutual dependence between workers and line management. These we discuss in the next section.

Informal bargaining

In all industrial societies that have existed up to now, both capitalist and Stalinist, the formal system of industrial relations is supported by a network of informal arrangements among workers, and between workers and line management, without which production could not be kept going, even in the most efficiently running factory. These involve tacit understandings over earnings, discipline, the organization of work, and effort, which set the limits within which management can apply the formal rules and workers can bend or circumvent them. These arrangements can be seen as a form of bargain, where management agrees to allow workers a certain leeway in exchange for workers' willingness to help out in times of difficulty. Obviously, the form and content of this bargaining vary considerably from factory to factory, and even from shop to shop. Where workers are badly organized and the nature of production or the state of the market make management's dependency on the cooperation of the workforce weak (as with women workers in the clothing industry), management is relatively free to adopt an authoritarian style and make few concessions. Where workers' organization is strong or management is highly dependent on workers' collaboration to meet orders, the informal agreements will be more highly developed and more transparent.[51]

Informal bargaining and its role in the ebb and flow of shop floor conflicts within capitalist industry have received a great deal of attention in the West, dating from the late nineteenth century, when Frederick Taylor began developing his ideas about so-called scientific management. Taylor based these on his own observations, as both a worker and a manager, of how workers fought to monopolize knowledge of production processes in order to restrict effort and output. It was the goal of scientific management to wrest this knowledge from the operatives and make it the exclusive province of management. This, in conjunction with a restructuring of production on functional lines, would, at least in theory, make it both impossible and unprofitable for workers to engage in output restriction.[52] The results of scientific management were mixed. The system did not succeed in eliminating output restriction, but it did lead to a long-term shift in the power relationships on the shop floor from labour to management, with devastating political consequences for workers and their shop floor organizations.[53] One other by-product of scientific management was the birth of industrial sociology, the aim of which was specifically to enhance managerial power. Largely as a response to this trend, there has developed over the past two decades a rich marxist, or at least 'pro-labour' literature on the subject, centring around the labour process debates initiated by the publication of Harry Braverman's pathbreaking work, *Labor and Monopoly Capital*.[54]

The nature of informal bargaining in Soviet industry shows important differences with capitalism, which reflect the specific origins and political economies of the two systems. David Montgomery, for example, describes how output restriction in the United States in the late nineteenth and early twentieth centuries was organized not just through workers' informal traditions, but through its codification in union rules.[55] Nothing could be further from the situation in the Soviet Union, where historically workers appropriated partial control over the labour process precisely as a response to their *inability* to mount a collective defence of their position at the workplace and within society at large. This control was subsequently sustained by two factors: the labour shortage and the absence of a market, which, by eliminating the threat of bankruptcy, did away with the incentive for enterprises not to hoard labour. Although bargaining on the shop floor focuses on issues similar to those in capitalist factories – namely, work organization and the protection of earnings – the dynamics of the process differ considerably. This derives from the fact that, given the high level of contradiction within the Soviet system and its inherent lack of stability, the mutual relations of dependency between line managers and workers have manifested themselves in more extreme fashion. At the general level, it has always been the case that neither managers nor workers could fulfil the formal requirements of the plan except by violating its specific conditions: concealing capacities, changing specifications of products, altering the product mix, allowing deterioration in quality, over-consuming resources, or hoarding labour power. At the concrete level, this has meant that managers could not meet their plans without gaining the tacit cooperation of significant sections of the workforce, whose occupations or position within the chain of production made it vital that they fulfil their assigned tasks within certain limits of efficiency and quality. This explains the repeated failure of all attempts to impose a centrally determined wages policy and to use this policy as a lever for controlling workers' behaviour within production: managers had to maintain the freedom to offer differential concessions to different groups of workers, depending on circumstances within the shop at any given time. The other pole of this relationship, however, is that workers had no political power, nor even the ability to develop their own collective organizations on the shop floor. They could neither strike nor organize collective protests to press their grievances. They were dependent on management both materially (for their money wage and for access to housing, scarce goods, and social benefits for themselves and their families) and politically. They could extract concessions from management, but only as individuals (or small groups of individuals), and so were dependent on personal connections and the arbitrariness of managerial decisions.[56]

This general description, though accurate in its broad outlines, must itself be nuanced. Some groups of workers are in a stronger position to extract concessions than others. As noted in chapter 5, women workers have far less bargaining power than male workers because of the technology which prevails within 'feminized' industries and the larger pattern of discrimination and exploitation of women in Soviet society. Even in defence industries, which have allegedly offered their workers the trade-off of stricter discipline in exchange for better privileges, there are important differentiations, depending on whether the defence plant concerned is open or closed, whether the workers are engaged directly in defence work or on civilian production, and the strictness with which quality controllers accept or reject what the workers have produced.[57]

The two issues at the centre of informal bargaining in Soviet factories – control over work organization and wages – find their most obvious link in the phenomenon of output restriction, where workers collectively reach informal agreement to retard productivity in order to stave off norm rises and cuts in piece rates. It was only during perestroika that this subject began to be discussed openly in the press and journals, although there is no reason to suspect that it was not a central part of wage bargaining throughout the Soviet period.[58] Despite the limited and admittedly unsophisticated nature of the surveys conducted, it is clear that piece workers routinely engage in the practice. According to one such study of machine tool operators in Gor'kii during 1986–7, over half said that they deliberately hold back productivity, and three-quarters admitted that their brigade could carry out the same volume of work with fewer people.[59] Other surveys reported similar results.[60] A number of factors contributed to this attitude. First, as already noted in the chapter on wages, the limited availability of consumer goods in the Soviet Union has meant that higher remuneration was a relatively weak incentive to better work. Kozlov's study found that brigades would stop work as soon as they had reached what they deemed a reasonable level of earnings. Second, workers saw little reason to exert themselves when, in their view, management did little to eliminate the myriad hitches and dislocations which plagued production and held back earnings.[61] Third, as in capitalist industry, workers restricted output in order to neutralize management attempts to use improvements in performance to raise norms and cut rates, and thereby claw back the bonuses workers had been encouraged to earn through norm overfulfilment.[62] This was part of both collective and individual consciousness. Workers in brigades studied by Kozlov found it profitable to have a few slow workers in the work team whose poor performance would act as a 'balance' by lowering average fulfilment for the brigade as a whole.[63]

The issue of control goes far beyond the regulation of earnings. It is embedded in the very nature of the work process itself. The most obvious division within the workforce is that between production and auxiliary workers. The former have traditionally enjoyed greater prestige and higher wages, but this is by no means a uniform process. Since the 1960s, the pay and 'prestige' of machine tool operators, one of the largest occupations and the key trade in engineering, have fared poorly compared to other trades, and factories have found it extremely difficult to recruit young people to the profession. Both in the 1960s and the present period, there has been a significant minority of skilled production workers who have been willing to give up their jobs for manual auxiliary work, even where the latter offered lower pay, so that they could exercise greater control over the intensity of labour.[64]

This also helps explain the traditional resistance of machine tool operators to working with machine tools with programmed controls. Although the latter provide a minority of operators with the chance to enhance their skills by learning how to programme, set, and repair the machines, for the bulk of operators they impoverish the job content, as there is little to do but mount the part to be machined, oversee the running of the machine, and take the finished part off again.[65]

There are also groups of workers, the nature of whose work gives them considerable scope to exercise independence and relative creativity. Tool-makers and pattern-makers regularly analyse their own jobs and make or invent their own tools or vital parts.[66] A minority of machine tool operators are also able to set their own machines, without being dependent on tool-setters.[67] Even workers whose work is not generally considered skilled have scope for developing and employing considerable expertise. Experienced loaders in meat packing accumulate over the years detailed knowledge of how to work most efficiently, which makes their cooperation essential to management when plan targets have to be met.[68]

By and large, however, work within Soviet industry has been subjected to an overly specialized division of labour, with workers performing repetitive, minute tasks. This system originated during the 1930s, when the regime was faced with the influx into industry of millions of ex-peasants. Operations were broken up into sub-tasks, often of just a few seconds' duration, ostensibly on the grounds that this would permit the extraction of maximum productivity from a workforce with little or no previous experience of industrial labour. Though this may have been part of the logic behind the strategy, it had a much more basic political motive. It was part of a much broader tendency to deprive workers of any and all input into decision-making on the job, lest this challenge the system of one-man management (*edinonachalie*), based on a rigidly authoritarian model of control. However efficacious this approach may have been for the elite in its formative years, by the 1960s it was clearly becoming a brake on productivity. It caused the loss of countless hours of work time, as machine-tool operators had to wait for tool-setters and tuners to make even the simplest adjustments. At a more basic level, it lay at the heart of the disenchantment and alienation which workers, especially younger and better-educated entrants to the labour force, felt as a result of the monotony of their jobs.[69] That this problem was still acute under perestroika is shown by an account of a machine shop at the ZiL truck and limousine plant in Moscow. Workers in the shop carried out a number of basic machining jobs, for example, polishing crankshaft journals (the part of the shaft which rests on the bearings) or machining cylinder sleeves. The work was monotonous and boring – a senior polisher could train a new worker to do the job in three days – and many of the young workers quit as soon as they had learned the trade. The shop was caught in a vicious circle. Because of the boredom it was becoming increasingly difficult to recruit machinists. The factory had to resort to what it called 'temporary contingents', that is, groups of totally unskilled workers. In order to use them productively and to maintain quality, the shop had to narrow job specifications even more, making the work even more unattractive and exacerbating recruitment problems still further.[70] According to the author of this article, ZiL was by no means unique in this regard. 'In many large-scale enterprises', she wrote, 'the process of splitting up technology into its most minute components is gradually proceeding, in planned fashion'. In short, the impoverishment of job content was likely to become worse, creating a corresponding drag on productivity.

In the view of one economist this polarization of production into a small stratum of highly skilled and a mass of semi-skilled was the real stumbling block to the democratization of the workplace, for it precluded the self-organization of workers directly in the process of production; instead, the worker became ever more closely bound to a rigid technological rhythm and was reduced to the position of a mere executor.[71] This hyper-specialization, linked as it was to the Soviet Union's slow pace of technical progress, also hampered attempts to introduce what in the West is known as flexible specialization, where workers have a broad profile of skills, allowing them to interchange jobs as required. But the authors of this view also noted social and political obstacles to this form of rationalization: large numbers of workers had their privileged pension rights tied to the particular trade in which they worked, thus making it difficult to eliminate the literally thousands of outmoded occupations in Soviet industry.[72]

In important respects the above picture is misleading. There were cases where groups of workers doing jobs of quite average skill were allowed to work out their own systems of job rotation, so as to equalize earnings and share out the burden of boring jobs more fairly.[73] Far more important, within the generally rigid division of labour and the impoverishment of job content, the conditions of Soviet production constantly forced workers to intervene in the production process merely to keep it going. This was most obvious in the case of skilled workers and foremen, who in many cases knew far more about the

production process than the technical specialists who planned and
designed their jobs. The experience of a woman foreman at the
machine-tool manufacturing association in Kuibyshev is illustrative in
this regard. Often, she said, the blueprints and drawings call for the
use of technology or materials to which her shop has no access. In this
case she has to sit down and work out how to do the job using
alternative materials and methods.[74] But such intervention was not
limited to workers in skilled trades. Virtually all production workers
were at some time or another called on to go beyond their formal job
profile in this fashion. According to one worker, this was inherent in
the piece rate system, which put pressure on workers actively to insert
themselves into the production process in order to cut losses of work
time and safeguard earnings. In his view, this was a double-edged
sword, since management took advantage of this situation to shift
some of its own responsibilities for organizing production on to the
workers.[75] A worker at another factory described how this operated:

> In the course of the month, you have to assemble the plan, say 1,000
> units. I assemble opera glasses. I could assemble the entire 1,000 in a
> week or so if I worked day and night, since I can do 40 in a shift. But
> that depends on how regularly I receive the parts. Besides, it happens
> that the parts are defective. It's hard to assemble the parts with them,
> but we do what we can. There is quality control, but it is all fiction.
> There is no control on incoming parts, only on finished output. For
> example, a controller in the machine shops spot checks the parts
> made there and sends them on. I might get 10 per cent defective
> parts, but since there can't be 10 per cent defective output, I have to
> assemble the units as best I can. I have to use my skills and ingenuity
> to put the binoculars together and have them passed.[76]

The point is that such interventions formed a vital part of informal
bargaining. In this particular factory, where the workers were mainly
women and not in a strong position, the only concession they received
was time off in lieu if they had to put in overtime, plus payment for the
extra hours. They were unable, for example, to win compensation for
stoppage time, in sharp contrast to workers at Leningrad's Lenin
engineering works, where management offered large top-up
payments as recompense for 'chronic stoppages'.[77] The specifics of the
bargain therefore varied from workplace to workplace, depending on
the power relations between workers and line management. Yet in
virtually all cases – even where workers were in a relatively strong
position – it took the form of an exchange of favours between individuals or small groups of individuals, rather than gains won through

collective struggles. The issues at the heart of the bargain might be overtime and storming, the agreement to help unblock bottlenecks or rectify faults in designs or construction, already described, or a willingness by key workers or foremen to expedite urgent orders. The concessions offered by management also depended on circumstances: managers might turn a blind eye to discipline violations, such as absenteeism, drunkenness, or theft; they might pass defective production; or, most commonly of all, they might simply pay workers for work they had not done (*pripiski*).

The complexity of the bargaining can be made clear by a few concrete cases. Metallurgical institutes in the Leningrad shipbuilding industry often had to have prototypes of different metals tested and put into production. Doing this through official channels – negotiating with the foreman of the steel works to have the steel smelted, rectifying any defects, waiting for a truck to cart it from the steel works to the machine shop where it would be machined, having prototypes made and then tested – could take literally months, but if favours were given to the relevant workers and foremen, the waiting time could be cut to two or three weeks. A metallurgical specialist described how he did this.

> I might go personally to the foreman, on the strength of the fact that I might have done him a prior favour or we had some common interest; or I might say to him that I would write an order for one ton of metal, that is, I needed one ton of metal smelted, but I would sign a form saying he'd done me two tons. Or, for example, before this, when he had given me defective metal I had always signed the form stating there were no defects and I had collected the metal – that is, I had done him a favour, allowing him to fulfil his plan.

Where he needed help from workers with whom he had not built up such good relationships, this specialist had to use more direct methods, including bribery with alcohol. This was standard procedure. Each month the laboratories of the shipbuilding industry's Scientific Research Institutes would incorporate substantial volumes of alcohol into their request for laboratory supplies, ostensibly for cleaning laboratory equipment. In reality the alcohol was kept in a safe and parcelled out to specialists who had to grease the palms of key workers in order to expedite urgent orders.[78]

The most common issue over which bargaining took place was overtime and storming. Workers knew they had to do the overtime, but management realized that they had to provide adequate compensation to keep discontent from spilling over into outright refusal to cooperate. We have already seen how the infamous Black Saturdays could erupt into open conflict. But there are occasions throughout the working day when management needs not an entire shift to put in extra time, but only one or a few workers, and this has to be negotiated. At AZLK, and presumably other factories, the system was quite complex. A foreman might approach a worker to do an extra shift, for which the worker will receive two job sheets, one for that worker's normal shift, and one for the overtime. For doing this the worker may demand payment for yet another shift which he or she has not in fact worked. Moreover, the foreman has to conceal the overtime, because it is technically illegal. Both needs can be met by taking advantage of the existence of substitute workers on the payroll of each section and whose task it is to cover for absent colleagues. The foreman waits for a day when someone has not shown up, and then writes up the job sheet as if the worker to whom he or she owes the favour for the overtime has filled in; in reality one of the substitutes has done it, but officially the substitute is listed as having been put on other duties, so that the payment goes to the worker to whom the foreman is indebted. By doing this two or three times the foreman can pay the worker back for the overtime and then make the extra payment the worker has demanded.[79]

As this same foreman pointed out, however, the bargain involves an equally intricate hierarchy, where each is beholden to his or her immediate superior. People thus have leverage over those in a weaker position than themselves, but are at the same time controlled by those higher up.

> A foreman has the right to pay a [good] worker one and a half times what he pays a bad worker, but no-one has explained to him how to do this. So, what does he do? Say you have two workers, and they turn out an equal number of cars. The foreman writes up that one worker did 100 cars that day, while the other did 150. In fact they turned out the same number of cars, but the one who did a hundred was drunk and the other was sober. Officially the foreman isn't supposed to let a worker into work drunk, he's supposed to bar him. But if you bar him there's no-one to do the work. And so the foreman, in order to punish the drunk, credits him with only 100 cars, and credits the sober one with 150. But he's broken the law, because he didn't bar the drunk, and they both did identical work. However, the shop superintendent turns a blind eye to all this. He says, 'I trust you, foreman – if you thought you had to write it up that way it must have been necessary'. But at the same time the foreman is guilty and is dependent on the shop super, because he's broken the rules. But the

> foreman can ask the worker to take on jobs that he's not obliged to
> do. For instance, if they've put a defective bolt on the conveyor,
> which it's difficult to turn. The worker has the right to refuse to work
> with this bolt, but now the foreman says, 'work with this bolt and I'll
> pay you more'. And so some drunk will quench his thirst.

The exercise of favours has given the foreman power over the
drunken worker and at the same time made him dependent on his
own immediate superior, who could fine him 100 rubles for not
sending this worker home, and will certainly come down hard on him
if the conveyor comes to a stop. Equally important, there are skilled
workers whose cooperation the foreman desperately needs, and to
their discipline infractions he has to take an altogether more defer-
ential attitude.

> The nature of our work is such that my workers are maintenance
> mechanics. There are no spare parts and I try to avoid conflicts with
> them, because there will be a time when something breaks and I have
> to ask them to show initiative, to run to the welder, to look for metal
> to do a repair, that is, to carry out those functions which the labour
> contract doesn't call on them to do.[80]

This same pattern of differential power relationships is observed even
in industries which rely largely on unskilled labour. Among loaders in
meat packing the more experienced workers are able to bargain for
various forms of monetary compensation if conditions do not allow
them to make their customary earnings, usually by threatening to
invoke routinely ignored safety regulations if management does not
cooperate. Younger and less experienced workers are simply not
well-enough organized to press such demands.[81] Even steps towards
marketization reinforced this trend. When shop managers set up
internal cooperatives, it was management who chose which workers
would receive the privilege of joining the cooperative and the higher
wages it offered. They selected those workers with whom they had
good personal relations, or who could be relied on for better discipline
and harder work. The cooperatives thus gave managers more power
over workers, through this system of individual rewards and penalties
– a fact which rank-and-file workers were quick to perceive, and to
resent.[82]

This analysis of informal bargaining raises an important question.
The limited interviews we have done, together with various press
reports and more substantial sociological studies from the Brezhnev
period, show that many workers perceive themselves to have an

essentially adversarial relationship with management, whom they accuse of speed up, wage cutting, unfair dismissal, and a readiness to victimize those who expose misdeeds or abuses of authority.[83] How can this be reconciled with the evidence of highly developed patterns of informal bargaining, through which substantial sections of the workforce are able to exercise a significant degree of control over their own labour process? There are a number of answers to this question. First, as we have noted, the bargaining power of different groups of workers is highly differentiated, depending on whether the workers are men or women, in heavy or light industry, skilled or unskilled, 'native' or migrants, production or auxiliary workers, or essential or peripheral to the production process. The examples we have cited show how within one and the same workplace some workers may be victimized while others are able to win adjustments to earnings or toleration of a lax work regime, depending on their standing in this hierarchy of mutual dependency.

Secondly, informal bargaining has very definite 'rules' and limits. Management may be forced to grant any number of concessions to workers, perhaps even to all the workers in a given shop or section, but these never go so far as to challenge management's ultimate authority. Informal bargaining, therefore, is not an equal relationship. Workers can partially attenuate managerial power and the efficacy of its decisions, but they cannot supplant that power or management's prerogative to make decisions. This means, of course, that within this constellation of power relations, management, too, finds its freedom of action constrained. It wants to have the clear and unchallenged right to dictate what happens on the shop floor, but the conditions of Soviet production are such that it cannot. Its own ability to achieve success depends on the cooperation of workers, which it can only win by granting certain concessions over earnings and the organization of production.

Thirdly, it is my view that management saw in perestroika the chance fundamentally to redress the balance of power on the shop floor through the promise of mass unemployment and the wage reform, and began acting in a more authoritarian direction, but this potential went largely unrealized because of the labour shortage and the internal chaos caused by *khozraschet*. On the contrary, political liberalization opened up new possibilities of shop floor action which tended to weaken managerial authority still further. The result was a political impasse. Management strove to impose a more rigid, top-down regime, and on issues concerning broader enterprise policy, for example, the issues of privatization or the powers that would be granted the STK, in many cases it did so. But where production itself was concerned, the elite and industrial management proved unable to impose their will on the working class. Workers, however, while blocking any fundamental restructuring of power relations on the shop floor, saw neither the need nor the means to assert their own preeminence either inside the factory or within society at large. This was not a situation of dual power: except for fleeting instances, the working class did not establish political, economic, or administrative structures paralleling official ones. Rather it was fast approaching a situation of nil-power, where even the repressive apparatus was becoming increasingly unable to function as the executor of the elite's policies. From the bottom to the top of society workers, either through organized protests or more commonly through spontaneous, inchoate, and often individual action, led elite policy into stasis. This was the fundamental and unresolvable contradiction of perestroika: the elite could no longer govern, but the working class could not fulfil the role of a universal class and take power in order to overcome the antagonisms within society.

The hybrid social form of the product under perestroika

The contradictions of a society are expressed in the social form of the product which emerges from the process of production. Under capitalism the product has the social form of the commodity, an object produced not for direct use by the producer, but for sale on the market – an act which can be completed only because the commodity embodies the social form of exchange value. The concrete properties of the product as a potential object of use – a use value – are secondary: they, too, can be realized only if the product can be sold and the exchange value embodied in it is transformed into money. These two properties of the product – as embodiment of both exchange value and use value – express the contradictory nature of capitalism as a mode of production. The aim of production is not the creation of useful things, but the creation of value. Society does not collectively determine which objects of use it requires and set about planning how to produce them; these decisions reside in the capitalist, who undertakes production only if what is produced can be sold, that is, realized as value. It is left to the spontaneous and crisis-ridden vicissitudes of the market whether these two needs – those of society and those of the capitalist – coexist in the same product, as witnessed by the bizarre, indeed obscene state of late-twentieth-century imperialism, where, despite the historically unprecedented development of technology since World War II, the mass of the world's population sinks deeper and deeper into starvation and destitution, amidst potential abundance. Thus the bulk of society stands in permanent contradiction with its capitalist mode of production: people labour and produce, yet their needs go unmet. For billions this means even the most basic needs of food and shelter, not to mention such 'luxuries' as education and health care. It was in recognition of this reality that Marx concluded that this contradiction could be abolished only by abolishing the capitalist mode of production itself. The acts of production and appropriation of the social product would have to be reunified, but not through the return to small-scale individual producers, but in the 'person' of society as a whole, which through its democratic self-government would collectively determine its needs and priorities and the methods by which it would meet them.

In marxist theory, the supersession of capitalism and of the category of exchange value would mean that the social form of the product becomes also its concrete form, use value, which expresses the abolition of the social contradiction between capitalists and proletariat. In the Soviet Union, because of the absence of the market and the production of exchange value, the social form of the product was also use value, but the form was distorted. Consumers acquired the product for its useful properties: the individual because she or he needed clothing or food; the factory because it needed steel, machinery, or raw materials in order to fulfil its plan. But because of the social contradictions within the process of production, what entered either productive or individual consumption was a deformed product, which could not be fully used as intended. Metal might be defective, possess the wrong physical properties, or be of the wrong size or type. Machinery would be badly assembled from defective components, so it, too, could not function as required.

The deformed product lies at the heart of the phenomenon of waste, that is, the tendency to consume means of production and labour power without a commensurate production of use values. The generation of waste is one of the primary forms in which the workforce limits the Soviet elite's ability to extract and dispose over the surplus product, since the size of the surplus is always below what is either planned for or possible. Thus in the mid-1980s the Soviet Union, according to its own official statistics, expended 1.5–2 times more energy and material resources per unit of national income than did developed capitalist countries. In order to produce a national income given by Soviet statisticians as 64 per cent of that of the United States (almost certainly an overestimate), the Soviet Union had to expend 1.8 times more fixed capital, 1.6 times more materials, 2.1 times more energy, and make twice as many shipments of freight.[84] In *Soviet Workers and De-Stalinization* we analysed in considerable detail the different forms of waste, their production, and their circulation through the system, and we intend only to summarize that discussion here, using illustrations from the perestroika period.[85]

A large part of the social product is simply lost in physical terms. In the mid-1980s every seventh cubic metre of natural gas was lost during transport and usage.[86] Between 7–10 million tons of coal each year were lost just falling off of coal trucks on the railways.[87] The USSR used to produce more cement than any country in the world, yet every fifth cement factory worked merely to replace what was lost in transport or blown away on building sites.[88] Physical losses occur also through the overconsumption of fuel, materials, and tools. Accounting of materials expenditures in factories is poor, making consumption difficult to monitor and supervise.[89] Materials, especially – but by no means exclusively – metal, come into shops the wrong shape and size, entailing huge wastage trimming them down to a usable size.[90] Moreover, the quality of Soviet metals and chemical products is a problem: designers have to compensate for their unreliability by increasing the weight of parts and components or doubling the number of circuits in electrical equipment to guard against possible failure,[91] a fact which helps explain why the metal content of Soviet products is so much higher than their Western counterparts.[92] Although high-grade steel is allegedly on a par with Western standards,[93] this is a relatively small proportion of Soviet output. On ordinary grades of steel officially set quality standards are extremely low, so that iron and steel works can produce metal which technically meets official requirements, but whose physical and mechanical properties are poor.[94] By way of illustration, in the late 1980s the USSR was turning out 17 million tons of pig iron castings per year, of which only 3 per cent were highly durable; this contrasts with the 6 million tons of these castings produced in the United States, of which a full half are of high durability.[95] At the same time, the Soviet Union is extremely backward in developing and using alternative, light-weight materials, such as clay or plastic. Roofs are covered in steel or zinc instead of tiles; the country still makes large quantities of zinc dishes, washbasins, buckets, and wash-tubs.[96] It produces plastics and polymers, but not in sufficient quantity. Perhaps more telling, their quality is also low, so that components and other articles made from them do not possess the appropriate characteristics to allow their widespread use in production.[97]

The other important manifestation of waste is defective production. A large part of the output of Soviet factories is simply unusable: it has to be scrapped, sent back through the production process, or put right by workers who are taken off general production in order to rectify faults. We have already described the huge losses this entails for production when discussing the use of work time. But outright defects, however great they may be, are not the most important manifestation of poor quality. The overwhelming proportion of products with defects are not scrapped, but continue to circulate through the economy. In the more severe cases, the products may be genuinely defective, but customer factories are so desperate for supplies that they will accept them anyway, even if they have to assign their own workers to making good the flaws. In other cases, the defects only show up during subsequent stages of production. Thus one Ukrainian construction trust discovered that the piles they had received from a supplier snapped 'like a match' as soon as they were driven into the ground.[98] More commonly, the products are still usable, but their physical characteristics are either not up to standard or of the wrong type for the production process being used. They enter as means of production into the manufacture of other products, whose quality is then also compromised. If these are consumer goods, their quality, too, will be bad,[99] and Soviet consumers will often refuse to buy them, even in the face of chronic shortages. If they are means of production, they will pass their deformations to subsequent products.[100] In this way defective production is constantly reproduced from one production cycle to the next.

Poor quality arises as a direct result of the conditions of production in Soviet factories. No small amount comes from workers' outright negligence and indifference, as workers – both production workers and quality controllers – consciously pass defective intermediate products to the next stage in production.[101] But much of it stems from the Soviet production cycle itself, in particular the mentality created by having to cope with chronic shortages. Machinery at Leningrad's Sevkabel' works suffered damage from water leaks because for two years the factory had been unable to acquire the materials needed to repair the roofs.[102] A new Italian assembly line at Moscow's AZLK was rendered unusable because the factory could not provide a supply of pure water for cooling filters. Its water was so contaminated that the filters became clogged and everything rusted.[103] More telling still were the defects in steering wheels and head-rests made out of resins. The factory was using resin which was too old and had started to season, but it was afraid to discard it for fear of shortages if future supplies did not arrive.[104]

In an attempt to combat the huge amount of defective production entering into circulation, the government in 1986 instituted a system of state certification of product quality at factory level, known as *gospriemka*. In 1990 it was wound up, having been a total failure. As one economist noted, 'putting up a barrier to defective production, it [*gospriemka*] could not change the established system of production.' State certifiers could catch poor quality goods and stop them from leaving the factory gates, but they simply piled up in storage, and factories wrote them off as part of production costs.[105] But there was another side to this story: *gospriemka* led to considerable shop floor conflicts over wage and bonus cuts, as managers tried to hold workers financially liable for rejected output, while workers resented being penalized for what in their eyes were managerial failings. Clearly the bitterness caused by the new system played no small part in its ultimate abandonment.[106]

A final manifestation of waste is the phenomenon of incomplete production. This occurs when the assembly of finished output cannot be completed because one or another essential component is missing, thus rendering the items virtually useless. Under the old planning system such production could help a factory register 90 or 99 per cent plan fulfilment, even though the utility of what it had made was zero. Garment factories, for example reported clothing that was '99.9 per cent' finished, but they could not despatch it because it lacked such trifles as elastic bands.[107] Expensive televisions could not be completed because of a shortage of resistors costing just a few kopeks.[108] New factory buildings could not be put into operation because they lacked equipment or even such basic, yet vital items as glazed windows.[109]

Like defective production, the effects of incompleteness (for which the Soviets even have a special term – *nekomplektnost'*, or incomplete batching) are far more pronounced within the production process. Indeed, incompleteness is endemic to the Stalinist planning system, with its emphasis on gross physical output at the expense of proper coordination of the different stages of production. This was graphically illustrated by the factory newspaper at AZLK: 'You see, the conveyor, as a rule, comes to halt not because all the parts are missing at once, but because of certain individual items, or even just one. The other parts are there, they have to pile up.'[110] In our discussion of work time we have already shown how the stoppages at AZLK had virtually a different cause each day. The pattern of incompleteness was similar. On some days the workers could not assemble cars because there were no gear boxes. On others there was no electrical wire. On still others there was a shortage of fastenings.[111] The pattern was the same in the tractor production shops of Leningrad's Kirov works. One particular machine shop had an excellent record of efficiency, but delays elsewhere meant that the parts it produced simply had to be stockpiled: for some parts a month's supply had already accumulated. In short, remarked the factory newspaper, its workers were producing simply for the warehouse.[112]

What are the implications of the different forms of waste for the political economy of the Soviet system? First, waste entails a huge squandering of labour power and means of production. An enormous amount of labour time is lost producing goods which cannot be used, rectifying defects, or repairing equipment. This overconsumption of resources, either directly in excess expenditures of fuel or metal, or indirectly through defective output, requires the creation and maintenance of a hypertrophied sector for the production of means of production. The Soviet Union uses more metal per unit of output than Western industry. Insofar as this extra demand for metal cannot be met out of spare capacity, its production requires the prior construction of new iron and steel mills. This in turn creates an excess demand for building materials and machinery. If this, too, cannot be met with existing capacity, new building materials and engineering factories will have to be erected as well, putting an even greater drain on society's resources. But the overconsumption of inputs does not end there. Once in operation, these steel works must have more coal and iron ore; thus the demand for mine construction and mining equipment is also raised. But these, in turn, require metal and machinery, so that the demand for steel and equipment goes up still further. In short, the economy is caught in a vicious circle, where it has to produce more and more just to stay in the same place, because so much of what it produces cannot be used, at least not in the form in which it emerges from production. It is this, far more than the political power of the industrial ministries, which explains the Soviet economy's permanent hypertrophy of department I and perpetual underdevelopment of light industry.[113] The generation of waste is, therefore, both a drive of the system – a motor force of its reproduction – and a source of its instability and tendency towards stagnation.

Secondly, this contradiction is reproduced in the social basis of waste. At a superficial level, the hypertrophy of department I can be seen as the historical genesis of the political dominance of the representatives of heavy industry within the elite, whose need to perpetuate this domination has acted to reinforce the structural rigidities between departments I and II. In this sense the specific contours of the class relations of Soviet society – an elite rooted in the hypertrophy of heavy industry and a workforce producing a social product the intrinsic deformities of which reproduce this very same hypertrophy – are also rooted in the phenomenon of waste. At another level, the manifest futility of this system of production – a system which takes high-quality imported Japanese steel and turns it into defective ball bearings[114] – has played a critical role in perpetuating the demoralization of the workforce. Waste is at one and the same time a product of workers' atomization and alienation and its cause. This was summed up succinctly by two mine workers following the strikes of 1989. According to N. Anokhin, a member of the Prokop'evsk City Workers' Committee in the Kuzbass:

> The miner moreover must see the use of his labour: that the coal went on heat, lighting, or something else sensible. But what does the miner see? That the coal went to make poor-quality metal which rusts. That the coal was transformed into a mountain of machines which fall to pieces. That the coal has been stockpiled in warehouses where it simply piles up. And after all this they say to him, 'Dear comrade, let's have more productivity, extract still more!' It's logical to ask: why extract still more if the coal that's been extracted isn't being used, but is being turned into smoke and ash?[115]

A similar argument was advanced by V. Golikov, an electrician at the Pervomaiskaya mine in Berezovskii (Sverdlovsk oblast):

> This is an economic riddle, a paradox: the richest territory, a developed industry, people who are in no way work-shy – and suddenly they are eternal debtors. Debtors to whom? Why? Who, for example, will say how much coal the country needs? Gosplan knows, you will answer. But how much is lost? No-one would venture even an approximate answer to this question. Tens of millions of tons of fuel pile up in coal stores or in slag heaps – and there's nothing to cart them away in. Tens of millions more tons go literally up the chimney due to defects in energy plants. They demand more extraction from the miners, but the more we extract the more is lost, and we become ever poorer.[116]

The elite's ability to stay in power depended on maintaining the atomization of the workforce, but this atomization – through the individualization of the work process and the alienation which it engendered – formed a central element of those shop floor relations which generate waste. However, insofar as waste is itself a factor perpetuating workers' political demoralization, it has been a political condition of the elite's continued rule. Thus waste is both an expression of the social conflicts within the system and a condition of that system's reproduction. But this very fact also made it a condition of the system's collapse: waste, as a precondition of the elite's political domination, at the same time led the system into stagnation and hence acted to undermine that domination.

The point of this discussion is not to catalogue the different forms of waste and to demonstrate their continued manifestation under perestroika. The issue is far more complex, for perestroika was not a simple continuation of what had gone before. Waste, or the deformed product, is the social form of the product in Soviet-type systems. The contradiction between this social form and the product's concrete existence as use value lies within the social form itself, that is, within use value. The product cannot function as an object of use in the fashion that was either intended or is required by either individual or productive consumers or by the system as a whole. This contradiction, we have argued, is an expression of the social contradiction within the society, between the elite and the workforce. Under perestroika the nature of this contradiction – between the product's social form and its function as use value – began to change. Through the imposition of *khozraschet* and its 'market mechanisms' the product 'aspired' to the social form of the commodity, but could not acquire this social form, because the old social relations, although modified, could not, as we have detailed throughout this book, be transformed into capitalist relations. Perestroika sought to achieve this and to replace the discipline of coercion and atomization with the discipline of the market and commodity production, but without the actual introduction of the market and commodity production and exchange. In other words, it tried to effect a transition from concrete labour to abstract labour (which gives rise to exchange value), without creating the structural preconditions of abstract labour. As this project proved unrealizable and the elite opted for a full-scale transition to capitalism, this opened up at least the hypothetical possibility of moving from an economy regulated by the production and circulation of deformed use values to one regulated by the production and circulation of exchange value.

This process, too, was abortive, and gave rise to yet another set of hybrid forms: a market that was not a market; a product that was supposed to function as a commodity but could not; labour power that was supposed to become abstract labour, but remained concrete.

Atomization eased, but workers' alienation from the means of production and the social product persisted. This, of course, is the case under capitalism, but in the USSR, the antagonism between the workforce and the elite still did not extend to the political arena or to struggles over the appropriation and division of the surplus product. Instead they remained largely confined within the labour process, over control over the labour process itself. It is true this began to change with the two miners' strikes and the emergence of localized conflicts, but this marked merely the beginnings of what will be a protracted historical process – such strikes have yet to become the dominant form of class struggle even in post-Soviet society. Within the labour process under perestroika little changed. Relations on the shop floor became even more unstable than they had been before, but within the same essential contours as existed before Gorbachev launched his reforms.

The failure to introduce commodity production meant that production continued to be production for use – of use values, that is, of goods acquired because of their concrete properties. As discussed at the close of chapter 4, exchange and barter relations between enterprises during perestroika were not based on exchange of value equivalents (abstract labour), but on the concrete utility of the objects that were traded. Insofar as this was the case, the old contradiction within use value was reinforced, but it was at the same time modified. In effect, there arose a contradiction within waste – if that is possible. Waste had been a driving force of the old Stalinist-bureaucratic system. It defined the nature of the product and was self-reproducing, in that it constantly called forth the conditions of its own reproduction: physical losses which had to be replaced; the circulation of defective or deformed products, which gave rise to new defects and deformities; the unproductive expenditure of labour power and means of production, which were perpetually overconsumed; an atomized workforce which created new deformed products with each cycle of production. With this came the constant renewal of a hypertrophied department I. With the breakdown of circulation under perestroika this process became blocked. The social relations within the enterprise continued to create and recreate waste, but its circulation and reproduction were distorted and in some cases halted. As coordination between industries and enterprises broke down, the continued hypertrophy of department I, essential for the production of the self-consuming social product, became choked off. Enterprises attempted to counter this trend through increasing reliance on barter relations, but this was not sufficient to call forth new production. The result was not just the stagnation inherent in waste, but actual declining repro-duction. Resources continue to be dissipated, but could not be fully renewed.

It is in this context that we need to assess the concrete forms of waste under perestroika. We see that both the phenomenal expressions of waste and the drives which create them were preserved, and derived in the last instance from the elite's failure to restructure the labour process. However, the economy was left without any driving force, even one which tended towards deformity and stagnation. Soviet society under perestroika became a society at an even higher level of contradiction than Stalinist society, but without throwing up any means of its supersession. Potentially this exists within the developing working class, but in the absence of the working class's political maturation and conscious recognition of this need, the society will remain stuck in stasis, even in its new capitalist integument.

Conclusion
The demise of perestroika and the emergence of class conflict

When Gorbachev came to power and launched his programme of economic and political reforms – perestroika and glasnost – many on the Western left mistakenly viewed this as an attempt to rejuvenate an innately progressive kernel buried beneath the distortions of Stalinism, and to restore to the Soviet Union the socialist traditions of its birth. The naivete of this view was soon made obvious, and Gorbachev would find few defenders on the left today. It would be equally mistaken, however, to see Gorbachev's policies as merely cosmetic, as window dressing designed to retain the Stalinist system beneath a new veneer. Perestroika was far more than this. It represented a recognition by the more pragmatic elements within the Soviet elite that the system had run into a dead end: economic growth had ceased and popular morale was at rock bottom. The process of surplus extraction had become so compromised as to endanger the source of the elite's privileges and perhaps also its long-term hold on political power. On this interpretation perestroika was above all else an attempt to reform the Soviet economy to allow the elite to exercise greater control over the creation and disposition of the surplus product, above all by making the reproduction of this process more regular and predictable. The main argument of this book has been that this required a restructuring of the Soviet labour process, since the behaviour of workers within production posed the primary limit to surplus extraction.

At all times both the broader goals of perestroika and the specific policies designed to achieve them were plagued by a high degree of internal contradiction. The reform wing of the elite, having identified the nature of the problems facing the economy and Soviet society, was equally aware that reforms, no matter how fundamental, would have to take place within the integument of that society's existing property relations. In the absence of private ownership of the means of production, the elite controlled the means of production only by virtue of its political control over the state. This was a legacy of the particular way in which the elite emerged out of NEP and Stalinist industrialization, where the elite had been able to secure its position in the face of opposition from both the working class and the peasantry by crushing independent political activity and atomizing society. Yet the reformers of perestroika appreciated that without overcoming this atomization and the alienation, low morale, and poor discipline within the workplace which it created, their plans would be still-born. This was the first contradiction of reformist policy: the strategy of reform could achieve its goal – to regularize and secure the elite's hold on power and privilege – only by partially negating what historically had been an essential precondition of that power.

This was encapsulated in the problem of the labour process. Restructuring the labour process would require a frontal assault on the network of defensive practices which workers had developed over decades as a way to insulate themselves, either as individuals or together with their immediate workmates, from the exploitation and repression of the Stalinist system. Yet such an attack on traditional work practices and the informal arrangements with line management on which they relied carried the risk of provoking both passive and open hostility on the shop floor. Reform would have to be multifaceted, involving the erosion of the basis of these work practices and broader political changes, which we described in our Introduction as an attempt to create a Soviet equivalent to bourgeois civil society. This had two aspects to it: the creation of the citizen, akin to the nominally free individual of capitalist society – a society which requires the free movement of capital and labour power, a freedom based on inequalities of power and wealth, a freedom to exploit and to be exploited; and more importantly, the creation of a hegemonic ideology through which the exploited classes would come to view their subordinate position as part of the 'natural' organization of society.

The idea that the elite could carry out this project was utopian. First of all, the ideological foundations of a Soviet 'civil society' could not be manufactured. They would take generations to develop, and would require the creation of a society on an upward trajectory of development with relative social stability. From where would such stability come? Political liberalization may have been an imperative for the elite's continued survival, but it was impossible to introduce liberalization into a society with such pent-up political frustrations and hostilities and expect that the elite would retain its political supremacy unchallenged. Second, the standard of living would have to rise, so that people would come to identify their well-being with the maintenance of the system. Here the elite was caught in a vicious circle. It could not raise the standard of living without a thorough modernization and streamlining of the economy. But this had as its precondition a restructuring of the labour process, which in turn could not be imposed without a higher standard of living, unless the elite were willing to risk massive social upheaval.

The specific labour policies of the Gorbachev period revealed the different sides of this contradiction: political liberalization as a condition of creating a reproducible and effective system of economic coercion, in place of the dysfunctional economic and political coercion of Stalinism.

Employment policy aimed to create a flexible labour market and free labour mobility; some reformers also wished to use mass unemployment and job instability to impose tighter labour discipline, although this group did not dominate the formulation of official policy. In the event, neither of these scenarios was realized. Some amongst the more vulnerable groups of workers – women with children, older workers near to retirement, young entrants to the labour force – faced redundancy and/or difficulties finding employment, but large-scale unemployment did not occur. During the early years of the reforms, those who were laid off were in the main redeployed within the same enterprise. But by 1990 even such token gestures were few and far between. Conjunctural factors – primarily the loss of workers to cooperatives paying higher wages and the small-scale, but nonetheless discernable exit of women from production – deepened the sectoral tendency towards permanent labour shortage. Only a financially ruthless and economically suicidal policy of imposing widespread bankruptcies could have reversed this trend, and this was neither a political nor an economic possibility. On the contrary, the large-scale temporary layoffs resulting from the supply shortage were neither anticipated nor welcomed, since they reflected the disintegration of the economy, rather than any trend towards technical modernization.

The wage reform was perhaps the most traditional policy of perestroika, and in many cases merely reiterated or attempted to reimpose changes in wages policies that had been tried at different times in the past. In this sense it presupposed no major changes in the organization of either the enterprise or the economy at large, the one exception being the long-term aim of tying wage funds to enterprise self-financing. Here, too, the result was failure. The twin pressures of a deepening labour shortage and a crumbling economy, combined with growing militancy on the shop floor as a result of political liberalization, made the reform virtually inoperable. The regime recognized this and officially abandoned it in 1990.

Enterprise democratization was the political centrepiece of perestroika. While the reformers prevaricated over just how far democratization could go within society at large, they hoped to provide workers with a political incentive to cooperate in the reforms and to accept its economic sacrifices by giving workers a limited say in the running of enterprise affairs. This, too, was doomed to failure. Either the campaign was simply empty rhetoric, in which case it would – and did – lead to increased cynicism among workers, or any genuine attempt to implement it would be racked by internal contradictions. The economic reforms of perestroika, at least in theory, gave managers the power and the rationale to rid themselves of surplus workers and to impose rigid financial discipline over wages. Managers quite correctly saw in this both the need and the opportunity to make an assault on workers' independence of action on the shop floor and to assert the type of rigid authority which they had always sought to impose, but which the nature of production and the labour process had made impossible. The implantation of such a new managerial 'style' was simply incompatible with political changes that might weaken managers' authority over their enterprises. Managers were in no way prepared to accept such a dilution of their powers with its inherent threat to their preeminence and privileges. In defending the economic logic of perestroika they were at the same time undermining the political preconditions for its long-term success. For many, if not most, industrial managers during the early phase of the reforms this did not appear as a contradiction, since at this stage their support for the reforms was lukewarm at best. The response of workers to this political stalemate within the factories was continued alienation if not outright hostility towards management. But there was another side of liberalization which acted to destabilize the individual enterprise and the economy at large, namely the rise of worker protests. Workers learned to press their demands and grievances through strikes or milder forms of industrial action, so that the mere threat of a stoppage was often sufficient to extract concessions from management. Such actions, not to mention the mass strikes of 1989 and 1991, made the reforms even more unworkable and their goals unobtainable.

The key to the failure of all these policies was *khozraschet*, which we have characterized as an attempt to reconstruct the economy using the financial discipline of capitalism without capitalism itself. Only in this way could the elite hope to introduce a dynamic into the economy and still maintain the political structures through which it perpetuated its own preeminence. Its choices were decidedly limited. Socialism was impossible, since genuine working-class power – even had there been a working class with the consciousness and preparedness to seize it – was excluded, as it would have displaced the elite once and for all as the ruling group within society. Capitalism was simply too risky, since the elite could not ensure that its members would survive the transition to the market and emerge as the new capitalists. The result was a deformed market, the encouragement of market logic and market behaviour without a market and the operation of the law of value.

The chaos to which this led confronted the elite with a stark dilemma. As the mechanisms of economic coordination came apart, the reform wing of the elite was confronted with little choice. In mid-1990 it abandoned perestroika in favour of a full-scale restoration of capitalism. But capitalism could not simply be imposed. The underlying institutions to sustain it did not exist. The lack of such things as financial markets, a stable and convertible currency, a stock exchange, and property law were merely symptomatic of the deeper problems: a transport and communications infrastructure which physically could not sustain the free circulation and exchange of commodities; a lack of labour mobility, without which labour power could not function as a commodity; and the absence of a capitalist class. Moreover, the reforms, which had been designed to create some of these prerequisites, had led to their opposite. The economic dislocations and the worsening supply crisis placed a premium on hoarding labour. Workers left their enterprises for work in the private sector (cooperatives), but while the scale on which this took place was enough to cause serious damage to the economy, it was too small to represent any fundamental change in patterns of labour mobility, and there was certainly no question of workers following investment into new lines of production. Shortages, too, meant that free exchange of commodities, including of labour power, became impossible. Exchange relations between enterprises contracted, rather than expanded. The anticipated growth of direct market transactions was stunted and barter arrangements became more common. In such a situation the historical evolution of an abstract measure of equivalence – value – and of money as a universal equivalent, medium of exchange, and measure of value were impossible. Goods continued to be acquired and 'exchanged' for their utility, irrespective of labour content or production costs. In short, there was no scope for the emergence of the law of value, without which there could be no capital, that is, money invested in the production of commodities whose sale realizes surplus value.

Managers and officials in the industrial ministries were quick to appreciate the new situation and to attempt to control it. The market was now inevitable. They dropped their resistance to perestroika and attempted to position themselves to become the new capitalists, but were able to accomplish only part of this task. They began appropriating state property as their own private property, but the process was haphazard and uncertain, and was only in its embryonic stages when perestroika was superseded by the breakup of the Soviet Union. Moreover, they could acquire their enterprises, but there was neither the incentive nor the compulsion to make them function profitably, other than through speculation and raising prices. Operating in the main as monopolistic producers amidst general scarcity, rationalization, new investment, and cost-cutting were simply unnecessary. Even if these goals had been seen as desirable, economic conditions did not allow for any assault on the labour process and a 'rationalization' of the mechanisms of exploitation, without which profitability in a genuinely competitive economy could not be ensured. The result was stasis, both politically within society as a whole, and within the enterprise. This was only unblocked by the attempted *putsch* of August 1991, and the ascendancy of El'tsin and the new Russian bureaucracy.

El'tsin's triumph after August 1991 had nothing whatsoever to do with democracy. It also had relatively little to do with his personal conflict with Gorbachev, although his grudge against the latter must have run very deep. In his past incarnation as a populist reformer inside the Communist Party, who consistently attacked bureaucratic privilege and bureaucratic opposition to change, El'tsin had been subjected to appalling humiliation, in which Gorbachev, his erstwhile ally, had openly participated. This, of course, was long before El'tsin had opportunistically discovered the wondrous benefits of capitalism and the market. But the antagonism between the two men transcended such personal rivalries and the settlement of old scores. It was about which faction of the bureaucratic elite – the old All-Union bureaucracy or the emergent apparatus of the Russian Republic – would inherit the state property about to be privatized. In a truly prophetic article, written in an obscure newspaper of the Leningrad oblast Komsomol a full three months before the attempted *putsch*, Boris Kagarlitsky characterized the growing conflict in the following terms:

> The fact is that the talk is not about democracy, the market, or Russia, but about things far more simple and prosaic, but for all that concrete and commonplace. The weak (but strengthening) Republican bureaucracy of Russia is trying to redistribute power and property in its own favour, removing them from the strong (but weakening) central and party bureaucracy. Both sides dream about appropriating what used to be state property, about privatization, but the question is, to whom this property is going to pass. Who will become the new master? And if for the basic mass of the population this question is essentially irrelevant, to those actually taking part in the carve-up it appears singularly important.[1]

This process emerged more clearly after August, as directors of leading enterprises began more openly and self-consciously to articulate their group interests and to pursue them through a unified, class organization. In early 1992 they formed the Russian Union of Industrialists and Entrepreneurs, which aspired to emulate – not totally successfully, as it turned out – the big employers' organizations of the West, such as the Confederation of British Industry or the Italian Confindustria.[2] The large ministries also started to form themselves into private corporations: the old USSR Ministry of Coal became Coal of Russia, uniting 88 of the former ministry's 112 Russian-based enterprises, including mines, enrichment plants, engineering works, and research and design institutes.[3] More significantly, the stance of management towards the workforce began to harden. In the wake of the August *putsch* and the subsequent ban on the activities of the Communist Party, a number of directors tried to bar trade unions from operating inside their enterprises.[4] More durably, line management has shown signs of taking a new, more stringent attitude towards some of the traditional bedrocks of informal bargaining: discipline has become tighter and foremen and shop superintendents are less prone to make concessions over wages when production conditions make it difficult for workers to sustain customary earnings.[5]

Although a bourgeoisie was beginning to crystallize, this did not make the future of Russian capitalism any more viable. The process of *nomenklatura* privatization was merely gaining ground, containing within it the seeds of a moribund capitalism, devoid of any dynamic towards development. The new capitalism would grow up on the foundations of the old command system, dominated by monopoly producers bonded by ties of personal power and connections, and operating within a shortage economy where huge profits were, and are, to be made through cutting production and speculative price rises. The tendency of such a capitalism is not towards investment and growth, but speculation, corruption, and the drive to amass personal fortunes at the expense of capital accumulation. This, coupled with the Soviet Union's endemic crisis of fixed capital could only produce a deep and chronic shortage of capital for investment. From what source was the capital for reconstruction to come? Western capital, mired in its own economic crisis and unable to bear even the costs of German unification, was simply unable, even had it been more willing, to throw billions of dollars into the purchase and reconstruction of Russian and Ukrainian factories. El'tsin appealed to the Western banking system for financial assistance, but the price was the hasty stabilization of the currency and a sharp reduction in the budget deficit. Even had such a strategy achieved its stated financial objectives – which it did not – it could not have solved the problems of production. On the contrary, it merely accelerated the decline. Supply problems worsened throughout 1992 and production continued to contract. The precarious financial position of most enterprises, coupled with the shortage of bank notes, meant that for millions of workers wages were paid weeks, if not months in arrears; high inflation, in many cases coupled with short-time work, caused living standards to plummet.[6]

Faced with such uncertainty, managers have themselves proven incapable of forging a genuinely class-based unity. Despite the pretensions of the Union of Industrialists to create the foundations of such a unity, during 1992 and 1993 most managers adopted survival strategies specifically aimed at enhancing their own power and wealth. Some responded by selling off enterprise assets and engaging in speculation. Others made genuine attempts to adapt to emerging market conditions by developing new lines of production for export, only to find these strategies blocked by internal power struggles within the administration over influence and the division of shares. Still others found that their tenuous efforts to adapt at least part of their production profile to the market were continually blocked by a lack of resources: their technology was too backward, their workforce lacked the required skills, and supplies of raw materials and machine parts continued to be highly irregular and of inadequate quality. The result has been that the economic crisis of the post-Soviet system has led to, and in turn become perpetuated by, an 'every man for himself' attitude on the part of individual factory managers, thus rendering their nascent class solidarity a chimera.[7]

For all this, managers have still been quicker to recognize their developing class interests than have the workers. When managers

throughout 1992 and 1993 demanded a slowdown in El'tsin's 'stabilization' programme and increased state funds for investment, this was
far from being an attack on privatization; rather, it was an attempt to
strengthen the source of their wealth and power, which ultimately
resides in production, not finance. By contrast, for all the hardships
suffered during the winter of 1992, including the non-payment of
wages and the breaking of collective agreements, there were no significant worker protests and no mass strike wave. On the contrary, the
tendency was for managers to claim to represent workers' interests
through their defence of the 'interests of the labour collective'.[8]
Workers on their part have in the main remained passive and demoralized – at least throughout 1993.

What we have seen is a major historical discontinuity between the
tasks thrown up by the current crisis and the ability of the contending
classes to resolve it in favour of one side or the other. Like the Russian
bourgeoisie prior to 1917, the new Soviet bourgeoisie will prove too
enfeebled and steeped in corruption and speculation to carry out the
tasks of what is in effect Russia's second 'bourgeois revolution'. Politically it cannot unify the country or generate a viable civil society.
Economically it cannot even reverse the terminal decline in industry
and agriculture, much less renew and expand the productive forces.
These tasks must, therefore, fall to the Soviet proletariat, which alone
has the potential to unite society, and to form the collective bodies of
political representation and worker self-management needed to revi-
talize production. But this is nothing more than a general orientation.
This proletariat is still in the process of its historical re-formation. It has
no organizational, political, or ideological independence or identity.
There is thus an historical void which the proletariat must fill but
cannot. It is a situation reminiscent of the late 1920s and early 1930s,
when European capitalism had clearly lost all vitality and was in a
state of long-term decline, but the proletariat – largely due to Stalinist
domination over the international workers' movement – was incapable of supplanting it.

It is essential, however, to see these developments not simply in a
Russian or Soviet context, but as part of a world process of capitalism's
decline. What we have witnessed since 1989 is not the death of
communism or socialism, but the death of Stalinism. It would be
impossible to overestimate the role that Stalinism played in ensuring
the political and ideological stability of twentieth-century imperialism.
It provided a continuing and all-too tangible referent for anti-
communism, while its hold over the international workers' movement

and its corrupting influence on socialist politics mortally weakened any possible challenge to capitalist rule. Even where the Soviet Union provided aid and assistance to anti-imperialist struggles, as in Viet Nam, this was at great cost. Its help was always tied to political concessions from the recipient movements, so that the politics of these movements tended to resemble those of the Soviet Union itself. The Soviet elite's interest in anti-imperialist wars was not ideological, but above all else a desire to reproduce regimes like itself, and if possible gain tactical advantage over the Western superpowers.

For this reason we would argue that in the long term the removal of Stalinism poses a fundamental threat to capitalist stability. This may seem an odd prediction given the rabid aggressiveness of the United States in the immediate wake of the Soviet Union's collapse, but it will prove true in the near future. First, within the old Soviet Union, perestroika unblocked what had been a static system, incapable of movement and therefore of any resolution of its inherent contradictions and conflicts. Perestroika never held out any promise of 'restoring socialism', but it did create the preconditions for the reemergence of class struggle, so that these conflicts, while becoming more open and increasingly more severe and brutal, can now at least potentially be resolved. Secondly, the fall of Stalinism has already led to growing economic and political crisis in the West as well as East, characterized by long-term economic decline and a rise of nationalism and nationalist wars. The two phenomena are inseparably linked: the economic crisis provoked by German unification has meant that Western capitalism cannot even begin to finance the restoration of capitalism in Eastern Europe. This will be a far more spontaneous, barbaric, and crisis-ridden process than any capitalist politician would have imagined in 1989. Finally, and most important of all, the end of the Cold War removes the basis of capitalism's ideological hegemony over the working class. For nearly five decades capitalism more or less successfully concealed the contradictions within its own system behind the rhetoric of anti-communism and the Cold War. This is now impossible. Capitalism's manifest failure to provide for its citizens, its pillage of global resources, and the destitution to which it has condemned the vast majority of the world's population will henceforth be transparent in a way not seen since the 1930s, or possibly even the early twentieth century.

In reality this process of ideological decomposition will unfold over generations, as the temporal discontinuity between the Soviet working class's tasks and capacities becomes mirrored in the working class in the West. For the Western proletariat, too, must undergo a period of historical reconstitution. It must overcome generations during which it lost its consciousness of itself as a class-for-itself and of socialism as an inspirational vision of a future where people could peacefully and collectively arrive at solutions to their fundamental problems. It must overcome generations of deep and cancerous divisions along lines of race, religion, nation, and gender. The contours of this process cannot as yet be predicted. Perhaps the working classes of the ex-Soviet Union will finally reclaim the historical promise opened up by the October Revolution, but which went unrealized. Perhaps the working classes in the advanced capitalist countries will rediscover their own lost traditions of anti-capitalist militancy and struggle for a different future. Perhaps the locus of class struggles will shift, to regions where capitalism has newly penetrated and a new proletariat is taking shape and maturing. Perhaps none of these will occur and humanity will at last descend into the barbarism which Engels deemed the only ultimate alternative to socialism. Whatever the case one thing is certain. We are entering a new epoch in world history. These promise to be difficult and dangerous times. There will be massive suffering and much human tragedy. But these are also times of great promise and potential, such as humanity has not seen for over three-quarters of a century. The old slogan of the 1960s may come to take on a meaning and relevance that its histrionic inventors could never have contemplated.

Seize the Time.

Notes

Introduction

1 Filtzer, *Soviet Workers and Stalinist Industrialization, Soviet Workers and De-Stalinization*.
2 For a more detailed discussion of the limits on surplus extraction within the Soviet economy, see Filtzer, *Soviet Workers and De-Stalinization*, chapters 5 and 6.
3 For the issues taken up in this paragraph see Braverman, Burawoy, Lupton, Knights and Willmott, Montgomery, Roy, and Wood. Aspects of these issues as they relate to Soviet industry are discussed in Filtzer, *Soviet Workers and De-Stalinization*, chapter 8, and more briefly in chapter 6 of the present book.

1 Attempts to create a labour market

1 For the historical origins of the labour shortage and the dynamics behind its reproduction in the Stalin and post-Stalin periods, see Filtzer, *Soviet Workers and Stalinist Industrialization*, ch. 2; *Soviet Workers and De-Stalinization*, ch. 3.
2 Simon Clarke, in a personal communication, has suggested that labour hoarding allows management to compensate for the loss of disciplinary control over the workforce which unemployment and an external reserve army of labour would provide. By keeping on hand a large internal pool of low-paid and low-skilled jobs, together with better-paid, but relatively non-taxing jobs in administration, management could use the threats of demotion or promotion as a disciplinary device. This is an intriguing thesis, but would need to be modified to take account of gender, regional, and ethnic rigidities within the factory workforce: many, if not most auxiliary jobs are performed by women and/or internal migrants (*limitchiki*); thus threats to transfer skilled male workers to lower-status auxiliary jobs would in many cases carry little force. Nevertheless, this issue clearly requires further investigation in future labour process studies.
3 *EZh*, no. 15, 1990, p. 12.
4 See, for example, the press conference held by V. I. Shcherbakov, head of Goskomtrud, reported in *Izvestiya*, 5 February 1991. Shcherbakov put this

argument in more detail in *EKO*, no. 1, 1990, p. 38, and *ST*, no. 1, 1991, p. 10. This did not keep him from describing unemployment as 'an inevitable evil under market conditions'. *EZh*, no. 15, 1990, p. 12.

5   Until recently a job [*rabochee mesto*] had little prestige in our country. Many people, knowing that they could always find work in their trade, did not value their job or their duties. Even though these workers did not always work conscientiously, the administration turned its head the other way, excused their indiscipline with the sole desire to keep them from leaving the enterprise and leaving the work place bare. This, to be sure, is one of the reasons for the ineffectiveness of many of the measures designed to strengthen labour discipline. Now the situation is gradually changing. A place to work has gone up in price, since the enterprise now has an economic interest in cutting the number of cadre. When this interest becomes general, the worker will constantly face the choice: either work well and be necessary to production, so that the question of dismissal never comes up, or work badly and become a candidate for dismissal. *ST*, no. 7, 1989, p. 74 (Yu. Orlovskii)

6 Literally, those on the *limit*, or authorizations made to enterprises allowing them to hire a certain number of outsiders on temporary residence permits.

7 *Trud*, 19 April 1990. On the unreliability of these estimates see the interview with V. Kolosov, head of Goskomtrud's Administration of Labour Resources and Employment of the Population, *Trud*, 29 March 1990.

8 *ST*, no. 10, 1990, p. 37 (I. Zaslavskii).

9 *EN*, no. 8, 1990, p. 71 (O. Osipenko).

10 *ST*, no. 8, 1989, p. 71 (V. Pavlov, V. Baryshev).

11 *Sots. issled.*, no. 1, 1989, pp. 38–41 (I. E. Zaslavskii, M. V. Moskvina).

12 Interview with V. Kolosov, head of the Administration of Labour Resources and Employment, Goskomtrud USSR, *Izvestiya*, 11 May 1990.

13 *Izvestiya*, 18 January 1991.

14 *LR*, 5 April 1991. I am grateful to Anna Temkina for making this reference available to me.

15 Interview with officials of the Moscow Labour Exchange, Moscow, 9 October 1991. See also *VE*, no. 9, 1991, p. 35 (I. Zaslavskii), and *RT*, 24 October 1991.

16 *RG*, 9 October 1991.

17 *KP*, 5 February 1991 (B. Vishnevskii).

18 *RG*, 28 March 1991 (V. Nikitchenko).

19 See the example of the Batumi woodworking combine, Adzhar ASSR, cited in *SI*, 27 September 1989. On leasing, see chapter 4.

20 *RT*, 21 July 1990. The campaign continued for several weeks. Ryzhkov pledged his support in the issue of 4 August. This was, of course, in the days before these same ministry officials and Party functionaries had decided that the market was not such a bad innovation, and began to use their power and position to facilitate their entry into the new class of private entrepreneurs.

21 *RT*, 26 January 1991 (Georgii Dolzhenko).

22 *RT*, 22 September 1990 (V. Noskov). According to the women the overtime was required because management was selling its above-plan output of

candy to the Volga Automobile Factory (VAZ) in Tol'yatti, in exchange for cars – which managers then appropriated for their own private use.

23 *SP*, no. 5–6, 1990, p. 46 (V. Povetkin).

24 *Trud*, 12 September 1989 (V. Pavlenko); *SG*, 6 October 1989; *RT*, 16 February 1990 and 31 January 1991 (V. Bogodelov). The latter article refers to 'mass unemployment' in the area, which first hit the gas pipeline workers, and extended to workers and specialists in the oil industry.

25 It is worth noting, however, that the pipeline was not the only budget're-lated issue to arise at this time. As we discuss in the chapter on self-financ-ing, also in late 1989 the government proposed to raise prices on fuel, transport, and energy, thus jeopardizing the financial position of countless factories, especially in the iron and steel industry. When these workers threatened to strike the price rises were postponed, only to be imple-mented later in 1990.

26 *RT*, 12 February 1991.

27 *Trud*, 23 January 1990.

28 *RT*, 28 March 1991 (Ali Naibov).

29 *EKO*, no. 6, 1990, p. 16.

30 *EN*, no. 12, 1990, p. 15 (V. Shustov). The exception was Tadzhikistan, where the non-working population had fallen to 25.7 per cent.

31 *ST*, no. 1, 1991, pp. 17–18 (M. Kuz'minova, V. Karev).

32 *Trud*, 30 April 1991 (B. Ashurov).

33 *ST*, no. 5, 1988, p. 27 (F. R. Filippov).

34 *ST*, no. 6, 1989, pp. 50, 59; *RT*, 28 March 1991 (Ali Naibov).

35 *ST*, no. 6, 1989, pp. 49–50, 59; *Trud*, 23 January 1990. In Dushanbe, Tadzhi-kistan, only five enterprises have dormitories for housing workers. *Trud*, 30 April 1990 (B. Ashurov).

36 *RT*, 28 March 1991 (Ali Naibov).

37 *ST*, no. 12, 1990, p. 63 (S. Beisenov).

38 *ST*, no. 12, 1990, p. 64 (S. Beisenov).

39 *RT*, 18 September 1990.

40 *Trud*, 10 November 1990. For a detailed account of the black labour market in the Russian city of Krasnodar, see *EZh*, no. 35, 1990, p. 11 (V. Ivanov).

41 *ST*, no. 6, 1989, pp. 53–4, no. 8, 1989, p. 61 (V. Skuratovskii), no. 2, 1990, pp. 45–6 (S. Blazhevich), no. 1, 1991, p. 26 (S. Blazhevich); *RT*, 9 September 1990 (Bryansk oblast).

42 *Sots. issled.*, no. 1, 1989, p. 39 (I. E. Zaslavskii, M. V. Moskvina).

43 *Pravda*, 2 July 1988.

44 *OT*, no. 9, 1989, p. 2. See also, *ST*, no. 8, 1989, pp. 64–5 (L. Shineleva).

45 According to one woman bookkeeper looking for work at a jobs fair in Moscow in November 1991, if you were over 40 or had children it was *do svidaniya*. *Exspress, Ltd.*, 28 November–4 December 1991. My thanks to Judith Shapiro for making this reference available to me.

46 *ST*, no. 6, 1989, p. 53, no. 7, 1985, p. 75 (Yu. Orlovskii); *Trud*, 10 January 1990 (B. Sarygulov).

47 *Sots. issled.*, no. 5, 1988, p. 28 (F. R. Filippov).

48 *EZh*, no. 35, 1990, p. 16 (I. Kirillov).

49 *Sots. issled.*, no. 5, 1988, p. 28 (F. R. Filippov); *SP*, no. 17–18, 1990, p. 86 (I. Dudukina); *ST*, no. 1, 1991, p. 24 (Z. Babkina).
50 *EZh*, no. 35, 1990, p. 16 (I. Kirillov); *ST*, no. 10, 1991, pp. 96–7 (Galina Grigor'yants).
51 *SP*, no. 17–18, 1990, p. 86 (I. Dudukina).
52 *EKO*, no. 1, 1990, p. 36 (V. I. Shcherbakov); *Trud*, 13 April 1990 (I. Travin), 2 September 1990; *ST*, no. 1, 1991, p. 26 (S. Blazhevich).
53 Law of the USSR, 'Ob osnovnykh nachalakh sotsial'noi zashchishchennosti invalidov v SSSR', 11 December 1990. *Trud*, 19 December 1990.
54 *Trud*, 13 April 1990 (I. Travin); *EZh*, no. 15, 1990, p. 13.
55 *Trud*, 2 September 1990.
56 *Ibid.*
57 *Trud*, 13 April 1990 (I. Travin).
58 *Sots. issled.*, no. 3, 1987, pp. 80, 84 (V. S. Dunin, E. A. Zenkevich).
59 Interview with D. Ya. Travin, Committee on Economic Reform, Leningrad City Soviet, 26 June 1991.
60 *Sots. issled.*, no. 3, 1987, p. 81 (V. S. Dunin, E. A. Zenkevich – ZiL); interview with S. A., foreman AZLK automobile factory, Moscow, 7 July 1991, *Trud*, 25 September 1990 (Serp i molot); *Trud*, 30 April 1991 (O. Osipov – building materials industry); *ST*, no. 3, 1991, p. 12 (Moscow margarine factory); *SP*, no. 11–12, 1990, p. 56 (T. Zykova – Moscow public laundries); *KP*, 1 May 1991 (S. Blagadorov – Moscow textile industry).
61 *Trud*, 14 September 1988.
62 *KP*, 16 February 1991 (L. Krutakov).
63 *Kabel'shchik* (Sevkabel', Leningrad), 22 March 1990.
64 Interview with D. Ya. Travin, Committee on Economic Reform, Leningrad City Soviet, 26 June 1991.
65 *SP*, no. 11–12, 1990, p. 56 (T. Zykova); *ZSM*, 1 December 1989; *Moskvich*, 31 May 1991.
66 *KP*, 16 February 1991 (L. Krutakov); *RT*, 18 July 1990 (L. Biryukova).
67 Interview with S. A., foreman at AZLK, Moscow, 7 July 1991.
68 *Rabotnitsa*, no. 2, 1990, p. 17 (A. Chizhevskii).
69 *Ritm*, 24 September 1990.
70 *Rabotnitsa*, no. 2, 1990, p. 17 (A. Chizhevskii); *Trud*, 25 September 1990.
71 *Rabotnitsa*, no. 2, 1990, p. 17 (A. Chizhevskii).
72 *Ibid.*; *Skorokhodovskii rabochii*, 28 August 1990.
73 *RT*, 16 August 1990 (E. Seregina).
74 *Trud*, 29 September 1990 (D. Romanov).
75 *Rabotnitsa*, no. 2, 1990, p. 23 (A. Chizhevskii).
76 *Trud*, 29 September 1990 (D. Romanov); *Rabotnitsa*, no. 2, 1990, p. 23 (A. Chizhevskii); interview with L. Tanova, staff sociologist, Krasnyi treugol'nik rubber-technical goods factory, Leningrad, 27 June 1991.
77 *KP*, 16 February 1991 (L. Krutakov).
78 *SP*, no. 11–12, 1990, p. 57 (T. Zykova).
79 *SP*, no. 11–12, 1990, p. 56 (T. Zykova).
80 *MP*, 6 September 1989.
81 *KP*, 16 February 1991 (L. Krutakov).

82 Interview with L. Tanova, staff sociologist, Krasnyi treugol'nik, Leningrad, 27 June 1991. Tanova herself came to the factory originally as a worker, and lived in the dormitories for fifteen years. A foreman at Moscow's AZLK car plant, who also came as a *limitchik* in 1971, lived in the dormitories for thirteen years, a full nine years after receiving permanent residence in Moscow. Interview with S. A., foreman at AZLK, 7 July 1991.

83 *RT*, 5 January 1991. In the case reported here, the wife was unable to obtain a Moscow residence permit, and hence could not work, because her husband had for ten years lived in a male-only dormitory. He could stay there with their 11-month old son, but she could not legally join him. As an 'illegal' she was not even entitled to the miserly 35–ruble child allowance, which she would have received had she been employed and able to take maternity leave. When she appealed to the local authorities for help they told her there was nothing they could do – there were thousands in Moscow in her situation.

84 *KP*, 1 May 1991 (S. Blagodarov). For another, equally grim report on the factory, see *Sobesednik*, no. 23, 1988, pp. 4–5. In the words of one woman worker, 'I'm 27 and I shudder to think what I'll be like in two or three years.'

85 David Mandel, interview with workers from the Lytkarino Optical Glass Factory, October 1990.

86 *ST*, no. 9, 1988, pp. 59–61.

87 *Ibid.*

88 *ST*, no. 1, 1989, p. 80 (R. Z. Livshits, V. I. Nikitinskii); no. 7, 1989, pp. 72–3 (Yu. Orlovskii); no. 8, 1989, pp. 95–6 (Yu. Volegov). According to Volegov (p. 95), managers were using transfers to deprive older workers in heavy or hazardous work of the higher pensions attached to these jobs. They shifted them to easier work on allegedly 'humanitarian' grounds one or two years before their retirement, thus denying them the extra money they would have received.

89 'Osnovy zakonodatel'stva Soyuza SSR i respublik o zanyatosti naseleniya', 15 January 1991, implemented by decree of the Supreme Soviet of the USSR, 'O vvedenii v deistvie Osnov zakonodatel'stva Soyuza SSR i respublik o zanyatosti naseleniya', 15 January 1991.

90 The trade union objections were contained in a number of sources. See, *EZh*, no. 15, 1990, p. 13; *Pravda*, 20 April 1990; *Trud*, 12 April, 19 April, 15 June, 25 September, and 7 December 1990. The issue of 15 June contained VTsSPS's alternative version of the law.

91 *RT*, 6 February 1991. In Ukraine, as already noted, the government delayed passing its own employment law, claiming it could not afford to pay the benefits. Yet the law, when it finally was passed, granted benefits slightly more generous than those at All-Union level. Law of the Ukrainian Soviet Socialist Republic, 'O zanyatosti naseleniya', 1 March 1991, *RG*, 20 March 1991. See also the interview with V. S. Vasil'chenko, Ukrainian Minister of Labour, *RG*, 5 February 1991.

92 *Trud*, 30 April 1991 (O. Osipov).

93 *RT*, 6 February 1991 (interview with V. Shcherbakov, chair of Goskomtrud).

94 *Sots. issled.*, no. 1, 1989, p. 41 (I. E. Zaslavskii, M. V. Moskvina).
95 *RT*, 14 December 1990; *EZh*, no. 19, 1991, p. 12 (V. Stashevskii).
96 *ST*, no. 6, 1989, pp. 54–6, no. 2, 1990, p. 46 (B. Blazhevich).
97 *ST*, no. 6, 1989, pp. 54–6.
98 *ST*, no. 6, 1989, pp. 55–6.
99 *ST*, no. 8, 1989, p. 62 (V. Matrokhina).
100 *EZh*, no. 15, 1990, p. 13; *RT*, 14 December 1990.
101 *ST*, no. 6, 1989, p. 58.
102 *ST*, no. 8, 1989, p. 59 (V. Ishin).
103 *ST*, no. 8, 1989, pp. 57–8 (A. Arzamastsev).
104 *ST*, no. 2, 1990, p. 46 (S. Blazhevich).
105 *ST*, no. 10, 1990, p. 41 (I. Zaslavskii).
106 *Izvestiya*, 18 June 1990 (S. Chugaev).
107 *Izvestiya*, 5 February 1991 (V. Romanyuk).
108 *Leningradskii rabochii*, 5 April 1991; interview with G. Golov, Standing Committee on Questions of Self-Administration, Work of Soviets, and State-Construction, Leningrad City Soviet, 21 June 1991. I am grateful to Anna Temkina for making the *Leningradskii rabochii* reference available to me.
109 *Nez. gaz.*, 13 June 1991; interview with officials of the Moscow Labour Exchange, 9 October 1991.
110 *Trud*, 22 November 1991 (A. Dzhapakov).
111 On the problems of the recruitment and training networks during the Khrushchev period, see Filtzer, *Soviet Workers and De-Stalinization*, pp. 70–5. On the growing gap between education and job prospects, see Yanowitch, *Work in the Soviet Union*, pp. 59–73.
112 *ST*, no. 3, 1990, p. 61 (I. Kochetkova), no. 5, 1990, p. 59 (V. Tomashkevich, S. Batekhin); *EZh*, no. 36, 1990, p. 6 (V. Tomashkevich).
113 *ST*, no. 3, 1990, pp. 65–6 (I. Bezgrebel'naya).
114 *EZh*, no. 46, 1990, p. 15; *ST*, no. 3, 1990, p. 62 (I. Kochetkova).
115 *ST*, no. 3, 1990, pp. 62–3 (I. Kochetkova). The study on which these figures are based, carried out in 1988 by Goskomtrud's Scientific Research Institute of Labour, found wide differentiations in the impact of retraining on earnings. At some enterprises as few as 3 per cent saw their earnings fall, while at others it was as high as 51 per cent, so that in these factories 'upgrading' one's skills could prove very costly indeed.
116 *ST*, no. 3, 1990, p. 64 (I. Kochetkova).
117 *Trud*, 26 November 1991.
118 *EN*, no. 4, 1990, p. 71 (E. Breeva).
119 On the Labour Reserve Schools and their successors in the Khrushchev period, see Filtzer, *Soviet Workers and De-Stalinization*, pp. 70, 72–3.
120 *RT*, 13 March 1991 (Igor' Smirnov).
121 *SP*, no. 2, 1991, p. 71 (V. Koltashev).
122 *EZh*, no. 35, 1990, p. 16 (I. Kirillov). The discrepancy here would appear to be even greater than Kirillov claims. According to Starikov, the PTU offered training in only 1,500 of the country's 6,500 enumerated trades. *ST*, no. 2, 1989, p. 72.

123 *SP*, no. 2, 1991, p. 72 (V. Koltashev). Another factor is the pressure on PTU
   to inflate their successes by awarding their students higher wage and skill
   grades (*razryady*) than their skills actually warrant, further compelling
   factories to retrain and regrade them once they start work.
124 *ST*, no. 2, 1989, p. 68 (I. Starikov).
125 *ST*, no. 2, 1989, p. 70 (I. Starikov); *MP*, 13 December 1989; *EZh*, no. 9, 1990, p.
   13 (V. Petrov). It is sad to say, but while this point is valid in principle, the
   reality is that, given the advanced age and depreciation of much of the
   equipment used in Soviet industry, the training these students received
   very probably corresponded quite closely to the jobs they would do once
   in the factory. On this point, see chapter 5.
126 *Sobesednik*, no. 29, 1988, pp. 12–13; *SI*, 23 September 1989 (Donetsk PTU);
   MP, 13 December 1989.
127 *Sobesednik*, no. 29, 1988, pp. 12–13; *SG*, 12 October 1989 (V. Tumanov).
128 *Sots. issled.*, no. 4, 1988, pp. 73–4 (E. Ya. Butko, N. A. Denisov). The figures
   cover the period 1981–5. *Sobesednik*, no. 29, 1988, p. 12, gives slightly lower
   figures for the share of outsiders in construction and textile PTU in
   Moscow: 81 per cent in construction and 84 per cent in textiles during
   1983–7.
129 *Sobesednik*, no. 29, 1988, pp. 12–13; *ST*, no. 2, 1989, p. 69 (I. Starikov), no. 6,
   1989, p. 56, no. 10, 1991, p. 95 (Galina Grigor'yants). By the same token, the
   small number of PTU cited by the press as being well equipped and
   offering their students adequate training also tended to be oversubscribed.
   See *ST*, no. 2, 1989, pp. 72–4 (I. Starikov) and *Trud*, 28 September 1990
   (GPTU No. 10, Lyubertsy).
130 *EZh*, no. 21, 1990, p. 9; *RT*, 13 October 1990. According to the latter some
   PTU were transferred to the budgets of the local soviets, some of which
   attempted to cut costs by not paying the instructors and foremen for two
   to three months, prompting a number of them to quit.
131 *RT*, 13 October 1990.
132 *Trud*, 25 January 1992.
133 For an outstanding early analysis of this issue, which foreshadows much
   of the recent discussion of the relationship between military spending and
   the endemic long-term crisis of modern capitalist production, see E. A.
   Preobrazhensky, 'Economic Equilibrium Under Concrete Capitalism and
   in the System of the USSR'.
134 *Sots. issled.*, no. 5, 1990, pp. 113–16 (V. L. Kunin).
135 *Sots. issled.*, no. 5, 1990, pp. 114–15 (V. L. Kunin); *LR*, 1 May 1991. I am
   grateful to Anna Temkina for making this last reference available to me.
136 *Tekhniko-ekonomicheskoe i sotsial'no-ekonomicheskoe obosnovanie leningradskoi
   zony svobodnogo predprinimatel'stva*, pp. 14–16.
137 'Strukturnaya perestroika i konversiya predpriyatii VPK', section 9, pp. 4–6.
138 *Izvestiya*, 11 April 1991 (E. Solomenko); interview with D. Ya. Travin,
   Committee on Economic Reconstruction, Leningrad City Soviet, 21 June
   1991; *RT*, 19 December 1991.
139 *Izvestiya*, 28 April 1990; *Trud*, 22 July 1990 (S. Strel'chenko) and 5 August
   1990.

140 *Trud*, 10 December 1991 (V. Dolgodvorov); 22 July 1990 (S. Strelchenko).
141 *Trud*, 5 August 1990.
142 *EZh*, no. 9, 1990, p. 15 (O. Stolyarov).
143 *Trud*, 20 March 1990 (Admiralty Production Association, Leningrad); *LR*, 31 May 1991 (Severnaya verf' shipbuilding factory). I am grateful to Anna Temkina for providing me with this reference.
144 *Mashinostroitel'* (Ivtekmash, Ivanovo), 21 January 1991.
145 *Za stal'*, 5 July 1990; *Trud*, 10 December 1991 (V. Dolgodvorov).
146 The fact that money wages rose quite sharply in this period does not, of course, mean that real wages followed suit. For most people the accelerating cost of living meant that living standards were falling, and it was this which reinforced workers' determination to win better pay.
147 *Sots. issled.*, no. 8, 1990, p. 8 (L. M. Martseva).
148 *ST*, no. 1, 1990, p. 53 (L. Dobrynina); *VE*, no. 9, 1991, p. 33 (I. Zaslavskii).
149 *Trud*, 16 April 1991 (construction); *RT*, 18 September 1990, and *Trud*, 7 May 1991 (iron and steel).
150 *ST*, no. 2, 1990, p. 45 (S. Blazhevich). The strain on resources was actually tighter than these figures indicate: 6 per cent of work places were held by people holding more than one job, and another 12 per cent were held by pensioners.
151 *Trud*, 26 November 1991.
152 In the Mid-Urals, for example, there were in November 1991 11,500 people looking for work through the oblast Employment Service, together with 27,000 unfilled job openings. The overwhelming proportion of those out of work were engineering and technical personnel. *Trud*, 21 November 1991. In Khar'kov the situation was almost identical: in November 1991 the oblast Employment Centre had 26,000 vacancies, including virtually all trades employing low-skilled workers, but only 1,220 for technical personnel. *Trud*, 26 November 1991. This was not, however, a new situation in Ukraine, but had been the case at least through all of 1991. *RT*, 26 January 1991 (Georgii Dolzhenko).
153 *VS*, no. 7, 1992, pp. 37–8.
154 *ST*, no. 5, 1988, pp. 34–7 (B. N. Belyakov). In coal mining *podsnezhniki* were workers listed on pit establishments, but put to work fulfilling personal services for colliery managers, such as house repairs and gardening. In return they were rewarded with minor privileges and jobs in the political or managerial bureaucracy. Friedgut and Siegelbaum, p. 17.
155 *SI*, 8 December 1989; *Trud*, 25 September 1990; *Izvestiya*, 23 April 1991 (V. Romanyuk).
156 *ZSM*, 27 November 1989, 21 March and 18 July 1990; *Moskvich*, 11 February and 31 May 1991. Tractor production at Leningrad's Kirov works was plagued by similar problems. During July and August 1990, tractor shops took on 622 workers but lost 973. *Kirovets*, 8 August and 14 September 1990.
157 *Izvestiya*, 11 February 1991 (V. Filippov). A former specialist in the Leningrad steel industry told a similar story: at his small enterprise, which was part of the ship-building industry, brigades of five workers had only three, and shop superintendents had to fill in for those missing. Interview with

A. K., metallurgical specialist, Leningrad, 21 June 1991. See also the case of the Fiftieth Anniversary of the USSR iron and steel combine, Cherepovets, which during 1989 lost 8,000 people (including technical staff) out of a total workforce of 45,000. *EZh*, no. 16, 1990, p. 12.

158 *Mashinostroitel'* (Malyshev Production Association, Khar'kov), 5 October and 23 November 1990; *RG*, 18 October 1991. Besides the Malyshev works, other plants affected were the Khar'kov Tractor Factory, the aviation factory, the electrical engineering factory, Serp i molot, and the Number Eight Ball Bearing factory.

159 *Baltiets*, 23 April 1991.

160 *Rezinshchik*, 17 July 1990, 5 March and 9 October 1991; *Priborostroitel'*, 30 January and 17 April 1991. Similar cases were reported in the power plant at Leningrad's Lenin engineering works (*Molot*, 20 December 1990), at the Strommashina factory, Kuibyshev (*Strela*, 20 July 1990), and among pattern-makers – a skilled trade – at the Ivtekmash textile-equipment association in Ivanovo (*Mashinostroitel'*, 17 September 1990).

161 See the example of the Ryazan' garment association, *SI*, 18 October 1989 (O. Berezhnaya).

162 *Trud*, 1 May 1990. Textiles, of course, was not alone here. The Skorokhod footwear production association was, as of mid-1990, a full 20 per cent below its full establishment. One of its constituent factories tried to solve the problem by enlisting home workers, but this was not copied elsewhere in the association. *Skorokhodovskii rabochii*, 17 August and 22 August 1990.

163 *Trud*, 16 September 1990. According to Tat'yana Sosnina, of the Textile and Light Industry Workers' Union, the total number affected throughout light industry came to between 750,000 and 1 million. *RT*, 23 January 1991.

164 *Trud*, 21 December 1991 (interview with M. V. Ikharlova, chairperson of the Central Committee of the Textile and Light Industry Workers' Union of the RSFSR); interview with officials of Textile and Light Industry Workers' Union of the RSFSR, Moscow, 2 July 1991. At one of the job fairs in Moscow held in November 1991 the majority of jobs being offered were for textile workers. *Ekspress Ltd.*, 28 November–4 December 1991 (I am grateful to Judith Shapiro for making this reference available).

165 *Molot*, 20 December 1990, 21 February 1991; *Kabel'shchik* (Sevkabel', Leningrad), 26 February 1990; *Kirovets*, 27 June 1990.

166 *Za stal'*, 24 July 1990. Because of the shop's low pay it had lost eight of its fourteen welders. *Za stal'*, 5 July 1990.

167 *SI*, 10 October 1989 (Znamya revolyutsii engineering factory, Moscow); *Trud*, 20 March 1990 (Krasnoe Sormovo, Gor'kii); *RT*, 25 December 1990 (Sverdlovsk construction); *LR*, 31 May 1991 (Severnaya verf' shipbuilding factory); *Kabel'shchik* (Sevkabel', Leningrad), 22 March 1990; interview with A. M., technical specialist, Lytkarino Optical Glass Factory, Moscow oblast, 12 June 1991.

168 Burawoy and Hendley, pp. 380–2.

169 *Baltiets*, 23 April 1991.

170 *ST*, no. 5, 1990, p. 60 (V. Tomashkevich, S. Batekhin); *Leningradskii rabochii*,

1 May 1991; David Mandel, interview with S., an electrical fitter at a large electrical equipment factory in Chelyabinsk, October 1991.

171 According to E. Katul'skii, Deputy Minister of Labour of the USSR, 40 per cent of young workers in industry and 60 per cent in construction quit their jobs without working out their initial contracts. *ST*, no. 9, 1991, p. 3. For specific cases involving factories in Leningrad and Moscow, see *Tribuna mashinostroitelya*, 4 April 1990; *SP*, no. 17–18, 1990, pp. 84–5 (I. Dudukina).

172 *Metallist*, 16 January 1991.

173 *Rezinshchik*, 24 July 1990; *Znamya*, 25 January 1991.

174 The factory paper at Sevkabel', for example, claimed that 130,000 highly-skilled workers over an unspecified period had quit jobs in Leningrad industry and gone into cooperatives. *Kabel'shchik* (Sevkabel', Leningrad), 22 March 1990.

175 *VS*, no. 2, 1991, p. 39.

176 We discuss the implications of this process in more detail in chapter 5.

177 *Ritm*, 27 August 1990. According to the factory paper, skilled workers were leaving because the factory paid practically the lowest wages in Khar'kov. Rather than putting office workers on jobs for which they could not possibly be trained in so brief a time, management would have been better off paying a decent wage. An attempt to solve the labour shortage in shop no. 12 of the Sverdlovsk instrument factory was of equally questionable utility: workers were drafted in from other shops to help clear out backlogs, but left behind masses of defective work which the shop's already hard-pressed workers had to rectify themselves. *Priborostroitel'*, 17 April 1991.

178 *KP*, 5 February 1991. This was not an exceptionally high wage at this time, but it was by no means a low wage either.

179 *RG*, 9 October 1991.

180 *Tribuna mashinostroitelya*, 28 February 1990.

181 *VE*, no. 9, 1991, p. 34 (I. Zaslavskii).

182 For example, the Serp i molot iron and steel works in Moscow, which was unable to employ many of its lower-skilled manual workers in its new, high-technology sections. *ST*, no. 2, 1991, p. 26 (Yu. Yakovets).

183 *SI*, 11 October 1989 (Oktava production association, Tula); *Trud*, 23 August 1990 (Dnepropetrovsk mining equipment factory); *Mashinostroitel'* (Ivtekmash, Ivanovo), 14 January and 8 April 1991.

184 See, for example, the cases of the Tyumen' plastics factory, *RT*, 12 June 1990; the atomic energy equipment factory in Volgodonsk, Rostov oblast, *RT*, 27 May 1990; the Nairit chemical association in Armenia, *RT*, 23 November 1990 (A. Bagdasaryan, V. Aidinyan); and the Tsentral'naya copper mine in Karabash, Chelyabinsk oblast, *RT*, 11 July 1991 (Mikhail Popov).

185 *Trud*, 16 September 1990 (A. Kozlov), 16 February 1991; *RT*, 28 September 1990, 26 January 1991 (Georgii Dolzhenko) and 27 February 1991; *RG*, 27 February 1991 (Sergei Il'chenko), 28 March 1991 (V. Nikitchenko), and 18 April 1991 (I. Donchenko). In St Petersburg in early 1992 the city's three

main confectionary factories were sending workers home because they could not buy sugar anywhere in Russia or Ukraine. *RT*, 13 February 1992 (Natal'ya Tyurina).

2 Economic incentives: the disintegration of the 1986 wage reform

1 Filtzer, *Soviet Workers and Stalinist Industrialization*, ch. 8; *Soviet Workers and De-Stalinization*, pp. 93–5.

2 'Technically based' norms are, at least theoretically, calculated on the basis of the optimal output that could be achieved using equipment at its full technological capacity within a rational, problem-free organization of labour. Their opposite are so-called empirically based norms, which are calculated from time-and-motion studies of the working day as it is actually used, that is, allowing for stoppages, breakdowns, problems with supplies, etc. In practice most 'technically based' norms are really empirical norms under the 'technically based' label.

3 Filtzer, *Soviet Workers and De-Stalinization*, ch. 4.

4 On the fate of the various experiments of the Brezhnev period, see Arnot, in particular ch. 9.

5 Already in the 1930s, our wages systems – borrowed in essence from the arsenal of capitalist production – did much to promote mass violations of labour discipline, pilfering, defective production, an indifferent attitude towards national property. Draconian laws were applied to overcome these abnormalities, which transformed people into virtual serfs and slaves but gave little to show for it. Tens, if not hundreds of different decrees and decisions appeared on improving the wages systems of both time and piece workers. The public was assured: just one more exertion and we shall overcome workers' indifference towards social property, we shall interest them in voluntarily revising norms (the Aksai method), in economising on raw materials and materials (the Zlobin method), in cutting the number of workers [needed to] fulfil production targets (the Shchekino method), etc. However, time passed and everything stayed as before: pilfering, defective work, absenteeism, workers worried, as before, only about profitable work, low norms, and high job rates, just like a waged worker. *SP*, no. 5–6, 1990, p. 30 (F. Shishkov, I. Ryazhskikh)

6 There were, of course, exceptions to this pattern. The Soviet press and interviews with workers offer no shortage of evidence of managers slashing rates, often because they could not otherwise meet their planned targets for productivity. This was the case, for example, in Novocherkassk, at the factory where Petr Siuda worked just before the strikes and demonstrations there in June 1992. David Mandel, interview with Petr Siuda, unpublished typescript, pp. 15–16. A worker at an electrical equipment factory in Chelyabinsk describes how in the mid-1980s, even before perestroika, management, by reporting fictitious improvements in equipment and work organization was given productivity targets by its parent ministry which it could only meet by constantly slashing rates or depriving workers of their bonuses. David Mandel, interview with S., an electrical repair fitter at the factory, October 1991. As will be clear when we discuss

the dynamics of informal bargaining and the labour process in chapter 6, these are exceptions to the general trend, often provoked by the same pressures which in most other circumstances have compelled managers to make concessions.

7 Where consumer goods and food were concerned, there was a marked increase in workers' reliance on the workplace during the latter half of perestroika. In the late 1980s 51 per cent of sewing machines, 51 per cent of soft furniture, 42 per cent of refrigerators, and 32 per cent of vacuum cleaners were purchased through the closed distribution system at people's places of employment. Nearly 30 per cent of the population was at least to some extent dependent on this system for access to foodstuffs. *Trud*, 14 November 1990 (V. Radaev).

8   It is hard to name any other country where the state power has turned out to be so powerless in the face of an inordinate increase in violations of labour discipline, mass drunkenness, public embezzlement and corruption ... These ugly phenomena were secretly consecrated by a 'second' ideology, which stood behind the first ideology proclaimed in official speeches and documents. Its plain content was expressed by Brezhnev in one of [his] confidential chats. In reply to a reference to the difficult material situation of low-paid groups of workers, Brezhnev declared: 'You know nothing about life. No one lives off their wages. I remember when I was young, when I was studying in the *tekhnikum*, we earned extra money by unloading freight cars. And how did we do it? For every three sacks or boxes, one was for us. That's how everyone in the country lives.' *EKO*, no. 9, 1989, p. 142 (V. Z. Rogovin), citing F. Burlatskii, 'Brezhnev i krushenie ottepeli', *Literaturnaya gazeta*, 14 September 1988

9 The basic provisions of the reform were laid out in a 1986 decree of the Central Committee of the Communist Party of the Soviet Union, the Council of Ministers of the USSR, and the All-Union Central Council of Trade Unions, 'O sovershenstvovanii organizatsii zarabotnoi platy i vvedenii novykh tarifnykh stavok i dolzhnostnykh okladov rabotnikov proizvodstvennykh otraslei narodnogo khozyaistva,' usually referred to simply as Decree No. 1115. *SP SSSR*, 1986, no. 34, art. 179. For details of the Khrushchev reform and its failures see Filtzer, *Soviet Workers and De-Stalinization*, ch. 4.

10 *Trud*, 21 December 1989. The regulations were slightly modified in February 1990. *EZh*, no. 9, 1990, p. 19.

11 As of the end of 1989, 8 per cent of industrial personnel (including clerical employees and technical staff) were on this second variant of *khozraschet* and another 3.3 per cent worked in enterprises on leasing. Together they accounted for just over 10 per cent of all industrial production and services. *EZh*, no. 31, 1990, p. 8 (A. Siginevich, I. Gurkov).

12 *ST*, no. 6, 1988, p. 28 (Yu. Shatyrenko).

13 *ST*, no. 8, 1989, p. 71 (V. Pavlov, V. Baryshev); *Izvestiya*, 7 May 1990.

14 See for example the accounts of the Tasma Production Association (chemical industry, Kazan), *ST*, no. 9, 1989, pp. 65–8 (V. Spirkin); the Volgograd Silicate Building Materials Combine, *ST*, no. 5, 1989, pp. 28–30 (V. Tinyakov, L. Mironenko) and *SG*, 17 September 1989; the Rabochaya odezhda

Production Association, Moscow, *ST*, no. 2, 1990, pp. 88–9 (L. Rzhanitsyna); and the Bryansk Technological Equipment Factory, *Trud*, 28 December 1989.

15 For a detailed discussion of this problem and its political implications in the pre-perestroika period, see Ticktin, 'Political Economy of the Soviet Intellectual'.

16 In 1987 there were 578,000 specialists with higher education, and 4,161,200 with a general specialized education, working as workers, or 9.6 per cent and 35.9 per cent of their respective cohorts. This was already a 9 per cent increase over 1985. Between 1987 and 1989 the figure expanded by a further 5.5 per cent. *EN*, no. 4, 1990, p. 68 (E. Breeva); *NK*, no. 1, 1990, p. 18 (F. R. Filippov); *Sots. issled.*, no. 9, 1990, p. 62 (S. N. Bykova, V. I. Chuprov).

17 Lane, *Soviet Economy and Society*, p. 59; Yanowitch, *Social and Economic Inequality*, p. 42 and ch. 3.

18 *ST*, no. 8, 1989, p. 73 (V. Pavlov, V. Baryshev).

19 See below, chapter 5, pp. 175–6.

20 See Holubenko, Belotserkovskii, Siuda.

21 *ST*, no. 1, 1990, pp. 54–5 (L. Dobrynina). Women are 58 per cent of engineers in the Soviet economy.

22 *ST*, no. 8, 1989, p. 73 (V. Pavlov, V. Baryshev), no. 8, 1990, p. 89 (V. Pavlov, L. Yurchikova); *MP*, 12 September 1989 (N. Volgin).

23 *ST*, no. 2, 1990, p. 91 (L. Rzhanitsyna); interview with trade union officials of the Elektron Institute, Leningrad, 21 June 1991.

24 *Sots. issled.*, no. 3, 1989, pp. 4, 6 (I. F. Belyaeva); *EKO*, no. 3, 1989, p. 14 (V. E. Boikov); *SP*, no. 7–8, 1990, p. 29 (Yu. Ovchinnikov).

25 *Sots. issled.*, no. 1, 1989, p. 52 (V. S. Dunin, I. Yu. Var'yash); *EKO*, no. 2, 1990, p. 87 (E. G. Yasin, S. V. Zenkin, S. V. Aleksashenko). The other side of this egalitarianism is workers' traditional hostility to rate busters. See the example of the refrigerator assembly section at the Arson factory (Arsenal production association, Leningrad), *Arsenal*, 24 June 1991.

26 *EKO*, no. 3, 1988, pp. 95–6 (L. I. Gol'din).

27 See, for example, the comments by I.N. Gubaidullin, director of the Chusovoi iron and steel works, *EKO*, no. 6, 1990, p. 96.

28 *ST*, no. 6, 1989, pp. 64–6 (K. Parmenenkov). For details of the various quality bonuses applied in sections of engineering see *ST*, no. 2, 1988, p. 72, and no. 4, 1988, p. 39.

29 *ST*, no. 4, 1988, p. 39.

30 *SI*, 25 November 1989 (Yu. Sagan').

31 *Sots. issled.*, no. 1, 1990, p. 86 (A. A. Mironov).

32 *RT*, 12 March 1990 (Chelyabinsk measuring-device factory). The dispute was followed up in *RT*, 15 March and 22 March 1990.

33 *EZh*, no. 45, 1990, p. 17 (V. Naumov).

34 *Materialy vsesoyuznogo monitoringa*, p. 10. For smaller local surveys showing the same trends, see *MP*, 12 September 1989 (N. Volgin), and *EKO*, no. 3, 1989, p. 14 (V. E. Boikov).

35 Filtzer, *Soviet Workers and Stalinist Industrialization*, pp. 212–13; *Soviet Workers and De-Stalinization*, pp. 97, 109; *ST*, no. 6, 1989, p. 62 (V. Alimova).

36 *ST*, no. 8, 1989, p. 72 (V. Pavlov, V. Baryshev); *MP*, 12 September 1989 (N. Volgin).
37 *ST*, no. 6, 1989, pp. 61–3 (V. Alimova).
38 *ST*, no. 6, 1988, pp. 38–9 (S. Petrova); *RT*, 13 May 1990 (letter from V. Prop'ko, Penza).
39 At one ceramics factory near Tashkent, in Uzbekistan, the workers were regraded downwards without any increase in wage rates. *ST*, no. 8, 1990, p. 89 (V. Pavlov, L. Yurchikova). At the textile machinery factory in Ivanovo painters were promised lower norms in exchange for moving down one skill grade: the workers were regraded, but the norms were never revised, prompting many of them to quit. *Mashinostroitel'* (Ivtekmash, Ivanovo), 17 September 1990.
40 *RT*, 2 May 1991 (Siberian ore mining).
41 *Sots. issled.*, no. 3, 1989, pp. 15–16 (D. I. Zyuzin); *ST*, no. 10, 1989, pp. 45–6 (D. Karpukhin).
42 See below, chapter 5, pp. 168–70.
43 *ST*, no. 10, 1989, pp. 71–72 (E. Leont'eva).

> Not letting the 'lower ranks' in on the algebra of incomes and expenditures, enterprise heads and specialists ultimately find themselves, to put it delicately, in a tricky situation. Receiving *'khozraschet'* wages which contain less than the usual number of bank notes, the outraged workers refuse to take up their place at their machines, to go down the pit, or to sit behind the wheel of the bus. Poor working conditions, undemocratic methods of electing managers, and inattentiveness by local authorities towards the social conditions of workers' lives are all pregnant with explosion. *Ibid.*, p. 72.

44 *ST*, no. 7, 1989, p. 113; no. 8, 1989, p. 72 (V. Pavlov, V. Baryshev); *SI*, 23 November 1989 (P. Myagkov).
45 *Izvestiya*, 7 May 1990.
46 *EZh*, no. 9, 1990, p. 6 (I. Manykina); no. 12, 1990, p. 13 (Yu. Yakutin). According to Yakutin's figures, the gap was narrowest in engineering, where average monthly wages went up 13 per cent faster than productivity, and greatest in fuel and energy (5 times faster) and metallurgy (4.8 times).
47 *EZh*, no. 6, 1990, p. 6 (I. Manykina).
48 Average wages at the Sverdlovsk instrument factory during 1990 rose by 14 per cent, while output *fell* by 7 per cent. This was made possible thanks to a 1 million ruble subsidy from its parent ministry to offset the effects of conversion, plus various financial and tax concessions, none of which were expected to be available in 1991. *Priborostroitel'*, 30 January 1991. For other examples, see *ST*, no. 8, 1990, p. 88 (V. Pavlov, L. Yurchikova).
49 *EZh*, no. 9, 1990, p. 6 (I. Manykina); no. 12, 1990, pp. 12–13 (Yu. Yakutin). Managers could also use such manoeuvres to boost their own personal incomes: a favourite device was to create bogus cooperatives as enterprise sub-units, with managers paying themselves a second salary as cooperative members. *Izvestiya*, 9 March 1990 (V. Romanyuk).
50 Interview with officials from the Textile and Light Industry Workers' Union of the RSFSR, 2 July 1991. According to these officials norms had

actually become tighter since the 1991 decentralization of wages, since factories were now free to set their own basic wage rates, and it was no longer necessary to use norms as a means of regulating minimum earnings. If this is true, it makes textiles an exception within Soviet industry.

51 *ST*, no. 5, 1988, p. 39.

52 *ST*, no. 6, 1988, p. 29 (Yu. Shatyrenko); no. 10, 1990, p. 14. Of 520 enterprises surveyed in 1989, norms were raised on average a mere 6.3 per cent, as against a 20–25 per cent rise in basic wage rates. *Ibid.*

53 *ST*, no. 8, 1989, p. 72 (V. Pavlov, V. Baryshev).

54 *ST*, no. 6, 1989, p. 32 (E. Antosenkov, N. Kovaleva, A. Makhmutova, Ya. Shagalov); no. 12, 1990, p. 44 (A. Fedorov); *EKO*, no. 9, 1990, p. 130 (Stanislav Mironchenko).

55 *ST*, no. 6, 1989, pp. 32–3 (E. Antosenkov, N. Kovaleva, A. Makhmutova, Ya. Shagalov).

56 *ST*, no. 5, 1988, p. 36.

57 *ST*, no. 10, 1990, p. 48 (V. Sekachev).

58 *ST*, no. 9, 1990, pp. 23–4. According to one specialist, lower management has resisted the computerization of factory information systems precisely because this would narrow the scope for concealing 'reserves' of resources, including slack norms. *EKO*, no. 6, 1990, p. 81 (V. M. Portugal).

59 *ST*, no. 12, 1990, p. 43 (A. Fedorov).

60 *ST*, no. 8, 1990, p. 88 (V. Pavlov, L. Yurchikova); no. 10, 1990, p. 14.

61 *ST*, no. 10, 1990, p. 14.

62 *ST*, no. 8, 1990, p. 89 (V. Pavlov, L. Yurchikova). This trend became especially pronounced in enterprises or enterprise sub-divisions which had transferred to leasing, and which, in order to maximize available wage funds, actually laid off their norm-setters and either abandoned norm setting or, in some cases, carried on using handbooks that were ten to fifteen years out of date. *ST*, no. 5, 1991, pp. 50–2 (V. Levitan, D. Rybakov).

63 I discuss here only those features of the contract brigades relevant to the wage reform. The contract system was also a centrepiece of the early phases of self-financing, and I examine it again in chapter 4.

64 On earlier forms of brigade organization see Arnot, ch. 9; Slider; and Filtzer, 'The Soviet Wage Reform' (unpublished paper, 1987), Appendix A.

65 Arnot, p. 221; *Sots. issled.*, no. 4, 1988, p. 72 (N. A. Sviridov).

66 *Sots. issled.*, no. 4, 1988, p. 72 (N. A. Sviridov).

67 *EKO*, no. 4, 1988, p. 126 (A. A. Prokhrov).

68 *Sots. issled.*, no. 4, 1988, p. 72 (N. A. Sviridov).

69 See the example of the Kineskop Production Association in L'vov, discussed in *ST*, no. 8, 1991, pp. 29–30 (S. Levitskii, V. Yakimchuk).

70 At the electrical equipment factory in Chelyabinsk previously referred to, women on the conveyor had over the course of many years worked out their own system of rotating jobs. Not all jobs were paid the same or involved the same degree of monotony, and this was a means of equalizing earnings and ensuring that no one would be stuck too long on the most boring operations. While management approved of this system, since it had no effect on wages and almost totally eliminated conflicts, it did mean that

attempts to introduce KTU collapsed, since the women changed jobs too frequently to obtain an accurate measure of their contribution to monthly production results. David Mandel, interview with S., an electrical repair fitter at the factory, October 1991.

71 *ST*, no. 8, 1991, pp. 29–30 (S. Levitskii, V. Yakimchuk); no. 1, 1990, p. 49 (A. Rogov).

72 'Osnovnye napravleniya stabliizatsii narodnogo khozyaistva i perekhoda k rynochnoi ekonomike', approved by the Supreme Soviet of the USSR, 19 October 1990. *Izvestiya*, 27 October 1990. An earlier Goskomtrud draft of this legislation was published in *Izvestiya*, 8 August 1990.

73 *Trud v SSSR* (1988), pp. 189, 199–204.

74 A. V. Kormilkin, an economist of the former official trade union confederation, VTsSPS, estimated that the poorest 15 per cent of the Soviet population – about 40 million people with an average per capita income of less than 75 rubles a month – consumed some 30–35 per cent less meat and dairy produce than they had in the mid-1960s, and about one-third the amount of meat consumed in relatively well-off families (those with a per capita monthly income of over 200 rubles). Their expenditures on clothing and footwear were about 30 per cent below the officially calculated necessary minimum; ownership of consumer durables, including such basics as radios and televisions, was between one-third and one-fifth the accepted norm. Moreover, because many of them either do not work, or work in low-prestige enterprises, the poor are less able to take advantage of state subsidies on food and basic services. Indeed, the low-paid are precisely the ones forced to make the greatest use of the private markets, where prices are far above those charged by state shops or enterprise closed distribution networks. *EKO*, no. 9, 1989, pp. 152–3 (A. V. Kormilkin); no. 7, 1990, pp. 57–9, 61–4 (A. V. Kormilkin).

75 *ST*, no. 3, 1989, pp. 47–8 (L. Zubova, D. Lantsev).

76 *EKO*, no. 7, 1990, pp. 56–7 (A. V. Kormilkin); Mandel, p. 202, n. 5.

77 *Trud*, 6 November 1991.

78 'N' stands for *novinka*, meaning literally a novelty, that is, a new product; 'D' refers to goods sold at *dogovornye*, or contract prices, that is, prices negotiated separately between the producer and customer (in this case, the trading network), considerably in excess of official state prices.

79 On some lines of 'N' class clothing in the RSFSR between 37 and 100 per cent were found to be defective. *Izvestiya*, 15 February 1990 (Yu. Rytov).

80 *EZh*, no. 14, 1990, p. 10 (V. Nefedov, V. Sevast'yanova).

81 *SP*, no. 9–10, 1990, p. 48 (Yu. Gushchin). At one enterprise, the Mayak garment factory, 'N' and 'D' items made up 80 per cent of its output as early as 1988.

82 *EZh*, no. 14, 1990, p. 10 (V. Nefedov, V. Sevast'yanova). Sometimes even production for low income groups was affected. The Kursk footwear factory in 1989 boosted its production of 'N' shoes and of its top-line styles by 54 per cent and 100 per cent respectively, while cutting output of shoes for the elderly by 21,500 pair. *Trud*, 14 March 1990 (L. Atamanova).

83 See below, chapter 5, pp. 168–70.

84 The Pobeda Production Association in Vladimir, for example, this way was able to report a 28 per cent increase in its 'volume of production' while physical output fell by 19 per cent. *SP*, no. 7–8, p. 28 (Yu. Ovchinnikov).

85 *SP*, no. 9–10, p. 48 (Yu. Gushchin); *Trud*, 14 March 1990 (L. Atamanova). The fruits of this policy, which dated back to the early years of perestroika, were obvious from the statistics for plan fulfilment in 1989 and early 1990, which showed many branches of light industry – primarily textiles and clothing – overfulfilling their plans while actually producing less than they had the year before. Consumer durables, such as washing machines and televisions, continued to increase production during this period, while still shifting production towards more expensive lines. *SI*, 29 October 1989; *EZh*, no. 14, 1990, p. 10 (V. Nefedov, V. Sevast'yanova); no. 18, 1990, p. 16.

86 *SP*, no. 1–2, 1990, pp. 33–4 (L. Zhelnina).

87 *SP*, no. 7–8, 1990, pp. 28–9 (Yu. Ovchinnikov).

88 *Trud*, 4 September 1988; *Tribuna mashinostroitelya*, 10 October 1990. It is traditional in Soviet industry for workers to receive one month's extra wages at the end of the year, paid for out of bonus or incentive funds, and workers have come both to expect and depend on it.

89 *Arsenal*, 15 January 1991; interview with personnel from the Arsenal Production Association, Leningrad, 24 June 1991. This was illustrated by the experience of shop no. 333 at the Association's Ars factory, which suffered such a drastic fall-off in defence orders that by May 1991 workers claimed to be making half, or even less than half, of what workers in other sections of the factory were earning. It is significant that, because of declining orders, the shop had a labour surplus. Although management had a policy of not sacking anybody, it did mean that the workers were in an extremely weak position when it came to pressing for a wage increase. They threatened to strike, but management was not overly perturbed. *Arsenal*, 16 May 1991.

90 This ability to win compensation at local level – and not just the working class's ideological and political demoralization – may partially explain why the price rises met with so few mass displays of public anger. For a fuller discussion of the 1991 price protests, see chapter 3.

91 For an interesting discussion of some of the points raised here see Rogovin.

92 Filtzer, *Soviet Workers and Stalinist Industrialization*, pp. 111–12, 134.

93 *SI*, 22 October 1989; *Trud*, 18 November 1990 (N. Chaikovskii).

94 At some textile factories in the Greater Moscow region, for example, the housing queue has not shortened for twenty years. One worsted cloth production association, for example, managed to put up a single block of just 143 flats between 1985 and 1989; of these, after the local soviet took its quota, only 25–30 flats were available for the association's own employees, despite the fact that it had 1,125 families on its waiting list. *Trud*, 5 September 1990.

95 *Sots. issled.*, no. 6, 1990, pp. 38–9 (L. L. Mal'tseva, O. N. Pulyaeva); *NK*, no. 2, 1990, p. 27 (L. S. Navodkin). In such regions as Vorkuta and the Far East miners could work twenty to thirty years underground and still be living with their families in a single room in a barracks. *SI*, 2 September 1989 (S. Lushchikov); *Trud*, 25 October 1990.

96 *KP*, 6 December 1990 (V. Sanatin).

97 See the remarks of S. V. Khromov of the independent trade union federation, Sotsprof, *Sots. issled.*, no. 2, 1990, p. 84.

98 An all-out steel strike in the Ukraine was only narrowly averted when the
government promised temporarily to guarantee workers' wages and to
review the price rises. *Trud*, 9 January, 23 January, 24 January, and 31
January 1990. We discuss these events in greater detail in chapter 3.

99 Indirect evidence of this is the fact that housing queues actually lengthened during 1989. Of the 14.3 million families and single persons (totalling
47 million people) waiting for 'an improvement in housing conditions', 1.9
million left the queues of local soviets, enterprises, or organizations, while
2.2 million joined. In all, during 1990 nearly a quarter of all urban families
were waiting for housing. *EZh*, no. 25, 1990, p. 13 (M. Panova). The crisis
prompted Gorbachev to issue a presidential edict, calling for housing
construction to be doubled, primarily by shifting investment away from
capital construction and lifting restrictions on private house building. 'O
novykh podkhodakh k resheniyu zhilishchnoi problemy v strane i merakh
po ikh prakticheskoi realizatsii', 19 May 1990. *Izvestiya*, 20 May 1990.

3 Political incentives: enterprise 'democratization' and the emergence of worker protests

1 *ST*, no. 10, 1989, p. 75 (E. Leont'eva).

2 There has been a great deal written about the labour movements, both
official and unofficial, which emerged under perestroika. For more general
accounts see Aves, Bova, Conner, Cook, Rutland, Sedaitis, and Teague.
Friedgut and Siegelbaum's case study of the 1989 miners' strike in the
Donbass is unique in its richness of detail, thanks to the authors' access to
extensive interviews with participants and the local press of the time.
Equally valuable is Anna Temkina's study of the labour movement in
Leningrad, which provides a rare insight into the diversity, as well as the
strengths and weaknesses of the workers' movement as it evolved over the
course of perestroika. The most comprehensive and penetrating analysis of
the history of the labour movement as a whole during perestroika remains
Mandel.

3 *Vedemosti Verkhovnogo Soveta SSSR*, 1983, no. 25, art. 302.

4 Yanowitch, *Work in the Soviet Union*, ch. 5, *Controversies*, pp. 20–4.

5 *ST*, no. 2, 1989, pp. 90–1, 93 (A. Kurennoi).

6 *ST*, no. 8, 1989, p. 95 (Yu. Volegov), no. 6, 1989, p. 38.

7 *Argumenty i fakty*, no. 41, 1988, p. 7.

8 Simon Clarke, in a personal communication, has suggested that the STK
had far less to do with efforts by the regime to incorporate the workforce
through 'democratization', than with Gorbachev's attempts to use worker
dissatisfaction to remove bureaucratic managers. If true this would help
explain some of the seeming inconsistencies in Gorbachev's policy towards
worker participation and the STK. However, the evidence for this interpretation is ambiguous at best. Few managers were actually displaced by the
elections and, as we have already noted, corporatist-type reforms, offering

workers a limited say in enterprise affairs had been experimented with even under Brezhnev.

9 Ryzhkov, as part of his speech to the Second Congress of People's Deputies, said that election of managers would henceforth be confined to non-state enterprises, that is, cooperatives and private firms. *Trud*, 14 December 1989.

10 *ST*, no. 2, 1989, p. 80; *VE*, no. 10, 1990, p. 103 (E. Torkanovskii).

11 *SI*, 8 July 1988.

12 Interview with S. A., foreman at AZLK, Moscow, 7 July 1991.

13 *Trud*, 14 February 1988.

14 *ST*, no. 2, 1990, p. 35 (A. Simakov).

15 *ST*, no. 12, 1989, p. 46 (A. Buzgalin, A. Kolganov).

16 Interview with S. A., foreman at AZLK, Moscow, 7 July 1991. Overall representation of workers on STK was hardly better than their share of chairpersons. A survey of 6,400 workers, including 2,746 STK members from 87 industrial enterprises (conducted between March 1988 and January 1989) found that workers were a mere 31.6 per cent of STK members, as against 23.9 per cent who were ITR, 15.7 per cent brigade leaders, 10.9 per cent shop or department superintendents, 7.2 per cent foremen, 6.3 per cent top management, and 4.6 per cent Communist Party and trade union officials. Women were also badly under-represented: they were 41 per cent of all the employed at these enterprises, but only 28.6 per cent of STK members. Andreenkova and Krotov, pp. 27–8.

17 *ST*, no. 8, 1989, pp. 52–3; no. 4, 1990, pp. 45 (N. Bolotina) and 47 (N. Lityagin).

18 *ST*, no. 1, 1990, p. 40 (O. Chumalo); *VE*, no. 10, 1990, pp. 105–6 (E. Torkanovskii).

19 *VE*, no. 12, 1990, p. 97 (V. Gerchikov).

20 *Trud*, 13 September 1988; *Sots. issled.*, no. 5, 1989, p. 72 (A. G. Aptip'ev); interview with S. A., foreman, AZLK, Moscow, 7 July 1991. A 1989 study of STK carried out by VTsSPS's Scientific Centre concluded:
   The processes of inertia have, unfortunately, been far from overcome. In practice labour collectives have, for the most part, still not assumed their proper place in the system of self-administration. Many of the production, economic, and social questions that are worrying people they neither investigate nor decide; on those questions which they do discuss, their decisions are merely recommendations, rather than binding. In other words, making the labour collective the legislative power within enterprises is a task which in large part still has to be solved. *ST*, no. 6, 1989, p. 36.

21 *ST*, no. 4, 1990, p. 48 (N. Lityagin); *Izvestiya*, 6 May 1990 (V. Mirolenich).

22 *Trud*, 27 June 1991 (Vladimir Kuz'mishchev). The title is a play on a scene from Bulgakov's *Master and Margarita*, where a sales attendant tries to pass off bad sturgeon as sturgeon of 'second freshness'.

23 *Sots. issled.*, no. 5, 1989, p. 72 (A. G. Aptip'ev); *ST*, no. 3, 1989, p. 117, no. 2, 1990, p. 36 (A. Simakov).

24 *Sots. issled.*, no. 5, 1988, pp. 74–5, and no. 2, 1989, pp. 30–2 (P. P. Reznikov); *EKO*, no. 3, 1989, pp. 11–13 (V. E. Boikov).

25 *Trud*, 13 September 1988.

26 *Sots. issled.*, no. 5, 1989, pp. 71–3 (A. G. Aptip'ev). Similar results were reported in a 1987 trade union survey (*Sots. issled.*, no. 4, 1989, p. 78 – A. N. Komozin), and by Burawoy and Hendley in their 1990–1 study of Moscow's Rezina rubber-technical goods factory. As elsewhere, Rezina's STK was dominated by middle-level management, who, although 'sincere in their efforts to understand and redress the concerns of ordinary workers ... lacked a direct link with these workers. Often the workers were unaware of the efforts being undertaken on their behalf by the STK.' Burawoy and Hendley, p. 389.

27 *RT*, 2 October 1990 (N. Kvizhinadze). For similar views see the letter from an STK member at the Minsk coach repair factory, *RT*, 6 January 1990; the letter from the chair of the STK at Zaporozhtransformator, *IZ*, 6 February 1990; and the comments of the head of the STK at the Irkutsk mica factory, reported in *ST*, no. 4, 1990, p. 47 (N. Lityagin). It is worth noting that all three of these people are workers.

28 Andreenkova and Krotov, pp. 6–7.

29 *Materialy vsesoyuznogo monitoringa*, pp. 3–19. It is interesting that this trend was already visible as early as 1987. A study comparing workers' attitudes towards the prospects for worker participation found them decidedly more pessimistic in 1987 than they had been in 1985. *ST*, no. 5, 1988, pp. 63–7 (A. Meshcherkin, E. Prudnik).

30 Interview with S. A., foreman at AZLK, Moscow, 7 July 1991.

31 *Lyublinskie Vesti*, 11 January 1991.

32 *RT*, 15 June 1990.

33 *RT*, 20 April 1990 (Kovrov); Temkina, p. 223, and *Izvestiya*, 11 April 1991 (Kirov works); *EKO*, no. 8, 1990, pp. 92, 95 (L. Shcherbakova; Sibelektrotyazhmash).

34 Law of the USSR, 'O predpriyatiyakh v SSSR', 4 June 1990; implemented by the decree of the USSR Supreme Soviet, 'O poryadke vvedeniya v deistvie Zakona SSSR 'O predpriyatiyakh v SSSR'.' *EZh*, no. 25, 1990, pp. 19–21. Procedures for hiring managers in state enterprises were laid down in a decree of the USSR Council of Ministers, 23 October 1990, no. 1073, 'O poryadke naima i osvobozhdeniya rukovoditelya gosudarstvennogo soyuznogo predpriyatiya'. *EZh*, no. 45, 1990, p. 19.

35 Similar laws were passed in the RSFSR and Ukraine, both of which assigned the labour collective a totally undefined role either in appointing the enterprise director (Russia), or 'determining the conditions' under which the director would be hired (Ukraine). In all cases management had sole authority to conduct enterprise business, including signing contracts, disposing over enterprise property and finances, and issuing orders and instructions binding on all enterprise personnel. Law of the RSFSR, 'O predpriyatiyakh i predprinimatel'skoi deyatel'nosti', 25 December 1990, *EZh*, no. 4, 1991, pp. 16–18. Law of the Ukrainian SSR, 'O predpriyatiyakh v Ukrainskoi SSR', 27 March 1991, *RG*, 6 May 1991.

36 Interview with V. Lamonov, a miner from Krasnodon, and V. Eliseev, of the Trade Union of Employees in the Coal Industry (the official miners' trade union), Moscow, 8 June 1991.

37 *RG*, 19 January 1991 (M. Baltyanskii).

38 *Znamya*, 26 September and 28 September 1990.
39 *VE*, no. 10, 1991, p. 37 (E. Klisho, I. Chuiko).
40 *EZh*, no. 32, 1990, pp. 4–5 (P. Korotkov, V. Ul'yanov). Sale of shares to outside individuals was to be allowed only after the creation of a functioning stock market (*ibid.*). In the meantime, the government was to retain a controlling interest. *ST*, no. 10, 1990, p. 6 (S. Zenkin).
41 *SP*, no. 8, 1991, pp. 30–3 (A. Kondrashov). Perhaps the most blatant move of this kind involved the Voskov instrument factory in Sestroretsk, Leningrad oblast. There the workforce, most of whom are women, voted by a 90 per cent majority to fire the director. The head of the factory's parent Production Association, 'Instrument', not only refused to accept the workers' decision, but even congratulated them on 'their' proposal to the USSR Council of Ministers (about which they knew absolutely nothing) to turn 'Instrument' into a private concern, with its director as its new head. *Trud*, 26 January 1991. If nothing else, this example calls into question government and management claims that such administrative privatization of enterprises had the workers' support.
42 The Petrograd District Soviet refused to register the Company after an appeal by workers at one of the Association's constituent factories, who had argued that such a major decision should be taken by a referendum of all the enterprise's workers, and not by a management-organized delegate conference. At this point management turned to the USSR Ministry of Finance, which had no legal authority in the case, but nevertheless issued a decree registering Lenpoligrafmash as a joint-stock company. *Tribuna mashinostroitelya*, 16 January, 7 February, 20 March, 27 March, 3 April, 22 May, 5 June 1991; interview with Andrei Tuchkov, Leningrad City Soviet, 27 June 1991.
43 *SP*, no. 7, 1991, p. 17 (A. Ivanov).
44 This was the case in a number of engineering enterprises, where a majority – and in some cases, all – of shares were reserved for sale to employees. See the examples of the L'vov conveyor factory, *ST*, no. 10, 1991, pp. 59–64 (Tamara Odinets, Aleksandr Maslak); the Poltava chemical equipment factory, *RG*, 2 November 1991; and the Kalinin pump factory, *Trud*, 1 November 1991 (A. Chereshnev).
45 *Nez. gaz.*, 8 June 1991.
46 *Trud*, 30 August 1990 (interview with A. A. Mel'nikov, first deputy chairperson, VAZ STK); *Trud*, 6 December 1990 (interview with V. A. Andrianov, deputy chairperson, VAZ STK); *EZh*, no. 2, 1991, p. 12 (V. Ul'yanov); *SP*, no. 6, 1991, pp. 40–3 (A. Turbanov).
47 *Izvestiya*, 13 February 1991 (S. Zhigalov); *KP*, 15 February 1991 (A. Kalinin).
48 *Nez. gaz.*, 8 June 1991.
49 *Trud*, 26 December 1991 (Yu. Orsov); *RT*, 6 February 1992. As of late 1992 the question of what proportion of VAZ shares would go to the collective was still being disputed, this time by management and the Russian government. *RT*, 9 October 1992.
50 *Trud*, 30 August 1990; *RT*, 4 September, 9 September; *VE*, no. 12, 1990, pp. 147–50. The latter contains the full text of the main conference documents.
51 *Trud*, 6 December 1990; *RT*, 8 December, 9 December, and 12 December 1990

(L. Biryukova, E. Mokhorov), and 23 January 1991; *Izvestiya*, 11 December 1990 (I. Demchenko).

52 *RT*, 9 December 1990, 10 January 1991 (interview with A. Gukanov), 23 January 1991.

53 *RT*, 12 December 1990 (L. Biryukova, E. Mokhorov).

54 *RT*, 23 January 1991 (interview with I. T. Akhmetov).

55 Temkina, pp. 220–5.

56 *RT*, 23 October 1991 (Vladimir Chuprin) and 14 November 1991 (Ol'ga Vlasova); *Prolog*, 28 November–4 December 1991, p. 4 (interview with Leonid Gordon). According to David Mandel, who interviewed a number of the movement's leaders, another factor in its demise was its cooption by the Russian government, which gave it premises and money, and helped ensure that its strategy was aimed at lobbying the government rather than building a rank-and-file movement. David Mandel, personal communication.

57 Perhaps indicative of this trend was the conflict at the Rezina rubber-technical goods factory in Moscow, played out before the Union of Labour Collectives was formed. At Rezina the STK, which represented middle management and technical specialists, attempted to undercut the position of the Association's general director by proposing to convert Rezina into a joint-stock company with shares issued free to all employees. At no time, however, did these specialists make any attempt to discuss their plan with production workers, and no workers were invited to the joint STK–management meetings held to debate it. When the June 1990 Enterprise Law put the STK's actual existence on the line, its leadership openly linked the question of the STK's continuation to Rezina's privatization and transfer to Russian jurisdiction. Burawoy and Hendley, pp. 390–3.

58 *EZh*, no. 31, 1990, p. 15.

59 *Izvestiya*, 24 October 1990. We should caution that these figures are very imprecise. According to this report the country was averaging 50,000 people off work each day due to strikes and inter-ethnic conflicts (the figure we have used to estimate the total days lost for January–September). Other reports quoted a daily average during January–May of 100,000 people not working (*EZh*, no. 31, 1990, p. 15), while Abalkin claimed that during January–March lost person-days averaged 200,000 per day (*EZh*, no. 17, 1990, p. 6). It would appear that some of these sources were using the number of work days as the basis for their calculations, while others used the total number of days in the year. The problem would have been solved, of course, if the press had simply reported the quarterly totals for strike days lost.

60 Filtzer, *Soviet Workers and Stalinist Industrialization*, pp. 82–7; Holubenko, pp. 8–10.

61 The coal fields in the Greater Moscow region did not strike.

62 We can only give here a very brief outline of the events surrounding the strike. For detailed accounts see Friedgut and Siegelbaum, and Mandel, ch. 3.

63 *Sots. issled.*, no. 1, 1989, p. 29; *NK*, no. 2, 1990, p. 22 (L. S. Navodkin); *Trud*,

5 May 1989. I am grateful to Simon Clarke for calling this last reference to my attention.

64 *ST*, no. 10, 1989, p. 72 (E. Leont'eva); *SI*, 2 September 1989 (S. Lushchikov).

65 *SI*, 7 November 1989.

66 Mandel, pp. 55–7; *NK*, no. 2, 1990, pp. 22–3 (L. S. Navodkin).

67 *NK*, no. 2, 1990, pp. 22–3 (L. S. Navodkin); Mandel, p. 57.

68 *NK*, no. 2, 1990, p. 27 (L. S. Navodkin).

69 *Sots. issled.*, no. 6, 1990, pp. 38–9 (L. L. Mal'tseva, O. N. Pulyaeva). For a more detailed discussion of working conditions in coal mining, see below, chapter 5.

70 *NK*, no. 2, 1990, p. 28 (L. S. Navodkin); *Sots. issled.*, no. 6, 1990, pp. 40–1 (L. L. Mal'tseva, O. N. Pulyaeva); *SI*, 4 October 1989.

71 *NK*, no. 2, 1990, pp. 25–6 (L. S. Navodkin).

72 In the procedures set up for the election of the new Congress of People's Deputies, one-third of seats were 'reserved' for the Communist Party, the official trade unions, the Soviet Women's Committee, and other Party-controlled bodies.

73 *NK*, no. 3, 1990, p. 27 (L. S. Navodkin); Mandel, pp. 58–60.

74 Mandel, p. 59; Friedgut and Siegelbaum, pp. 20–1.

75 In Vorkuta the miners had also demanded that 25 per cent of hard currency earnings from coal exports be kept within the region. Mandel, p. 59.

76 The accord was codified in a decree of the USSR Council of Ministers, 3 August 1989, 'O merakh po obespecheniyu vypolneniya sovmestnykh reshenii, prinyatykh pravitel'stvennymi komissiyami s uchastiem VTsSPS i zabastovochnymi komitetami trudyashchikhsya ugol'nykh regionov strany', subsequently known simply as Decree No. 608.

77 For example, the mining regions were to receive improved supplies of soap. Dutifully 45 tonnes of soap were shipped to the Donbass – not bath soap, however, but highly alkaline 'industrial' grade soap which irritates the skin and was unusable. *SI*, 9 September 1989.

78 *RT*, 1 June 1990.

79 *SI*, 27 October 1989; *Trud*, 18 November 1989.

80 *Trud*, 19 November 1989.

81 *SI*, 27 October, 28 October, and 16 November 1989; *Trud*, 14 November and 19 November 1989.

82 *RT*, 16 February 1990. In October 1989 there was a 24–hour warning strike in Mezhdurechensk, but it was not extended. *SI*, 24 October 1989.

83 Mandel, pp. 65–7; Friedgut and Siegelbaum, pp. 10–13.

84 *SI*, 21 November 1989 (A. Parshintsev); *RKSM*, no. 1, 1990, pp. 191–4 (A. Katsva); *RT*, 3 January 1990 (A. Parshintsev); *VE*, no. 2, 1990, p. 85.

85 In the Kuzbass, for example, over 200 participants in the 1989 strike were elected to local trade union committees. *Trud*, 25 February 1990 (V. Korovitsin). There was also considerable pressure on many pit managers to resign. In Donetsk oblast forty-two directors (about one third of the total) were subjected to votes of no confidence; twenty-seven had to face reelection and ten were forced to give up their jobs. *SI*, 1 October 1989.

86 Law of the Supreme Soviet of the USSR, 9 October 1990, 'O poryadke

razresheniya kollektivnykh trudovykh sporov (konfliktov)', *Trud*, 14 October 1989.
87 Mandel, p. 56.
88 See, for example, the interviews with Leonid Gordon in *NG*, 26 January 1991 and *KP*, 8 February 1991.
89 *Trud*, 4 April 1990.
90 In support of their charge they pointed out that among the delegates were 319 dismissed trade union officials, 56 colliery directors and general directors of production associations, 19 Communist Party and soviet officials, 52 technical specialists, 50 workers of non-mining trades, and only 123 actual miners. In addition, 92 other miners had been invited to attend, including 50 from the commission charged with overseeing the implementation of the July accords. *Izvestiya*, 1 April 1990. Given this composition, the delegates' hostility to the old Central Committee is all the more amazing.
91 In the words of one delegate, a tunneller from Vorkuta, 'If we want fundamental changes in miners' lives we must understand clearly that the organization and conduct of the congress cannot be entrusted to the official trade union. For it is under the thumb of bureaucrats [*chinovniki*] and is incapable of defending the workers' interests to the end'. *Trud*, 5 June 1990 (N. Mokrishchev).
92 *Izvestiya*, 16 June 1990; *Trud*, 17 June 1990.
93 'Resolyutsiya Pervogo S'ezda Shakhterov po voprosam sotsial'no-ekonomicheskogo polozheniya, vypolneniya postanovleniya SM SSSR No. 608 i perspektivam perekhoda k rynku.' I am grateful to Leonid Gordon for providing me with a copy of this resolution.
94 This was based on a survey of delegates' views carried out by a team of sociologists headed by Leonid Gordon. *Delovoi mir*, no. 7 (24), 15 January 1991; *Smena* (Leningrad), 28 June 1990. I am grateful to Anna Temkina for providing me with both of these references.
95 *Izvestiya*, 11 July 1990; *RT*, 12 July 1990; *Trud*, 12 July and 13 July 1990.
96 David Mandel, personal communication. Mandel was present at the Congress. The report in *Trud*, 30 October 1990 (N. Mokrishchev), claimed that the Kuzbass and Vorkuta delegates did not gain majority support and staged a walkout, thus implying that the formation of the new union was a unilateral act by an isolated rump.
97 Again, we cannot give a full account of the history of the strikes here. The most detailed discussion is Mandel, ch. 7.
98 *RT*, 8 January 1991; *Izvestiya*, 8 January 1991.
99 *Izvestiya*, 9 January 1991 (Nikolai Lisovenko); *RG*, 19 January 1991.
100 *Izvestiya*, 13 February, 26 February, and 27 February 1991; *RT*, 14 February and 28 February 1991; *RG*, 27 February 1991.
101 *Izvestiya*, 1 March 1991; *Trud*, 2 March 1991; *RG*, 7 March 1991.
102 *Trud*, 1 March, 2 March, 5 March, 8 March, 14 March, and 16 March 1991; *Izvestiya*, 5 March, 14 March, and 16 March 1991; *RT*, 19 March, 21 March and 3 April 1991.
103 *Izvestiya*, 8 April and 9 April 1991.

104 *Izvestiya*, 1 March 1991; *Trud*, 2 March 1991.
105 *Izvestiya*, 4 March 1991; Mandel, p. 162.
106 *Izvestiya*, 15 March 1991. According to Vyacheslav Golikov, chair of the Council of Workers' Committees of Kemerovo oblast, the Kuzbass miners were not asking any economic concessions from the government, and would not even negotiate with it, since their main demand was for that government to resign. Instead they were pressing for economic independence, which in his view would grant mines the conditions needed to support substantial wage rises. *RT*, 26 March 1991.
107 *Trud*, 1 March, 5 March, 13 March, 15 March, and 9 April 1991; *Izvestiya*, 15 March and 16 March 1991.
108 *Trud*, 5 March, 8 March, 13 March, 15 March, 26 March, and 27 March 1991; *RT*, 30 March 1991. According to Mandel, p. 169, Vorgashorskaya had received the right to export its above-plan coal for hard currency, and its miners were reluctant to jeopardize this by striking. In a similar incident in Western Siberia, the Chernigovskii open cast mine, which in the wake of the 1989 strike had won the right to conclude contracts directly with customers without any *goszakaz*, refused to join the 1991 strike, on the grounds that it could not violate its contracts. *RT*, 27 March 1991 (Anatolii Parshintsev). Both these examples show how potentially divisive was the demand for economic independence for individual pits.
109 *Trud*, 15 March and 16 March 1991; *RT*, 19 March 1991.
110 *RT*, 5 April 1991.
111 *Trud*, 9 April 1991; *Izvestiya*, 8 April, 9 April, and 24 April 1991; *RT*, 9 April 1991.
112 *Izvestiya*, 19 April 1991; Mandel, pp. 181–2.
113 *Izvestiya*, 1 May and 5 May 1991.
114 *Izvestiya*, 5 May 1991.
115 Mandel, p. 189.
116 Mandel, p. 172.
117 This was particularly true of the unions in iron and steel and engineering, which were most dependent on deliveries of coal to keep their own production going. *Trud*, 13 March 1991. See also *RT*, 29 March 1991 (Mefodii Martynov). The All-Union official union body, the General Confederation of Trade Unions (VKP, which VTsSPS had renamed itself in October 1990), also never gave the miners more than token support. On the other hand, the strike did win the backing of the official Russian trade union federation, the FNPR, which at the time was attempting to forge an informal alliance with El'tsin so as to stengthen its own political and financial position *vis-à-vis* the VKP. The FNPR not only publicly gave a modest donation of 300,000 rubles to the miners' strike fund (*Trud*, 5 March 1991; *RT*, 11 April 1991), it channelled some 41 million rubles of Russian government money to the independent mineworkers' union in Vorkuta as a reward for their demanding Gorbachev's resignation. See, Kagarlitsky, p. 92. I am grateful to Simon Clarke for calling this reference to my attention.

118 Despite the official position of their union, workers in metallurgical factories and ore mines in Sverdlovsk and Chelyabinsk held meetings in solidarity with the miners and collected money for their strike fund. The factory newspaper at Sverdlovsk's Turbo-Motor factory even felt obliged to publish the bank account number into which people could make contributions. *Trud*, 19 April and 23 April 1991; *Znamya*, 5 April 1991.

119 *Nez. gaz.*, 9 July 1991.

120 *Pravda*, 20 March 1991.

121 *RG*, 15 May 1991 (N. Andrusenko); interview with V. M., loader at the Moscow Meat Combine, 12 June 1991. In both cases salami that had started to spoil was recycled into cheap sausage meat and put back on sale. As *RG*'s reporter commented, this should have come as no surprise, since in the aftermath of the Chernobyl catastrophe the authorities had allowed people to eat radioactive food, assuring them that it was safe.

122 *Trud*, 5 April and 12 April 1991.

123 The Russian trade union federation, FNPR, called for a day of action on 26 April, but this was almost certainly an empty gesture. The federation did nothing to prepare it, and it received little response. *Trud*, 24 April, 26 April, and 27 April 1991; *RT*, 30 April 1991 (Viktor Yurlov).

124 *Moskvich*, 26 April and 6 May 1991.

125 *Trud*, 5 April 1991 (Yu. Kotlyarov).

126 *RT*, 18 April 1991 (Ali Naibov); *Znamya*, 5 April 1991; *Impul's*, 30 May 1991.

127 *Priborostroitel'*, 22 May 1991.

128 *Izvestiya*, 9 May 1991 (Evgenii Solomenko).

129 *RT*, 5 April and 19 April 1991.

130 *Izvestiya*, 15 April 1991 (N. Matukovskii). David Mandel, in a personal communication, has suggested that another factor might have been the relatively well-supplied state retailing network in Belarus', which even in 1991 was selling at prices far lower than the free prices prevailing on most goods in Russia. Thus the April price rises were more strongly felt in Belarus' than elsewhere.

131 *Trud*, 5 April 1991 (S. Vaganov); *RT*, 5 April and 6 April 1991 (Vasilii Roshchin); *Izvestiya*, 5 April 1991 (M. Shimanskii).

132 Mandel, p. 178.

133 *Izvestiya*, 9 April and 18 April 1991 (M. Shimanskii).

134 *Izvestiya*, 9 April, 10 April and 11 April 1991 (M. Shimanskii); *Trud* 11 April 1991 (S. Vaganov).

135 *Izvestiya*, 11 April 1991 (M. Shimanskii).

136 'Polozhenie o Stachechnom Komitete Belorussii', adopted at a Conference of the Belorussian Strike Committee (SKB), Minsk, 13 April 1991. Duplicated copy.

137 *Izvestiya*, 24 April, 25 April, and 26 April 1991 (M. Shimanskii).

138 *Izvestiya*, 24 April, 25 April, 26 April, and 29 April 1991 (M. Shimanskii); Mandel, p. 185; Informatsionnoe Agenstvo SMOT IAS, *Informatsionnyi Byulleten'*, no. 61, May 1991, p. 2.

139 Mandel, p. 185. Part of the answer may lie in the close ties between the Strike Committee and the Belorussian Popular Front, which no doubt

wished to use the strikes to further an essentially nationalist political agenda somewhat divorced from the issues which precipitated the workers' original anger. There were certainly bitter disputes within the Strike Committee over the wisdom of its tactic to suspend the strikes after 23 April. By the time the Strike Committee reissued its call to resume the strikes on 21 May few workers responded, and for good reason: management at the large industrial plants had used the breathing space thus allowed to reach settlements with their workers. For an account of these events, which does not, however, share the interpretation we have presented here, see the two articles by Mihalisko.

140 Mandel, pp. 183–4.

141 *SP*, no. 10, 1991, pp. 21–2 (A. Krest'yaninov). These wage rises, as those achieved through more spontaneous local action, were to be financed by allowing enterprises to sell 30 per cent of their output at contract prices, thus feeding the general inflation and making it harder for other enterprises still bound by the fixed prices of *goszakaz* to acquire metal. In a separate accord with the Ukrainian government, Ukrainian iron and steel works were allowed to meet wage demands out of profits. *Trud*, 6 April 1991. On the background to the strike threat and how both management and the official trade union moved in to coopt it, see the articles by I. Ostrovskii, *Trud*, 19 January and 9 February 1991.

142 The phrase was used as the title of a round-table discussion published in *Sots. issled.*, no. 1, 1989. For a discussion of early strikes during 1987–8, see Mandel, pp. 19–33 and Cook, pp. 47–8.

143 For interesting examples, see, *Polis*, no. 1, 1991, p. 112 (A. A. Shkreba) and *Sots. issled.*, no. 1, 1989, p. 29.

144 *ST*, no. 8, 1988, p. 41.

145 *ST*, no. 10, 1989, pp. 74–5 (A. Kravchenko); no. 7, 1991, p. 73 (A. Lopatin); *SP*, no. 2, 1991, pp. 46–9 (Yu. Antropov); Mandel, pp. 28–9.

146 *SG*, 13 December and 16 December 1989; *ST*, no. 10, 1989, p. 75 (A. Kravchenko).

147 *SP*, no. 7, 1991, p. 28 (A. Mitin); *Trud*, 20 February 1991. Management further inflamed the conflict by filing a suit in court to have the strike declared illegal.

148 *Arsenal*, 15 January and 16 May 1991; *Priborostroitel'*, 17 April 1991; *Trud*, 10 January and 28 July 1990.

149 Interview with personnel from the Arsenal Production Association, Leningrad, 24 June 1991. This also helps explain workers' intense hostility to management-sponsored internal cooperatives, which received preferential allocation of resources to the detriment of ordinary workers, or were allowed to earn higher pay for the exact same work. *EKO*, no. 8, 1990, pp. 91–2 (L. Shcherbakova); Burawoy and Hendley, p. 381; *Trud*, 27 November 1991 (G. Sazonov).

150 *RT*, 18 January 1990 (G. Dolzhenko); *RG*, 2 December 1990.

151 *Izvestiya*, 5 March 1991 (Yu. Perepletkin). Tensions were temporarily eased by a government decision to allow oil enterprises to sell a portion of their output abroad and to use the hard currency thus earned to buy food and

consumer goods. This clearly had little long-term impact on conditions in the fields, because in August 1991, just after the unsuccessful *putsch*, El'tsin signed an edict allotting the territory a 10 per cent quota of all oil and gas extracted from the region for sale abroad, with the right to use the proceeds to improve conditions. The edict, however, was never implemented, and in early 1992, the oil workers again were threatening industrial action. *RT*, 14 February 1992 (Sergei Petrov).

152 *Trud*, 4 October 1990 (Yu. Dudkov, Yu. Kotlyarov).

153 See, for example, the discussion in Yanowitch, *Work in the Soviet Union*, ch. 7.

154 *ST*, no. 10, 1989, pp. 74–5 (A. Kravchenko); no. 7, 1991, p. 73 (A. Lopatin); *SP*, no. 2, 1991, pp. 46–9 (Yu. Antropov).

155 *SP*, no. 2, 1991, p. 49 (Yu. Antropov).

156 Interview with S. A., foreman at AZLK, Moscow, 7 July 1991.

157 *Trud*, 16 September 1990 (V. Konstantinov), 3 October 1990 (F. Emchenko), 13 October 1990 (F. Emchenko), 23 March 1991 (V. Kozlov).

158 Surveys of public attitudes towards the trade unions carried out during 1989 and 1990 found, not unexpectedly, that most people still considered the unions to be tools of management or the Communist Party. Some 40 per cent felt that expanding the legal rights of trade unions would not help the situation, since they would be structurally incapable of using them. *Trud*, 26 October 1990.

159 Thus the strikes in the metallurgical industry during the 1991 miners' strike, already referred to, were in many cases led by local leaders of the official union. *SP*, no. 10, 1991, p. 21 (A. Krest'yaninov).

160 *RT*, 25 January 1990; *SP*, no. 5–6, 1990, p. 47 (V. Povetkin); no. 17–18, 1990, pp. 66–9 (K. Kamenev). A similar situation arose in early 1990 in Poltava, where workers at the city's chemical equipment factory struck over alleged corruption by the head of its trade union. When the demands of the workers, which expanded to include calls for the resignation of local Communist Party and city soviet officials, were taken up by other factories in the town, and plans were set for a city-wide strike, the oblast trade union council stepped in and defused the situation by negotiating a complex agreement between the chemical equipment factory's workers, management, and its parent production association. *Trud*, 11 April 1990.

161 *Izvestiya*, 14 October 1990.

162 *Trud*, 9 January, 23 January, 24 January, 31 January, 10 February, 11 February 1990; *RT*, 1 February 1990; *Izvestiya*, 2 February 1990.

163 The supply crisis is discussed in greater detail in ch. 4.

164 *Trud*, 21 November 1990 (A. Bogomolov).

165 *Trud*, 10 January 1990 (interview with M. V. Ikharlova, then chairperson of the union).

166 Despite its title, this was the official trade union federation of the RSFSR and, at least at its inception in April 1990, was heavily influenced by old-line conservatives in both VTsSPS and the Communist Party. It later assumed greater political independence, and became the principal trade union federation within Russia after the breakup of the Soviet Union.

167 *Trud*, 21 November and 25 December 1990; *RT*, 23 December 1990.
168 Nikolai Preobrazhensky; Clarke, *et al.*, ch. 10.

4 'Market mechanisms' and the breakdown of economic regulation

1 E. A. Preobrazhensky, *The New Economics*.
2 See in particular Rakovsky and Braginskaya.
3 Filtzer, *Soviet Workers and De-Stalinization*, ch. 5.
4 Cook is certainly correct when she points out (pp. 42–5) that from late 1988 Gorbachev retreated from pushing self-financing to its ultimate limits and began issuing renewed credits to enterprises threatened with bankruptcy. She is also right to attribute this move to the regime's fear of the political repercussions of massive job losses. She does not, however, seem to appreciate the conclusion which the Gorbachev wing of the elite drew from this experience: the need for a total restoration of capitalism.
5 On the Enterprise Law and the decentralization of wages see pp. 88 and 71, respectively.
6 'Osnovy zakonodatel'stva ob investitsionnoi deyatel'nosti v SSSR', 10 December 1990. Implemented by a decree of the USSR Supreme Soviet, 'O vvedenii v deistvie Osnov zakonodatel'stva ob investitsionnoi deyaitel'-nosti v SSSR', 10 December 1990. *Izvestiya*, 16 December 1990.
7 Draft legislation, 'Osnovy zakonodatel'stva Soyuza SSR i respublik o raz-gosudarstvlenii sobstvennosti i privatizatsii predpriyatii', *EZh*, no. 7, 1991, pp. 18–19. Plans to draft a new law on bankruptcy, 'O nestoyatel'-nosti [bankrotstve] predpriyatii', were discussed in an interview by A. Sukhanov, a high-ranking Gosplan official, *Izvestiya*, 12 February 1991.
8 See, for example, the comments by Yurii Prokof'ev, leader of the Moscow City Communist Party, as reported in the *Financial Times*, 5 February 1991. According to Prokof'ev, the Soviet Union could not afford the prolonged process of capital accumulation characteristic of the older capitalist powers, but had to develop its market infrastructures quickly, within ten to fifteen years. Its model of development should, therefore, be countries like Japan, Spain, South Korea, 'and even' Chile.
9 We discuss this problem in detail below, pp. 139–41.
10 See, for example, the experiments at the Volgograd Silicate Building Materials Combine discussed in *ST*, no. 5, 1989, pp. 28–30 (V. Tinyakov, L. Mironenko) and *SG*, 17 September 1989; and the Svetlana Production Association in Leningrad, *EKO*, no. 5, 1989, pp. 107–8 (O. A. Mozhzhukhin, A. F. Tyagushev).
11 *ST*, no. 3, 1988, p. 96 (G. Knykhin); no. 7, 1988, p. 46 (P. Petrochenko); no. 5, 1989, pp. 35–6 (V. Korolev).
12 *ZSM*, 31 October 1990.
13 *ST*, no. 4, 1988, p. 60 (V. Kolosov).
14 *ST*, no. 5, 1989, pp. 36–7 (V. Korolev); *ZSM*, 12 February 1990.
15 *ST*, no. 1, 1990, p. 50 (A. Rogov). See also the experience of the Kirov engineering works in Gorlovka, discussed in *ST*, no. 2, 1991, pp. 67–8 (S. Chernyavskii).

16 *Trud*, 3 January 1990.
17 *ST*, no. 9, 1988, p. 18.
18 *ST*, no. 4, 1988, p. 60 (V. Kolosov).
19 See, for example, *Moskvich*, 1 April 1991.
20 See the experience of the Tripol'skii biochemical factory, where those sections deemed not yet ready for leasing were put on collective contracts. But even here they used the second, more 'radical' variant of *khozraschet*. *ST*, no. 12, 1991, pp. 19–20.
21 *ST*, no. 7, 1990, p. 22 (I. Borodin, U. Gil'manov).
22 Burawoy and Hendley, pp. 378–87. The Moscow low-voltage equipment factory, for example, had 900 of its 1,500 workforce in a cooperative in 1989, with plans to convert the factory entirely into a cooperative at a later date. *ST*, no. 2, 1990, p. 20 (V. Illarionov). For the possibilities of corruption latent in such arrangements, see ch. 3, note 149.
23 *EZh*, no. 31, 1990, p. 8 (A. Siginevich, I. Gurkov).
24 *ST*, no. 7, 1990, p. 21 (I. Borodin, U. Gil'manov).
25 *EZh*, no. 14, 1992, p. 1. The reference does not cite the number of enterprises on full *khozraschet*.
26 In 1989 enterprises on leasing achieved a 1.3 per cent decline in costs per ruble of output relative to 1988, versus a 0.3 per cent rise for industry as a whole. Average wages in leasing enterprises were a bare 12 rubles a month higher. *EZh*, no. 31, 1990, p. 8 (A. Siginevich, I. Gurkov).
27 *ST*, no. 2, 1990, pp. 18–20 (V. Illarionov); *Arsenal*, 26 November 1990, 21 January 1991, 24 June 1991. See also the report on the Chusovoi iron and steel works, *ST*, no. 12, 1990, pp. 16–17. Among the enterprises which claimed successfully to have applied the leasing system were several building materials factories which went on leasing during 1988 and 1989, some on long-term contracts of from five to seven years. One, the Butovskoe building materials combine in the Greater Moscow region, did away with wage rates and salaries, and instead made earnings dependent on employees' personal contributions to total revenues. *EKO*, no. 6, 1989, p. 6 (M. A. Bocharov). Another, the Revda brick factory in Sverdlovsk oblast, abolished profits as its main indicator, in favour of total income, from which it financed new investment, wages, and a fund for social development. *SG*, 27 October 1989. For other reports on the building materials industry see *RT*, 4 January 1990 (reinforced concrete factories in Frunze), and *EZh*, no. 22, 1990, p. 12 (Kotlasskii silicate brick factory, Arkhangel'sk oblast).
28 *SI*, 27 September 1989 (Batumi woodworking combine, Adzharskaya ASSR); *SG*, 27 October 1989 (Revda brick factory, Sverdlovsk oblast); *RT*, 16 October 1990 (Frunze production association, Penza).
29 *EKO*, no. 12, 1989, pp. 69–73 (V. N. Malyshev, V. F. Borovskii). This same system of shops selling output to one another at internal prices was applied at the Tashkent textile combine. *EZh*, no. 43, 1990, p. 9 (B. Irgashev, V. Levina).
30 See, for example, the cases of the Foton Production Association in the Crimean city of Simferopol', *SP*, no. 7–8, 1990, p. 24 (F. Shishov, I. Ryazhskikh); and the Gomel' Agricultural Equipment Production Associa-

tion (Gomsel'mash), *ST*, no. 1, 1991, p. 40 (A. Dulina. G. Kobrinskii). At the Strommashina factory in Kuibyshev sections were accused of resorting to internal litigation simply to deflect responsibility for their own failures. *Strela*, 22 June and 6 July 1990.

31 *ST*, no. 2, 1990, p. 21 (V. Illarionov), no. 11, 1990, p. 9 (V. Illarionov, citing the example of the Odessa refrigeration equipment scientific-production association).

32 *RT*, 10 December 1991; Bizyukov and Bel'chik, pp. 5–6.

33 *ST*, no. 2, 1990, p. 22 (V. Illarionov).

34 *Arsenal*, 25 April 1991.

35 *ST*, no. 8, 1990, p. 41 (V. Korolev).

36 *Izvestiya*, 29 January 1990. The collective at the Stroipolimer factory in Moscow oblast, which went on leasing in 1987, eventually had to buy the factory out, its lease payments were so high. Of the 3 million rubles in profits earned in its first year on leasing, it paid 1.5 million as lease payments and another 1 million to the central budget, keeping only 500,000 rubles for its own use. It eventually succeeded in increasing the share of retained profits to nearly two-thirds, but employees still found it more profitable to purchase the factory. *EZh*, no. 42, 1990, p. 4 (A. Matveev, O. Mikhal'chuk).

37 *ST*, no. 7, 1990, p. 24 (I. Borodin, U. Gil'manov).

38 *ST*, no. 8, 1990, p. 42 (V. Korolev).

39 *Trud*, 14 January 1990 (Kursk ball bearing factory). For other reports on this factory after its transfer to leasing, see *Trud*, 5 October 1989, and 28 March 1990.

40 *ST*, no. 8, 1990, p. 42 (V. Korolev). Korolev's observations were based on a survey of fifteen Moscow enterprises on the leasing system, carried out by the Department of Political Economy at the Tsiolkovskii Institute of Aviation Technology. An identical problem with incentives arose at the Chusovoi iron and steel works. *ST*, no. 12, 1991, p. 17.

41 *Molot*, 19 July 1990. See also the account of the Kuznetsk iron and steel works, reported in *ST*, no. 9, 1990, p. 35 (N. Afrikantov). This problem was not specific to leasing collectives. The Sverdlovsk rubber technical goods factory kept no accounting of materials consumption at shop level or as materials passed through various stages of the production process. There is no reason to believe that this factory was exceptional. *Rezinshchik*, 10 July 1990.

42 *EKO*, no. 9, 1990, p. 131–2 (Stanislav Mironchenko).

43 *RT*, 14 November 1990 (Promstroimekhanizatsiya, Azerbaijan); *Izvestiya*, 4 February 1991 (Verkhnesaldinskii metallurgical association); *Trud*, 23 August 1990 (Dnepropetrovsk mining-equipment factory), 18 April 1991 (Lianozov woodworking factory, Moscow oblast), and 21 November 1991 (Syamzha timber combine, Vologda oblast).

44 *EZh*, no. 9, 1990, pp. 12, 21 (A. Gnidenko, V. Ul'yanov).

45 *ST*, no. 10, 1989, pp. 14–15 (A. Shadrina, T. Tsvetkova, S. Kosyak), and no. 8, 1990, p. 42 (V. Korolev).

46 See the examples of the Kazan'rezinotekhnika association, cited in *EZh*, no. 9, 1990, p. 12, and Moscow's Krasnaya ploshchad' garment factory reported

in *RT*, 3 January 1991 (Lyudmila Biryukova). The latter was not actually on leasing, but had been bought out by its workers, after which its parent association decided to try to claim the factory back.

47 Such was the case with a consumer goods shop at Arsenal, which refused to go on leasing because of the general supply crisis and the absence of a coherent schedule of internal prices. *Arsenal*, 18 April 1991. See also the examples of the Novocheboksary bread factory (Chuvash ASSR), reported in *SP*, no. 13–14, 1990, pp. 43–4 (A. Smirnov) and the Kuibyshevkabel' Production Association, *Kabel'shchik* (Kuibyshevkabel'), 13 July, 20 July, and 17 August 1990; 25 January 1991.

48 *EZh*, no. 18, 1990, p. 17; no. 43, 1990, p. 16.

49 *Izvestiya*, 13 April and 14 May 1991 (V. Romanyuk).

50 *RT*, 2 March 1991 (Mikhail Popov).

51 *ZSM*, 28 March and 20 August 1990; *Moskvich*, 11 March 1991; *Stankostroitel'* (Ivanovo), 12 April 1991; *Arsenal*, 28 February 1991; *Kabel'shchik* (Sevkabel', Leningrad), 30 May and 1 August 1990; *RT*, 10 April 1991 (Rostov Agricultural Equipment Factory); *Izvestiya*, 21 December 1990; *Trud*, 16 April 1991; *LR*, 12 April 1991. I am grateful to Anna Temkina for making the latter reference available.

52 *Izvestiya*, 5 January 1991 (V. Romanyuk).

53 A similar, but equally illustrative chain affected the Irtysh Production Association in Omsk, which manufactured televisions. Its production came to a total standstill because it could not obtain transformers from a factory in Vilnius. The latter could not manufacture them because it was waiting for ferrite cores from Belaya Tserkov'. But the factory in Belaya Tserkov' was in turn waiting for raw materials from the Donetsk chemical combine. *Trud*, 21 July 1990. See also the experience of the Kommunar automobile factory in Zaporozh'e, reported in *RG*, 15 March 1991.

54 *RT*, 27 November 1990.

55 *RT*, 2 October 1990 (N. Kvizhinadze).

56 *RT*, 25 April and 30 April 1991 (Metrovagonmash); *RG*, 7 May 1991 (Ternopol'); *Kirovets*, 5 December 1990; *Stankostroitel' o. 6, 1990, p. 6 (I. Manykina).*

56 *RT*, 25 April and 30 April 1991 (Metrovagonmash); *RG*, 7 May 1991 (Ternopol'); *Kirovets*, 5 December 1990; *Stankostroitel'* (Ivanovo), 15 June 1990; Burawoy and Hendley, p. 376 (Rezina).

57 *RG*, 7 May 1991 (V. Litvin); *Trud*, 13 November 1990 (N. Roi).

58 *Izvestiya*, 19 March 1990 (V. Tolstenko).

59 *SP*, no. 7, 1991, p. 16 (A. Ivanov); *RG*, 7 May 1991 (V. Litvin). The Novotrubnyi pipe factory in Pervoural'sk drove an especially hard bargain, refusing to provide either factories or farms with metal unless they paid in advance with meat, sausage, or other hard-to-acquire produce. When one farm offered to pay the factory back over time, with meat it would raise using supplies received from Novotrubnyi, the latter simply refused. *RT*, 20 August 1990 (V. Noskov); *Izvestiya*, 19 March 1990 (V. Tolstenko).

60 *Arsenal*, 26 November 1990.

61 *Trud*, 24 April 1991 (Z. Tereshkova); *RT*, 22 January 1992.

62 *RT*, 18 July 1990. In theory these barter arrangements should have favoured food factories, but this was not always so, since some had their entire output gobbled up by *goszakaz* and had nothing with which to barter. *Trud*, 27 March 1991 (D. Romanov).
63 *RT*, 23 January 1991. For a similar example at the Yunost' garment production association in Kiev, see *RT*, 11 October 1990 (G. Dolzhenko).
64 Edict of the President of the USSR, 14 December 1990, 'O merakh po predotvrashcheniyu desorganizatsii proizvodstva v svyazi s neudovletvoritel'nym sostoyaniem zaklyucheniya khozyaistvennykh dogovorov na postavku produktsii v 1991 godu', *Trud*, 15 December 1990.
65 *RG*, 20 February 1991.
66 *RT*, 18 November 1990 (G. Belotserkovskii).
67 *RT*, 8 March 1990 (G. Belotserkovskii), and 7 December 1990; *RG*, 10 January 1991 (N. Andrusenko); *Izvestiya*, 5 March 1991.
68 Edict of the President of the USSR, 'O chrezvychainykh merakh po obespecheniyu material'nymi resursami predpriyatii, ob"edinenii i organizatsii', 12 April 1991. *Izvestiya*, 13 April 1991.
69 See chapter 3, pp. 119–20.
70 *Trud*, 8 September 1990 (interview with M. Ikharlova, chairperson of the Central Committee of the Union of Workers in Textiles and Light Industry).
71 *SI*, 25 October 1989 (L. Biryukova).
72 *Izvestiya*, 2 June 1990 (I. Demchenko).
73 *Trud*, 21 November 1990 (A. Bogomolov).
74 *Izvestiya*, 21 February 1991.
75 *Krasnaya talka*, 3 January 1991; *Golos Dzerzhintsa*, 18 January and 25 January 1991; *RG*, 29 November 1991 (I. Pashchuk). Cotton users in heavy industry faced a similar problem. The Rezina rubber-technical goods plant in Moscow threatened to halt the manufacture of conveyor belts because the price of cotton, essential to their production, had tripled, while the belts themselves continued to be sold at fixed prices on *goszakaz*. Burawoy and Hendley, p. 378.
76 *Trud*, 12 January 1991 (I. Ostrovskii) and 16 November 1991 (A. Kozlov); *RT*, 27 February 1991 (Sergei Il'chenko); *RG*, 28 March 1991 (V. Nikitchenko). The problem of imported materials was not confined to textiles. The Lutsk footwear factory in Ukraine had to put its workforce on unpaid leave because the glue it used was not made in the USSR and the Ukrainian Ministry of Light Industry did not have the foreign currency to continue importing it. *RG*, 20 February 1991.
77 In addition to examples already cited, see *Izvestiya*, 19 March 1991 (Aprelevka phonograph record factory) and 29 March 1991 (Bikin knitwear factory); *RG*, 1 March 1991 (Baltskii garment factory, Odessa oblast, and Chernovtsy rubber footwear factory).
78 *Trud*, 16 February 1991.
79 *RT*, 23 December 1990 (L. Biryukova).
80 *RT*, 23 January 1991; *Trud*, 16 November 1991 (A. Kozlov).
81 *EZh*, no. 35, 1990, p. 2 (I. Donchenko); *RT*, 22 December 1990; *Trud*, 3 August 1990, 10 April 1991.

82 See chapter 3, p. 119.
83 *Trud*, 19 January 1991 (I. Ostrovskii); *Izvestiya*, 11 February 1991 (V. Fillipov).
84 For a fuller discussion of this issue, see Filtzer, *Soviet Workers and De-Stalinization*, pp. 161–2.
85 *RG*, 9 February 1991 (V. Nikitchenko), 6 April 1991 (V. Kovriga); *EZh*, no. 2, 1991, p. 3; *Izvestiya*, 5 March 1991.
86 *EZh*, no. 5, 1991, p. 11; *RG*, 28 February 1991 (I. Donchenko).
87 *Trud*, 15 March 1991; *EZh*, no. 5, 1991, p. 11; *RG*, 5 January 1991 (Azovstal', Mariupol').
88 *Trud*, 27 October and 12 December 1990; *RT*, 1 June 1990; *RG*, 20 February 1990. The situation with roofing timbers worsened during 1991. Miners were put on short time and earnings fell. By the end of 1991, when the Soviet Union was officially dissolved, timber deliveries from Russia to Ukrainian mines had come to a virtual halt. *RG*, 2 October and 11 October 1991, and 23 January 1992; *RT*, 18 December 1991.
89 *Izvestiya*, 14 May 1991 (V. Romanyuk).
90 *RG*, 12 March, 22 March, 23 March, 29 March 1991; *Trud*, 16 March and 20 April 1991.
91 *RG*, 18 April 1991 (I. Donchenko).
92 *RT*, 22 March and 18 April 1991; *Izvestiya*, 22 April 1991; *Moskvich*, 8 May 1991.
93 *RG*, 20 November and 25 December 1991.
94 *RT*, 22 January 1992.
95 *RG*, 2 October 1991.
96 *RT*, 11 February 1992 (articles by Elena Ponomareva and Ivan Mordvintsev).
97 The situation was neatly summed up in a letter to *RT* from a worker at an unnamed factory.
> They say that in Japan the factories have no storerooms for components. They regularly deliver however many are needed, say for each shift. We, too, have no need for storerooms, since we've nothing to store. During two weeks our shop has come to a standstill five or six times: first parts didn't arrive from the Caucasus, then from Moldova, then from Central Asia, then from the Baltic. There's always some sort of problem: customs, blockades, leap-frogging prices. We feel the breakup of the Union on our own skin twice a month, in our pay check – if we weren't standing idle, we'd earn a lot more. *RT*, 7 November 1991.
98 The other side of this was that managers used the situation to reinforce old paternalistic relations with the workforce, and their claims to speak for their 'labour collectives' became an important factor in the power struggles between industrialists and monetarists in Russia during 1992 and 1993.

5 The labour process under perestroika: 1 The political economy of working conditions

1 Following Marx's terminology, used in his analysis of capitalist reproduction in *Capital*, volume II, we refer to that branch of the economy which produces means of production as department I, and that which produces means of consumption as department II. In the 1920s Soviet statistics

divided the economy into two large groups which roughly, but not precisely, corresponded to Marx's departments. Group A comprised the production of means of production, but excluded construction and agricultural
raw materials, both of which Marx included in department I. Group B was
similar to Marx's department II. Carr and Davies, p. 422, fn.

2 The most important of these are described in Nove, pp. 63, 163–4. For the
problem of the waste and its impact on maintaining the swollen size of
department I, see Filtzer, *Soviet Workers and De-Stalinization*, ch. 6.

3 This is discussed in more detail in pp. 168–70 of this chapter.

4 *VE*, no. 8, 1991, p. 6 (S. Pervushin). A perhaps extreme case which illustrates
Pervushin's point is the yeast industry, some of whose factories have been
working with fixed capital 80 per cent depreciated, yet the USSR did not
have a single enterprise manufacturing equipment for yeast-making. *Trud*,
21 November 1990 (D. Struzhentsov).

5 For a detailed discussion of the investment crisis of NEP, see E. A. Preobrazhensky, 'Economic Equilibrium in the System of the USSR'. In both NEP
and the present crisis the only solution lay in the infusion of investment
from outside. In the 1920s this was precluded by the political hostility of the
capitalist world (hence Preobrazhensky's affirmation of the impossibility of
'socialism in one country' and the need for proletarian revolutions in
Europe to end the USSR's isolation). Under perestroika and the reforms
which have succeeded it, a number of Soviet (and post-Soviet) economists,
politicians, and even workers' leaders staked a great deal on the assumption that Western investment would make up for the domestic shortage.
However, the developed capitalist powers, even were they not facing their
own period of economic downturn (in part accelerated, as in the case of
Germany, by the collapse of Stalinism), simply do not possess the surplus
capital to meet the large volume of investment required.

6 *Rabotnitsa*, no. 7, 1990, p. 11 (Nina Karpovna Kul'bovskaya).

7 *ST*, no. 3, 1988, pp. 31–2. Other examples from the late 1980s and early 1990s
will display the gravity of the situation here. The power-cable shop at the
Kuibyshevkabel' cable works in Kuibyshev (now Samara) was using paper-
cutting machines installed in 1942 and presses and insulation equipment
dating from the 1950s and 1960s. *Kabel'shchik* (Kuibyshevkabel'), 13 July
1990. The bulk of equipment at the same city's Steel Foundry had not been
replaced since the 1940s. *Za stal'*, 5 July 1990. In the motor vehicle industry,
40 per cent of equipment at Moscow's ZiL Association had been in service
for over twenty years. *Sots. issled.*, no. 3, 1987, p. 84 (V. S. Dunin, E. A.
Zenkevich). Presses in the foundry and press shops of the AZLK car factory
in Moscow, which manufactures the Moskvich, were from thirty to forty
years old. *ZSM*, 17 December 1990, *Moskvich*, 11 February 1991. One textile
factory in the Greater Moscow region was using German machinery made
in 1932: a group of West Germans visiting the mill wanted to buy the
equipment for their factory museum! *Trud*, 5 September 1990. Other textile
mills were in an even worse state: Moscow's fulling and felting factory was
using machinery dating back to 1911 (*ST*, no. 3, 1991, p. 11), while some of
the equipment at Moscow's Osvobozhdennyi trud fine-cloth factory

(originally built in 1860) was described as 'of purely archeological interest'. *KP*, 1 May 1991 (S. Blagodarov).

8 Nove, *Soviet Economic System*, p. 165. In the chemical industry, for example, despite the advanced age of the fixed capital stock, only 2–4 per cent was being replaced each year. *RG*, 10 January 1991; *Trud*, 6 February 1991 (E. Varshavskaya).

9 *VE*, no. 8, 1991, pp. 11–14 (B. Lavrovskii).

10 *Tekstil'naya promyshlennost'*, no. 4, 1991, p. 39 (K. V. Kutepova); *ST*, no. 5, 1990, pp. 33–4 (N. Khrulev, L. Salomatina).

11 Thus the share of equipment in total capital investment was only 48 per cent in the USSR, as opposed to over 70 per cent in the USA. *EZh*, no. 10, 1990, p. 19 (G. Zholudev).

12 *EZh*, no. 10, 1990, p. 19 (G. Zholudev). In fact, the volume of unfinished construction was worse than the official figures suggested, since many projects, both in capital and housing construction, were accepted as 'complete' by ministry or oblast officials, when they were in fact unfit for use or habitation. Sometimes this was the result of pressure to improve 'plan fulfilment' results; in other cases it involved outright corruption and the receipt of bribes to falsify reports. *Izvestiya*, 27 March 1990; *RT*, 16 May 1990.

13 Officially there were 14 billion rubles worth of uninstalled machinery as of 1 January 1989, including 4.6 billion rubles worth of imported machinery. Just three factories in Zaporozh'e oblast held between them 30 million rubles in unused foreign equipment. *Trud*, 19 October 1990; *PKh*, no. 2, 1990, p. 88 (Yu. Tushunov); *RT*, 7 October 1990 (V. Tsekov).

14 *EKO*, no. 8, 1989, p. 87 (V. D. Roik).

15 *PKh*, no. 2, 1990, pp. 85–6 (Yu. Tushunov). In the chemical industry in 1989 expenditures on equipment repair and maintenance came to 1.5 billion rubles, nearly 80 per cent of the entire annual volume of capital investment. *SI*, 13 October 1989.

16 *SI*, 21 June 1988 (Kalinin excavator factory); *RT*, 25 December 1990 (Sverdlovsk housing construction). For a discussion of this phenomenon in the Brezhnev period, see Nove, *Soviet Economic System*, pp. 157–8.

17 *ST*, no. 12, 1990, pp. 41–2 (A. Monusov); *PKh*, no. 2, 1990, pp. 83–4 (Yu. Tushunov).

18 *ST*, no. 6, 1990, p. 47 (A. Semenov). In the case of machine tools with numerically programmed controls the discrepancy was even more striking: these machines cost some ten to fifteen times the equipment they were designed to replace, far in excess of the increase in productivity which they might yield. *ST*, no. 8, 1988, pp. 40–1.

19 *ST*, no. 9, 1989, p. 54 (L. Sitnikova), no. 1, 1990, p. 51 (G. Amelina, E. Zhukova), no. 5, 1990, p. 35 (N. Khrulev, L. Salomatina); *SP*, no. 2, 1991, p. 71 (V. Koltashev). At the Strommashina factory in Kuibyshev (Samara), numerically controlled machine tools were used to machine pig iron and ordinary castings, a situation the factory newspaper likened to using machine tools made of gold to turn sledge hammers! *Strela*, 13 July 1990.

20 *ST*, no. 5, 1990, p. 35 (N. Khrulev, L. Salomatina).

21 Kats and Pavlychev, p. 22. In some ministries the prospects were not so

gloomy: the pay-off was calculated as 38 years in the automobile industry and 196 years in heavy engineering. See also *SR*, 1 June 1988.

22 *ZSM*, 20 November 1989, 9 July 1990. A similar situation arose at the Krasnyi treugol'nik rubber goods factory in Leningrad (Boris Maksimov, Institute of Sociology, Leningrad, personal communication).

23 *ZSM*, 27 December 1989.

24 For a more detailed discussion of this point see chapter 4.

25 *SI*, 1 October 1989; *VE*, no. 8, 1991, pp. 14–16 (B. Lavrovskii).

26 *VE*, no. 18, 1991, pp. 16–18 (B. Lavrovskii).

27 Filtzer, *Soviet Workers and De-Stalinization*, pp. 85–9.

28 *Sots. issled.*, no. 1, 1990, pp. 48–53 (V. Ya. Belen'kii); *ST*, no. 8, 1989, p. 73 (V. Pavlov, V. Baryshev), no. 10, 1990, p. 14, and no. 12, 1991, pp. 35–6 (Valentin Illarionov).

29 *SP*, no. 15–16, 1990, p. 36 (V. Gotlober, I. Shevchenko); *ST*, no. 12, 1991, p. 35 (Valentin Illarionov).

30 *ST*, no. 8, 1988, p. 29 (Yu. Kalmykov); *ibid*, p. 39; *ST*, no. 12, 1991, pp. 36–9 (Valentin Illarionov).

31 The most common measure of equipment utilization is the so-called 'shift index' (*koefitsient smennosti*), which measures the average number of shifts worked by each piece of equipment. It is calculated by dividing the total number of machine-shifts worked by the total number of machines. Thus a factory with 100 machine tools working without interruption over 3 shifts would have a shift index of 300 machine-shifts/100 machines = 3.0, a perfect score. Conversely, if this same factory worked only 1 shift, its shift index would be 1.0, which was relatively low.

32 *EKO*, no. 8, 1989, p. 87 (V. D. Roik).

33 *ST*, no. 8, 1988, pp. 41–2; no. 9, 1989, p. 54 (L. Sitnikova).

34 *EKO*, no. 8, 1989, p. 87 (V. D. Roik); *Sots. issled.*, no. 1, 1990, pp. 55–7 (N. D. Baranovskii, T. A. Ribkinskii); *ST*, no. 12, 1991, pp. 40–1 (Valentin Illarionov). Cook, p. 42, attributes the multi-shift campaign to the regime's desire to lessen the impact of redundancies. While this may have been a factor, the main drive behind it was, as we have argued here, the long-standing need to improve equipment use. Moreover, the campaign was by no means specific to *perestroika*. A similar campaign in the Khrushchev period met with equal lack of success. Filtzer, *Soviet Workers and De-Stalinization*, pp. 85–9.

35 *IAN*, no. 1, 1991, p. 64 (V. D. Roik).

36 *Kabel'shchik* (Sevkabel', Leningrad), 11 March 1990.

37 *RT*, 17 May 1990.

38 *Trud*, 28 April 1990, 29 April 1990; *Izvestiya*, 29 April 1990 (Nizhnii Tagil); *RT*, 26 November 1991 (A. Suvorov – Kuzbass). A campaign to curb similar levels of pollution in Zaporozh'e oblast in Ukraine led, in early 1990, to 32 shops and production sub-units being issued orders to halt production, while 379 enterprise managers had their bonuses withheld for pollution violations. *IZ*, 21 February 1990.

39 *Rabotnitsa*, no. 7, 1990, p. 10; *RT*, 5 December 1990 (V. Vas'kova, E. Poluyanov, K. Kotov), and 8 May 1991; *Trud*, 29 December 1990 (V. Popov), and

1 May 1991 (Grigorii Volovich); *IAN*, no. 1, 1991, p. 65 (V. D. Roik). By contrast, in Great Britain there are some 700 work-related deaths each year; allowing for the smaller size of its population, this is still about one-quarter the Soviet average.

40 In the agro-industrial complex of Voronezh' oblast (which includes not just farmers, but many workers in the food-processing and chemical fertilizer industries) 103 employees died in 1990 and another 68 during the first eight months of 1991. *RT*, 1 November 1991 (Aleksei Pavlov). In February 1990 127 people died in accidents within industry proper. *Trud*, 18 March 1990. If this were a typical month it would suggest that some 90 per cent of deaths occur outside of industry. Judging from the descriptive accounts of factory working conditions appearing in the Soviet press this would seem, however, to be an underestimate.

41 In 1988 I met a worker at a large engineering works in Moscow who had suffered a concussion as a result of falling from a roof. His foreman, fearing repercussions if the accident was reported, refused to grant the man permission to see the factory doctor. Instead he worked out the rest of his shift and travelled home by public transport. Later that night he was rushed to the hospital in critical condition, where he remained for several weeks. After his convalescence he was fired from his job for alleged malingering. It was only after the intervention of his local Communist Party committee, in turn brought about by the relentless petitioning of his wife, that he was given his job back. According to the Ukrainian newspaper, *Rabochaya gazeta*, it is routine practice for pit doctors to understate the severity of the occupational diseases of coal miners, to prevent them from taking early retirement and thereby exacerbating labour shortages in the industry. *RG*, 13 November 1991 (A. Afanas'ev). The same practice occurs at the Arsenal Production Association in Leningrad: factory doctors, while privately advising women with occupational diseases to switch to less dangerous work, nonetheless refuse to certify them as suffering from a work-related illness. Interview with personnel from the Arsenal Production Association, Leningrad, 24 June 1991. For another case in the engineeriing industry, see *Trud*, 3 December 1991 (N. Sivkova; O. Posdnyakova).

42 *RT*, 12 May 1990; *Trud*, 2 June 1990 (N. Mokrishchev); *KP*, 18 December 1990 (A. Ermakov).

43 *RT*, 3 February 1990, 12 May 1990; *Trud*, 2 June 1990 (N. Mokrishchev).

44 *SWB*, 15 June 1990, citing *Trud*, 8 June 1990. This issue of *Trud* was not available to me for verification.

45 *RT*, 26 February 1991.

46 *Gudok*, 23 April 1991 (I am grateful to Nikolai Preobrazhenskii for this reference).

47 *EN*, no. 2, 1990, p. 30 (V. D. Roik).

48 *Trud v SSSR* (1988), pp. 63–5, 249; *Znamya*, no. 9, 1991, p. 211 (Evgenii Starikov). Taking industry as a whole, the high share of workers on low-skilled manual jobs shows an actual decline from the levels of the mid-1960s, when nearly half of all workers (excluding maintenance person-

nel) did their jobs by hand. However, this fall has been partially offset by an increase in the number of repair personnel, from 11.2 per cent in 1965 to 14.2 per cent in 1987. *Trud v SSSR* (1988), p. 250.

49 *RT*, 23 March 1990. This job was done by women, who allegedly found it embarrassing to have to way-lay men walking past to ask for help wielding the sledge hammer. More indicative of the times is the fact that the French have a hydraulic cutter to perform this operation, but the factory chose not to buy it in order to save on hard currency.

50 *Kirovets*, 17 September 1990, 26 December 1990, 28 February 1991.

51 *VE*, no. 12, 1990, p. 137 (N. Kul'bovskaya).

52 At Leningrad's Krasnyi treugol'nik rubber goods factory, which belongs to the chemical industry, some 50 to 60 per cent of jobs are done by hand. Conveyors exist, but most of the operations which the workers carry out are still done manually. Moreover, the USSR had only one factory which manufactured equipment for the rubber industry, in Tiraspol in Moldova. With Moldovan independence it was unclear (as of mid-1991) whether it would carry on supplying rubber factories in Russia. Interview with L. Tanova, staff sociologist, Krasnyi treugol'nik, Leningrad, 27 June 1991.

53 *Trud*, 31 January 1991 (Yu. Rogozhin). Rogozhin's account was based on the experience of the chemical industry, where a 1990 survey of some 15,000 chemical installations passed a mere 607 as safe, primarily, although not exclusively, due to the worn-out state of equipment.

54 *Molot*, 19 April 1990.

55 David Mandel, interview with S., foreman at the AZLK automobile factory, Moscow, July 1988.

56 *EN*, no. 2, 1990, p. 32 (V. D. Roik); *RKSM*, no. 3, 1989, p. 12 (V. D. Roik, citing *Izvestiya*, 4 September 1988). Not all the victims are industrial workers. The USSR's inability to manufacture tractors with protective cabins allegedly accounts for 400 farm deaths a year.

57 *ST*, no. 1, 1990, pp. 47–8 (M. Begidzhanov, V. Kargashevskii, Yu. Kuz'-menko), no. 3, 1990, p. 33 (Z. Molokova, A. Mironenkov).

58 Thus at the Moscow Meat Combine a German conveyor designed to assist with unloading blocks of meat, which had cost the factory DM330,000, could not be used because it would not fit inside the combine's refrigeration lockers. Interview with V.M., a loader at the Moscow Meat Combine, 12 June 1991. Similarly, after the Sverdlovsk instrument factory had spent $12,000 on new American painting equipment for one of its shops, it discovered that, in order to use it, the factory would have to spend a further 60,000 rubles expanding the work area and installing painting cabins and ventilation equipment. As of April 1991 the American machinery was still not in operation. *Priborostroitel'*, 17 April 1991.

59 *ST*, no. 12, 1990, p. 41 (A. Monusov); *IAN*, no. 1, 1991, p. 67 (V. D. Roik).

60 David Mandel, interview with S., a repair fitter at a large electrical equipment factory in Chelyabinsk, October 1991.

61 *Rabotnitsa*, no. 7, 1990, p. 10 (interview with Nina Karpovna Kul'bovskaya).

62 *RT*, 1 November 1991 (Aleksei Pavlov).

63 *RT*, 5 December 1990 (V. Vas'kova, E. Poluyanov, K. Kotov). This is assuming that the enterprise's culpability can be proven, something which is not always guaranteed.

64 *ST*, no. 9, 1991, p. 39 (Natal'ya Vladova).

65 *Trud*, 16 October 1990 (A. Surkov).

66 In Volgograd oblast, of the twenty-four physicians hired by the oblast committees of the different unions to monitor conditions and deal with cases of occupational disease, by the end of 1991 the *obkomy* had retained only two. *Trud*, 3 December 1991 (O. Posdnyakova).

67 *OT*, no. 3, 1990, pp. 12–13 (S. Belozerova). Belozerova based her claims on her study of the Upper Volga Cable Works (Verkhnevolzhskkabel'), where a combination of dilapidated equipment, labour shortages, and a substantial rise in its production plan resulted in extensive overtime: some workers were putting in fourteen-hour shifts, and the average worker worked an extra twenty-five to thirty-five days per year. As a result illness rates at the factory rose from eleven days per year in 1986 to seventeen in 1989. She claims that other enterprises surveyed in engineering, instrument making, electrical engineering, metallurgy, and automobile manufacture showed a similar portrait. Without knowing the basis of the survey to which she refers it is impossible to judge just how typical these enterprises were. Certainly my own picture derived from reading factory newspapers from 1990 and 1991 indicates that the intensification of labour to which she refers was at least partially compensated for by increased stoppages due to the supply crisis. See chapter 4.

68 *Trud v SSSR* (1988), p. 139. Perhaps surprisingly, far fewer workers in construction received these 'privileges', despite the inherent dangers of their work.

69 *IAN*, no. 1, 1991, p. 69 (V. D. Roik).

70 *EN*, no. 2, 1990, pp. 31–3 (V. D. Roik); *Rabotnitsa*, no. 7, 1990, pp. 10–11 (interview with Nina Karpovna Kul'bovskaya).

71 *EKO*, no. 1, 1990, p. 35 (V. I. Shcherbakov); *ST*, no. 6, 1991, p. 41 (I. Molokanova); David Mandel, interview with S., repair fitter at a large electrical equipment factory in Chelyabinsk, October 1991.

72 See, for example, the case of two women at the Khimprom Production Association in Sayansk, Irkutsk oblast, reported in *Trud*, 7 July 1990 (A. Komarov).

73 *VE*, no. 12, 1990, p. 142 (N. Kul'bovskaya); *Trud*, 3 December 1991 (O. Posdnyakova).

74 *Rabotnitsa*, no. 7, 1990, p. 10 (interview with Nina Karpovna Kul'bovskaya).

75 Some of the empirical material used in this section has been cited previously in the article by my colleague Judith Shapiro (Shapiro, 'The Industrial Labour Force'). Shapiro and I have regularly shared each other's research notes and discussed the issues surrounding women workers in great detail. Since both the focus and main argument of Shapiro's article differ considerably from those presented in this chapter, I feel justified in asking the reader to tolerate a certain amount of duplication.

76 Filtzer, *Soviet Workers and De-Stalinization*, ch. 7.

77 *SP*, no. 13–14, 1990, pp. 50–1 (L. Glebova). Dots in the original.
78 *VE*, no. 9, 1991, p. 35 (I. Zaslavskii); interview with officials of the Moscow
    Labour Exchange, 9 October 1991; *RT*, 24 October 1991; *Ekspress, Ltd.*, 28
    November–4 December 1991 (I am grateful to Judith Shapiro for making
    this last reference available).
79 *EN*, no. 1, 1990, p. 34 (A. Chuikin).
80 *EKO*, no. 8, 1988, pp. 144–5 (Tat'yana Boldyreva), citing *Narodnoe khozyaistvo
    SSSR na 70 let* (Moscow, 1988). In 1963 Soviet women were doing roughly
    thirty-nine hours per week of housework, as against fifteen hours for men.
    For detailed time budget statistics from the early 1960s see Filtzer, *Soviet
    Workers and De-Stalinization*, pp. 196–204.
81 Gruzdeva and Chertikhina, 'Soviet Women', p. 163. This article originally
    appeared in *RKSM*, no. 6, 1982.
82 *VS*, no. 2, 1991, pp. 51–2. According to this survey, the amount of free time
    available to women had already fallen by 60 per cent since 1980, leaving
    women with only half the free time enjoyed by men.
83 *EZh*, no. 34, 1990, p. 12.
84 *Trud*, 12 January 1990.
85 *Izvestiya*, 15 February 1990 (Yu. Rytov). In 1989, 20 per cent of phonographs,
    17 per cent of televisions, 7 per cent of radios, and nearly 6 per cent of
    refrigerators and washing machines were returned for repair during their
    warranty period. As *Izvestiya* remarked, 'everyone knows how much
    energy, time, nerves, and money we have to expend putting right faulty
    goods. We curse the grey economy, but even when goods are still under
    warranty, we have to turn to craftspersons working "on the left", choosing
    the lesser of many evils.'
86 *SP*, no. 111–12, 1990, pp. 55–58 (T. Zykova).
87 *VS*, no. 2, 1991, p. 39. These data are based on the 1989 population census
    and list the proportion of women 'employed primarily in physical labour',
    without explaining what this category entails, although it is clearly a far
    narrower definition than that of 'worker' used in other statistical hand-
    books. In some industries, such as footwear, the percentage of women
    doing 'primarily physical labour' is well below the share of women
    workers. In others, such as the food industry, it is much higher. In the case
    of engineering the census gives women as only 15 per cent of those doing
    physical labour, one-third of their percentage of workers listed in *Trud v
    SSSR* and older statistical compendia. Without knowing just how this
    category is defined it is impossible to explain these discrepancies, and these
    data should be used with some caution.
88 *VS*, no. 1, 1990, p. 42.
89 *ST*, no. 3, 1991, p. 8; Gruzdeva and Chertikhina, 'Polozhenie zhenshchiny',
    p. 153.
90 Calculated from Gruzdeva and Chertikhina, 'Polozhenie zhenshchiny',
    p. 154; *Trud v SSSR* (1988), pp. 106, 249. According to *OT*, no. 9, 1989, p. 2,
    there were 4.2 million women in industry working manually without any
    mechanical assistance, or approximately 30 per cent of women workers
    (calculated from *Trud v SSSR*, 1988, pp. 47 and 106). However, this excludes

those women doing manual labour in connection with mechanized operations.

91 Statistics on the occupational breakdown of women industrial workers for the 1950s and 1960s appear in Filtzer, *Soviet Workers and De-Stalinization*, pp. 182–8.

92 Interview with L., a woman assembly-line worker at AZLK, Moscow, June 1988; interview with A., technical specialist, Lytkarino Optical Glass Factory (Moscow oblast), 12 June 1991; interview with personnel from Arsenal Production Association, Leningrad, 24 June 1991; interview with L. Tanova, staff sociologist, Krasnyi treugol'nik, Leningrad, 27 June 1991.

93 For example, the brigade of women electricians who repair electric motors at the Dzerzhinskii spinning and weaving factory, Ivanovo. *Golos Dzerzhintsa*, 1 February 1991. According to a maintenance electrician at a large electrical equipment factory in Chelyabinsk, women repair fitters tend to work on simpler types of equipment, rather than repairs which demand a detailed knowledge of electronics. David Mandel, interview with S., October 1991.

94 Filtzer, *Soviet Workers and De-Stalinization*, p. 187; *Trud*, 27 October 1989 (V. Zakharov).

95 *EKO*, no. 8, 1988, p. 149 (Tat'yana Boldyreva).

96 Filtzer, *Soviet Workers and De-Stalinization*, p. 188; *EKO*, no. 8, p. 142 (Tat'yana Boldyreva); Rosenbaum, p. 59.

97 *EKO*, no. 8, 1988, pp. 128–9 (E. E. Novikova, O. L. Milova, E. V. Zalyubovskaya).

98 *Sobesednik*, no. 29, 1988, pp. 12–13. At Leningrad's Krasnyi treugol'nik rubber goods factory, some two-thirds of workers are women *limitchitsy*, many employed in dangerous jobs which men will not do. Interview with L. Tanova, staff sociologist, Krasnyi treugol'nik, Leningrad, 27 June 1991.

99 *Trud*, 24 October 1990; *EKO*, no. 9, 1989, p. 153 (A. V. Kormilkin). An even worse disparity exists in the leather and hide industry: At the Zhitomir hide factory in 1990 a seamstress making sheepskin coats earned 1.40 rubles for a coat which sold for 140 rubles at official prices and for 500 rubles on the black market. *RT*, 11 October 1990 (G. Dolzhenko).

100 The Orekhovo cotton textile combine in the Greater Moscow region was perhaps an extreme, but otherwise typical case, when it had to pay its entire 1990 material incentives fund to the state in taxes. *Trud*, 5 September 1990.

101 *SI*, 25 October 1989 (L. Biryukova); *Trud*, 10 January 1990, 14 March 1990, 1 May 1990; *EZh*, no. 14, 1990, p. 10 (V. Nefedov, V. Sevast'yanova); *Izvestiya*, 15 February 1990 (Yu. Rytov), 9 March 1990 (V. Romanyuk).

102 Gruzdeva and Chertikhina, 'Polozhenie zhenshchiny', p. 160.

103 *EKO*, no. 8, 1988, p. 142 (Tat'yana Boldyreva).

104 *VS*, no. 1, 1990, p. 41.

105 *EKO*, no. 8, 1988, p. 142 (Tat'yana Boldyreva). At the Kama River Motor Vehicle production association (KamAZ) in Naberezhnye Chelny, where women are half the Association's 140,000 employees, there are ten times more men than women in grades 5 and 6, and four times more women than men in grades 1 and 2. *SP*, no. 6, 1991, p. 67 (T. Galiev).

106 *Rabotnitsa*, no. 1, 1991, p. 10 (Ol'ga Laputina). A shop in the Number Five Building Materials Combine, belonging to the Chelyabinsk metallurgical construction association, imposed, in the words of one author, 'a rather original form of regrading', when implementing the wage reform: all men were put in the fifth *razryad* and all women in the third, a move which management justified on the grounds that the skills of men must be two skill grades higher than those of women. The action was reversed only after protests from the women. *ST*, no. 6, 1989, p. 61 (V. Alimova).

107 *Znamya*, 25 January 1991. Women knurling dowells were paid 53 kopeks per 1,000. As it was physically impossible to turn out more than 10,000 or 11,000 dowells per shift, their earnings were limited to a paltry 120 rubles a month, barely half the average wage in engineering in 1987, and far below the 235 to 314 rubles which turners in Moscow were averaging in early 1991, when this report appeared. See *VE*, no. 9, 1991, p. 33 (I. Zaslavskii).

108 Filtzer, *Soviet Workers and De-Stalinization*, p. 189. Even in the 1960s this argument lacked credibility. As Lupton observed while working in a British engineering plant in the late 1950s, limited formal education was no barrier to workers becoming skilled at their particular trades. Lupton, pp. 113–14 and table 4.

109 Gruzdeva and Chertikhina, 'Soviet Women', pp. 157–8; Rosenbaum, pp. 45–7.

110 Gruzdeva and Chertikhina, 'Soviet Women', p. 158.

111 *Ibid.*, pp. 157–8.

112 *VS*, no. 2, 1991, p. 54. At KamAZ in 1989 3.6 per cent of women workers went on courses to improve their qualifications, as opposed to 27.1 per cent of men. *SP*, no. 6, 1991, p. 67 (T. Galiev). An earlier, 1988, study of workers in the agricultural machinery, iron and steel, non-ferrous metallurgy, electrical engineering, and footwear industries, carried out by Goskomtrud's Scientific Research Institute of Labour, found that men were three to four times more likely than women to undergo retraining and acquire new skills. *ST*, no. 3, 1990, p. 62 (I. Kochetkova).

113 *VS*, no. 2, 1991, p. 55.

114 *EKO*, no. 8, 1988, p. 129 (E. E. Novikova, O. L. Milova, E. V. Zalyubovskaya); *VS*, no. 2, 1991, p. 53.

115 *VS*, no. 1, 1990, p. 41.

116 *OT*, no. 9, 1989, p. 2; *ST*, no. 8, 1989, pp. 63–4 (L. Shineleva), and no. 3, 1990, p. 33 (Z. Molokova, A. Mironenkov). According to *Okhrana truda*, there were only 275,000 women doing heavy physical labour, but this figure is impossibly low. If women were 44 per cent of workers doing heavy physical labour or working in unsafe conditions, and if just under half of all industrial workers fell into this category, there would have been at least 6.5 million women in this group in the late 1980s. If the figure of 3.4 million in hazardous conditions was even remotely accurate, this would imply another 3 million on heavy work. See *VS*, no. 1, 1990, p. 41, and *Trud v SSSR* (1988), pp. 45 and 139.

117 *ST*, no. 3, 1991, p. 8.

118 *ST*, no. 4, 1989, p. 70 (A. Abramova); *EZh*, no. 10, 1991, p. 14. New regulations were to have been drafted during 1991, but to the best of my knowledge they did not reach the statute book. Decree of the USSR Supreme Soviet, 'O neotlozhnykh merakh po uluchsheniyu polozheniya zhenshchin, okhrane materinstva i detstva, ukrepleniyu sem'i', 10 April 1990.

119 *EZh*, no. 10, 1991, p. 14; *IAN*, no 1, 1991, p. 66 (V. D. Roik), citing *Rabotnitsa*, no. 3, 1989, p. 10. At the Semiluki refractory materials factory (Voronezh oblast), attempts to apply these limits led to such a fall in the women's wages that the trade union agreed to wave their enforcement. *EZh*, no. 10, 1991, p. 14.

120 *RG*, 13 November 1991 (A. Afanas'ev); *Molot*, 12 April 1990; *Skorokhodovskii rabochii*, 7 August 1990; *KP*, 1 May 1991 (S. Blagodarov).

121 *Pravda*, 11 June 1988; *Trud*, 7 July 1990 (Khimprom Production Association, Sayansk, Irkutsk oblast); *Rezinshchik*, 14 August 1990; *Stankostroitel'* (Machine-Tool Manufacturing Production Association, Kuibyshev), 17 September 1990; *ST*, no. 3, 1991, pp. 10–11, 13. At Khimprom in Sayansk management attempted to cover up the dangers to which women cleaners in its mercury electrolysis shop were exposed by changing their job title to 'deactivators'. When four women protested about conditions and management's generally authoritarian conduct they were fired (with trade union connivance) under the pretext of removing them from dangerous work.

122 David Mandel, interview with workers at the Lytkarino Optical Glass Factory (Moscow oblast), October 1990.

123 *OT*, no. 9, 1989, p. 3; *SP*, no. 1, 1991, p. 42 (N. Ermolaeva). In the case of Kazakhstan, the operating manual of the machine in question actually stated that for every 100 spindles 10 runners would fly off. Miraculously, the accident rate on the equipment was surprisingly low, despite its nickname.

124 *SI*, 22 January 1988 (Lyudmila Telen'); *Rabotnitsa*, no. 1, 1990, pp. 15–16 (Ada Levina). Women in the paint shop of Kuibyshev's Machine-Tool Manufacturing Association made a similar complaint: on some equipment they could not reach the upper areas for cleaning or servicing; on others they had to erect special trestles to avoid having to crawl around on their hands and knees. *Stankostroitel'*, 17 September 1990.

125 Z. P. Pukhova, Chair of the Soviet Women's Committee, addressing the 19th Conference of the Communist Party of the Soviet Union, 1 July 1988, *Pravda*, 2 July 1988; *EKO*, no. 8, 1988, p. 139 (Tat'yana Boldyreva).

126 *SI*, 22 January 1988 (Lyudmila Telen'); *ST*, no. 3, 1991, p. 9.

127 *ST*, no. 4, 1989, p. 70 (A. Abramova).

128 *SP*, no. 6, 1991, p. 67 (T. Galiev).

129 *Trud*, 14 September 1988.

130 *EKO*, no. 8, 1989, pp. 89–91 (V. D. Roik).

131 *EKO*, no. 8, 1988, p. 139 (Tat'yana Boldyreva).

132 *EKO*, no. 8, 1989, p. 91 (V. D. Roik); *SI*, 22 January 1988 (Lyudmila Telen'); *Trud*, 14 September 1988. According to an official of the Russian Textile and

Light Industry Workers' Union, workers receive an unpaid dinner break
of 30–40 minutes, plus two paid breaks of 10–15 minutes each. Interview
with Anatolii Kol'makov, Moscow, 2 July 1991. Textiles, of course, is not
the only industry where women are subjected to such a high intensity of
labour. Women rollers in a calendering section of the Sverdlovsk rubber-
technical goods factory work an 8–hour shift without a single rest break,
despite the large amount of heavy physical labour their jobs involve.
Rezinshchik, 14 August 1990. On the general use of work time within
industry as a whole, see chapter 6.

133 *Trud*, 14 September 1988; *EKO*, no. 3, 1988, p. 98 (L. I. Gol'din).
134 *ST*, no. 9, 1990, p. 27.
135 *SP*, no. 1, 1991, p. 41 (N. Ermolaeva).
136 *Trud*, 14 September 1988. Sometimes the problem is caused, or at least
exacerbated, by negligence and poor storage facilities, so that raw materials are damaged by exposure to bad weather. *Zarya*, 5 April 1991.
137 *SI*, 22 January 1988 (Lyudmila Telen'); *ST*, no. 3, 1991, p. 11; *SP*, no. 1, 1991,
p. 42 (N. Ermolaeva). According to Soviet pension law, textile workers
could retire five years early if they had worked twenty years in industry,
at least ten of them in textiles. *Ibid.*, p. 43.
138 *Golos Dzerzhintsa*, 26 April 1991.
139 *Trud*, 14 September 1988. On the specific problems of Vietnamese workers
in light industry see *RT*, 16 August 1990 (E. Seregina).
140 *Trud*, 8 September 1990; *VS*, no. 2, 1991, p.39.
141 Filtzer, *Soviet Workers and De-Stalinization*, p. 192; *EKO*, no. 8, 1988,
pp. 139–40 (Tat'yana Boldyreva).
142 *VS*, no. 2, 1991, p. 56.
143 *ST*, no. 8, 1989, p. 66 (L. Shineleva). These average figures overstate the
gravity of the position of urban workers, since living and working conditions in the countryside, and the resulting death rates, are far worse
than in the towns. According to Shineleva, the death rate in Soviet rural
areas is 20 per cent above that in towns; among children it is 50 per cent
higher.
144 *EKO*, no. 8, 1988, pp. 140–1 (Tat'yana Boldyreva); *ST*, no. 8, 1989, p. 64
(L. Shineleva).
145 *Trud*, 9 August 1990.
146 *ST*, no. 3, 1991, p. 13. Women painters at the Kuibyshev Machine-Tool
Manufacturing Association similarly claimed that they could not afford to
give up this type of work. *Stankostroitel* (Kuibyshev), 17 September 1990.
The foundry worker at ZiL also pointed out that there were many other
trades at ZiL – press operators, painters, and furnace operators – which,
despite the hazardous nature of the work, were not classified as unsafe
and thus earned these workers no compensatory privileges.
147 *Rabotnitsa*, no. 1, 1991, p. 12 (Ol'ga Laputina); *SP*, n. 1, 1991, p. 41
(N. Ermolaeva), no. 7, 1991, p. 17 (A. Ivanov); *ST*, no. 3, 1991, pp. 8–9; *Trud*,
27 October 1989.
148 Lapidus, ed., *Women, Work, and Family*, pp. xxv–xl.
149 *Pravda*, 11 June 1988.

150 *EKO*, no. 7, 1988, p. 11 (N. M. Rimashevskaya), and pp. 24–5 (Yu. N. Lachinov).

151 Mason, part 1, pp. 102–5.

152 It is characteristic that even such a traditionally docile organization as the Soviet Women's Committee felt compelled to protest against the back to the home campaign. In a startlingly forthright address to the Communist Party's 19th Party Conference in July 1988, the Committee's chair, Z. Pukhova, defended the principle that equal access to work was the main avenue of social advancement for women, cited the country's economic backwardness as the main source of pressure on family stability, and insisted that men must assume a more equal share of domestic responsibility. *Pravda*, 2 July 1988.

153 Decree of the USSR Supreme Soviet, 'O neotlozhnykh merakh po uluchsheniyu polozheniya zhenshchin, okhrane materinstva i detsva, ukrepleniyu sem'i', 10 April 1990. *Izvestiya*, 13 April 1990.

154 Law of the USSR, 'O vnesenii izmenenii i dopolnenii v nekotorye zakonodatel'nye akty SSSR po voprosam, kasayushchimsya zhenshchin, sem'i i detstva', 22 May 1990. *ST*, no. 11, 1990, pp. 60–1, citing *Vedemosti S"ezda narodnykh deputatov SSSR i Verkhovnogo Soveta SSSR*, 1990, no. 23, art. 422.

155 *EKO*, no. 8, 1988, pp. 131–3 (E. E. Novikova, O. L. Milova, E. V. Zalyubovskaya). Although, according to the survey, only 3 per cent of workers wanted to give up their jobs completely, the authors make the curious statement that over a quarter claimed 'frequently' to have the desire to leave their jobs and concentrate on their homes and families. The cause of this discrepancy remains a mystery.

156 *SP*, no. 6, 1991, p. 67 (T. Galiev). The author, who was deputy chairperson of the trade union committee in the association's press and chassis factory, found the low share of women ready to give up work lamentable.

157 *EKO*, no. 8, 1988, pp. 131–2 (E. E. Novikova, O. L. Milova, E. V. Zalyubovskaya).

158 *Izvestiya*, 7 June 1990 (V. Bodrova, O. Podkolodnaya, V. Sazonov); *ST*, no. 1, 1991, p. 19 (M. Kuz'minova, V. Karev); *VS*, no. 2, 1991, pp. 56–8.

159 *ST*, no. 8, 1989, pp. 66–7 (L. Shineleva).

160 *EKO*, no. 7, 1989, p. 9 (N. M. Rimashevskaya); *EZh*, no. 47, 1990, p. 15. In 1989, 23 per cent of the children in the pre-school centres run by the State Committee for Education (Gosobrazovanie) were looked after in buildings which required major capital repair; another 4 per cent were in buildings which should have been pulled down. A third of the buildings did not have running water, a quarter had no central heating, and nearly a third had no sewerage.

161 *Sobesednik*, no. 23, 1988, pp. 4–5; *ST*, no. 10, 1989, pp. 14–15 (A. Shadrina, T. Tsvetkova, S. Kosyak); *SI*, 18 October 1989 (O. Berezhnaya), and 25 October 1989 (L. Biryukova); *Trud*, 30 November 1989 (N. Nadezhdina).

162 *SI*, 25 October 1989 (L. Biryukova).

1

6 The labour process under perestroika: 2 The failure of restructuring

1 We have analyzed this process in extensive detail for both the 1930s and the post-war period. See Filtzer, *Soviet Workers and Stalinist Industrialization*, ch. 6, and *Soviet Workers and De-Stalinization*, ch. 6.

2 We are leaving out of account here time lost off work due to excused absences, such as diversion to agricultural work or urban building projects, looking after sick children, or time off work sick. At the end of the 1980s these amounted, on a rough estimate, to approximately two weeks per employed person each year. *EZh*, no. 32, 1990, p. 19; *SG*, 1 September 1989; *Golos Dzerzhintsa*, 26 April 1991.

3 *RT*, 28 July 1990.

4 *ST*, no. 7, 1991, p. 72 (A. Lopatin); Filtzer, *Soviet Workers and De-Stalinization*, p. 136.

5 *LP*, 13 October 1989.

6 *Arsenal*, 28 February 1991. This same article claimed that workers were also leaving work 20 minutes before the end of shift, without any valid excuse.

7 Interview with personnel from the Voskresensk fertilizer factory, 9 July 1991. Perhaps the most bizarre case of such maladministration, however, was the trade union meeting held in the middle of working hours at a Moscow textile mill on the theme, 'How to Save the Working Minute'. *EKO*, no. 9, 1990, p. 69.

8 *Kabel'shchik* (Sevkabel', Leningrad), 7 February 1990; *Priborostroitel'*, 20 February 1991.

9 In addition to the ensuing discussion of AZLK, see *Kirovets*, 6 August and 14 September 1990; *Trud*, 10 February 1990 (Yaroslavl' Avtodizel'); *Ritm*, 6 October 1990.

10 *Moskvich*, 17 May 1991.

11 *Moskvich*, 26 April 1991.

12 *ZSM*, 25 May 1990.

13 *ZSM*, 22 August 1990.

14 *ZSM*, 20 November 1989, 29 June, 19 September, and 17 October 1990.

15 See chapter 3, p. 114.

16 *ZSM*, 28 March and 27 April 1990.

17 *Moskvich*, 21 January 1991; *ZSM*, 14 November 1990.

18 *Moskvich*, 24 April 1991.

19 *ZSM*, 11 July 1990; *Moskvich*, 21 January 1991.

20 *ZSM*, 25 December 1989, 18 July 1990.

21 *ZSM*, 10 January, 20 June, and 25 June 1990. This also gives some indication of the extent to which enterprises under-reported actual losses of work time. On one morning when the shop did not turn out a single gear box until nearly two hours after the start of the shift, the shop log recorded only one stoppage. *ZSM*, 10 January 1990.

22 *ZSM*, 15 January 1990.

23 *ZSM*, 27 November 1989. Another interesting footnote to this saga was the fact that many pieces of equipment had no working drawings, so that if a spare part needed making the shop had first to hunt down a designer.

This was far from straightforward, since with *khozraschet* AZLK had laid off many of its designers, leaving just twelve to service the entire enterprise.

24 *ZSM*, 27 April 1990; *Sputnik*, 15 November 1990.
25 *ZSM*, 27 December 1989.
26 *Kirovets*, 4 July 1990.
27 *Rezinshchik*, 17 July 1990.
28 Between 1965 and 1985 the total number of industrial workers as listed by occupational censuses grew by 32 per cent, as opposed to a 64 per cent rise in the number of repair fitters. During this same period the number of electrical fitters, most of whom work in repair and maintenance, more than doubled. *Trud v SSSR* (1988), pp. 63–5. Unfortunately, we have no way to determine the number of machine-tool operators working for the repair sector in factory machine shops.
29 For a detailed analysis of the repair and maintenance sector during the 1960s, but which is still valid today, see Filtzer, *Soviet Workers and De-Stalinization*, pp. 167–71.
30 *ST*, no. 3, 1991, p. 14; *ZSM*, 20 November 1989.
31 *Moskvich*, 22 March 1991. On the economic impact of poor repair work see also *Stankostroitel'* (Kuibyshev), 10 September 1990.
32 At AZLK, for instance, there was a running dispute between maintenance mechanics and tool-setters over who was responsible for dismantling and reassembling machinery prior to, or upon completion of repairs. *ZSM*, 21 November 1990.
33 Filtzer, *Soviet Workers and De-Stalinization*, pp. 26–8.
34 *Rezinshchik*, 17 July 1990; *ZSM*, 25 December 1989, 13 May 1991.
35 *Moskvich*, 9 January 1991.
36 *Sots. issled.*, no. 3, 1989, pp. 3–4 (I. F. Belyaeva).
37 *EKO*, no 6, 1989, p. 203 (R. B. Gitel'makher).
38 *Izvestiya*, 24 October 1990. The link between unauthorized and excused absenteeism has always been close, since managers often sanction unauthorized truancy after the fact, in order to avoid having to penalize workers whom they do not wish to alienate.
39 Interview with A. K., metallurgical specialist, Leningrad, 21 June 1991.
40 *Moskvich*, 18 March and 20 May 1991; *ZSM*, 17 January 1990.
41 *Raduga*, 19 April 1991; *Moskvich*, 25 January 1991.
42 *Rezinshchik*, 26 June 1990; *Zarya*, 5 April 1991; *ZSM*, 29 November 1989, 15 January and 31 October 1990; *Mashinostroitel'* (Ivanovo), 17 September 1990; *Kirovets*, 25 June 1990.
43 Interview with A., Moscow, June 1991.
44 *Ritm*, 3 December 1990.
45 *Molot*, 19 April 1990.
46 *Arsenal*, 26 November 1990, 7 January 1991.
47 Interview with A., Moscow, June 1991. It is fascinating to compare this account with Peter Linebaugh's outstanding study of crime and the proletariat in eighteenth-century London, in particular, the relationship between 'theft' and what workers felt to be an integral – and rightful – part

of their incomes. Writing of shipyard workers' customary right to remove wood scraps, or 'chips', for their own personal use, Linebaugh notes:

It was observed of the dockyard workers that their dwellings were constructed of materials formerly of His Majesty's Naval Stores, and after the naval defeats of the War of American Independence it was remarked that more ships were lost piecemeal in women's aprons than to enemy action at sea ... The nominal monetary wage was not at this time a matter of much contention ... But against this stability in wages must be set the vigour of protracted struggle that defended the men's control over the pace of work, the materials of labour and the structure of the labour force in the yards. In these fields of contention the men enjoyed a power – especially in wartime – that compensated for the low nominal monetary wage. Slow-downs, absenteeism, tippling and baseying [climbing over the walls and absenting oneself during work time] were complained of constantly by Deptford Yard supervisors. Linebaugh, pp. 376–7.

According to one source, only a sixth of the timber entering the Deptford Naval Yard 'left it afloat'. The appropriation of materials helped explain the lack of standardization in size and shape of allegedly identical classes of ships. Essentially, shipwrights and other skilled workers tailored the components to maximize the amount of wastage that they could carry home. *Ibid.*, pp. 380, 389. On the importance of such customary 'depredations' in other trades, see Linebaugh, chs. 5 and 7.

48 A study of the Severnaya mine in the Kuzbass in the wake of the 1991 miners' strike (the authors of which are sympathizers of the workers' movement) found that for many miners the substantial wage rises won as part of the strike settlement caused discipline and motivation to fall, since the minimum wage now far exceeded what previously they could only have dreamt of earning. The fact that rapid inflation would have rendered this a highly temporary state of affairs does not negate the authors' observations. Bizyukov and Bel'chik, pp. 5–8.

49 Interview with L. Tanova, sociologist, Krasnyi treugol'nik, Leningrad, 27 June 1991. Similar, but less graphic accounts appear in *Stankostroitel'* (Kuibyshev), 10 September 1990, 8 October 1990.

50 *Stankostroitel'* (Kuibyshev), 8 October 1990.

51 This distinction is the subject of Lupton's excellent study, *On the Shop Floor.*

52 According to Taylor, 'We propose to take all the important decisions and planning which vitally affect the output of the shop out of the hands of the workmen, and centralise them in a few men, each of whom is especially trained in the art of making those decisions and in seeing that they are carried out, each man having his own particular function in which he is supreme, and not interfering with the functions of the other men'. F. W. Taylor, *The Art of Cutting Metals* (New York, 1906), sect. 124, cited in Linebaugh, p. 400. This functional system of management, where each manager was a specialist in his or her own section and enjoyed relative autonomy from meddling and control from outside, can be contrasted with the Stalinist principle of one-man management (*edinonachalie*), where the enterprise director was the supreme authority over all areas of production. This was one among many reasons why, despite official rhetoric about

scientific management, Taylorism was never successfully applied in Soviet industry. The various 'rationalization' campaigns, such as shock work and Stakhanovism, were nothing more than crude attempts to impose speed-up, without any functional reorganization of production or lines of authority. As such they were pre-Taylorist, and were the breeding ground for exactly the types of restrictive practices which Taylor sought to undermine.

53 For detailed accounts of this process see Braverman, and Montgomery.

54 For participatory observation studies by sociologists who took jobs in industry, see Roy, Lupton, and the various studies by Michael Burawoy. For an introduction to the modern labour process debates see Braverman, Littler, Wood, and Knights and Willmott.

55 Montgomery, chs. 1 and 2.

56 Some of these differences between informal bargaining in capitalist and Soviet-type factories are explored by Burawoy, who generalizes on his experiences as a machine-tool operator in American and Hungarian factories in Burawoy and Lukacs.

57 David Mandel, interview with S., an electrical repair fitter at a large electrical equipment factory in Chelyabinsk, October 1991.

58 My conclusion in *Soviet Workers and De-Stalinization*, that output restriction was not an important factor in shop floor bargaining under Stalin and Khrushchev, is certainly wrong, and was based on a false distinction between output restriction as a means of fending off norm rises and rate cuts, and the more general repertoire of devices used to reduce the effort expenditure required to achieve an accepted level of earnings.

59 *Sots. issled.*, no. 2, 1990, p. 53 (V. D. Kozlov).

60 *Sots. issled.*, no. 10, 1990, p. 8 (A. N. Komozin), no. 5, 1992, pp. 23–32 (Yu. L. Neimer); *SP*, no. 7, 1991, p. 27 (A. Mitin).

61 *Sots. issled.*, no. 2, 1990, p. 54 (V. D. Kozlov). Similar conclusions are drawn in *Sots. issled.*, no. 1, 1990, p. 19 (V. E. Gimpel'son, V. S. Magun).

62 *ST*, no. 6, 1989, p. 67 (V. Vikhornov, V. Vvedenskii), no. 10, 1990, p. 46 (V. Sekachev); *Sots. issled.*, no. 10, 1990, p. 8 (A. N. Komozin).

63 *Sots. issled.*, no. 2, 1990, p. 53 (V. D. Kozlov).

64 Filtzer, *Soviet Workers and De-Stalinization*, pp. 80–2; *Sots. issled.*, no. 4, 1990, pp. 51–2 (V. V. Neugodov).

65 *ST*, no. 5, 1990, p. 35 (N. Khrulev, L. Salomatina); *IAN*, no. 1, 1991, pp. 65–6 (V. D. Roik); *Strela*, 13 July 1990.

66 *Molot*, 21 February 1991.

67 *Metallist*, 9 January 1991.

68 Interview with V. M., Moscow Meat Combine, 12 June 1991.

69 Filtzer, *Soviet Workers and De-Stalinization*, pp. 152–6.

70 *RT*, 18 July 1990 (L. Biryukova).

71 *VE*, no. 12, 1990, pp. 99–100 (V. Gerchikov).

72 *ST*, no. 3, 1990, pp. 6–7 (Yu. Anan'eva, S. Kolobaev, A. Stepanov).

73 See the example of women conveyor line workers in Chelyabinsk, cited in chapter 2, note 70.

74 *Stankostroitel'* (Kuibyshev), 8 October 1990. The lighter side of this process is revealed by an anecdote from the tractor-trailer factory in Kurgan. After programmers constantly failed to obtain decent results from a newly installed machine tool with programmed controls, an experienced fitter was called in who, by making a number of minor, common-sense adjustments, was able to get the equipment running properly. As the fitter commented, 'besides a diploma you still need a brain'. *SP*, no. 2, 1991, p. 71 (V. Koltashev).

75 David Mandel, interview with S., electrical fitter at a large equipment factory in Chelyabinsk, October 1991. It is worth recalling that this was a major grievance in Soviet industry, including among the miners during the 1989 strike; workers felt managers were overpaid for the amount of work they did (or did not do). This worker also noted that with the disintegration of production during 1990–1, workers at his factory no longer had the time or energy to take this responsibility, and were pushing management to take a more active role in sorting out problems. This, too, was a common event, as noted in chapter 3, pp. 114–15.

76 David Mandel, interview with workers from the Lytkarino Optical Glass Factory, October 1990.

77 David Mandel, interview with workers from the Lytkarino Optical Glass Factory, October 1990; *Molot*, 19 July 1990.

78 Interview with A. K., metallurgical specialist, Leningrad, 21 June 1991.

79 Interview with S. A., foreman, AZLK, Moscow, 7 July 1991.

80 *Ibid.* Burawoy identified a similar differential distribution of favours and concessions in his Hungarian factory, where he worked as a radial drill operator in 1984: 'core' workers, by virtue of their position in the labour process or their particular skills and experience, could exercise countervailing power to that of the foreman, while so-called peripheral workers could not. Burawoy and Lukacs, p. 76.

81 Interview with V. M., Moscow Meat Combine, 12 June 1991.

82 Burawoy and Hendley, pp. 380–1.

83 On the growing sense of 'them' and 'us' which emerged during the Brezhnev period, see Yanowitch, *Work in the Soviet Union*, pp. 156–7. For examples of wage cutting, see *RT*, 29 May 1990 (Yaroslavl' motor factory); *Trud*, 1 May 1990 (60 Years of the Soviet Union cotton textile combine); *RG*, 29 November 1991 (Dobropol'eugol' Production Association, Donetsk oblast); *Stankostroitel'* (Kuibyshev), 9 October 1990. Workers interviewed by David Mandel from the Lytkarino Optical Glass Factory and the electrical equipment factory in Chelyabinsk also tell of managers cutting rates or refusing to pay for stoppages. For cases of unfair dismissal, see *Trud*, 26 October 1989 (butter factory, Arkhangel oblast), 3 December 1989 (Volga Automobile Factory), and 7 July 1990 (Khimprom Production Association, Sayansk, Irkutsk oblast); *RT*, 27 May 1990 (Association of the Unemployed of the Ukraine); *SP*, no. 13–14, 1990, pp. 55–6 (L. Bukhtoyarova).

84 *EN*, no. 7, 1990, p. 16 (Z. Reinus).

85 Filtzer, *Soviet Workers and De-Stalinization*, ch. 6.

86 *EN*, no. 7, 1990, p. 21 (Z. Reinus).
87 *KP*, 18 December 1990 (A. Ermakov).
88 *SG*, 5 October 1989. In fact, this is just a rough estimate since many building materials factories had no scales and did not actually know how much they were loading on to rail cars for outward shipment.
89 *Rezinshchik*, 10 July 1990; *EKO*, no. 9, 1990, p. 129 (Stanislav Mironchenko).
90 *ST*, no. 3, 1988, pp. 31–2; *Moskvich*, 22 May 1991.
91 *EKO*, no. 7, 1990, p. 127 (E. G. Repin).
92 Volga cars weigh 220 kg. more than comparable Western models; Zhiguli cars weigh from 130–440 kg. more. *ST*, no. 5, 1988, p. 35.
93 Interview with J. Preskey, John Brown, Moscow, July 1991; interview with A. K., metallurgical specialist, Leningrad, 21 June 1991.
94 *EKO*, no. 7, 1990, p. 129 (E. G. Repin).
95 *SI*, 8 July 1988. It is no accident that 1991 saw the first ever sale of Soviet rolled steel to the United States – a fact explained far more by the quality of Soviet metal than by Cold War trade restrictions. *RT*, 8 October 1991.
96 *SI*, 23 September 1989.
97 *EKO*, no. 7, 1990, p. 128 (E. G. Repin).
98 *RG*, 29 December 1990 (M. Tulivskii).
99 *Krasnyi tekstil'shchik*, 31 August 1990.
100 *ZSM*, 11 December 1989, 16 April 1990.
101 *Skorokhodovskii rabochii*, 10 July 1990; *Kabel'shchik* (Sevkabel', Leningrad), 17 May 1990.
102 *Kabel'shchik* (Sevkabel', Leningrad), 19 April 1990.
103 *Moskvich*, 5 June 1991. According to the factory paper, the filters became so clogged up with green 'that it looks like a frog will jump out'.
104 *Moskvich*, 4 January 1991.
105 *EKO*, no. 2, 1991, pp. 133–4 (M. Budovnich). For an earlier critique, see *LP*, 10 November 1989 (E. Kurochka).
106 For an account of some of these conflicts, see Cook, pp. 46–7.
107 *RT*, 6 March 1991.
108 *MP*, 3 September 1989.
109 *Znamya*, 22 March 1991; *Rezinshchik*, 31 July 1990.
110 *Moskvich*, 20 March 1991.
111 *ZSM*, 17 January and 8 October 1990.
112 *Kirovets*, 14 February 1991.
113 'We extract five times as much iron ore as the Unites States. And we continue to increase the production of metals, which, like a spiral, dictates an increased output of equipment for these purposes. Is it any wonder that other industries like light industry or the food industry are technologically neglected?' *SI*, 8 July 1988.
114 *Trud*, 20 October 1989.
115 *SI*, 9 September 1989.
116 *SI*, 7 November 1989.

Conclusion: The demise of perestroika and the emergence of class conflicts

1 *Novaya gazeta*, no. 17, 29 May–6 June 1991 (B. Kagarlitsky).
2 *RT*, 14 January 1992 (Aleksandr Krotkov), 11 February 1992.
3 *RT*, 24 December 1991.
4 *Trud*, 27 November and 21 December 1991, 8 February 1992 (A. Isaev).
5 Interviews with personnel from the Samara Metallurgical Factory and the Samara Aviation Factory, May 1993; interview with N. Prostov, chair of the trade union committee, Arsenal Production Association, St Petersburg, May 1993. I am grateful to Pavel Romanov for his assistance in organizing and conducting the interviews in Samara.
6 Coal miners, for example, were to have their wages indexed when prices rose by 40 per cent. However, by early 1992 prices had risen by several hundred per cent, and the miners received no increase. *RT*, 24 January 1992. A review of several factory newspapers suggests that for most workers money wages rose as much as ten-fold over the course of 1992, but this still produced a fall in real wages of around 50 per cent.
7 I have based this account on the preliminary results of a research project into enterprise responses to privatisation, being carried out by Simon Clarke and Peter Fairbrother of the University of Warwick. Their findings are drawn from case studies of a number of enterprises in Moscow, Samara, the Kuzbass, and the Komi Republic. I am grateful to Drs Clarke and Fairbrother and to their Russian collaborators (in particular to Pavel Romanov in Samara) for allowing me access to this material. They are not, of course, responsible for the interpretation I have given it. Their findings are partly confirmed by the experience of the Arsenal engineering Production Association in St Petersburg, where the general engineering plants within the association have been privatized while the weapons factories have remained in state hands. Under these circumstances the association has found it impossible to develop a unified economic strategy, since the interests of the privatized and state factories simply do not coincide. Interview with N. Prostov, chair of the Arsenal trade union committee, St Petersburg, May 1993.
8 Nikolai Preobrazhensky, p. 21.

Bibliography

The bibliography lists all sources consulted in the preparation of this book. The abbreviations of journal and newspaper titles used in the notes appear below, next to the full title. In general, the notes do not give the titles to Soviet journal articles, but merely the journal issue number, the page number of the specific reference, and the author's name in parentheses at the end.

Abbreviations

Journals

EKO	
EN	*Ekonomicheskie nauki*
IAN	*Izvestiya Akademii Nauk SSSR, Seriya ekonomicheskaya*
NK	*Nauchnyi kommunizm*
OT	*Okhrana truda i sotsial'noe strakhovanie*
PKh	*Planovoe khozyaistvo*
Polis	*See RKSM*
RKSM	*Rabochii klass i sovremennyi mir* (from 1 January 1991, *Polis*)
	Sobesednik
Sots. issled.	*Sotsiologicheskie issledovaniya*
SP	*Sovetskie profsoyuzy*
ST	*Sotsialisticheskii trud*
SWB	BBC *Summary of World Broadcasts*, Weekly Economic Report, Part 1, USSR.
TP	*Tekstil'naya promyshlennost'*
VE	*Voprosy ekonomiki*
VS	*Vestnik statistiki*

National and Local Newspapers

	Argumenty i fakty
EZh	*Ekonomika i zhizn'*
IZ	*Industrial'noe Zaporozh'e*
	Gudok
	Izvestiya

KP	*Komsomol'skaya pravda*
LP	*Leningradskaya pravda*
LR	*Leningradskii rabochii*
	Lyublinskie Vesti (paper of Lyublin raion Council of People's Deputies)
MK	*Moskovskii komsomolets*
MP	*Moskovskaya pravda*
NG	*Nasha gazeta*, paper of the Union of Kuzbass Toilers
Nez. gaz.	*Nezavisimaya gazeta*
	Novaya gazeta, paper of the Leningrad oblast organization of the All-Union Lenin Komsomol
	Pravda
RG	*Rabochaya gazeta* (Kiev)
RT	*Rabochaya tribuna*
SG	*Stroitel'naya gazeta*
SI	*Sotsialisticheskaya industriya*
SR	*Sovetskaya Rossiya*
	Trud

Factory newspapers

Arsenal	Arsenal Production Association, Leningrad
Baltiets	Baltiiskii [shipbuilding] Production Association, Leningrad
Golos Dzerzhintsa	F. E. Dzerzhinskii Spinning-Weaving Factory, Ivanovo
Golos shveinika	Kalinin Garment Production Association, Kalinin city
Impul's	Arzamas radio parts factory
Kabel'shchik	Kuibyshevkabel' Cable Communications Production Association, Kuibyshev (Samara)
Kabel'shchik	Sevkabel' Production Association, Leningrad
Khimik	October Revolution Chemical Production Association, Rostov-on-Don
Kirovets	Kirov Factory, Leningrad
Krasnaya talka	Krasnaya talka [textile] factory, Ivanovo
Krasnyi tekstil'shchik	O. A. Varentsova Weaving and Finishing Factory, Ivanovo
Mashinostroitel'	Ivtekmash Production Association, Ivanovo
Mashinostroitel'	Malyshev Production Association, Kharkov
Meridian	Sverdlovsk precision-machining factory
Metallist	Izhevsk machine factory
Molot	Lenin factory, Leningrad
Moskvich	See *Za sovetskuyu malolitrazhku*
Priborostroitel'	Sverdlovsk instrument-making factory
Raduga	Pigment Production Association, Leningrad
Rezinshchik	Sverdlovsk rubber-technical goods factory
Ritm	Khark'kov Tractor Motor Factory (paper closed down by management at end of 1990)

Sputnik	Irkutsk Relay Factory
Skorokhodovskii rabochii	Skorokhod footwear Production Association, Leningrad
Stankostroitel'	50 Years of the USSR Machine Tool Production Association, Ivanovo
Stankostroitel'	Stankostroitel'noe Production Association, Kuibyshev (Samara)
Strela	Strommashina factory, Kuibyshev (Samara)
Tribuna Mashinostroitelya	Printing and Publishing Machinery Production Association (Lenpoligrafmash), Leningrad
Turbinist	Kaluga Turbine Factory Production Association
ZSM: Za sovetskuyu malolitrazhku	Lenin Komsomol Automobile Factory (Production Association Moskvich). From 1 January 1991 title changed to *Moskvich*
Za stal'	Kuibyshev (Samara) Steel-founding factory
Zarya	Lenin Worsted Combine, Ivanovo
Znamya	Sverdlovsk Turbo-Motor factory Production Association

Books and articles

Andreenkova, N. V. and Krotov, P. P., *Sovet trudovogo kollektiva i demokratizatsiya upravleniya* (Moscow: Akademiya Nauk SSSR, Institut Sotsiologii, Tsentr Povysheniya Kvalifikatsii Sotsiologov, 1989).

Arnot, Bob, *Controlling Soviet Labour: Experimental Change From Brezhnev to Gorbachev* (London, 1988).

Aves, Jonathan, 'The New Russian Labour Movement', *Slovo*, vol. 3, no. 2, pp. 16–17.

Avis, George, 'Access to Higher Education in the Soviet Union', in J. J. Tomiak, ed., *Soviet Education in the 1980s* (London, 1983), pp. 199–239.

Belotserkovsky, Vadim, 'Workers' Struggles in the USSR in the Early Sixties', *Critique*, no. 10/11 (1979), pp. 37–50.

Bizyukov, P. V. and Bel'chik, I. A., 'Kratkii otchet ob izuchenii sotsial'noi situatsii na sh. "Severnoi"', unpublished paper, Laboratoriya ekonomicheskoi sotsiologii, Kemerovo State University, 1991.

Bova, Russell, 'Worker Activism: The Role of the State', in Judith B. Sedaitis and Jim Butterfield, eds., *Perestroika From Below: Social Movements in the Soviet Union* (Boulder, 1991), pp. 29–42.

Braginskaya, Yu., 'Pobeda plana i rekord besplannovosti', *Sotsialisticheskii vestnik*, 27 September 1930.

Braverman, Harry, *Labor and Monopoly Capital. The Degradation of Work in the Twentieth Century* (New York, 1974).

Burawoy, Michael, *Manufacturing Consent: Changes in the Labor Process Under Monopoly Capitalism* (Chicago, 1979).

The Politics of Production (London, 1985).

Burawoy, Michael, and Hendley, Kathryn, 'Between *Perestroika* and Privatisation: Divided Strategies and Political Crisis in a Soviet Enterprise', *Soviet Studies*, vol. 44, no. 3 (1992), pp. 371–402.

Burawoy, Michael, and Lukacs, Janos, *The Radiant Past. Ideology and Reality in Hungary's Road to Capitalism* (Chicago, 1992).

Buzgalin, A. V. and Kolganov, A. I., *Samoupravlenie – klyuch k ekonomike XXI veka* (Moskovskii Gosudarstvennyi Universitet im. M. V. Lomanosov, Obshchestvennaya laboratoriya samoupravleniya, 1991).

Carr, Edward Hallett, and Davies, R. W., *Foundations of a Planned Economy 1926–1929* (London, 1969).

Clarke, Simon, Fairbrother, Peter, Burawoy, Michael, and Krotov, Pavel, *What About the Workers?* (London, 1993).

Connor, Walter D., *The Accidental Proletariat: Workers, Politics, and Crisis in Gorbachev's Russia* (Princeton, 1991).

Cook, Linda J., 'Brezhnev's "Social Contract" and Gorbachev's Reforms', *Soviet Studies*, vol. 44, no. 1 (1992), pp. 37–56.

Filatochev, Igor, Buck, Trevor, and Wright, Mike, 'Privatisation and Buy-outs in the USSR', *Soviet Studies*, vol. 44, no. 2 (1992), pp. 265–82.

Filtzer, Donald, *Soviet Workers and Stalinist Industrialization. The Formation of Modern Soviet Production Relations, 1928–1941* (London, 1986).

'Labour', in Martin McCauley, ed., *Khrushchev and Khrushchevism* (London, 1987), pp. 118–37.

'The Soviet Wage Reform of 1956–1962', unpublished seminar paper, Soviet Industrialization Project Seminar, Centre for Russian and East European Studies, University of Birmingham, October 1987 (Appendix A).

'The Soviet Wage Reform of 1956–1962', *Soviet Studies*, vol. 41, no. 1 (January 1989), pp. 88–110.

'The Contradictions of the Marketless Market: Self-financing in the Soviet Industrial Enterprise, 1986–90', *Soviet Studies*, vol. 43, no. 6 (1991), pp. 989–1009.

Soviet Workers and De-Stalinization: The Consolidation of the Modern System of Soviet Production Relations, 1953–1964 (Cambridge, 1992).

Friedgut, Theodore, and Siegelbaum, Lewis, 'Perestroika From Below: The Soviet Miners' Strike and its Aftermath', *New Left Review*, no. 181 (May–June 1990), pp. 5–32.

Gruzdeva, E. B. and Chertikhina, E. S., 'Soviet Women: Problems of Work and Daily Life', in Murray Yanowitch, ed., *The Social Structure of the USSR: Recent Soviet Studies* (Armonk, NY, 1986), pp. 150–69.

'Polozhenie zhenshchiny v obshchestve: konflikt rolei', in *Obshchestvo v raznykh izmereniyakh* (Moscow, 1990), pp. 147–67.

Holubenko, M., 'The Soviet Working Class: Discontent and Opposition', *Critique*, no. 4 (1975), pp. 5–25.

Kagarlitsky, Boris, 'Russia on the Brink of New Battles', *New Left Review*, no. 192 (1992), pp. 85–92.

Kats, I. Ya. and Pavlychev, V. V., *Uskorenie nauchno-tekhnicheskogo progressa v ob"edinenii: Opyt Ivanovskogo stankostroitel'nogo proizvodstvennogo ob"edineniya im. 50–letiya SSSR* (Moscow, 1989).

Knights, D., and Willmott, H., eds., *Labour Process Theory* (London, 1990).

Kontorovich, Vladimir, 'Discipline and Growth in the Soviet Economy', *Problems of Communism*, November–December 1985, pp. 18–31.

'Labor Problems and the Prospects for Accelerated Economic Growth', in Marice Freidberg and Heyward Isham, eds., *Soviet Society Under Gorbachev* (Armonk, NY, 1987), pp. 30–51.

Lane, David, *Soviet Economy and Society* (Oxford, 1985).

Lapidus, Gail Warshofsky, *Women in Soviet Society* (Berkeley, 1978).

Lapidus, Gail Warshofsky, ed., *Women, Work, and Family in the Soviet Union* (Armonk, NY, 1982).

Linebaugh, Peter, *The London Hanged. Crime and Civil Society in the Eighteenth Century* (London, 1991).

Littler, C., *The Development of the Labour Process in Capitalist Societies: A Comparative Study of the Transformation of Work Organization in Britain, Japan and the USA* (London, 1982).

Lupton, Tom, *On the Shop Floor* (Oxford, 1963).

McAuley, Alistair, *Women's Work and Wages in the Soviet Union* (London, 1981).

Malle, Silvana, 'Planned and Unplanned Mobility in the Soviet Union Under the Threat of Labour Shortage', *Soviet Studies*, vol. 39, no. 3 (July 1987), pp. 357–87.

Mandel, David, *Perestroika and the Soviet People* (Montreal, 1991).

Marx, Karl, *Capital*, vol. II (Moscow, 1967).

Mason, Tim, 'Women in Germany, 1925–1940: Family, Welfare and Work', part I, *History Workshop Journal*, no. 1 (1976), pp. 74–113.

'Women in Germany, 1924–1940: Family, Welfare and Work', part II, *History Workshop Journal*, no. 2 (1976), pp. 5–32.

Materialy vsesoyuznogo monitoringa po voprosam sotsial'no-ekonomicheskogo razvitiya promyshlennykh predpriyatii (Moscow: Akademiya Nauk SSSR, Institut Sotsiologii, Tsentr Povysheniya Kvalifikatsii Sotsiologov, 1990).

Mihalisko, Kathleen, 'The Workers' Rebellion in Belorussia', Radio Free Europe/Radio Liberty *Report on the USSR*, 26 April 1991, pp. 21–5.

'Workers and Soviet Power: Notes from Minsk', Radio Free Europe/Radio Liberty *Report on the USSR*, 5 July 1991, pp. 15–21.

Montgomery, David, *Workers' Control in America: Studies in the History of Work, Technology, and Labor Struggles* (Cambridge, 1979).

Moses, Joel C., 'Consensus and Conflict in Soviet Labor Policy – the Reformist Alternative', *Soviet Union/Union Sovietique*, vol. 13, part 3 (1986), pp. 301–47.

'Worker Self-Management and the Reformist Alternative in Soviet Labour Policy, 1979–85', *Soviet Studies*, vol. 39, no. 3 (July 1987), pp. 205–28.

Nove, Alec, *The Soviet Economic System* (London, 1977).

Peers, Jo, 'Workers by Hand and Womb – Soviet Women and the Demographic Crisis', in Barbara Holland, ed., *Soviet Sisterhood* (London, 1985), pp. 116–44.

Pietsch, Anna-Jutta, 'Shortage of Labour and Motivation Problems of Soviet Workers', in David Lane, ed., *Labour and Employment in the USSR* (Brighton, 1986), pp. 176–90.

Preobrazhensky, E. A., *The New Economics* (Oxford, 1965).

'Economic Equilibrium in the System of the USSR', in E. A. Preobrazhensky, *The Crisis of Soviet Industrialization* (White Plains, 1979), pp. 168–235.

'Economic Equilibrium Under Concrete Capitalism and in the System of the USSR', in E. A. Preobrazhensky, *The Crisis of Soviet Industrialization* (White Plains, 1979), pp. 134–67.

Preobrazhensky, Nikolai, 'The Disarray of Social Forces and Political Perspectives for the Workers' Movement', *Bulletin in Defence of Marxism* (September 1992), pp. 18–23.

Problemy sotsial'noi spravedlivosti v raspredelenii zhiznennykh blag (Moscow, 1988).

Rakovsky, Khristian, 'The Five-Year Plan in Crisis', *Critique*, no. 13 (1981), pp. 13–53.

Rogovin, V. Z., 'Problemy sootnosheniya otraslevogo (proizvodstvennogo) i territorial'nogo printsipov v upravlenii sotsial'noi infrastrukturoi', *Problemy sotsial'noi spravedlivosti v raspredelenii zhiznennykh blag* (Moscow, 1988), pp. 46–79.

Rosenbaum, Monika, *Frauenarbeit und Frauenalltag in der Sowjetunion* (Münster, 1991).

Roy, Donald, 'Quota Restriction and Goldbricking in a Machine Shop', *American Journal of Sociology*, vol. 52 (March, 1952), pp. 427–42.

'Work Satisfaction and Social Reward in Quota Achievement: An Analysis of Piecework Incentive', *American Sociological Review*, vol. 18 (October 1953), pp. 507–14.

'Efficiency and the "Fix": Informal Intergroup Relations in a Piecework Machine Shop', *American Journal of Sociology*, vol. 60 (November 1954), pp. 255–66.

Rubin, I. I., *Essays on Marx's Theory of Value* (Detroit, 1972).

Rutland, Peter, 'The Shchekino Method and the Struggle to Raise Labour Productivity in Soviet Industry', *Soviet Studies*, vol. 36, no. 3 (July 1984), pp. 345–65.

'Productivity Campaigns in Soviet Industry', in David Lane, ed., *Labour and Employment in the USSR* (Brighton, 1986), pp. 191–208.

'Labor Unrest and Movements in 1989 and 1990', *Soviet Economy*, vol. 6, no. 3 (1990), pp. 345–84.

Schlögel, Karl, *Der renitente Held: Arbeiterprotest in der Sowjetunion 1953–1983* (Hamburg, 1984).

Sedaitis, Judith B., 'Worker Activism: Politics at the Grass Roots', in Judith B. Sedaitis and Jim Butterfield, eds., *Perestroika From Below: Social Movements in the Soviet Union* (Boulder, 1991), pp. 13–27.

Shapiro, Judith, 'The Industrial Labour Force', in Mary Buckley, ed., *Perestroika and Soviet Women* (Cambridge, 1992), pp. 14–38.

Siuda, Petr, unpublished interview with David Mandel, 1988.

Slider, Darrell, 'The Brigade System in Soviet Industry: An Effort to Restructure the Labour Force', *Soviet Studies*, vol. 39, no. 3 (July 1987), pp. 388–405.

'Strukturnaya perestroika i konversiya predpriyatii VKP'. Partly reproduced in *Tekhniko-ekonomicheskoe i sotsial'no-ekonomicheskoe obosnovanie leningradskoi zony svobodnogo predprinimatel'stva*. Leningradskii gorodskoi sovet narodnykh deputatov – ispol'nitel'nyi komitet – komitet po ekonomichekoi reforme, 1991, pp. 43–48.

Teague, Elizabeth, 'The USSR Law on Work Collectives: Workers' Control or Workers Controlled?' in David Lane, ed., *Labour and Employment in the USSR* (Brighton, 1986), pp. 239–55.

'Workers' Self-Management and the Enterprise Law', *Radio Liberty Research Bulletin*, November 1988.

'Perestroika and the Soviet Worker', *Government and Opposition*, vol. 25, no. 2 (1990), pp. 191–211.

Tekhniko-ekonomicheskoe i sotsial'no-ekonomicheskoe obosnovanie leningradskoi zony svobodnogo predprinimatel'stva. Leningradskii gorodskoi sovet narodnykh deputatov – ispol'nitel'nyi komitet – komitet po ekonomichekoi reforme, 1991.

Temkina, Anna, 'The Workers' Movement in Leningrad, 1986–91', *Soviet Studies*, vol. 44, no. 2 (1992), pp. 209–36.

Tezisy nauchno-prakticheskoi konferentsii 'Perestroika i rabochii klass', Leningrad, 21 November 1989 (Leningrad: Leningradskii Institut Mashinostroeniya, 1989).

Ticktin, Hillel, 'Towards a Political Economy of the USSR', *Critique*, no. 1 (1973), pp. 20–41.

'Political Economy of the Soviet Intellectual', *Critique*, no. 2 (1973), pp. 5–21.

'The Contradictions of Soviet Society and Professor Bettelheim', *Critique*, no. 6 (1976), pp. 17–44.

'The Class Structure of the USSR and the Elite', *Critique*, no. 9 (1978), pp. 37–61.

Trud v SSSR. Statisticheskii sbornik (Moscow, 1988).

Wood, Stephen ed., *The Degradation of Work? Skill, Deskilling and the Labour Process* (London, 1982).

Yanowitch, Murray, *Social and Economic Inequality in the Soviet Union* (White Plains, NY, 1977).

Work in the Soviet Union: Attitudes and Issues (Armonk, NY, 1985).

Controversies in Soviet Social Thought. Democratization, Social Justice, and the Erosion of Official Ideology (Armonk, NY, 1991).

Yanowitch, Murray, ed., *The Social Structure of the USSR. Recent Soviet Studies* (Armonk, NY, 1986).

Index of industrial, mining, and construction enterprises

General index

absenteeism, *see* labour discipline
abstract labour, 146–7, 211–12
  see also waste
agricultural machinery industry
  training in, 267, n112
All-Union Central Council of Trade
  Unions (VTsSPS), *see* trade unions
All-Union Society of Blind Persons, 26
All-Union State Standards (Gosstandart),
  159
Andropov, Yurii, 79, 82
atomization, *see* workers
automotive industry
  organization and use of work time in,
    183–8
  supply problems in, 136, 143
auxiliary workers, *see* industry –
  occupational structure

Baltic States
  suppression of demonstrations in, 103,
    128
barter, 137–8, 140, 256, n59, 257, n62
  undermining emergence of exchange
    value, 146–7, 213, 218
Bases of Legislation of the USSR and
  Republics on the
  Denationalization of Property and
  the Privatization of Enterprises
  (draft legislation), 129, 253, n7
Bases of Legislation on Investment
  Activity in the USSR (1990), 129,
  253, n6
Belorussian Federation of Trade Unions,
  see trade unions
Black Saturdays, *see* overtime and
  storming
bonus systems, *see* wage reform – failure
  of incentive systems
Brezhnev, Leonid, 236, n8
brigades, 57, 60, 70–1
budget deficit, 43

building materials industry
  gender inequalities in, 170
  supply problems in, 136
  working conditions in, 172
Burawoy, Michael, 274, nn54, 56

capitalism
  failures of, 204–5, 222–4
  nature of in ex-Soviet Union, 89, 128,
    220–1, 222
  moves to restore, 9, 88, 122, 130, 218–19
cellulose and paper industry
  gender inequalities in, 170
Centres for Job Placement, Retraining,
  and Vocational Guidance of the
  Population, *see* job placement
  centres
certification of workplaces, 154
chemical industry
  supply problems in, 136
  wages in, 169
  working conditions in, 173, 175, 263,
    nn52, 53
Chernobyl disaster, 111, 112
  childcare provision, 178, 270, n160
Clarke, Simon, 225, n2, 242–3, n8, 277,
  n7
coal industry
  supply problems in, 141–4
  strikes in, *see* strikes and worker
    protests
  wages in, 169
  working conditions in, 156, 160–1, 172
collective payment systems, *see*, contract
  system
command system, 126, 127
  see also planning
concrete labour, 146–7, 211–12
Conference of Kuzbass Workers'
  Committees, 107
construction industry
  supply problems in, 136

impact of on supply crisis, 142–4, 258,
n88
political impact of, 113–14
in light industry, 119–20
in metallurgical industries, 113, 119,
227, n25, 241, n98, 251, n141, 252,
n159
limited nature of, 115–22, 212, 213
Novocherkassk (1962), 79, 235, n6
over April 1991 price rises, 75, 95, 106,
108–13, 241, n90, 250, nn123, 130,
250–1, n139
over Nagorno Karabakh, 94
over privatization of state enterprises,
81, 87, 88–93
over consumer shortages, 115, 251–2, n151
over wage cuts, 67, 114–5, 238, n43
over wages lost due to disruptions to
production, 114–5, 184, 251, n147,
275, n75
repression of under Stalin, 94
supply shortages, 9, 24, 35, 52, 54, 69, 216
and losses of work time, 182
and republican protectionism, 138–9,
144, 258, n97
and system of self-financing, 127–8,
135–47, 256, nn53, 59, 257, nn62, 64,
68, 75, 76
and utilization of equipment, 154
as cause of prices protests in Belarus',
110
as cause of strikes, 115, 119–20
in light industry, 50, 54, 74, 119–20, 130,
139–41, 165
in post-Soviet period, 221
surplus product
production and appropriation of, 4, 7,
148, 162, 163–4, 205, 214

Taylor, Frederick, 194
and Taylorism in the USSR, 273–4, n52
trade unions, 92, 168, 177, 220
All-Union Central Council of Trade
Unions (VTsSPS), 33, 84, 119, 129,
159, 229, n90
and control over benefits, 75, 76, 116
Belorussian Federation of Trade
Unions, 111, 112
Federation of Independent Trade
Unions of Russia (FNPR), 120, 249,
n117, 250, n123, 252, n166
General Confederation of Trade
Unions (VKP), 108, 249, n117
Independent Union of Mineworkers
96, 101–3, 105, 156, 248, n96
role of in curbing worker militancy,
116–20, 252, nn158, 160

Trade Union of Coal Industry Workers
(later Trade Union of Coal
Industry Employees)
and 1991 miners' strike, 104, 105
discredited by 1989 miners' strike, 95,
96, 97, 100, 247, n85
extraordinary 15th congress, 101–2,
248, nn90, 91
Union of Metallurgical Workers, 119
Union of Workers in Textiles and Light
Industry, 119–20, 175
textile industry
wages in, 169, 170
working conditions in, 163, 173
see also light industry

underaccumulation, see industry
undermechanization, see industry
unemployment, 7, 16, 18–21, 53
alongside unfilled vacancies, 48
among disabled workers, 26–7
among gas pipeline workers, 21
among older workers, 216, 229, n88
among specialists, 19–20, 48
among women workers, 21, 24, 165, 216
among young workers, 25–6, 216
and job placement centres, 35–8
and layoffs due to environmental crisis,
54, 234, n184
and layoffs due to supply shortages,
50, 54, 140–1, 216, 233, n163, 234–5,
n185
as disciplinary device, 16, 31, 226, n5
impact of on labour discipline, 20–1
in Central Asia, 19, 21–3
in Kazan, 20
in Leningrad, 20
in Moscow, 19–20
in Ukraine, 20
in Zaporozh'e, 20
regulations governing, 32–5, 229, n91
see also employment policy, labour
shortage, Law on Employment,
perestroika
unfilled vacancies, 48–9, 51
Union of Councils of Labour Collectives,
92–3, 246, n56
Union of Kuzbass Toilers, 99
uninstalled equipment, see industry
unskilled labour, see industry –
occupational structure
use value
in capitalist economy, 204–5
in Soviet Union, 205, 211–13, 218–19
see also waste

Vietnamese workers, 28–9, 269, n139

Cambridge Russian, Soviet and Post-Soviet Studies

Series list continued

Lightning Source UK Ltd.
Milton Keynes UK
UKOW04f0612110316

270015UK00001B/82/P